FOCUS
MADE EASY
The Complete Focus® Handbook
for Users and Programmers

RICHARD R. TAHA

University of California, Berkeley

San Francisco Center

Prentice Hall, Englewood Cliffs, New Jersey 07632

Library of Congress Cataloging-in-Publication Data

TAHA, RICHARD R.
    Focus made easy: the complete Focus handbook for users and
programmers/Richard R. Taha.

        p.   cm.
    Includes index.
    ISBN 0-13-322108-3
    1. FOCUS (Computer program language)   I. Title.
QA76.73.F23T34 1992   91-2533
650'.0285'5133—dc20   CIP

Editorial/production supervisor
  and interior designer: **Karen Bernhaut**
Cover designer: **Ben Santora**
Prepress buyer: **Kelly Behr**
Manufacturing buyer: **Susan Brunke**
Acquisitions editor: **Paul W. Becker**

 © 1992 by Prentice-Hall, Inc.
A Simon & Schuster Company
Englewood Cliffs, New Jersey 07632

The publisher offers discounts on this book when
ordered in bulk quantities. For more information,
write:
    Special Sales/Professional Marketing
    Prentice-Hall, Inc.
    Professional & Technical Reference Division
    Englewood Cliffs, New Jersey 07632

Focus is a registered trademark of Information Builders
Incorporated.

Printed in the United States of America

10 9 8 7 6 5 4 3 2 1

ISBN   0-13-322108-3

Prentice-Hall International (UK) Limited, *London*
Prentice-Hall of Australia Pty. Limited, *Sydney*
Prentice-Hall Canada Inc., *Toronto*
Prentice-Hall Hispanoamericana, S.A., *Mexico*
Prentice-Hall of India Private Limited, *New Delhi*
Prentice-Hall of Japan, Inc., *Tokyo*
Simon & Schuster Asia Pte. Ltd., *Singapore*
Editora Prentice-Hall do Brasil, Ltda., *Rio de Janeiro*

To
My wife, Maureen
my son, Darian and my daughter, Emma
and
my parents

CONTENTS

Contents   vii

Appendices

PREFACE

This book is written to teach you Focus and to be used as a Focus reference manual. Focus is the major fourth-generation language in use today. It is available on practically every type of business computer system from small personal computers to huge IBM mainframe computers with thousands of users.

Focus is a very easy tool to use. In fact, you do not even have to learn Focus to use it. Anyone who can operate a computer keyboard or a mouse can use Focus. Users can produce reports and even create files by using very simple Focus facilities such as TableTalk and FileTalk.

Learning Focus can be fun. This is especially true since you can start seeing results from the first day of working with Focus. Like learning to drive a car, you will get more competent and will find more interesting things to do as each day goes by.

One of the nice features of Focus is that it works in very much the same way with all types of computers. If you develop a Focus program on an $800 PC, you can easily execute the same program on a multimillion-dollar supercomputer, the only difference being that on the bigger computer your application will run much faster. What is interesting is that the reverse is also true. In other words, you can transport Focus programs from large computers and execute them on smaller, much cheaper computers. As personal computers become very powerful, many businesses are in the process of moving their business applications from large, expensive computers to small, inexpensive, very powerful personal computers. This concept, which has become very popular in recent years, is known as downsizing. There have been reports of companies saving millions of dollars in personnel and equipment costs by downsizing to PCs. Focus is a major tool in this area, because the code is almost totally portable between computers.

This book is designed to be both a tutorial for people who want to teach themselves Focus and a reference manual for people who are professional programmers. The book is written in a very simple and readable style. In fact, I have used the same technique that I have used in my computer classes at the university, guiding the user step by step through the learning process. I assume no prior computing or programming knowledge on the part of the reader. If you know some Focus and are looking for a refresher course, you can skip Chapters 1 and 2.

The book has two main sections and appendices. The first section introduces the novice user to data processing concepts and to Focus and teaches him or her how to use the report writer features of Focus to produce perfect reports. The book is designed to build on the experience of the user as the chapters progress.

The second section deals with more advanced features of Focus, such as file creation and update. It teaches the reader how to create online screens for updating files. The entire process is explained so easily that the reader can learn the process almost effortlessly. This section is especially useful for people who have studied the first section or have previous Focus experience and would like to upgrade their knowledge.

There is also an appendix section at the back of the book which includes a TableTalk tutorial. You can actually use the TableTalk tutorial to start using Focus to prepare reports on the first day that you purchase the book.

The book can be used as a reference manual by Focus programmers. It covers practically every useful aspect of Focus and will make an excellent reference manual. This is made even more significant by the fact that there are nearly 200 Focus programs of various complexities in the book. These programs cover a variety of business functions. All the programs have been fully tested and can be used by readers to help them solve business problems. About 180 of the most important programs are available on a diskette for $25. See Appendix D for details on ordering the diskette.

If you have ever wanted to buy just one book to help you learn about computer information systems from the very beginning to the most sophisticated online programming, this is it.

Audience

This book was written with the following users in mind:

End users. These are persons whose primary responsibility is analyzing and managing functions in various departments of organizations. Accounting, human resources, treasury, engineering, operations, customer services, and marketing departments are prime examples of user areas. There is usually a wealth of information available inside an organization's computers, but the data processing (or MIS or information systems) department is usually so backlogged with work that it would take months before they can start work on a new request. In addition, many data processing departments use the older third-generation languages which are cumbersome. By using Focus you can develop your own reports the way you want them in a fraction of the time and cost of the traditional methods.

Systems analysts/designers and managers. Focus is the ideal tool for prototyping new applications. In prototyping, the analyst must quickly be able to develop a model of a complex application and to modify the results with ease. For example, in developing an online financial system to keep track of security holdings of your clients, there would be many screens, databases, and reports. The major parts of the system could be prototyped with Focus in 2 to 3 weeks and reviewed with the user for accuracy. After completing user revisions, the application could be completed in Focus or in a third-generation language. It would not be possible to conduct any meaningful prototyping with third-generation languages such as COBOL, C, or CICS. If the same application were developed using a third-generation tool such as CICS, it would take several months for the user to see the result, and then it would be too costly to make major changes to the programs.

Professional programmers. Focus can be mastered in a brief period of time. Because you are an experienced programmer, you do not need to attend a class to learn Focus. Just read this book and you can pick up the most important skills in no time at all. Since Focus is both a database manager and a programming language, you will find that your productivity will increase because you will not have to use other tools with Focus. In addition, because Focus is available in both an IBM mainframe and IBM PC version, it provides an ideal opportunity and career path for PC programmers to break into the mainframe world, where salaries are higher and career opportunities greater.

Students and educators. This book is ideally suited for teaching a college-level programming and database design course. I have been instructing university-level students in Focus Report Writer and Focus database design. This book is developed with the needs of students in mind. It can also be used as an independent, self-teaching study course.

Reference book. Last but not least, this book is intended as a refresher course and a reference book for everybody who uses Focus. The book is divided into two sections. The first section deals with Focus Report Writer and the second section deals with database design and file maintenance.

Everyone will find Focus an easy and exciting tool to use. It is so satisfying to be able to design a report or create a screen for entering data in 1 or 2 hours. I am sure that you will get the same feeling of achievement and gratification that I get every time one of my programs produces the results requested. Why use anything else?

I welcome your comments and suggestions. I can be reached through the publisher. You can also contact me through BITNET or INTERNET. My BITNET address is EXTN3$4 at UCBCMSA. My INTERNET address is EXTN3$4@CMSA·BERKELEY·EDU.

ACKNOWLEDGMENTS

At Information Builders Inc., I would like to gratefully thank Gerald Cohen, President, Merv Adrian, Chris Gerrard, and Cheryl Wolhar for their kind support and assistance in this project.

At Prentice Hall, I would like to thank Karen Gettman for first suggesting the idea, Paul Becker, the Executive Editor, for encouraging me throughout this project, and Karen Bernhaut, my production editor, for all her valuable assistance and generous advice.

My sincere thanks to Bonnie Stiles of The University of California for her encouragement. My heartfelt thanks to Santiago Tula, a true friend indeed.

CHAPTER 1

OVERVIEW OF COMPUTER SYSTEMS AND INTRODUCTION TO FOCUS®

MAIN TOPICS:

- OVERVIEW
- COMPUTER SYSTEM COMPONENTS
- OPERATING SYSTEMS BASICS
- FOCUS BASICS
- THE FOCUS ENVIRONMENTS
- THE FOCUS DATABASE STRUCTURE

This section is intended for those of you who are new to the field of information systems or who need a refresher course covering the various parts of a computer system and how they work together to get things done.

COMPUTER SYSTEM COMPONENTS

Computer systems are generally divided into three groups: personal computers or PCs, the minicomputers, and mainframe computer systems. Although they differ in size and number of attachments, all computers have the same major components (see Fig. 1.1).

Central processing unit (CPU) or processor. Simply put, the CPU is the brains of any computer system. The processor contains very tiny electronic circuits to perform mathematical and logical functions. Other devices, such as printers, disk units, and display terminals, are attached to it. The CPU is also the traffic cop (monitor) of the computer system. It has channels to direct information among all its attachments. Any information first passes through the CPU and is then directed to its final destination.

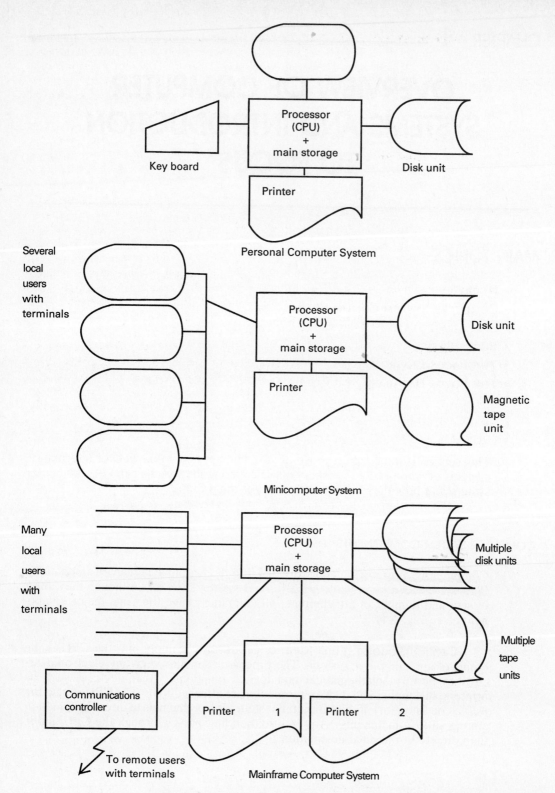

Processor
(CPU)
+
main storage

Key board

Disk unit

Printer

Personal Computer System

Several
local
users
with
terminals

Processor
(CPU)
+
main storage

Disk unit

Printer

Magnetic
tape
unit

Minicomputer System

Many
local
users
with
terminals

Processor
(CPU)
+
main storage

Multiple
disk units

Multiple
tape
units

Communications
controller

Printer   1

Printer   2

To remote users
with terminals

Mainframe Computer System

Figure 1.1 Diagram of various types of computer systems.

Memory or main storage. The computer's memory is another piece of electronic circuitry. The CPU sends small electric currents through the memory's circuits to create magnetic fields and store data. The CPU places programs and data in the main storage area for execution. Main storage is also known as *central storage* or *real storage*. In the PC world, the main storage area is known as *random access memory* (RAM). Every time the computer system is turned off, the memory is wiped clean.

Secondary storage. Secondary storage is usually either a disk unit or a tape unit. In the IBM mainframe environment, disk storage is referred to as a *direct-access storage device* or DASD (pronounced "dazdee"). Disk units are platters of magnetized surfaces that can hold computer information. These platters are similar to phonograph records and serve basically the same purpose—capture and store information and play it back on demand. The secondary storage area is used to file user information such as accounting or payroll data and programs that manipulate this information. Disk units can hold anywhere from a few hundred thousand to billions of characters of information. A character is defined as any of the letters A through Z, numbers 0 through 9, and special symbols such as $, +, −, %, &, *, and @. By the way, you may hear the term *bytes* used rather than *characters*. One byte is equivalent to one character of data.

Display terminals. Terminals are TV-like screens with keyboards that allow you to enter information into or retrieve information from storage areas. You also use a terminal's keyboard to issue commands to print reports, key in business information, and write programs. Most terminals can display 80 characters of information on each line of screen. The total number of lines per screen is usually 24 or 25. Other names for terminals are:

Monitor
Screen
CRT (cathode ray tube)
VDU or VDT (visual display unit or visual display terminal)
Display unit

Printer. The output device is usually a printer. It can be a *laser printer*, which prints one page of information at a time, or an *impact printer*, which prints one character or one line of information at a time.

A personal computer has all of the components described previously. It is usually dedicated to one user—hence the term *personal*. Mainframe computer systems have exactly the same functional units as those of a personal computer, but are faster and there are more of them. Mainframe memories are larger, and high-speed printers can produce up to 120 pages of information per minute. Mainframe systems are typically shared by tens, hundreds, or even thousands of users. The minicomputer fills the gap between the mainframe and the personal computer.

If you are using a fourth-generation language such as Focus, you should understand the basics of computer systems. However, as a Focus programmer, it is not necessary for you to become intimately familiar with the differences between various groups of computer systems. Focus works the same way on all of them.

OPERATING SYSTEMS BASICS

Definition of a program. A program is a series of instructions that tell a computer to perform specific tasks. In Focus a program is also called a *request* or a *procedure*.

Every computer needs an *operating system* (OS) or *control program* (CP) to make it work. An operating system consists of a series of programs that control operation of the computer and external devices such as disk drives, display terminals, and printers. The operating system also allows user programs to run in the computer and provides the computer resources that the programs might require. Focus works with most known operating systems, so there is no need to review specific operating systems here. However, the major operating systems in use are described below.

PC/DOS, MS/DOS, and OS/2. MS/DOS is the most widely used operating system on IBM personal computers. MS/DOS is essentially a single-user operating system. However, it can also work in networked environments where several computers are linked together and users simultaneously share the same files and programs. It is an easy operating system to use. In many cases it is loaded into the main storage area when you switch on a computer and you are not even aware of its presence.

VM/CMS. Many IBM System/370 computers operate under the VM/CMS (Virtual Machine/Conversational Monitor System) operating system. In the virtual machine environment, each user thinks that he or she has a real computer at his or her disposal—hence the term *virtual*. In effect, each user shares a central CPU and is provided with his or her own main storage and a slice of disk storage area called a minidisk. *Minidisk* is really a misnomer. Depending on your requirements, the minidisk size could range from less than 100,000 characters to hundreds of millions of characters of storage. The user is also allocated a simulated or virtual printer, a simulated card reader, and a simulated card punch. Of course, card readers and card punches are rarely used anymore. These virtual devices are used to send and/or receive electronic messages and other communications between the users and the central computer system.

There may be hundreds of users in a VM/CMS environment, all believing that they have a complete system at their disposal. In reality, there is only one big mainframe computer, a few disk units (DASDs), and one or perhaps two printers. The operating system arranges for sharing these resources among the various users. VM/CMS was designed to be very user friendly. It is almost as easy to use as a PC, yet it has the power of a mainframe. A small VM installation could actually operate without a full-time support staff such as operators or systems programmers. Extensive help facilities are available under VM/CMS. All you need to do is to type HELP or press the PF1 key almost any time during your *session*, the period of time that you are connected to the computer system.

MVS, MVS/XA, and MVS/ESA. These three products are the operating systems for the large IBM System/370 mainframe systems. MVS stands for "multiple virtual storage," XA for "extended architecture" and ESA for "enterprise systems architecture." All these operating systems are the direct descendents of the original IBM operating system called OS/370. As the word *multiple* indicates, the MVS operating system divides the computer into a number of separate regions that could execute several programs, also known as *jobs,* concurrently. These regions are constantly monitored by the operating system, and as soon as one job is completed, it is rolled out and another job that has been waiting for computer resources is rolled in and begins executing. Unlike VM/CMS and PC/DOS, these operating systems are complicated and are costly to maintain. A medium-sized MVS data center requires at least seven support persons (two operators, a systems programmer, a security administrator, a CICS/communications programmer, a production controller/tape librarian, and an operations manager) to stay operational. MVS has interactive features such as CICS and TSO/ISPF that allow users to access MVS facilities, but basically it is batch-process oriented. Batch processing is usually suited for heavy volumes of repetitive transactions such as nightly check processing, utility billing, or biweekly payroll updates. Batch processing usually takes place overnight. VM/CMS, on the other hand, was designed for interactive use. However, as a Focus user, you do not have to be concerned with such intricacies of operating systems. Focus works inside the operating system of a computer and you are usually protected from its complexities.

DEC VMS and MicroVMS. These are the operating systems of choice for Digital Equipment Corporation's VAX and MicroVax computers.

MPE XL. This is the operating system for Hewlett-Packard's HP 3000 computer.

GUARDIAN 90. This operating system is used to run Focus in Tandem computer systems.

Wang VS. This operating system is used by Wang minicomputers.

UNIX. This operating system works on a range of computers, from PCs to mainframes.

OS/400. This is the operating system designed for the IBM AS/400 series minicomputers. Focus has just recently become available for use on this computer.

As I said before, Focus works across various computer systems. Focus is very user friendly and does not require extensive knowledge of any particular computer system. All you really need to know is how to get into your computer system and invoke Focus. In most sites, the systems programmer or PC coordinator will set up the procedures for getting into the system and starting Focus. On mainframes and minicomputers, you will first have to type your identification and a password to get into the computer system. This is known as *logging in*. Next, you will either select Focus from a menu or type the word "Focus" to enter the

Focus domain. On PCs, access is determined at installation time. Normally, all you have to do is to type "Focus" and press the Enter or Return key and you are in Focus. Focus is sophisticated application software; however, like all other application software, it is completely under the control of the computer's operating system.

FOCUS BASICS

Focus was developed in the mid-1970s by a group of computer professionals. The group had developed the first commercial fourth generation language a few years earlier and this time set about developing a new language with enhanced features and new commands. Whether by design or by accident, Focus turned out to be both a powerful and a very easy language to use.

Focus has been revised and improved extensively over the years. It is now a major database management system and an application development tool, in addition to being a general-purpose report writing language. Focus is currently available on most major brands of personal computer, minicomputer, and mainframe computer systems. Following is a partial list of the computer systems that work with Focus.

IBM PC/XT and PS2
Compaq
Toshiba
AT&T
Other IBM PC-compatibles
Tandem
Hewlett-Packard HP 3000
Digital Equipment Vax, MicroVax
IBM 9370 and 4300 midrange mainframe series
IBM 3080 and 3090 large mainframe series
IBM system/390 Enterprise series
IBM AS/400
Wang/VS

Another advantage of Focus over traditional languages such as COBOL, Basic, and C is its portability. A Focus application developed on any of the computers on the list above can usually be executed successfully on any of the other computer systems on the list. For example, if we had developed a payroll application on an IBM personal computer, we could later have transferred (or ported) the same programs and executed them on an IBM mainframe or a Digital Equipment system. There are two primary advantages to this capability. One is that an organization can start on a small scale with Focus and gradually expand its computer size without incurring a major software conversion cost. The other is the possibility of prototyping major new applications on a personal computer and then developing them fully either with Focus or with traditional languages such as COBOL and CICS. *Prototyping* is the process of developing working models of applications. Users are given the opportunity to try out and modify the application model and finalize their requirements during the prototyping phase, before the system is developed. Prototyping is a concept that has been carried over to data processing from manufacturing. Aircraft manufacturing provides a good analogy. After a new aircraft is designed, a prototype is built, flown thousands of miles under rigorous conditions, and modified countless times before a commitment to a production model is made. The role of the prototype does not end there. It is kept as a test bed to try out new enhancements and modifications before they are applied to the production line. The same techniques could be used in developing computer systems.

Additionally, Focus has opened the door to a new area in computing commonly referred to as *application downsizing*. Some users are now transferring their mainframe applications to small clusters of personal computers that are linked together (these clusters are usually called local area networks or LANs). This approach could result in tremendous cost savings for users. This is because personal computer prices are only a fraction of mainframe prices. Also, personal computers do not require the same degree of power and airconditioning as do mainframes, and PCs do not need the same number of programmers and operators for upkeep. Downsizing usually results in major reductions in management information system (MIS) department personnel costs. It is beneficial to users also, since they can do some of the work themselves without waiting for mainframe programmers.

THE FOCUS ENVIRONMENT

It may be a good idea to make copies of the following few pages and keep them for future reference. You do not always use all the available features of Focus and it is good to have a source of quick reference when you need to refresh your memory about features that you may need for new applications.

Focus has many components. These are usually called *environments*. You could use most of these environments independently without using other parts of Focus. In the next few pages I provide an overview of the most common Focus environments.

TED (Short for "Text Editor")

This is the Focus text editor. It is very powerful and can be used to write procedures and programs to create reports, update files, create graphs, and even to access non-Focus files. You can also use TED to create files for testing purposes. It is not always necessary to use TED for your work. On personal computers, you could use any ASCII-compatible word processor such as Volkswriter or Wordperfect. ASCII (American Standard Code for Information Interchange) is one the two major standards for data representation in mainframe and personal computers. The other standard is EBCDIC (Extended Binary-Coded Decimal Interchange Code), which is used on all IBM mainframe systems. Both standards refer to the internal representation of data within the computer. To write programs, it is not necessary for you to know how they work. It is, however, good to know the terminology. On mainframe and minicomputer systems, you could use standard system editors such as Xedit in VM/CMS, the ISPF editor in MVS, EDT in the VAX, and EDIT in the Tandem environment. However, it is highly recommended that you use TED because it is integrated with Focus and, therefore, has other advantages.

Help Facility

Focus has a rather limited online help facility. There are several ways of invoking the Focus HELP. One is to press the PF1 function key (F1 on the PC) on the keyboard. Another is to type "HELP" from the Focus command line. A third way, available on PC/Focus, is to invoke HELP from the PC/Focus main menu.

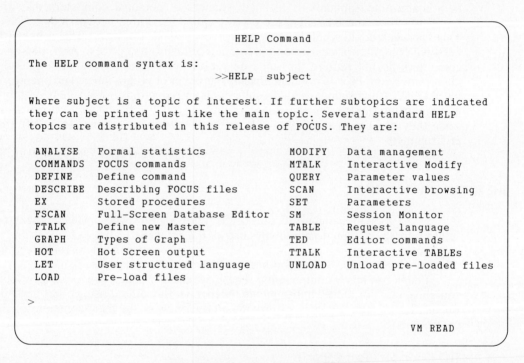

```
                              HELP Command
                              ------------
The HELP command syntax is:
                          >>HELP    subject

Where subject is a topic of interest. If further subtopics are indicated
they can be printed just like the main topic. Several standard HELP
topics are distributed in this release of FOCUS. They are:

    ANALYSE    Formal statistics          MODIFY    Data management
    COMMANDS   FOCUS commands             MTALK     Interactive Modify
    DEFINE     Define command             QUERY     Parameter values
    DESCRIBE   Describing FOCUS files     SCAN      Interactive browsing
    EX         Stored procedures          SET       Parameters
    FSCAN      Full-Screen Database Editor SM       Session Monitor
    FTALK      Define new Master          TABLE     Request language
    GRAPH      Types of Graph             TED       Editor commands
    HOT        Hot Screen output          TTALK     Interactive TABLEs
    LET        User structured language   UNLOAD    Unload pre-loaded files
    LOAD       Pre-load files

>

                                                      VM READ
```

Figure 1.2   Example of Focus HELP menu.

TABLE Environment

Information stored in Focus files and in most other types of files (dBase and Lotus in personal computers, and most mainframe files and databases such as DB2, IMS, and VSAM) can be retrieved and displayed on a formatted report with the Focus TABLE command. The TABLE command permits access to these files and allows us to manipulate the data with simple, yet powerful English-like commands such as PRINT, SUM, and COUNT. The TABLE environment also provides basic statistical functions such as minimums, maximums, averages, and others. The following is an example of the TABLE command:

```
TABLE FILE STAFF
PRINT LAST_NAME AND FIRST_NAME
BY EMPLOYEE_ID
END
```

Hot Screen

Output from the TABLE commands could be viewed on the display terminal, saved in a file on disk, or sent to the system printer. The default is the terminal. If you decide to view your report on the screen, the Hot Screen facility could be invoked by pressing the PF1 function key (F1 key on the PC).

```
PAGE      1

                LIST OF APPLICANTS AND THEIR SOFTWARE EXPERIENCE
LAST_NAME                   FIRST_NAME    SW_XPRTISE
---------                   ----------    ----------

BOCHARD                     CARLOS        COBOL ASSEMBLER JCL MVS ISPF CMS ROSCOE
BORGIA                      CESARE        DW4
CLAXON                      KEITH         COBOL, CICS, BASIC
FREEMAN                     MAUREEN       WORDSTAR DBASE IV
                            RICHARD       DBASE II, COBOL
JACOBY                      DAVID
KASTOR                      BARBARA       MSDOS COBOL UNIX  VAX
KRANSTON                    JUDITH        COBOL, IMS/VS
LAMARGO                     INDALECIO     COBOL MVS JCL VSAM IMS SPF CMS ROSCOE
LAMBACK                     JENNIFER      WORDSTAR VOLKSWRITER
TAHA                        RICHARD       IMS/VS,COBOL,DBASEIII,CICS/VS,MSA,UCC
TURPIN                      BEN           DISPLAYWRITE
ZARKOV                      VLADIMIR      DBASEIII UNIX PASCAL MSDOS




                                                              MORE
```

Figure 1.3 Displayed report without invoking the Hot Screen facility.

```
PAGE     1

              LIST OF APPLICANTS AND THEIR SOFTWARE EXPERIENCE
LAST_NAME                FIRST_NAME    SW_XPRTISE
---------                ----------    ----------


BOCHARD                  CARLOS        COBOL ASSEMBLER JCL MVS ISPF CMS ROSCOE
BORGIA                   CESARE        DW4
CLAXON                   KEITH         COBOL, CICS, BASIC
FREEMAN                  MAUREEN       WORDSTAR DBASE IV
                         RICHARD       DBASE IV, COBOL
JACOBY                   DAVID
KASTOR                   BARBARA       MSDOS COBOL UNIX  VAX
KRANSTON                 JUDITH        COBOL, IMS/VS
LAMARGO                  INDALECIO     COBOL MVS JCL VSAM IMS SPF CMS ROSCOE
LAMBACK                  JENNIFER      WORDSTAR VOLKSWRITER
TAHA                     RICHARD       IMS/VS,COBOL,DBASEIII,CICS/VS,MSA,UCC
TURPIN                   BEN           DISPLAYWRITE
ZARKOV                   VLADIMIR      DBASEIII UNIX PASCAL MSDOS


                                                    ┌─ Hot Screen
                                                   ↓  help line


KEYS: 1HELP  2FENCE 3END  4OFFLINE  5LOCAT 6SAVE  7BACK  8FORWA 9LEFT 10RIGHT
```

Figure 1.4   Displayed report after invocation of Hot Screen facility.

This is done as soon as the first page of your report is displayed on the screen. The Hot Screen help line is then displayed at the bottom of the screen. By pressing the various function keys, you could scroll backward and forward or left and right on the report. Function keys allow you to browse through very long or wide reports—remember that most display terminals can only display up to 80 characters across the screen. You could search and locate any item and even save selected data to a disk file for future review.

GRAPH Environment

This feature is very similar to the TABLE environment. The main difference is that the output of the GRAPH command is a graph. In fact, depending on your request, you can produce all the usual graphs with Focus, including the following:

> Pie chart
> Scatter diagram
> Histogram
> Bar chart
> Connected point plot

MODIFY Environment

This Focus facility allows you to add, change, and delete records from Focus and many non-Focus files and databases. MODIFY comes in several flavors. You can update a file in the batch mode or interactively, one field at a time. Formatted full-screen updating is also supported. Another Focus product, called FIDEL (Focus Interactive Data Entry Language), works within the MODIFY environment to produce additional features, such as scrolling, better field highlighting, and multiple-screen facilities.

Dialogue Manager

The Dialogue Manager consists of a series of English-like control statements that are used to direct the flow of Focus requests. For example, a payroll application contains several programs. There is a program for entering the data, the update program, and several programs to print the pay vouchers, the pay register, and the federal and state withholding reports. Without the Dialogue Manager, you would have to leave detailed instructions for the operator to load and execute each program individually to make sure that the application is run correctly. The programs have to run in correct sequence and the operator has to check that the payroll master file is for the current month and is loaded with data. With the Dialogue Manager, all these functions can be automated into a simple procedure with statements that control the sequence of programs, make sure that all the files are current and are not empty, and guide the operator through the operation.

SCAN and FSCAN Facilities

SCAN and FSCAN allow users to get inside Focus files and make changes, additions, and deletions. You can even change the key fields. At this time FSCAN is available only on some versions of Focus.

The features described above are the basic Focus facilities. Other features are described below.

SQL Translator

You can use the SQL translator of Focus to convert SQL programs to Focus. This means that if you knew only SQL, you could still access Focus files and extract information for reports.

```
SQL
SELECT LAST_NAME, FIRST_NAME, AGENCY, REQ_SALARY
FROM MASTER1
WHERE LAST_NAME > 'K'
ORDER BY LAST_NAME ;
ECHO ON
TABLE HEADING CENTER
"SQL APPLICANT LISTING"
END
```

Focus will automatically translate the SQL program above to the following Focus program and will execute it immediately.

```
TABLE FILE MASTER1
PRINT LAST_NAME FIRST_NAME AGENCY REQ_SALARY
BY LAST_NAME NOPRINT
IF LAST_NAME GT 'K'
HEADING CENTER "SQL APPLICANT LISTING"
END
```

The result of this request is as follows:

```
PAGE     1

                   SQL APPLICANT TRACKING REPORT
LAST_NAME          FIRST_NAME  AGENCY                    REQ_SALARY
---------          ----------  ------                    ----------
KASTOR             BARBARA     NONE                          22,500
KRANSTON           JUDITH      INTERNATIONAL SEARCH          42,000
LAMARGO            INDALECIO   INTERNAL REFERRAL             36,000
LAMBACK            JENNIFER                                  22,000
TAHA               RICHARD     FTA COMPUTERS                 52,500
TURPIN             BEN         EXECUTIVE CASTING             55,000
ZARKOV             VLADIMIR    MID WEST EXECUTIVE INC        46,800
```

Screen Painter

This is a tool for creating screens for data entry and inquiry. You can basically paint the screen with the help of function keys and menus. Focus will generate the necessary code to create these screens.

Report Painter

This is similar to the Screen Painter, except that it helps you create free-format reports such as forms and letters in Focus.

Import/Export Facility

This tool allows you to transfer data between mainframe and a PC/Focus file and between dBase and Lotus files and Focus files.

Financial Reporting Language (FRL)

This is an extension of the basic TABLE command. FRL is used primarily to create row-oriented reports such as budgets, balance sheets, and profit and loss statements.

Statistical Analysis with ANALYSE

Focus provides a complete tool for the statistician in the ANALYSE environment. As noted above, the basic TABLE environment provides standard statistical functions. The ANALYSE environment allows you to perform complex statistical operations such as multiple linear regression, exponential smoothing, time-series analysis, and correlations.

Window Environment

Focus is an optional facility which allows the programmer to design and develop user friendly pop-up windows, menus, and help screens.

Focus Talk Technology

Focus offers several utilities to assist both first-time users and experienced programmers to build applications, generate reports, and update files. The Talk utilities offer a selection of intelligent choices in a menu form. Users are prompted to point and select from little pop-up bar menus or windows. These selections are automatically converted into Focus requests. The requests can be saved and reused again and again. The Talk utilities are as follows:

TableTalk.   This utility allows you to develop a report program by pinpointing your requirements on the TableTalk menus. TableTalk prompts you with small menus as you progress through the building process. TableTalk can be used by beginners with little data processing background to create useful reports in a few minutes.

FileTalk. This utility follows the same principles as those of TableTalk. You use FileTalk to create new Focus files. You are constantly prompted and guided during a FileTalk session. The result is a Focus Master File Description that could be used for loading data.

ModifyTalk. This is the most sophisticated of the Talk technology utilities and is usable by both the beginners and seasoned programmers who need to develop custom update and inquiry programs. ModifyTalk menus ask a series of questions about user needs. Focus generates a complete update and/or inquiry program.

PlotTalk. This is very similar to the TableTalk utility. The output of a PlotTalk session is a program to create a Focus-supported graph.

THE FOCUS DATABASE STRUCTURE

To understand any concept it is important to understand the foundation on which it is built. Next, we review the structure of Focus files. This understanding will be needed when we write application programs or requests.

Any filing system needs certain rules to make it work. First, let us consider a simple manual filing system. We will assume that we have a drawer full of folders with information about our customers and their current balances. All these records will have to be organized in a certain way (e.g., in customer name or account number order); otherwise you would be spending half of your time trying to find the right customer file. In addition, for any filing system to be usable, the information on the records will have to be logically related. In other words, you would not expect to find company payroll information in the customer files. In our example, each customer record will consist of:

    Customer Name
    Account Number
    Customer Phone Number
    Customer Address
    Year-to-Date Purchases
    Outstanding Balance
    Comments

In addition, each record must have the same type of information in the same place. You would not expect to have the balance first, followed by comments, followed by the customer address in one record, and name, followed by comments, followed by the balance on another record. To be of any use, records must be organized logically. This is also true for computer files and databases.

The Focus database management system consists of two components or parts: (1) the Master File Description and (2) the Focus file.

Master File Description (MFD)

This is where you describe the organization of the data that you are going to store in the Focus file. For example, if you are going to create the customer file mentioned in the preceding paragraph, you should first put it together in an organized fashion, as shown in the following table.

Name of Field of Information	Type	Size
1. Customer Name	Alphabetic	20 characters
2. Customer Account Number	Numeric	9 characters
3. Customer Phone Number	Numeric	10 characters
4. Customer Street Address	Alphabetic	20 characters
5. Customer City	Alphabetic	18 characters
6. Customer State	Alphabetic	2 characters
7. Customer Zip Code	Alphabetic	5 characters
8. Year-to-Date Purchases	Numeric with two decimal places	12 characters
9. Outstanding Balance	Numeric with two decimal places	12 characters
10. Comments	Alphabetic	60 characters

From this information, you could then create a Master File Description:

```
FILENAME=CUSTOMER,SUFFIX=FOC
SEGNAME=CUSTOM,SEGTYPE=S1
FIELDNAME=CUSTOMR_NAME,ALIAS=LN,FORMAT=A20,$
FIELDNAME=ACCOUNT_NO,ALIAS=ACNO,FORMAT=I9,$
FIELDNAME=PHONE_NO,ALIAS=FN,FORMAT=A10,$
FIELDNAME=STREET,ALIAS=STR,FORMAT=A20,$
FIELDNAME=CITY,ALIAS=TOWN,FORMAT=A18,$
FIELDNAME=STATE,ALIAS=ST,FORMAT=A2,$
FIELDNAME=ZIP,ALIAS=ZIP,FORMAT=A5,$
FIELDNAME=YTD_PURCHASE,ALIAS=YTD,FORMAT=D12,$
FIELDNAME=OUTSTANDING,ALIAS=BAL,FORMAT=D12,$
FIELDNAME=COMMENTS,ALIAS=COMM,FORMAT=A60,$
```

This will let Focus know the names, types, relative locations, and sizes of all the fields of information. This is done only once, at the file design stage. Usually, an analyst or an experienced Focus programmer will undertake the task of designing the file. Thereafter, every time that you execute a program, Focus will automatically refer to the Master File Description and extract the needed information. By the time you finish this book, you will be able to design and code your own Focus Master File Description.

Focus File

The information that you or other people enter into the computer system will be stored in a Focus file or database. Focus will use the Master File Description as a template (mold) to store and retrieve data from Focus files. When you execute a Focus program, Focus will use the Master File Description, the Focus file, and your program together to extract the information requested and to print your report or update your file. Observe the following example:

```
TABLE FILE CUSTOMER
HEADING CENTER
"CUSTOMER NAME, ACCOUNT NO, YTD PURCHASE, AND OUTSTANDING
BALANCE"
PRINT ACCOUNT_NO AND YTD_PURCHASE AND OUTSTANDING
BY CUSTOMER
END
```

In this example Focus has to undertake five tasks:

1. Look at the Master File Description for the CUSTOMER file to see if the fields that you asked for actually exist.
2. Open the Focus file. (This is like opening the drawer in a manual filing system.)
3. Look at your program and select fields of information requested by your program. In this case it is the CUSTOMR_NAME, ACCOUNT_NO, YTD_PURCHASE and OUTSTANDING FIELDS.
4. Print the information retrieved.
5. Close the Focus file. (This is like closing the drawer in a manual filing system.)

The output of such a request is as follows:

```
PAGE     1

CUSTOMER NAME, ACCOUNT NO, YTD PURCHASES, AND OUTSTANDING BALANCE

CUSTOMR_NAME            ACCOUNT_NO      YTD_PURCHASE      OUTSTANDING
------------            ----------      ------------      -----------
BC MANUFACTURING        423421222             78,000           14,500
B.TURPIN ACADEMY        891244888             87,455           24,999
FISCHETTI ENTERPRISE    567180024            423,500           34,600
GREENSTREET ASSOC.      678891245             98,600           13,000
KESSLER AND CO.         981435888            897,000          234,000
STARRET AND BABBAGE     901888100          1,235,600          567,000
```

SUMMARY

In this chapter we reviewed the basic data processing concepts, the hardware, and the Focus environments. The following items were specifically addressed in the chapter.

1. Computer hardware:
   a. The CPU
   b. Main storage
   c. Disk units
   d. Printers
   e. Terminals.
2. Various operating systems and their differences
3. Focus basics
4. Focus Environments:
   a. TED
   b. HELP facility
   c. TABLE environment
   d. Hot Screen
   e. GRAPH environment
   f. MODIFY environment
   g. Dialogue Manager
   h. SCAN and FSCAN
   i. SQL Translator
   j. Screen Painter
   k. Report Painter
   l. Import/Export facility
   m. Financial Reporting Language
   n. ANALYSE statistical analysis
   o. WINDOW environment
   p. Focus Talk technology
5. The two components of Focus database:
   a. Master File Description
   b. Focus file

CHAPTER 2

THE FOCUS® PROGRAM
EDITOR: TED

MAIN TOPIC:

- THE FOCUS TEXT EDITOR (TED)

INTRODUCTION

TED is the text editor for Focus. It is also a word processor and can be used for writing letters and long reports. You will need a text editor for creating Focus programs. You may also need to use a text editor to create test data for testing your programs. There are other text editors around and some of them are probably available on your system. They are probably as good as TED in many respects. In fact, Xedit, the VM/CMS text editor, is almost identical to TED. However, since TED is integrated with Focus, it has the following advantages over many other text editors:

1. You can execute or RUN your Focus program directly from the TED text editor. When you finish coding your statements, you can move your cursor to the command line (see below), type RUN, and then press the Enter key. This command will execute your program. Additionally, it will automatically store your program on disk. You cannot do that from inside any other text editor.

2. Following execution of your Focus program, you can return to the program that you were executing simply by typing TED followed by the Enter key. This feature saves you time and allows you to modify your program while the events are still fresh in your mind.

3. If your program fails during execution due to a logic error, you will get a message from Focus indicating the possible reason for the error. Focus also displays the line number of the suspect statement. If you use a text editor that does not provide automatic line numbering of text lines, you will have a problem finding your statement. An automatic line-numbering option is available on mainframe editors but not on most PC word processors.

4. We said earlier that you can look at your program immediately after it is executed simply by typing TED. If you do this after your program fails due to an error, Focus will highlight the suspect statement. Also, the statement will be displayed at the top of screen, so you cannot miss it.

5. Online help is available with TED. All you need to do is press the PF1 key (F1 key on the PC).

6. A screen painting facility is available with TED. This feature will allow you to create screens for online data entry and inquiry applications.

7. On some versions of Focus, TED has a split-screen facility that allows you to display up to four files concurrently. You can also move lines of information from one file to the next.

TED TUTORIAL

Some of you may already be familiar with TED. In many cases it may already be set up for you. The following is intended for those of you who do not know TED and would like to use it as your main text editor in Focus.

> *Step 1: Invoke Focus.* As stated earlier this step usually involves typing the word "FOCUS," followed by pressing the Enter key. On some systems, Focus may be an option on a preprogrammed menu.
>
> *Step 2: Set up your TED PROFILE.* PROFILE is a file that you personalize to your needs. Focus will use this file every time you invoke Focus. You can use PROFILE to automate many user functions. For now, we create this file and set it up to ease data entry and edit tasks. Depending on the version of Focus that you are using, there may be a slight variation in the method of setting up PROFILE.

Setting Up TED Under PC/Focus

In PC/Focus version 4.0, select the TED option from the main menu.

```
           Menu Presentation of FOCUS facilities

  What would you like to do?
  ────────────────────────────────────────────────────────

  TableTalk     Build column-oriented report
  PlotTalk      Build a graph
  FileTalk      Describe a new database file
  Modify Talk   Build a MODIFY Procedure
  Painters      Build free-format reports or screens
 (Ted           Create/edit a file )
  Scan          Browse/update a database file
  Link          Communicate with other computers
  System        Issue a DOS command
  Windows       Create, maintain, & run WINDOWS
  Exec          Create, maintain, & run FOCEXECS
  Help          Display help information
  Other         Focus utilities (QUERY, JOIN, etc.)
  Commands      Issue interactive FOCUS commands
  Exit          Leave FOCUS and return to DOS

  Select options with ↑ ↓ and ENTER .. or ESC to back up
```

Next, press the Enter key; and the TED bar menu will be displayed on the screen.

```
          Menu Presentation of FOCUS facilities


     What would you like to do?
     ─────────────────────────────────────────────────

  Enter a file name to CREATE/EDIT:
  ──────────────────────────────────────────────────────
  PROFILE.TED

        Ted           Create/edit a file
        Scan          Browse/update a database file
        Link          Communicate with other computers
        System        Issue a DOS command
        Windows       Create, maintain, & run WINDOWS
        Exec          Create, maintain, & run FOCEXECS
        Help          Display Help information
        Other         Focus utilities (QUERY, JOIN, etc.)
        Commands      Issue interactive FOCUS commands
        Exit          Leave FOCUS and return to DOS


     Select options with ↑ ↓ and ENTER .. or ESC to back up
```

Type PROFILE.TED and press the Enter key. This will present you with an almost blank screen. There will be one line at the top of the screen which displays the file name and size, and two short lines at the upper left-hand side of the screen:

```
C:PROFILE.TED                    SIZE=0    LINE=0    ← File identification
                                                         line
 * * * TOP OF FILE * * *
 * * * END OF FILE * * *       File  area




===>         ← TED  command  line
                                                     TYPING MODE
```

The line at the top of the screen is called the *file identification line* or *status line*. The two lines surrounded by three asterisks on each side are the top of the file and end of the file. At this time, there is no information in your PROFILE file, so the file is empty. There is also a line at the bottom of the screen. This line with the arrow (====>) is the TED command line.

    1. The cursor should be positioned on the command line. If it is not already there, press the Enter key twice and the cursor will move to the command line in front of the arrow (====>). Next, you should type "num on" and press the Enter key once.

```
   PROFILE   TED        A1                      SIZE=0     LINE=0
   * * * TOP OF FILE * * *
   * * * END OF FILE * * *

















   ====> num on
                                                      TYPING MODE
```

This will generate a column of numbers starting from ''00000'' on the left side of the screen.

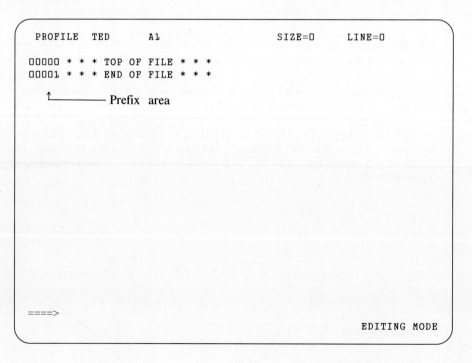

```
   PROFILE   TED        A1                      SIZE=0     LINE=0
   00000 * * * TOP OF FILE * * *
   00001 * * * END OF FILE * * *

   ↑_____ Prefix  area















   ====>
                                                    EDITING MODE
```

This area is called the *prefix*. The prefix area is used extensively in writing programs. You will use this area to insert, delete, add, and move lines of program around the screen. You can also perform block adds, deletes, copy, and move operations by making use of simple commands in the prefix area.

2. While you are still on the command line, type "add 2" and then press the Enter key. This will add two blank lines to the text area on top of the screen. It will also move the cursor to the top of the page and position it for data entry on the first line.

```
   PROFILE   TED        A1              SIZE=0     LINE=0

   00000 * * * TOP OF FILE * * *
   00001 * * * END OF FILE * * *

















   ====> add 2
                                                    EDITING MODE
```

3. On the first line, where the cursor should currently be positioned, type "NUM ON" and press the Tab key, which is located on the left side of the keyboard, twice. This will bring the cursor to the second line. Next type "CASE U" and press the Enter Key. The cursor will now move down to the command line. "NUM ON" is short for "number on." "CASE U" is short for "case upper."

```
  PROFILE   TED       A1                    SIZE=2   LINE=0

  00000 * * * TOP OF FILE * * *
  00001 NUM ON
  00002 CASE U
  00003 * * * END OF FILE * * *

















  ====>
                                               EDITING MODE
```

4. Type "file" and press the Enter key.

```
  PROFILE   TED       A1                    SIZE=2   LINE=0

  00000 * * * TOP OF FILE * * *
  00001 NUM ON
  00002 CASE U
  00003 * * * END OF FILE * * *
















  ====> file
                                               EDITING MODE
```

This will store PROFILE for you. By typing "NUM ON" you have told Focus that, in future, every time that you type TED to do programming, you will want to get a screen with sequence numbers in the Prefix area. By typing "CASE U" you have told Focus to convert whatever you type into uppercase automatically. This is important because Focus does not recognize commands typed in lowercase.

PC/FOCUS VERSION 5.5

The initial main menu under version 5.5 of PC/Focus is somewhat different. The following four screens show you (1) the main menu (2) the selection menu and (3) making the TED selection. The rest of the menus and instruction for creating the profile are the same as version 4.

The following figures display the PC/Focus Release 5.5 Menu System.

PC/FOCUS RELEASE 5.5 MAIN MENU

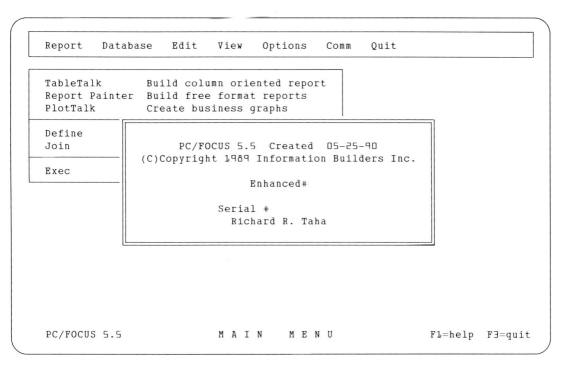

Figure 2.1 The Main Menu immediately after Focus is invoked.

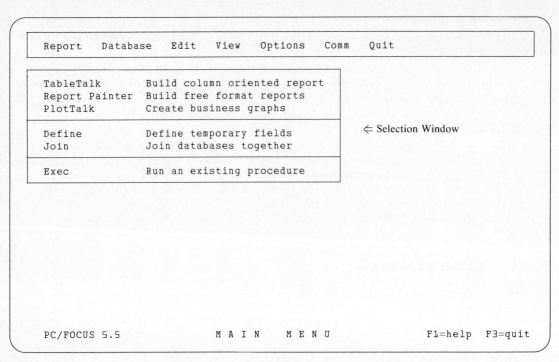

```
  Report   Database   Edit   View    Options   Comm   Quit

  TableTalk        Build column oriented report
  Report Painter   Build free format reports
  PlotTalk         Create business graphs
                                                    ← Selection Window
  Define           Define temporary fields
  Join             Join databases together

  Exec             Run an existing procedure




  PC/FOCUS 5.5              M A I N   M E N U          F1=help  F3=quit
```

Figure 2.2 The Main Menu with Sub Menu Selection Window.

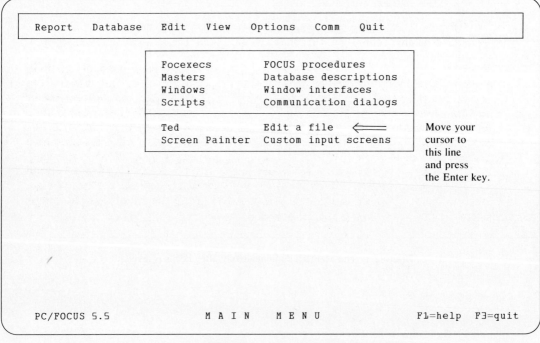

```
  Report   Database   Edit   View    Options   Comm   Quit

          Focexecs         FOCUS procedures
          Masters          Database descriptions
          Windows          Window interfaces
          Scripts          Communication dialogs

          Ted              Edit a file     ⟸         Move your
          Screen Painter   Custom input screens       cursor to
                                                       this line
                                                       and press
                                                       the Enter key.




  PC/FOCUS 5.5              M A I N   M E N U          F1=help  F3=quit
```

Figure 2.3 The Options Selection Window.

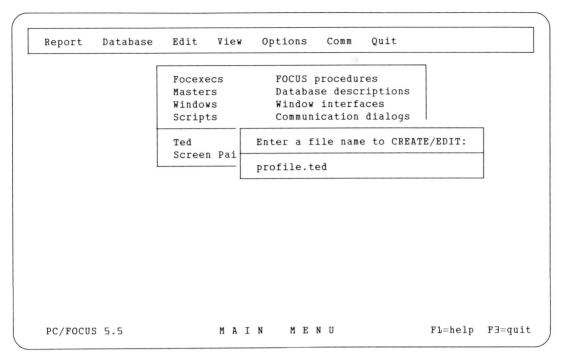

```
 ┌──────────────────────────────────────────────────────────────────┐
 │                                                                    │
 │  ┌──────────────────────────────────────────────────────────┐     │
 │  │ Report   Database   Edit   View   Options   Comm   Quit   │     │
 │  └──────────────────────────────────────────────────────────┘     │
 │         ┌─────────────────────────────────────────────────┐        │
 │         │ Focexecs        FOCUS procedures                │        │
 │         │ Masters         Database descriptions           │        │
 │         │ Windows         Window interfaces               │        │
 │         │ Scripts         Communication dialogs           │        │
 │         ├──────────────┬──────────────────────────────────┤        │
 │         │ Ted          │  Enter a file name to CREATE/EDIT:│        │
 │         │ Screen Pai   ├──────────────────────────────────┤        │
 │         └──────────────┤    profile.ted                   │        │
 │                        └──────────────────────────────────┘        │
 │                                                                    │
 │   PC/FOCUS 5.5           M A I N   M E N U      F1=help  F3=quit   │
 └──────────────────────────────────────────────────────────────────┘
```

Figure 2.4   Selection of PROFILE.TED Menu.

Setting Up TED under IBM Mainframes and Most Minicomputers

If you are using the mainframe version of Focus, where there are usually no main Focus menus, you must get into the Focus environment first. This differs from site to site. Generally, you get into Focus by first logging onto your host computer system. Focus may be an item on the main system menu that you could then select. Alternatively, there may be no system menu. On some systems you just get a prompt line indicating that you have established contact with your host computer. For example, with IBM VM/CMS, you get a READY prompt, which is displayed as "READY;" near the top of the screen. At that point you should type the word "FOCUS" and press the Enter key to get into Focus. Once you get into Focus you will see the Focus banner at the top of the screen and the Focus prompt sign (> or >>) on the line directly below it:

```
┌─────────────────────────────────────────────────────────────┐
│  FOCUS  6.0      10/31/91  16.13.07  9688.05      ← Banner line │
│  >          ← Focus prompt                                      │
│                          ·                                     │
│                                                                │
│                                                                │
│                                                                │
│                                                                │
│                                                                │
│                                                                │
│                                                                │
│                                                                │
│                                                                │
│                                                                │
│                                                                │
│                                               VM READ          │
└─────────────────────────────────────────────────────────────┘
```

This is the Focus command line. Please note that on some mainframe versions of Focus the cursor will be near the bottom of the CRT screen. Next to the cursor you should type the following command:

```
TED PROFILE TED
```

Next, press the Enter key. You can then follow the same steps as shown previously for PC/Focus to establish your PROFILE. You can, of course, change your TED PROFILE any time you wish by following the steps already mentioned.

Note to MVS Users: On MVS systems issue the following command from the Focus > prompt:

```
TED FOCEXEC(PROFILE)
```

Also, to tell Focus to place numbers on the Prefix area, you will need a TEDPROF file. To create this file issue the following command from the Focus > prompt:

```
TED FOCEXEC(TEDPROF)
```

The TEDPROF Focexec should only contain the NUM ON statement. See the following figure:

```
  FOCEXEC(TEDPROF)                    SIZE=1     LINE=0

  00000 * * * TOP OF FILE * * *
  00001 NUM ON
  00002 * * * END OF FILE * * *













  ====>
                                                 EDITING MODE
```

Figure 2.5 The TEDPROF file for MVS/TSO users.

Writing Programs under TED

We will now write our first Focus program. I am assuming that you are already in
Focus. If you are in the mainframe version of Focus, you should be at the command level with the Focus > prompt. In PC/Focus, choose the Commands option
from the main Focus menu and press the Enter key. This will put you in the
command mode. Your cursor should now be positioned in front of the Focus
double-arrow prompt sign (> >). Mainframe Focus uses the single arrow (>) or
spaced double arrows (> >) as a prompt sign, whereas PC/Focus uses the double
arrow (>>).

   We will try to use realistic and useful Focus examples throughout this
book. One of these files will be a credit card registration system called Registry.
You may have been offered the services of a card registration firm in the past.
The service usually costs $15 or more per year. Basically, this is how it works.
You send to the company a list of all your charge cards and their emergency phone
numbers. If you lose your cards, you make one phone call to the registration
company. The registration company in turn will call all your charge card companies to cancel your cards and request replacement cards.

   The first program will print a list of all the cardholders and the issuing
company, expiration date, and credit limit of each card.

   The first program will be coded as follows:

   1. At the Focus command line, on VM/CMS type "TED REGIST1
FOCEXEC." On the PC/Focus version, type "TED REGIST1.FEX." On
MVS/Focus type "TED FOCEXEC(REGIST1)." "FOCEXEC" and "FEX"

are the suffixes that identify Focus programs to Focus. We will learn more about them later. Focus will present you with an almost blank screen. However, since we have already set up a PROFILE, a prefix area will also be displayed on the left-hand side of the screen. As before, you must expand the file size. You do this by typing "add 6" on the command line. Then starting from the top of the screen, you code the program (as shown). Note that in TED you should use the Tab key to go from one line to the next, not the Enter key. The Enter key will move the cursor to the TED command line.

```
-* REGI1
-* PROGRAM TO LIST THE CARDHOLDERS AND THEIR DATA
TABLE FILE REGISTER
PRINT LAST_NAME
AND ISSUER AND EXPIRE_DATE
AND CREDIT_LIMIT
END
```

2. Once the coding is finished, you should press the Enter key twice. This will bring the cursor down to the command line. Next you should type "file" and then press the Enter key. This will file the program away for future use. Obviously, you cannot execute this program because you do not have the Master File Description and the Focus data file for the card registration application. Later I will show you several ways to create Master File Descriptions and to load data into Focus files. However, the following list is an example of the report that you might expect from executing the preceding program.

```
PAGE     1


LAST_NAME          ISSUER                     EXPIRE_DATE  CREDIT_LIMIT
---------          ------                     -----------  ------------
TURPIN             CARTE BLANCHE                09/30/92          8,000
TURPIN             MUTUAL STUDIOS C.U.          09/30/90          5,000
GREENSTREET        AMEX                         09/30/91          6,500
```

TED Prefix Commands

These are the letter and symbol commands that you key in on the prefix column (see Table 2.1). Focus will take specific actions depending on letters or symbols that you use. To use these commands, you use the Tab and the cursor keys. Suppose that you want to use the MOVE command to move one line of text (e.g., a report heading or a line of code) from one place in a program to another. You just keep pressing the Tab key until you arrive at the prefix area of the line that you want to move:

```
00120  PRINT LAST_NAME AND FIRST_NAME
```

Then put the letter M anywhere in the prefix area and press the Enter key:

```
0M120  PRINT LAST_NAME AND FIRST_NAME
```

TABLE 2.1 TED PREFIX COMMANDS

Symbol or letter	Meaning
C	Copy one line of text or program from one location to another in the same program.
CC	Copy a block of lines from one location to another. You will need one "CC" to mark the beginning of the block and another "CC" to mark the end of the block of lines.
M	Move one line of text or data from one location to another
MM	Move a block of lines from one location to another. You will need one "MM" to mark the beginning of the block and another "MM" to mark the end of the block of lines.
D	Delete the current line.
DD	Delete a block of lines. You will need one "DD" to mark the beginning of the block and another "DD" to mark the end of the block of lines.
"	The double quotation mark repeats the current line directly below itself.
"n	The combination of a double quotation mark and a number in the prefix area will repeat that particular line that many times. For example, "5 means "repeat this line five times."
A or I	Insert one blank line at the current line position. This actually creates a blank line directly below the current line.
An or In	Insert n blank lines at this (current) line. For example, I5 means insert five blank lines at this position. These prefix commands are used extensively to insert program code or text that you may have forgotten to enter previously.

Next, Tab over to the prefix area of the line to which you want to move the data and type either the letter "P" for "preceding" or the letter "F" for "following" and then press the Enter key. "P" means that you want the line moved to the line preceding the one you are now on. "F" means that you want it moved to the following line.

Use two letters or symbols in a block command. For example, in a block move, you should mark off the area that you want to move by typing "MM" in the prefix areas at the beginning and end of the group of lines that are to be moved. The TED display screen is only 19 lines long. If your block is longer than one screen full of data or you are starting near the end of the screen and the remainder of the data are on another screen, you should use the two-letter prefix commands with TED's scroll commands. Just mark the beginning of the block with a prefix command such as DD, MM, or CC and then use the PF8 or the F8 key to scroll down the pages until you reach the end of the block. Then enter the corresponding prefix command (e.g., DD) and press the Enter key. The rest of the move is just like a single-line move.

What happens if you make a mistake? Well, there are three ways that you can reverse entries.

1. You can cancel pending prefix operations after making a selection but before pressing the Enter key. To cancel an operation, move your cursor to the TED command line by using the Tab key, type the RESET command, and press the Enter key.

2. If you have already pressed the Enter key, you can recover deleted lines by moving the cursor to the TED command line and typing the RECOVER command in one of three formats:

```
RECOVER      ← Undeletes the latest deleted line.
RECOVER n    ← Undeletes the last n deleted lines (e.g., RECOVER 4).
RECOVER *    ← Undeletes all deleted lines.
```

The recovered lines are placed at the top of the screen starting on the first line of the file. It is then up to you to move them back to their appropriate location. RECOVER works only for deleted lines. It does not reverse other operations, such as move and copy.

3. Sometimes during a session you make a number of changes, such as adding, moving, copying, and deleting lines. You may modify the contents of some lines and then change your mind and decide to go back to the original program. To restore the original program, you should type "QQUIT" or "QQ" on the TED command line. This command will nullify all the changes that you have made during the session. This will work only if you have not saved your files during the session. If you save your files, as you should, every 5 minutes or so, this command will restore only the changes that you have made since the last SAVE command.

There are other prefix commands that I have not reviewed here. Table 2.1 is a list of the most useful commands. Take some time now and play around with TED and these commands. You should first create a document and then try to manipulate it by using the commands until you feel confident that you can handle TED.

Other TED Commands

There is another class of TED commands that you either issue from the TED command line (=====>) or invoke by pressing one of the function keys. Each of these commands executes a specific function. Function keys are known as *program function keys* (PF keys) in the mainframe world. In the PC world they are known simply as *function keys* (F). Unfortunately, only some of the function commands are the same across all Focus versions. The good news is that the most important function commands (Table 2.2) are identical in all versions.

The following commands can only be issued from the TED command line. Just type the command and press the Enter key.

TOP. This command will take you back to the first screen of your program or data file. Suppose that you had a 50-page data file and you wanted to go to the first page from page 44. You could press the PF7 key over 40 times, or alternatively, you could type the word "TOP" or the letter "T" and press the Enter key once.

TABLE 2.2 FUNCTION COMMANDS

Important function key commands	Meaning
PF1 or F1	This command activates the help message lines.
PF3 or F3	Pressing the PF3 will terminate your TED session. Alternatively, you could type "QUIT" in the TED command line. PF3 or "QUIT" will work only if you have not made any changes in the program file.
PF4 or F4	Paint.
PF7 or F7	PF7 will move the screen backward one full screen (18 lines).
PF8 or F8	PF8 will move the screen forward one full screen (18 lines).

BOTTOM. This command is the reverse of the TOP command. Typing the word "BOTTOM" or the letter "B" will take you to the last line of the program or file.

FILE. This command will file the current program and will return you to the main Focus command environment. When you enter this command, the current file is stored on disk and you are returned to the main Focus menu or the Focus command line.

SAVE. This command will store the current file. However, you will continue to stay in the TED edit environment. It is good practice to issue the SAVE command every 5 minutes or so during program entry so that data are not lost due to a power failure or system problems. You can save your file under a different name. If your file name is PROGRAM1 and you type "SAVE PROGRAM2," another program file called PROGRAM2 is created.

QUIT. This command will take you out of the TED environment and back to the Focus > prompt. This command will work only if no changes have been made in the current file.

QQUIT or QQ. This command is similar to QUIT except that it will take you out of TED even if you have made changes to the file. It will reverse all changes, additions, and deletions that you may have made during your session to the file in question.

LOCATE. The LOCATE command is the slash symbol /. This command will search for a string of characters starting from the current position. For example, if you wanted to find the word "balance" in your code, you would move your cursor to the TED command line and type "/BALANCE" or "LOCATE/BALANCE." The editor will search your file for the first line that contains the word "BALANCE" and will display that line at the top of the screen. "LOCATE /" or "/" works only from the current position of the file. For example, if you are on page number 5 of a program, it will not search the previous pages. It is therefore best first to go to the top of the file by issuing the TOP command and then issue the LOCATE command. Alternatively, you could type "-/BALANCE" to search backward through a file.

RUN. This command will execute your Focus program directly from the TED command line. After you finish coding your program in TED, press the Enter key twice to move your cursor to the TED command line. Next, type "RUN" and press the Enter key. Focus will file the program first and will then execute it. It is not necessary to execute your Focus program directly from TED, but it is a useful feature that could be used during the program testing and error correction phase.

Repeat last command. To repeat any command, type the equal sign (=) on the TED command line and press the Enter key. For example, if you have used the LOCATE command (/) to find the first occurrence of the word "BALANCE," you can keep entering the "=" on the command line to execute the same command automatically and try to find other occurrences of the word "BALANCE" farther down the file until you reach the end of the TED file or the program.

There is another way of repeating the commands even faster. If you know that you will need to repeat a command many times, precede it with an ampersand sign (&). Thereafter, all you need to do is press the Enter key and the command will be executed. For example, type "&/BALANCE" and press the Enter key. The first occurrence of the word "BALANCE" will be displayed at the top of the screen. If you keep pressing the Enter key, all other occurrences will be displayed at the top of the screen one after another until you reach the end of the file.

Show last command. After you enter a command and press the Enter key, the command will disappear from the screen. To recall the command that you have just executed, enter a question mark (?) symbol and press the Enter key.

SUMMARY

In this chapter we discussed the basics of TED. The VM/CMS Xedit editor is almost identical to TED, so you could use the foregoing material to learn Xedit commands and functions. The ISPF text editor on the IBM MVS systems is also similar to TED but is not a direct match. Following are the topics that we discussed in this chapter.

1. Advantages of using TED instead of your regular system's text editor
2. Setting up your own TED Profile under PC/Focus and mainframe Focus
3. Writing your first Focus program with TED
4. TED prefix commands
5. Storing and executing Focus programs
6. Recovering changed data with RESET, RECOVER, and the QQUIT commands

7. Function key commands

8. TED command line commands:
   a. TOP
   b. BOTTOM
   c. FILE
   d. SAVE
   e. QUIT
   f. QQUIT (or QQ)
   g. LOCATE (or /)
   h. RUN
   i. Repeat last command (or =)
   j. Automatic repeat (or &)
   k. Show last command executed (or ?)
   l. PC/Focus Release 5.5 Main Menu

CHAPTER 3

DESIGNING AND CREATING DATABASES IN FOCUS®

MAIN TOPICS:

- MANUAL FILING SYSTEMS
- AUTOMATED FILING SYSTEMS
- DATABASE MANAGEMENT SYSTEMS
- FOCUS FORMATS
- STAFF FILE
- MASTER FILE CREATION

It is not necessary for every Focus user to understand the concept of database design and structure. However, I feel very strongly that every user will benefit from reading this chapter, especially the section about Focus record types and formats. You can, however, proceed to Chapter 4, if you wish, without studying this chapter.

Figure 3.1 displays a simplified version of the information found in the master file of a typical personnel management system. We will call this the STAFF file and review it for the next few pages.

MANUAL SEQUENTIAL FILING SYSTEMS

Each employee in the company is identified by a number. Often, the social security number is used for this purpose. Other pertinent information is also recorded. This information is usually gathered at the time an employee is hired. The salary, job title, department, and address information may change over time. In a manual personnel system, this information is kept in manila folders and ledger cards. To make filing and retrieval of data manageable, the information is usually kept in some sort of sequence. Some organizations file the information by date of hire, some by last name, and some by employee ID number. Probably, the best method would be to file the records in employee ID number sequence, which is always a unique number. This method of filing the information in order by one of the fields is also known as a *sequential filing system*. Any other method, such

Name of Field
Employee ID
Last Name
First Name
Street Address
City
State
Zip Code
Telephone Number
Date of Birth
Date of Hire
Job Title
Salary
Percentage Increase
Vacation Hours
Department ID
Department Name
Section ID
Section Name   **Figure 3.1** STAFF file.

as filing the records by employee name within respective sections and departments, would be very cumbersome to do manually.

Let us consider a company that has 7000 employees, 10 departments, and four sections within each department. We will assume that the information is filed in the employee ID number sequence. If we wanted to find the names and salaries of employees in the collections section of the accounting department, we would have to read each of the 7000 records and locate employees who work in the section requested. This approach is time consuming but is practically the only way to produce reports under a manual system.

AUTOMATED THIRD-GENERATION FILING SYSTEMS

In a third-generation application development environment, you would be using magnetic files such as disk units, excellent access methods, and powerful languages such as COBOL. However, the problem with third-generation application development tools is that they essentially copy the manual systems that they are replacing. So while the accuracy is improved, the sorting of data is much faster, and more reports can be generated, the basic foundation and structure of data have not changed. This is because these application development tools are very similar in concept to manual systems. They view and store the data in the same way that a manual system does, and each field of each record is treated equally throughout the system. If your company has 7000 employees and only 10 departments, the department name and department ID will have to be repeated and stored 7000 times with each employee record. This is a function of a sequential filing organization, where each record must be filed separately and sequentially (see Fig. 3.2). IBM and other computer companies have developed other file

Field Name	value	value	value
Employee ID	1234	1235	1236
Last Name	Trask	Anders	Greene
First Name	Ben	Christine	Sam
Street Address	100 Vista	55 Villa	22 A. St.
City	Santa Ana	E. Orange	Chicago
State	CA	NJ	IL
Zip Code	91234	102355	432899
Phone No.	7145551234	2015551256	7085550989
Date of Birth	03/15/44	12/22/52	06/09/48
Date of Hire	10/30/88	08/15/85	07/17/82
Job Title	Analyst	Auditor	Engineer
Salary	64500	43500	55400
Percent Incr.	.04	.08	.10
Vacation Hours	100	50	20
Department ID	MIS	ACC	ENG
Department Name	Info syst	Accounting	Engineering
Section ID	PR1	Col	Mai
Section Name	Systems	Collections	Maintenance
	Record 1	Record 2	Record 3

Figure 3.2 Sequential file organization.

access methods that could retrieve records randomly. These access methods use an indexing system. The index points to the position of a block of records. This is very much like the index in a book. If you are searching for a key word, you would first locate the respective page number in the book's index. Then all you will have to do is to search through that particular page for the word. Indexing in computers works pretty much the same way. It can help a program locate the block of records that contains the record requested. Then the program only has to search sequentially for that record within that block. Each block would normally be, say, 100 records long instead of 7000 or more, as would be the case with sequential filing systems. One of the most popular indexed filing systems is IBM's Virtual Storage Access Method (VSAM).

Even with the best indexed filing systems, all the records would still have to be filed completely. In other words, you would still have to record the department name and the section name with each employee record. However, it will be much faster to access each record because an indexed filing system will automatically maintain an index file of where each record is located. In any case, this unnecessary duplication of the same data throughout the system will exist with all of the filing systems already described. Duplication of data is commonly known as *data redundancy*. The filing concept is known as *flat file structure*, because all fields are at the same level and are treated equally.

Database management systems and fourth-generation languages such as Focus use different structures. These structures are known as *hierarchical, network,* and *relational*. Focus is a hierarchical database management system (DBMS) with relational capabilities.

Hierarchical Organization

A hierarchical organization resembles the organization chart of a corporation (see Fig. 3.3). There is usually a president at the top with several vice presidents. Each vice president may have one or several departments under him. Some vice presidents may have no departments reporting to them. In each department there are one or more employees performing daily activities. The hierarchical structure is also very aptly called the *parent–child structure*. Each parent may have none, one, or several children. The children in turn could be parents and have other children. Without parents there would be no children. Another name for the hierarchical structure is the *inverted tree structure*. Unlike other types of database management systems, hierarchical organization is intuitively easy to understand because our culture is based on hierarchies.

How does all this relate to Focus? Well, we will use this structure to demonstrate how easy it is to improve upon the way we built our original STAFF file. To understand any subject you must be familiar with its terminology. So next, we review certain concepts and terms used in Focus.

Field. A field is the basic building block of a database. It is usually defined as the smallest unit of information that can be stored in and retrieved from computer storage by a program. We work with fields of information every day of our lives. Your last name is a field of information, as is your social security number. In Focus and other programming languages, each field must be named individually to differentiate it from other fields. Also, unlike manually based systems, in data processing, everything must be defined exactly. So each field must have a fixed size. Another important factor is the type of data that the field contains. A field can be alphanumeric or numeric. An alphanumeric field is a field that contains alphabet letters or a mixture of letters, numbers, and special characters. A part number such as A2234-12 or a name such as Richard are examples of alphanumeric fields. A numeric field can contain only the digits 0 through 9, a decimal point, and either a positive (+) or a negative (−) sign. Table 3.1 displays examples of valid and invalid numeric fields.

In a manual system, we do not need to define the format and type of fields because we know intuitively that you cannot divide a name by another name. In most computer languages, you must define the type of the field in your program. In COBOL and other third-generation languages, any attempt to perform mathematical operations on nonnumeric fields will cause the program to crash immediately. Focus is more forgiving and will tolerate certain user mistakes.

Field value. The field value or data value comprises the contents of a field of information. Probably the best example of this concept is a social security number. Every one has a social security number, which is a field of information.

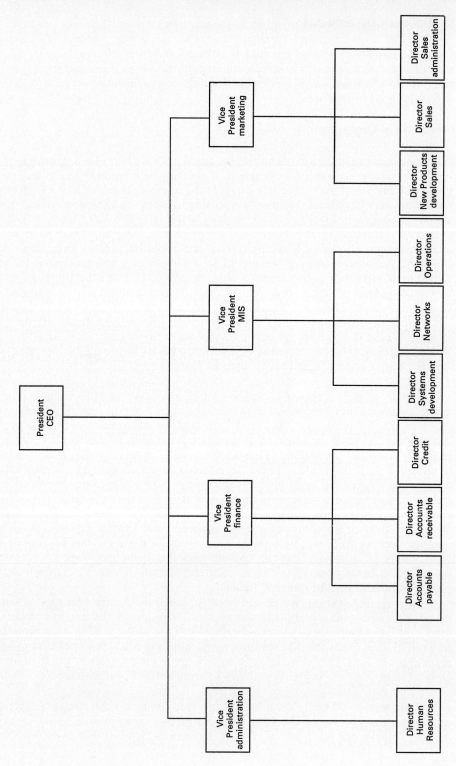

Figure 3.3 Typical organization chart.

TABLE 3.1 VALID AND INVALID NUMERIC FIELDS

Valid numeric fields	Invalid numeric fields
12345	1234−4 (minus sign not allowed in the middle of field)
+9123	9+912 (plus sign not allowed in middle of field)
345.00	345.00. (only one decimal point allowed)
12.245	12,245 (comma not allowed in a numeric field)
.00123	12/31/91 (slashes not allowed)
−564.12	''124'' (quotes not permissible)

The value is the contents of the field, which is different in every case. Sometimes, the field values are similar. The value of the branch number of a bank would be the same for all customers of that branch.

Segment. A segment is a combination of several related fields. It can sometimes be a single field. In personnel files, information such as department name, department ID, and department location could be lumped together to form one segment. We will call this the *department segment*. Information about people in each department, such as names, addresses, phone numbers, and salaries could be grouped together to form another segment, which we will call the *employee segment*. It is important to realize the concepts of one-to-one and one-to-many. Within each segment, fields have a one-to-one relationship. For each department there is only one department ID, one department name and one department manager—hence the term *one-to-one*. For each employee, there is only one social security number, one salary and one address. Again, this is considered a one-to-one relationship. However, within each department, there could be many employees. Therefore, the relationship of the department segment to the employees segment is called *one-to-many*.

Record. A combination of several fields of data logically related to each other is called a *record*. In our case the combination of the fields in the STAFF file is called a *staff record*.

File. A file is a combination of records.

Database. In data processing, the term *database* is used very loosely. There is no universal agreement. Any vendor of a filing system could claim that their filing system is a database. Generally, any combination of records that is filed hierarchically could be referred to as a database. It could also be called a file. Flat sequential files are not referred to as databases, but even here there is no agreement. If you combine several files, the result is usually called a database.

In Focus, the combination of the Master File Description (which identifies fields and segments and their relationships) and the Focus data file (which contains the actual data) is a database management system.

Our next task is to take the STAFF file in Fig. 3.1 and design a more efficient structure with the same information. Figure 3.4 shows the same information reorganized using a hierarchical structure. In this example, the file is divided into three levels. In each level there is one segment. As you will notice, the related fields are grouped together in each segment. If a department has four sections and 200 employees, there will be only one segment for the department. That segment will contain the department name and the department ID. There would be four instances of section segments under the department. This would be followed by

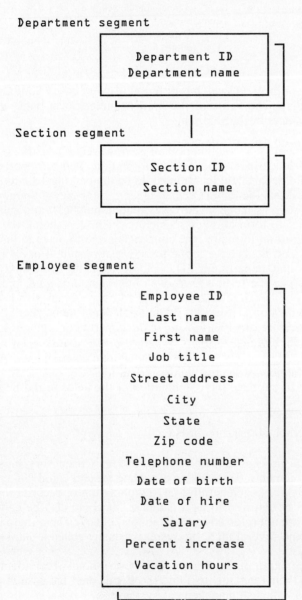

Department segment

Section segment

Employee segment

Figure 3.4 Hierarchical organization of the STAFF file. The double box indicates that this segment is repeated several times.

Designing and Creating Databases in Focus®   Chap. 3

many occurrences of employee segments for each section. There may be one or many instances of employee segments for each section segment. Therefore, in our hypothetical company, we would have 10 department segments, 40 section segments, and 7000 employee segments. We have created a definite relationship between employees and departments, and if you want to create a report of employees in one department, you simply look for that department segment and search for the employees there.

The top segment in a hierarchical organization is called the *root segment*. All the segments below it are subordinate segments called *descendent* or *child segments*. Each descendent segment is dependent on its parent segment. It may also be a parent to another segment. In Figure 3.4, the department segment is the root segment. It is also the parent segment to the section segment. The section segment is the descendent of the department segment and is the parent of the employee segment. The parent of the last segment, the employee segment, is the section segment. The employee segment has no descendents. All these terms are used in Focus and it is important to comprehend them fully.

Rules for Designing Hierarchical Databases

Many articles have been written about designing databases and there are many complex algorithms for segment design. Frankly, some of the rules are so complex that they may not be worth using except for very large databases. Anyway, there are several basic rules that you should remember:

1. Study the data thoroughly. Try to understand the purpose of structure and the relationship of various fields to each other. You may need to interview users to understand the requirements fully. If you decide to conduct an interview, always have your questions ready ahead of time, and if possible, send an advance copy to the person being interviewed to help him or her get the answers ready for you.

2. Put the related fields together as one segment. In other words, salary is a field that is related to an employee and should be in the employee segment. There is no reason to put it in the department or section segments.

3. Put the data that occur least in the top segment. This will make navigation through the database easier. In our example, there are 10 departments, 40 sections, and 7000 employees. The department segment should be at the top because it occurs only 10 times. The section segment should be next because it occurs 40 times. The employee segment should be next because it occurs 7000 times. If you write a program to find the records of employees in the engineering department, Focus will ignore all the other departments, sections, and employees and start from the engineering department. By using this technique, you are also improving the efficiency of your computer system by speeding up the data access.

4. Create a new level every time the relationship between the fields changes from one-to-one to one-to-many. In our example this happened between department and section and between section and employee segments. However, do not go overboard with new levels, because that could slow down your processing time.

5. Within each segment, put the key fields at the top. We will talk more about the key fields later. However, let us take a look at the employee segment. In this case, employee ID is the field that Focus will use to sequence and locate employees by. If you are searching your file, it is easier and faster for Focus to find the records requested if they are in a logical order. So, in effect, by using good design techniques, you are speeding up the processing of data.

6. In each segment, keep the fields that are used frequently for reporting as high as possible.

7. Consider reserving some fields on each level for future expansion.

8. To speed up processing, put as few fields as possible in the root segment.

.9. If you are adding date to the Focus file, make the date the key field in the segment, if possible. Also, use a segment type of SH1, which will keep the key field in the high-to-low order sequence. This will place the later dates at the beginning of the file and Focus will not be forced to traverse the entire group of segments while it is reading records or is adding records to the file.

10. Consider indexing heavily accessed fields. As we discussed earlier, indexing can speed up processing of data.

11. Do not use too many key fields. Unnecessary key fields can slow down processing of records in the Focus file.

FOCUS FORMATS OR USAGE TYPES

We discussed earlier that in a computerized system, each field must have certain characteristics or attributes. These requirements are detailed below.

- Type of data (i.e., alphanumeric or numeric).
- Size or length of the data (i.e., is the field 20 characters long, such as a name, or 10 characters long, such as a balance field?).
- The decimal accuracy of numeric data. Is this a balance field with two decimal places, or is it an interest field that needs six decimal places to be accurate? If data are numeric, they could be defined as one of the four types of numeric data that are allowed within Focus.

A list of permissible types of data and sizes in Focus is displayed in Table 3.2.

TABLE 3.2 PERMISSIBLE TYPES OF DATA AND SIZES

Type of data	Examples	Format[a]	Length of data	Maximum size
Alphanumeric: any	San Francisco	A	13	Up to 255
combination of	A-546228-Z	A	10	characters
alphabetic and/	Newmount Manufacturing	A	46	
characters	T	A	1	
	1$X%2	A	5	

TABLE 3.2 (*Continued*)

Type of data	Examples	Format[a]	Length of data	Maximum size
or numeric and/ or special	and Smelting Corpora-tion			
Numeric				
Integer: no deci-	1234	I	4	Up to nine
mal points	2	I	1	digits
allowed; could	921215	I	6	
be any digit	−1234	I	5	
from 0 to 9	123456789	I	9	
Decimal: could	45.16	D	5	Up to 15
be any digit	123456	D	6	digits[b]
from 0 to 9 plus	6	D	1	
a decimal				
point; the				
decimal point is				
counted in the				
total length, so				
41.16 has a				
length of five				
digits				
Packed decimal:	84.05	P	5	Up to 15
could be any	123456	P	6	digits[b]
digit from 0 to	7	P	1	
9 plus a deci-				
mal point; the				
decimal point is				
counted in total				
length of the				
filed, so 128.05				
has a length of				
6; packed				
decimal takes				
almost half the				
storage area of				
decimal type				
Floating point:	67.12	F	5	Up to nine
could be any	2	F	1	digits
digit from 0 to				
9; it is similar				
to the decimal				
D type, but its				
maximum size				
is limited to 9;				
F-type data are				
of limited use				
Date formats:	920131	I	6YMD	
there are sev-	013192	I	6MDY	
eral date for-	310192	I	6DMY	
mats, the most	31011992	I	8DMYY	
useful ones are	01311992	I	8MDYY	
shown here[c]				

a A, alphanumeric; I, integer (whole number); D, numeric (with decimal point); F, floating point; P, packed decimal (same as D except that it takes roughly half the space to store numbers in packed decimal format).

b Up to 16 digits if you can be sure that data will always be positive.

c If a field is defined with the date format, Focus will automatically insert slashes between the dates when printing. Therefore, a date stored as 013192 will be printed as 01/31/92.

We are now ready to complete converting our STAFF file into a Focus database. Figure 3.5 displays the new file structure with formats that show the type, size, and decimal position of numeric fields.

Department Segment

Field Name	Format	Example
Department ID	A6	315
Department Name	A20	Information Systems

Section Segment

Field Name	Format	Example
Section ID	A6	3151
Section Name	A20	Program Development

Employee Segment

Field Name	Format	Example
Employee ID	A9	364567476
Last Name	A20	Rocklin
First Name	A10	James
Job Title	A20	Lead Programmer
Street Address	A30	100 La Cienega Blvd.
City	A16	Santa Ana
State	A2	CA
Zip Code	A5	94070
Telephone Number	A10	7145551212
Date of Birth	I6YMD	440315
Date of Hire	I6YMD	881015
Salary	D9.2	65000.00
Percent Increase	D5.2	.05
Vacation Hours Accrued	I4	112

Figure 3.5 STAFF file with format attributes.

DETAILED EXPLANATION OF FIELDS AND FORMATS OF STAFF FILE

Department Segment

1. *Department ID.* Department ID is defined as a field six characters long. Because each department ID is unique and it is going to be a key field, it is placed at the top of the segment. Although department ID could be defined as a numeric field, the rule of thumb is that only fields that will be involved in arithmetic operations are defined as numeric. Fields such as zip code and social security number are best defined as alphanumeric. Alphanumeric data are much easier to manipulate and less likely to cause problems with the system during data manipulation.

2. *Department Name.* This is an alphanumeric field, such as "engineering," "accounting," or "information systems." The department name has been defined as having a length of 20 characters. It could be blank with nothing in it, or be up to 20 characters long. It will, however, occupy the same amount of space in main storage and secondary storage regardless of the field value. Since this field is defined as alphanumeric, it could also hold numbers or special characters, such as $, &, or *. Alphanumeric fields are left-justified. In other words, they start from the leftmost position of the field and fill up the characters in the field. The remaining positions, if any, are left blank. Figure 3.6 displays how alphanumeric data fill a field.

Section Segment

3. *Section ID.* This identification field is just like the department ID field except that it identifies a section within the department. Section ID should be unique within the department. In other words, you should not have two sections with the same ID number in the same department.

4. *Section Name.* This is a section within a department. The same rules as department name applies here also.

Employee Segment

5. *Employee ID.* This is usually the nine-digit social security number. It is unique for each individual and that is why it is the first field of the employee segment.

6. *Last Name.* Since last name is not as unique as the social security number, it is seldom used as a key field.

Figure 3.6 Department name field.

7. *First Name.* We have allocated 10 characters to this field. This should be enough for most names.

8. *Job Title.* Each employee has a job title. It could be as short as "clerk" or as long as "engineering manager." The alphanumeric rules as discussed in the department name apply here also.

9. *Street Address.* This field is usually a combination of numbers and alphabetic characters. Examples are "100 Beverly Drive" or "345 Avenue of the Americas." Here again, alphanumeric rules apply and the street address is left-justified.

10. *City.* We have allocated 16 characters for this field. If dealing with a city name of length greater than 16 characters, the person entering the data must abbreviate the name.

11. *State.* We will use the standard two-character state code here. If this file was designed for an international company, additional fields for the name of the country, province, and special postal codes would be added.

12. *Zip Code.* We decided to declare this field alphanumeric because it is highly unlikely that the zip code would be used in mathematical computations.

13. *Telephone Number.* The telephone number is entered without spaces, dashes, or parentheses between the area code and prefix numbers. This saves space. Parentheses and dashes can be inserted by the program at print time.

14. *Date of Birth.* This is a six-digit integer (whole-number) field in date format. Additionally, we have specified the YMD format, which means year/month/day (e.g., 91/11/25). A date defined as such will be entered as 911125, but Focus will display it as 91/11/25 at report time. Many Focus files are developed in the YMD format. This is known as the *metric date.* Metric dates are not as easy for people to use, at least initially, but are far easier for programmers to sort. For instance, consider 11/25/91 and 05/12/92. We intuitively know that the second date is later than the first, but to the computer these are just two numbers and 112591 is greater than 051292. In the metric format they would be entered as 91/11/25 and 92/05/12, and of course 920512 is greater than 911125. Most third-generation computer languages such as COBOL can easily sort metric dates but do not have the built-in facility to sort dates in the MDY format and have to convert them to another format by using a programmer-written algorithm prior to sorting them. Focus files could be read by Focus Report Writing language and also by COBOL. So it may be better to define the dates in Focus files in the YMD format if there is the likelihood that someone using COBOL may need to access them later. In this book we use the YMD format for most of our application development.

15. *Date of Hire.* This is similar to the date of birth and has the same constraints.

16. *Salary.* This is a numeric field with two decimal places. We have defined it as D9.2. This means that this field is nine digits long, including a decimal point and two decimal positions. So the integer part of this field is only six digits.

The largest amount this field could hold is

$$\$999999.99$$

We assumed that a salary of one penny under $1 million would be the maximum that anybody could earn in our company.

17. *Percent Increase.* This is a numeric field with two decimal places. We have defined it as D5.2. An increase of .10 means that the person received a 10 percent increase in salary, so in almost every case, the value of this field will be less than 1.

18. *Vacation Hours Accrued.* This is a numeric field with no decimal places. We defined it as I4.

KEY FIELDS

In the example given, we stated that department ID was unique and we placed it as the first field in the segment. We did the same with section ID and employee ID. We must also tell Focus that these fields are key fields. *Key fields* are defined as fields in a segment whose values are used to keep the information in the segment in sequence. These are the first few fields of a segment. So if the employee ID is declared a key field, all the employee information will be logically stored in the employee ID sequence. If this was not done, information would be logically stored in the order in which it was entered into the system. It is very easy to declare a field as a key field, as we shall soon see. Unless you are creating a file for archiving, you should at least have the first field declared a key field. However, there must be a reason for creating additional key fields, because there is an internal overhead associated with keeping track of all these fields. For example, in our STAFF file, there is no reason to declare the first-name field a key field since we will not achieve anything by keeping our segments in that order.

Regardless of the order of key fields, you can still sort the data in any order that you want through your Focus program. You can also sort your records in order of fields that are not key fields. So I could still print a list of my employees and their phone numbers in employee first-name sequence by using a simple Focus command. I show you how to perform these sorts and more in the next few chapters.

MASTER FILE DESCRIPTION

Every Focus database needs a Master File Description (MFD). The MFD contains information about the names and formats of the fields in each segment. It also holds information about the relationship of fields and segments to each other. At execution time, Focus uses the information from the MFD and the instructions from the program to locate the data in the Focus database and print the report requested or display it on the screen. MFD is like a template that Focus uses to locate and access the data from Focus and non-Focus files. We have so far performed three functions for our STAFF file: (1) we have identified the information that is needed in it, (2) we have designed the structure of it in Focus, and (3) we have determined the format of all the fields. All we have to do now is to define a Master File Description and later create the file.

Each Focus Master File Description consists of three distinct parts or attribute statements. The parts of statements are separated by a comma. The field name statements end with a dollar sign ($). This is like a period that identifies the end of a sentence. An example of a typical MFD is shown below:

```
FILENAME=CUSTOMER,SUFFIX=FOC        ← File statement (1)

SEGNAME=CUSTOM,SEGTYPE=S1           ← Segment statement (2)

FIELDNAME=CUSTOMR_NAME,ALIAS=LN,FORMAT=A20,$
FIELDNAME=ACCOUNT_NO,ALIAS=ACNO,FORMAT=I9,$
FIELDNAME=PHONE_NO,ALIAS=FN,FORMAT=A10,$      ←       Field
FIELDNAME=STREET,ALIAS=STR,FORMAT=A20,$            statements (3)
FIELDNAME=CITY,ALIAS=TOWN,FORMAT=A18,$
FIELDNAME=STATE,ALIAS=ST,FORMAT=A2,$
FIELDNAME=ZIP,ALIAS=ZIP,FORMAT=A5,$
FIELDNAME=YTD_PURCHASE,ALIAS=YTD,FORMAT=D12,$
FIELDNAME=OUTSTANDING,ALIAS=BAL,FORMAT=D12,$
FIELDNAME=COMMENTS,ALIAS=COMM,FORMAT=A60,$
```

1. The first part of the Master File Description is the *file statement*. The file statement consists of two parts or attributes. The first part is the *file name*, which is the name that you have decided to give the Focus file. You are limited to eight characters for the file name. You can use any letter or digit, but special characters or embedded blanks are not allowed. At least one of the eight characters must be alphabetic. If you are creating a Master File Description for a non-Focus file (remember that Focus can also access most non-Focus files), you must enter the name that has already been assigned to that file. The second part is the *suffix*. The suffix tells Focus the type of file it is dealing with. For most parts it will be FOC, which is short for Focus. However, with Focus you can read information from other non-Focus files, such as standard sequential data files, VSAM (Virtual Storage Access Method) and SQL (Structured Query Language). In that case you should identify it with FIX, VSAM, or SQLDS suffixes, respectively. This will allow Focus to access those files according to their native organizations. There is only one File statement in a Master File Definition.

2. The second part of the Master File Definition is the *segment statement*. This also consists of two parts. The first part is the *segment name attribute*. This is the name that you give to your segment. You are limited to a maximum of eight characters for the segment name. Just like the filename, you can use any letter of alphabet and/or digits, but no special characters or embedded blanks are permitted. The second part of the segment statement is the *segment type statement*. It is shortened to *Segtype*. Segment type is usually selected as type S or SH. This is the way it works: If there are any key fields, there will be a letter "S" or the letters "SH" followed by the number of key fields in the segment. S1 means that there is one key field in this segment and the first field is the key field. It also means that the key fields are in ascending sequence order (i.e., Adams is logically put ahead of Brown even if Adams was entered after Brown). SH means that the key fields are in descending order (i.e., Brown will be before Adams). Most key fields are the S type, but certain key fields such as dates are recorded in the SH format. There are other segment types in Focus, but they are not as highly used as S or SH. There could be many segment statements in a Focus file. The theoretical limit is 64, but most files do not exceed 10.

3. The third part of the Master File Description is the field-name statement, and it consists of three parts: field name, alias, and format. *Field names* could be up to 12 characters long. Again the rules are the same as file names. However, the use of an underscore (_) is permitted to separate the two parts of the field name but embedded blanks are not allowed. For example, "LAST_NAME" is acceptable but "LAST NAME" is not. Do not use a minus sign (−), as this would cause problems in Focus. An *alias* is optional and it is usually either a shortened version of the field name or a different name for the same field. For example, LN is often used to mean "last name." "PART_NO" may be used as an alias for "ITEM." If you decide not to enter the alias, you should enter an extra comma in its place. Therefore, both of the following statements are correct:

```
FIELDNAME=LAST_NAME,ALIAS=LN,FORMAT=A20,$
FIELDNAME=LAST_NAME,,FORMAT=A20,$
```

The final part of the field-name statement is the FORMAT statement. FORMAT will tell Focus the type of data, the size of data, and any special editing that may be required. There could be many fields in each segment.

MASTER FILE CREATIONS

There are two ways to create a Master File Description.

Using TED to Create a Master File Description

The first method is by creating a file with the suffix of Master or MAS:

```
TED STAFF MASTER        ← Mainframe Focus (VM/CMS)
```

or

```
TED MASTER(STAFF)       ← Mainframe Focus (MVS/TSO)
```

or

```
TED STAFF.MAS           ← PC/Focus
```

You then type in the Master File Description and save it like any other Focus file, as we have seen in Chapter 2.

The FileTalk Facility

The easiest and the most efficient way to create a Master File Description is through the Focus FileTalk facility. FileTalk is available on all versions of Focus and is very easy to use. FileTalk generates a Master File Description that could later be modified by you through TED or other system editors. To use FileTalk you have to be in Focus first. If your version of Focus has a selection menu such as the one shown below, select the FileTalk option and press the Enter key. If you do not have a selection menu, you must type FileTalk at the Focus > prompt.

```
┌─────────────────────────────────────────────────────────────────┐
│          Menu Presentation of FOCUS facilities                    │
│                                                                   │
│    ┌──────────────────────────────────────────────────────┐      │
│    │ What would you like to do?                            │      │
│    │ ─────────────────────────────────────────────────────│      │
│    │ TableTalk      Build column-oriented report           │      │
│    │ PlotTalk       Build a graph                          │      │
│    │(FileTalk       Describe a new database file)          │      │
│    │ ModifyTalk     Build a MODIFY Procedure               │      │
│    │ Painters       Build free-format reports or screens   │      │
│    │ Ted            Create/edit a file                     │      │
│    │ Scan           Browse/update a database file          │      │
│    │ Link           Communicate with other computers       │      │
│    │ System         Issue a DOS command                    │      │
│    │ Windows        Create, maintain & run WINDOWS         │      │
│    │ Exec           Create, maintain & run FOCEXECS        │      │
│    │ Help           Display help information               │      │
│    │ Other          Focus utilities (QUERY, JOIN, etc.)    │      │
│    │ Commands       Issue interactive FOCUS commands       │      │
│    │ Exit           Leave FOCUS and return DOS             │      │
│    └──────────────────────────────────────────────────────┘      │
│                                                                   │
│   Select options with ↑ ↓ and ENTER .. or ESC to back up          │
└─────────────────────────────────────────────────────────────────┘
```

Regardless of the way you select the FileTalk option, Focus will display the main FileTalk menu. This will be similar to the following example:

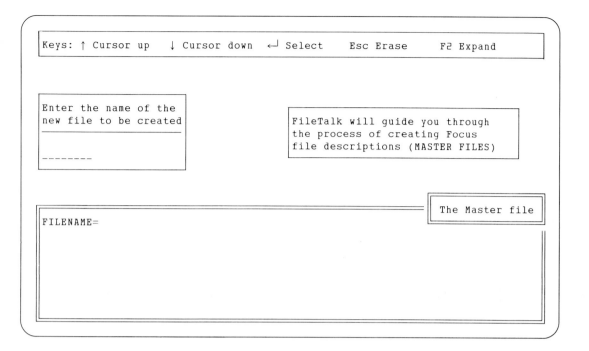

```
Keys: ↑ Cursor up    ↓ Cursor down   ↵ Select      Esc Erase      F2 Expand
```

```
Enter the name of the
new file to be created              FileTalk will guide you through
                                    the process of creating Focus
_____                            file descriptions (MASTER FILES)

_____
```

```
                                                       The Master file
FILENAME=
```

The FileTalk menus in PC/Focus and mainframe Focus are almost identical. The only difference is in the way certain keys on your terminal keyboard are defined. In PC/Focus, the Escape key is used for backing out of your selections. In mainframe Focus, PF3 performs the same function. In PC/Focus you use the Page Up and Page Down keys to scroll through your Master File Description if it is longer than one screen (up to 19 lines in Focus). In mainframe Focus, you would use the PF7 and PF8 function keys instead.

Before we start, make yourself a copy of Fig. 3.5 and have it handy so that we can follow the progress together. Now, let us return to the FileTalk menu and start creating our first Focus Master File Description. It is always so much easier to have the file designed with all the respective names, fields, formats, and lengths before attempting to create a Master File description. The 28 actions itemized are the steps you will need to follow. Read the instructions first and then try to follow through with me. If you make a mistake, you can always back out all the way to the beginning by repeatedly pressing the PF3 key on the mainframe or the Escape key on the PC.

The FileTalk screen is divided into two sections. The upper half of the screen is devoted to small interactive menus. Here Focus will use small pop-up menus or windows to ask you relevant questions about your file, segments, and fields. In the lower half of the screen, Focus builds the Master File Description based on your responses. Since you can always see the code that is being produced, you have the opportunity to back out and make corrections on the fly.

1. The first question you must answer is the Focus file name. In this case, we will call our file the STAFF file. Type the word "STAFF" and press the Enter key. On the lower half of the screen you will see the following line:

```
FILENAME=STAFF,SUFFIX=FOC
```

For the rest of this session, when you make a selection, you do so by using the cursor or the Tab keys. You must then press the Enter key to confirm your selection. So I will not mention this process again.

2. A new pop-up window will open up and Focus will ask you the following questions:

```
Do you want to create....

A Single segment file (A Relational Table)?
A Multi segment file?
QUIT
```

You should select the multisegment file option. As you can observe from Fig. 3.5, we have three segments in this file.

3. The next pop-up menu will ask for the segment name. Let's look at Fig. 3.5 again. Our first segment is the department segment. However, we are limited to eight characters for the segment name, so we must abbreviate the name to something short and meaningful, such as DEPRTMNT. Use only letters of the alphabet and any digit from 0 to 9.

4. The next menu will ask you to select a sort option for your segment.

```
Select the segment type

Sorted low to high
Sorted high to low
```

Focus wants to know if you plan to enter and keep the information in the segment in any particular order. Normally, the first field or the first two fields of each segment are sorted to speed up the data retrieval process. Whether you declare a field sorted or not does not affect your ability to sort the fields later and produce a desired output. In most cases, this selection is low to high, which is also known as the *ascending sequence*. In some cases, the sort may be high to low. For date fields, the key field is usually sorted high to low because for efficiency considerations, you may want to place the later dates first (i.e., at the beginning of the file). This is known as the *descending sequence*. The key field selection affects only the database design and computer response time and does not affect your program. So select low to high.

5. The next menu will ask how many key fields you need in this segment. The menu allows up to three key fields.

```
Key fields are specified first.
How many key fields are there?

One
Two
Three
```

In Focus, you are allowed many more, up to 255 key fields in ascending-sequence key fields or S segment type and up to 99 key fields in descending-sequence fields or SH segment type. However, in FileTalk you are allowed up to three key fields. It is unlikely that you would need more than three key fields per segment. If that were to happen, you should select three key fields in FileTalk and modify the number with TED or your system's editor after the FileTalk session was completed. In our example we will choose one key field. This means that the first field (i.e., department ID) will be sorted.

You now have the second line of your Master File Description completed:

```
FILENAME=STAFF,SUFFIX=FOC
SEGNAME=DEPRTMNT,SEGTYPE=S1
FIELDNAME=
```

Focus will now ask you for the name of your first field. You are limited to 12 characters for the field name. Our first field is department ID. Focus does not accept embedded blanks between parts of a field name. You must either join the two parts together (i.e., DEPARTMENTID) or use an underscore (_) to connect them (i.e., DEPRTMNT_ID). Please remember that a dash (-) is not acceptable because it is interpreted as a minus sign and you will run into lots of trouble later. So we will use an underscore and call our field DEPARTMNT_ID.

6. Focus will next ask for an optional alternate name or an alias.

```
Enter an optional alternate name for this field
              (maximum 12 characters)
```

Aliases are optional in Focus. You could use up to 12 characters to define an alias. They are used as either shortened versions or alternate names for field names. DOB is the shortened version of date of birth. Town is an alternate name for city. We will use DID as an alias for department ID. The next menu will ask for the data format:

```
Select the data format of this field:

Alphanumeric characters
Integer (numeric with no decimal places)
Numeric (with decimal places)
Date
```

Choose the alphanumeric option. Focus will next ask for the length of this field.

```
Enter the length (1-250)
```

You are really allowed up to 255 characters or bytes of data in an alphanumeric field. FileTalk menu suggests 250 characters as maximum, but you can enter 255 anyway and it will be accepted by Focus. It is very unlikely that you would ever want to design a file with a field that large. Most alphanumeric fields are less than 40 characters long. We know that department ID is six characters long, so you should enter the number 6.

7. The next pop-up menu will ask if we want to index this field.

Do you want to index this field?

```
No
Yes
```

Indexing is required if you want to join a Focus file to another Focus or non-Focus file. It is also used to speed up processing and retrieval. We will learn more about the Focus JOIN command in a later chapter. For now, select the ''No'' option.

The Master File Definition at the bottom of the screen should look as follows:

```
FILENAME=STAFF,SUFFIX=FOC
SEGNAME=DEPRTMNT,SEGTYPE=S1
FIELDNAME= DEPRTMNT_ID,ALIAS=DID,FORMAT=A6,$
```

8. Focus will ask if there are any more fields.

Any more fields?

```
Yes
No
```

Select the ''Yes'' option. As you will notice, it is very easy to answer the questions if you have done your homework and have the design document handy. The next field is the department name. Choose DEPT_NAME as the field name. For the alias, choose DEPT. The data format is alphanumeric. The length should be entered as 20 characters long. No indexing is required here.

9. The next pop-up menu will ask if there are any more fields.

Any more fields?

```
Yes
No
```

Select ''No'' because there are no more fields in this segment.

10. Focus will ask if there is another segment.

Do you want to describe....

```
Another SEGMENT?
Another FIELD?
END
```

Select the Another SEGMENT option. Focus will next ask for the name of this segment. Based on our file layout in Fig. 3.5, we should enter ''SECTION'' as the name of the segment.

11. The next pop-up menu will ask for the name of the parent segment. Remember that all segments except the first (the root segment) must have a parent segment. We know that the section segment is the descendent of the DEPRTMNT segment. This is the only segment name that Focus will accept. Try any other name and the system will reject it. Focus will next present you with another minimenu:

```
Select the segment type

Sorted low to high
Sorted high to low
Unique
```

We will discuss the Unique sort key later. For now select the low to high option.

12. Focus will next ask for your key field selection.

```
Key fields are specified first.
How many key fields are there?

One
Two
Three
```

We only have one key field in this segment and that is the segment ID. So select "One."

13. The next menu will ask for the field name. The first field name in this segment is the section ID, so enter "SECTION_ID." Don't forget to use the underscore to connect the two parts of the field name. For the alias, which is the next pop-up menu, select SECID. The data format is alphanumeric in this case. The length of field is 6. No indexing is required for this field.

14. The next menu will ask if there are any more fields. You should select the Yes option. In response to the next five menus, enter "SECTION_NAME" as the field name and "SECN" as the alias for this field. Select "alphanumeric" as the data format of this field and "20" as the length. No indexing is required in this segment. You should now have the following at the lower half of your screen.

```
FILENAME=STAFF,SUFFIX=FOC
SEGNAME=DEPRTMNT,SEGTYPE=S1
FIELDNAME=DEPRTMNT_ID,ALIAS=DID,FORMAT=A6,$
FIELDNAME=DEPT_NAME,ALIAS=DEPT,FORMAT=A20,$
SEGNAME=SECTION,PARENT=DEPRTMNT,SEGTYPE=S1
FIELDNAME=SECTION_ID,ALIAS=SECID,FORMAT=A6,$
FIELDNAME=SECTION_NAME,ALIAS=SECN,FORMAT=A20,$
```

15. The next pop-up menu will ask if there are any more fields.

Any more fields?

Yes
No

Select "No" because there are no more fields in this segment.

16. Focus will now ask if there are any more segments.

Do you want to describe....

Another SEGMENT?
Another FIELD?
END

Select the "Another SEGMENT" option, because we still have another section to go. In response to Focus, we will call this section Employee.

17. The next pop-up window will ask for the parent's name. Look at Fig. 3.5 again. Employee segment's parent is the section segment; it is *not* the department segment. Focus will accept either as parent. One is wrong and will create a different database from the one we had in mind when we developed our structure (see Fig. 3.7). If you were to choose the Department segment as the parent, no direct relationship between sections and employees will ever exist in our file. The correct answer is "section."

18. The next pop-up menu will ask you about the sorting selection.

Select the segment type

Sorted low to high
Sorted high to low
Unique

You should select the "Sorted low to high" option since the employee ID field will be in ascending sequence. The response to the next question about the number of key fields should be "One."

19. At this point the Master File Description at the bottom of your screen should look like this:

```
FILENAME=STAFF,SUFFIX=FOC
SEGNAME=DEPRTMNT,SEGTYPE=S1
FIELDNAME=DEPRTMNT_ID,ALIAS=DID,FORMAT=A6,$
FIELDNAME=DEPT_NAME,ALIAS=DEPT,FORMAT=A20,$
SEGNAME=SECTION,PARENT=DEPRTMNT,SEGTYPE=S1
FIELDNAME=SECTION_ID,ALIAS=SECID,FORMAT=A6,$
FIELDNAME=SECTION_NAME,ALIAS=SECN,FORMAT=A20,$
SEGNAME=EMPLOYEE,PARENT=SECTION,SEGTYPE=S1
FIELDNAME=
```

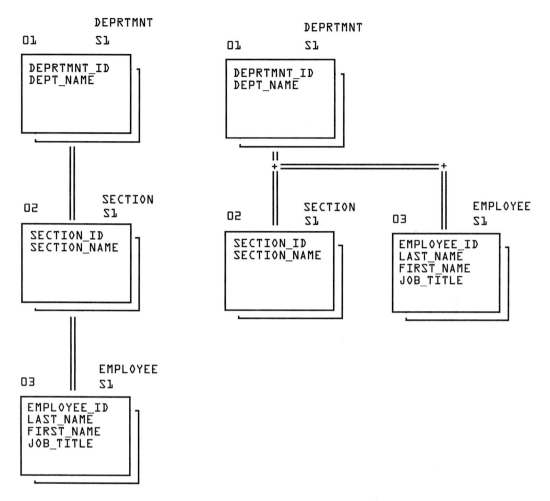

Figure 3.7 Effect of declaring a parent segment on the structure of database.

20. The next pop-up menu will ask about the field name. The field name is EMPLOYEE_ID. Choose "EID" as the alias for this field. The format is alphanumeric and the length is 9. No indexing is required.

21. The next few fields should be simple to enter. You should continue from the last-name field all the way through to the telephone number field with no problems. Suggested names and entries follow.

```
FILENAME=STAFF,SUFFIX=FOC
SEGNAME=DEPRTMNT,SEGTYPE=S1
FIELDNAME=DEPRTMNT_ID,ALIAS=DID,FORMAT=A6,$
FIELDNAME=DEPT_NAME,ALIAS=DEPT,FORMAT=A20,$
SEGNAME=SECTION,PARENT=DEPRTMNT,SEGTYPE=S1
FIELDNAME=SECTION_ID,ALIAS=SECID,FORMAT=A6,$
```

```
FIELDNAME=SECTION_NAME,ALIAS=SECN,FORMAT=A20,$
SEGNAME=EMPLOYEE,PARENT=SECTION,SEGTYPE=S1
FIELDNAME=EMPLOYEE_ID,ALIAS=EID,FORMAT=A9,$
FIELDNAME=LAST_NAME,ALIAS=LN,FORMAT=A20,$
FIELDNAME=FIRST_NAME,ALIAS=FN,FORMAT=A10,$
FIELDNAME=JOB_TITLE,ALIAS=TITLE,FORMAT=A20,$
FIELDNAME=STREET,ALIAS=STR,FORMAT=A30,$
FIELDNAME=CITY,ALIAS=TOWN,FORMAT=A16,$
FIELDNAME=STATE,ALIAS=ST,FORMAT=A2,$
FIELDNAME=ZIP_CODE,ALIAS=ZIP,FORMAT=A5,$
FIELDNAME=TELEPHONE_NO,ALIAS=PHONE,FORMAT=A10,$
```

22. In response to the question about the date of birth, I entered "DATE_BIRTH" as the field name and "DOB" as the alias. When a date format is selected, the following menu appears:

```
Select a date format:

month/day/year
year/month/day
day/month/year
month/year
month
```

I selected the date format with the year/month/day (YMD) option, which means that dates entered will be in the year, month, and day format. I named the date of hire "DATE_HIRE" with an alias of "DOH." The format again was date with the year/month/day (YMD) option. No indexing was required.

23. The next field is the salary field. This is a numeric field. I responded to the pop-up menu that I wanted the name salary for my field name. In response to an alias name selection, I chose "Income."

```
Select the date format of this field:

Alphanumeric characters
Integer (numeric with no decimal places)
Numeric (with decimal places)
Date
```

In response to format selection, I chose "Numeric." I also chose nine digits as the total length of this field. The nine digits include the decimal point and two decimal places. With numeric data, there are two other pop-up menus to go through. The first will request the number of decimal places.

```
How many digits after the decimal point?
```

I chose two decimal places. In most business applications, two decimal places is enough. The next pop-up menu will ask about the display option that you would want to use.

What display options do you want to use?

```
None or no more
Floating dollar
Nonfloating dollar
Comma inclusion
Zero suppression
Bracket negative
Credit negative
Leading zeros
```

You do not have to choose any. That is the first option. I selected "Comma inclusion." With this option, every time that you print this field, a comma will be inserted after every third significant digit. This is not necessary, but it will make the report look better. Requesting any display option will not in any way alter the number of characters that you have requested. As the name implies, it is for display purposes only. You can select more than one option from this menu. For example, you could choose "Comma inclusion" and then the "Credit negative" option.

24. The next field is the percentage increase field. This is the percentage of increase that the employee received last time that he or she was reviewed by his or her manager. It is a numeric field. I selected "PCT_INC" as my field name and "PIN" as my alias.

Select the data format of this field:

```
Alphanumeric characters
Integer (numeric with no decimal places)
Numeric (with decimal places)
Date
```

In response to the menu above, I selected "Numeric." I chose five digits as the total length of this field. In response to the next menu:

How many digits after the decimal point?

I selected two decimal places. This will give you a range of 00.00 to 99.99. This represents a minimum of 0 percent increase and a maximum of 99 percent in the decimal part of the field. A 5 percent increase would be entered as 00.05, a 45 percent increase would be entered as 00.45, and a 100 percent increase would be entered as 01.00.

The next menu asks about the display option.

What display options do you want to use?

```
None or no more
Floating dollar
Nonfloating dollar
Comma inclusion
```

```
Zero suppression
Bracket negative
Credit negative
Leading zeros
```

I selected the "None or no more" option. Sometimes it is preferable to use the "Leading zeros" option for percentage fields. It would have been correct to use it here. No indexing is required for this field.

25. The last field is the vacation hours accrued. This is the number of hours of vacation that each employee has earned, but not used, since the beginning of his or her employment with this company. It is a numeric field. I selected "VACATION" as the field name and "VAC" as the alias for this field.

Select the data format of this field:

```
Alphanumeric characters
Integer (numeric with no decimal places)
Numeric (with decimal places)
Date
```

In response to the menu above, I selected the integer data format. The VACATION field does not contain fractions of hours, so an integer number would be appropriate.

The next menu will ask for the number of digits:

Enter the number of digits (1–10)

I entered 4.

The next menu will ask the display option.

What display options do you want to use?

```
None or no more
Floating dollar
Nonfloating dollar
Comma inclusion
Zero suppression
Bracket negative
Credit negative
Leading zeros
```

I selected the "None or no more" option.

I did not select indexing for this field.

26. At this point, the Master File definition that you have created should look as follows:

```
FILENAME=STAFF,SUFFIX=FOC
SEGNAME=DEPRTMNT,SEGTYPE=S1
```

```
FIELDNAME=DEPRTMNT_ID,ALIAS=DID,FORMAT=A6,$
FIELDNAME=DEPT_NAME,ALIAS=DEPT,FORMAT=A20,$
SEGNAME=SECTION,PARENT=DEPRTMNT,SEGTYPE=S1
FIELDNAME=SECTION_ID,ALIAS=SECID,FORMAT=A6,$
FIELDNAME=SECTION_NAME,ALIAS=SECN,FORMAT=A20,$
SEGNAME=EMPLOYEE,PARENT=SECTION,SEGTYPE=S1
FIELDNAME=EMPLOYEE_ID,ALIAS=EID,FORMAT=A9,$
FIELDNAME=LAST_NAME,ALIAS=LN,FORMAT=A20,$
FIELDNAME=FIRST_NAME,ALIAS=FN,FORMAT=A10,$
FIELDNAME=JOB_TITLE,ALIAS=TITLE,FORMAT=A20,$
FIELDNAME=STREET,ALIAS=STR,FORMAT=A30,$
FIELDNAME=CITY,ALIAS=TOWN,FORMAT=A16,$
FIELDNAME=STATE,ALIAS=ST,FORMAT=A2,$
FIELDNAME=ZIP_CODE,ALIAS=ZIP,FORMAT=A5,$
FIELDNAME=TELEPHONE_NO,ALIAS=PHONE,FORMAT=A10,$
FIELDNAME=DATE_BIRTH,ALIAS=DOB,FORMAT=I6YMD,$
FIELDNAME=DATE_HIRE,ALIAS=DOH,FORMAT=I6YMD,$
FIELDNAME=SALARY,ALIAS=INCOME,FORMAT=D9.2C,$
FIELDNAME=PCT_INC,ALIAS=PIN,FORMAT=D5.2,$
FIELDNAME=VACATION,ALIAS=VAC,FORMAT=I4,$
```

27. After you enter the information about the format for the salary field, a pop-up menu will ask if there are any more fields.

```
Do you want to describe....

Another SEGMENT?
Another FIELD?
END
```

You should select the END option. The next menu will ask if the Master File definition should be saved or discarded:

```
Do you want to:

Save this MASTER file?
Quit without saving?
```

Select the ''Save'' option.

28. The final pop-up menu or window will give you three choices:

```
Do you want to....

Check your file description for errors?
Add data to your file?
End?
```

The second option, ''Add data to your file'' may not be available on some versions of Focus. We definitely want to know if we have made any errors and if Focus will accept our efforts so far. So select the first option, which will allow you to check your Master File Description for errors. When you choose this option, the screen may go blank for a second or two while Focus works on your file. In a few seconds Focus will display the result of checking the file:

```
NUMBER OF ERRORS=       0
NUMBER OF SEGMENTS=      3   ( REAL=      3   VIRTUAL=     0 )
NUMBER OF FIELDS=       18   INDEXES=     0   FILES=       1
TOTAL LENGTH  OF ALL FIELDS= 204
```

This will be followed by a picture of your file and the hierarchical relationships (see Fig. 3.8). Up to four fields per segment will be displayed. The level number and name of each segment will be displayed on top of each segment (i.e., level 01 and DEPRTMNT segment). Also displayed are the number and the location of key fields within each segment. S1 means that the first field (i.e., DEPRTMNT_ID) is the key field in the DEPRTMNT segment.

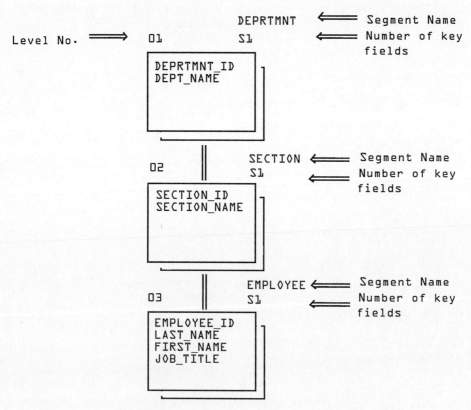

Figure 3.8 Pictorial display of STAFF file's structure.

Each box indicates a segment. A double box indicates that there may be many instances (occurrences) of this segment. In other words, you could have several departments and many sections within each department and maybe hundreds of employees in each section. As your company adds new departments, sections, and employees, Focus will automatically add new segments to the database. Of course, you will have to write a program to tell Focus to add, change, or delete the data, but you do not have to keep track of the number of segments. In effect, each descendent segment could occur (be repeated) as many times as necessary.

In third-generation filing organizations, there is a finite limitation to the number of times that a field or group of fields could be repeated. It could be as high as 5000 or more, but the limit must be stated in the program, and once coded, it cannot be exceeded unless the program is modified.

If you discover that you have made a mistake and need to modify your Master File Description, you could go back to FileTalk and edit your MFD. Alternatively, you could use TED or your system's editor to modify the MFD. If you wanted to change the MFD for the Staff file, you could go back to the Focus > prompt and issue the following command:

```
TED STAFF MASTER          ← Mainframe Focus (VM/CMS)

or

TED MASTER(STAFF)         ← Mainframe Focus (MVS/TSO)

or

TED STAFF.MAS             ← PC/Focus
```

Focus will put you in the TED edit mode and you could make all your changes, additions, or deletions to the Master File Description.

Once you have finished with the file, you should request Focus to check it again. To do this, you issue the following command from the Focus > prompt:

```
Check file STAFF picture.
```

Focus will check the file, give you the statistics (as we saw earlier), and draw another picture of your file. You could issue this command with any Focus file. In case of errors, Focus will display one or more error messages. You should then go back to the Master File Description and make the required corrections.

If you are satisfied, you should then create the Focus file. Remember that a Focus database system consists of a Master File Description which tells Focus the field attributes and a file. You should then issue the following command from the Focus command line:

```
Create file STAFF.
```

This will create a Focus file for you. It will be empty at this time, but the structure of the file will be created and later you could load data into it.

Note to MVS users: In MVS, you must allocate a file first. Therefore, before issuing the Create command in Focus, you should use option 3.2 in ISPF/PDF to allocate the STAFF file.

SUMMARY

The most important part of learning to use Focus effectively is understanding the one-to-one and one-to-many relationships. You could reduce redundancy by using the techniques offered in this chapter. This would in turn reduce computer storage requirements, which in turn would improve your computer efficiency. This is because for a given task, the central processing unit would be handling fewer data but producing the same information. Additionally, fewer data would be written to and/or read from disk units.

For certain applications, any other filing structure would be cost prohibitive. For example, in the securities industry (stock and bond trading), there are millions and millions of individual stock and bond certificates that are being kept in safekeeping by banks, federal agencies, and brokerage houses. A simple Focus system to keep track of these securities would be to have a small parent segment that identifies the bank or the brokerage company and a descendent securities segment which would have details such as the security ID number, issue date, par value, market value, and collateral value for each security. In other words, for each brokerage house or bank, there would be one segment followed by thousands of descendent security (bonds or stocks) segments. It would then be relatively easy to access this file for reporting and updating.

In an alternative third-generation filing system, each stock or bond record would have all the broker information appended to it. Another third-generation alternative would be to create two files: one file for the securities and another file for the brokers' information. You would then need to build and maintain extensive cross-references between the two files to keep them synchronized so they point to each other correctly. Both these approaches would be costly and difficult to maintain.

FileTalk is an excellent facility for both the newcomers and professional programmers. It creates the basic Master File Description and because it is done under program control, the majority of typographical and logical errors are captured while you are creating your file. You should still do a visual check of your Master File Description, because FileTalk does not catch all logical errors. If you want to add a feature to your MFD that FileTalk does not offer, such as increasing the number of your key fields beyond three or changing your data type from decimal (D) to packed decimal (P), you could always modify it by using TED or your system's editor. Some versions of FileTalk also provide a rudimentary facility for adding data to your Focus file immediately after completion of the Master File Description.

CHAPTER 4

DESIGNING AND CREATING REPORTS WITH FOCUS®

MAIN TOPICS:

- WRITING FOCUS PROGRAMS
- CODING YOUR FIRST TABLE REQUEST
- FOCUS VERBS
- HOT SCREEN FACILITY
- TABLETALK

Focus makes it easy to retrieve information from Focus and non-Focus files. The reports could be displayed on your terminal, printed on your computer's printer, or saved on a disk unit as a magnetic file to be used later. You use the TABLE command and the four action words associated with it to perform all your printing needs in Focus. The word "TABLE" has a specific meaning. It activates the TABLE environment, which is a series of internal Focus programs that will help you produce reports. We review the internal operations of Focus in a later chapter. It is worth noting that the word "TABLE" refers to the tabular nature of reports that Focus produces. In other words, the values of fields retrieved from a file are listed in columns.

Writing Focus programs or Focus TABLE requests is very easy. Like any other language, there are certain rules of grammar that we must learn to master Focus. Unlike most other languages, Focus has very few hard-and-fast rules. In fact, you do not even have to be very good at English to learn Focus. It also has some help and error-catching facilities built in, so if you make a mistake, it will probably help you correct it.

WRITING FOCUS PROGRAMS

By now, you should be familiar with getting in and out of Focus and using the TED or your own system's editor. Before writing a report, one of the first things a good programmer needs to do is to identify the file, the fields, and the relationships of fields to each other. It is important to know the purpose of the report, because you may be able to help prepare the requested report in a different way, or another program may already be producing a similar report. Unfortunately, you do not often get all the information that you may require. This is especially true if you are a contract programmer or consultant. Even if you are a full-time employee, you may not get the cooperation that you will need. Focus has several facilities that you could use to make your task easier.

Check File

The first such facility is the Check File utility. Check File with the picture clause allows you to verify that the file that you have been given to use for your reports actually exists and is error free. The Picture clause will display a pictorial repre-

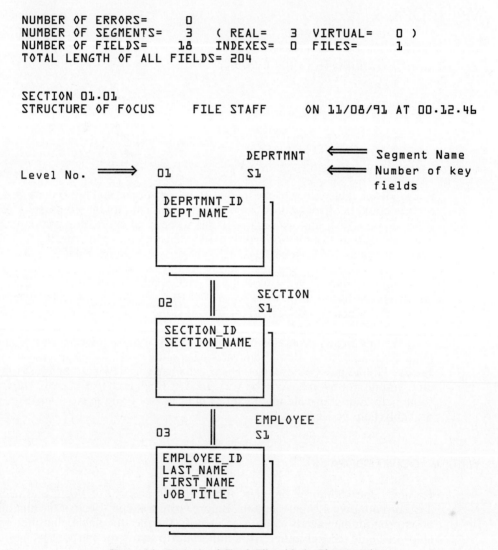

```
NUMBER OF ERRORS=       0
NUMBER OF SEGMENTS=     3   ( REAL=   3  VIRTUAL=   0 )
NUMBER OF FIELDS=      18   INDEXES=  0  FILES=     1
TOTAL LENGTH OF ALL FIELDS= 204


SECTION 01.01
STRUCTURE OF FOCUS      FILE STAFF      ON 11/08/91 AT 00.12.46
```

Figure 4.1 Example of Check File with the Picture option.

sentation of the file on your display screen or the printer. For example, if we issue the command.

```
Check file STAFF picture.
```

the information in Fig. 4.1 will be displayed on the terminal. The listing and diagram in Fig. 4.1 tell us that no errors were detected while checking the Master File Description of this file. It also tells us that each record has three segments and 18 fields and is 204 characters long.

Describe

Describe is another useful utility program that is available on most versions of Focus. Describe will produce a comprehensive record layout with field names, relationships, levels, and formats. The format of Describe is

```
Ex Describe filename.
```

For example:

```
Ex Describe STAFF.
```

Following is an example of the Describe output.

```
SECTION 01
       STRUCTURE OF FOCUS     FILE STAFF     ON 06/08/91 AT 13.09.07

             DEPRTMNT
   01      S1
 *************
 *DEPRTMNT_ID **
 *DEPT_NAME   **
 *            **
 *            **
 *            **
 *************
  *************
         I
         I
         I
         I SECTION
   02    I S1
 *************
 *SECTION_ID  **
 *SECTION_NAME**
 *            **
 *            **
 *            **
 *************
```

```
    **************
         I
         I
         I
         I EMPLOYEE
    03   I S1
    **************
    *EMPLOYEE_ID  **
    *LAST_NAME    **
    *FIRST_NAME   **
    *JOB_TITLE    **
    *            **
    **************
    **************
```

PAGE   1

```
INDEX OF FOCUS     FILE STAFF     ON 06/08/91 AT 13.07.28
SEGNO  SEGNAME    SEGTYPE  PARENT     CRKEY        CRFILE
-----  -------    -------  ------     -----        ------
 FLDNO  FIELDNAME    ALIAS         FORMAT    ACTUAL    INDEX
 -----  ---------    -----         ------    ------    -----


    1  DEPRTMNT  S01
       1  DEPRTMNT_ID   DID           A6        A006
       2  DEPT_NAME     DEPT          A20       A020
-------------------------------------------------------------


    2  SECTION   S01       DEPRTMNT
       3  SECTION_ID    SECID         A6        A006
       4  SECTION_NAME  SECN          A20       A020
-------------------------------------------------------------


    3  EMPLOYEE  S01       SECTION
       5  EMPLOYEE_ID   EID           A9        A009
       6  LAST_NAME     LN            A20       A020
       7  FIRST_NAME    FN            A10       A010
       8  JOB_TITLE     TITLE         A20       A020
       9  STREET        STR           A30       A030
      10  CITY          TOWN          A16       A016
      11  STATE         ST            A2        A002
      12  ZIP_CODE      ZIP           A5        A005
      13  TELEPHONE_NO  PHONE         A10       A010
      14  DATE_BIRTH    DOB           I6YMD     A006
      15  DATE_HIRE     DOH           I6YMD     A006
      16  SALARY        INCOME        D9.2C     A009
      17  PCT_INC       PIN           D5.2      A005
      18  VACATION      VAC           I4        A004
-------------------------------------------------------------
```

While Describe is similar to Check File, it has some additional features:

1. Each segment of the file is listed separately.
2. The parent segments are clearly identified.
3. Section names are printed two columns to the left of other fields to make them easier to locate.
4. All fields are itemized starting from number 1.
5. Aliases are listed.
6. The field format is displayed.
7. Index fields are identified.

There is also an ''actual size'' column, which shows the actual length of each field. You may notice that the DATE_BIRTH field with a format of I6YMD has an actual format of A006, which means that it is six characters long. You will need this information to format your report correctly.

Focus files can be cross-referenced to each other. That is the purpose of the CRKEY (cross-reference key) and CRFILE (cross-reference file) fields. In the case above, the file is not cross-referenced to other files, so those entries are blank. We talk more about cross-referencing and joining Focus files in Chapter 10.

Whenever you are given a Focus project, you should request a copy of the Focus file's record layout. This can easily be generated by executing the Describe program.

? FILE (Query File) Command

Another tool at your disposal is the ? FILE filename command. You will issue this command from the Focus prompt >. This command will provide information about the actual number of each type of segment and the total size of the file. It will also give you information about the last time that each segment was updated or deleted.

```
? FILE STAFF

STATUS OF FOCUS FILE:STAFF
```

SEGNAME	ACTIVE COUNT	DELETED COUNT	DATE OF LAST CHG	TIME OF LAST CHG	LAST TRANS NUMBER
DEPRTMNT	5		09/02/91	20.46.50	16
SECTION	8		09/02/91	20.46.50	16
EMPLOYEE	16		09/19/91	12.13.30	
TOTAL SEGS	29				
TOTAL CHARS	2796				
TOTAL PAGES	3				
LAST CHANGE			09/19/91	12.13.30	

Getting Out of the Table Environment and Focus

Before we go any further, you must remember how to get out of the TABLE environment or Focus. Sometimes, you enter a line of code and for some reason you get stuck in a loop and seem unable to get out. In these cases the best thing to do is to remember the following:

1. Typing "END" or "QUIT" or "QQUIT" will get you out of most serious situations. You may have to type these commands more than once to step through and out of a loop.

2. Typing "FIN" will get you out of Focus. However, you cannot get out of Focus from the TABLE environment. If you are stuck in the Table mode, you will first have to type "END" or "QUIT" or "QQUIT" to get back to the Focus > prompt. You can then enter the FIN command to leave Focus.

3. If your report keeps going on and on and you want to cancel it, you should type one of the two Focus terminate commands, KX (Kill Execution) or KT (Kill Typing). You should interrupt Focus before issuing these commands. The interrupt key on IBM mainframe system terminals is the PA1 key. On a PC, the Ctrl key and the Break key should be pressed simultaneously first. "KX" will terminate the execution of the report and return you to the > prompt. "KT" will suspend execution of the report temporarily. To resume execution of the report, you should type "RT" (Resume Typing).

4. If all else fails, in a PC you could always re-boot or reset the system. On a mainframe, switching the terminal on and off does not reset the system. It may even cause more problems. In fact, if you switch your terminal on and off in midsession, the processing will continue. All you have done is disconnect your terminal from the mainframe, so call the system operator and ask to be forced off the system. The operator has special commands to use to log you off. On VM/CMS systems you can force the log off from almost anywhere in Focus or CMS by typing

```
#CP LOGOFF
```

You could even issue this command in the middle of a report and the system will log you off. On MVS operating systems, if the interrupt key "PA1" does not work, your best bet is to call the system operator and ask to be logged off.

CODING YOUR FIRST TABLE REQUEST

Let's assume that we have found that a file exists and we have reviewed the record layout and relationship of the fields and segments with each other. The next step is to write the program or the TABLE request. A TABLE request is a series of instructions to the computer to perform a task. The definition of a program and a TABLE request are therefore identical. There are basically two ways of writing programs in Focus. You could code your program interactively (i.e., directly from the Focus > prompt) or you could use TED or your system's editor to create a program file. The programs created by TED or an editor could be stored and executed over and over. Most of the time, you should use the second method. Of course, you could always modify a saved program. However, if you are writing a simple ad hoc report program, you could key it directly from the Focus > prompt. We will discuss the interactive process first.

Interactive TABLE Requests (Programs)

For the purpose of this example, let us assume that we are writing a program to print the names and salaries of the employees in each department of the company. The code follows:

```
TABLE FILE STAFF
PRINT DEPT_NAME AND LAST_NAME AND FIRST_NAME AND SALARY
END
```

1. The first word that you must type is the word "TABLE." This is a key word that tells Focus that you are requesting a report. TABLE is followed by the word "FILE" and the name of the file that you are accessing. The TABLE command must be on a line by itself. After typing each line, you must press the Enter key. Focus will position the cursor on the next line and you could continue typing your program. Each line could be as long as the available width of the screen, which is about 72 characters. But you should never try to cram a lot of code into one line. Keep your lines to about 30 to 40 characters. One advantage of keeping the lines short is that if you mistype a field name, you do not have to wait until the end of a long line to find out that you have made a mistake.

2. The filename will identify the file that will be used in this program. Focus will use this name to search for and locate the Master File Description and its associated Focus data file. If the file does not exist or if you type the name incorrectly, Focus will inform you that it cannot process your request. Focus error messages start with the letters FOC and a three- or four-digit number inside parentheses. This is followed by a very short, sometimes cryptic message which notifies you of the reason for the error. In the example above, if the file did not exist, Focus would have displayed the following message:

```
(FOC205) DESCRIPTION CANNOT BE FOUND FOR FILE NAMED: STAFF
REPLY :>
```

At this point, Focus will stop and await a reply to the message. There are several possible actions that you could take at this time. You could respond by typing in the correct name if you had mistyped the filename in the first place, you could type "QUIT" and abandon the program, or if you feel that you will need more information and the message is not clear enough, you could ask for further explanation by typing in a question mark (?) or the word "HELP" next to the REPLY :> prompt symbol:

```
REPLY :>?
```

This will display a paragraph of additional explanation as follows:

```
No data description can be found for the file requested.
Check the master files allocated or available, or the
spelling of the filename.
```

In this case there is not much that you can do at this time. You should type "QUIT." This will return you to the Focus > prompt. You must then check your file listing or directory to discover the reason for the nonexistence of the file. Most of the time, an error message is printed because of a typing error. Another common reason has to do with file directories. In most computer systems, you usually have several file directories or paths. Your Focus file and the Master File Description may reside in one directory, whereas your Focus program may reside in a different directory or path. To avoid this problem, you should link all the related directories together before running a Focus application. This is done with the PATH statement in PC and the LINK statement in mainframe VM/CMS. On the MVS/TSO systems, you must use the ALLOCATE command to access files and/or programs. By the way, this situation is not peculiar to Focus: You need to link your files like that any time that you execute jobs where programs and files reside in different disk directories.

In addition to linking all needed directories together, you must issue the USE command from within Focus to make sure that you are pointing to the right file. Examples of issuing the USE command follow:

```
USE
STAFF FOCUS M       ←This is an example of accessing your Focus file, which is on
END                    the M disk in VM/CMS. You will still have to issue the
                       LINK command prior to invoking Focus.
```

or

```
USE
STAFF FOC D:        ← This is an example of accessing the STAFF file, which is on
END                    the D directory on the PC. You will still have to issue the
                       DOS path command first.
```

It is always a good idea to issue the USE command before starting to execute a program. This will ensure that you are pointing to the right Focus file.

3. The last line should contain only one of the words "END," "RUN," or "QUIT." If at any time during interactive program development, you decide that you want to abandon the work, you just type "QUIT" on a line by itself and you will be back at the Focus > prompt. The END command will execute the Focus program that you have just typed. If the execution is successful, you will see a report on your screen. If for any reason the program does not work, a FOC error message will be printed on the screen. Some typical FOC error messages are:

```
(FOC003)  THE FIELD NAME IS NOT IN THE DICTIONARY: fieldname

(FOC009)  INCOMPLETE REQUEST STATEMENT

(FOC016)  THE TRUNCATED NAME DESCRIBES MORE THAN ONE FIELD:
fieldname
```

In any event, you will be returned to the Focus > prompt. If you want to access the same file again, you will have to start your TABLE command from the beginning. Every time that you type the TABLE command, Focus will have to start searching to find the Master File Description and its associated Focus data file all over again. This puts a burden on the computing resources. It also means that you will have to wait a few seconds for Focus to find the file again and make it available for use. If you are trying to fix a report, you may have to do this repeatedly. To avoid these repeated delays, you should use the RUN command to terminate your program. The RUN command in the Focus Report Writer is very similar to the END command. The only difference is that the Master File Description and the data file remain active, so you do not have to repeat the TABLE file command. The following examples show the way RUN works.

```
TABLE FILE STAFF
PRINT LAST_NAME AND FIRST_NAME
RUN
```

Focus will display the report on the terminal and will return you to the T > prompt. You can then enter another TABLE request as shown:

```
T>PRINT SECTION AND LAST_NAME AND SALARY
RUN
```

Focus will display the report on the terminal.

```
T>PRINT LAST_NAME AND DATE_BIRTH AND DATE_HIRE
END
```

Focus will display the report on the terminal, but this time it will leave the TABLE environment and will return to the Focus > prompt.

```
>
```

The T> symbol, also known as the TABLE prompt, indicates that Focus is now in the TABLE mode. The T> is the prompt symbol used on VM/CMS Focus. On the PC/Focus, the prompt is TAB> instead of T>. In MVS/Focus the prompt is T> >.

Using TED to Write TABLE Requests (Programs)

In Chapter 2 we discussed the procedures for using TED to create and store files. Typing a TABLE request or program is similar to what we have already learned in that chapter. Focus programs, data files, and Master File Descriptions have to follow a certain naming convention. They are identified to Focus by two parts. One part of the filename is the name that you have given that data file, Master File Description, or program (TABLE request). The second part is known as the *file type*. File type tells Focus if the file is a data file, a Master File Description, a program (TABLE request), or a non-Focus file. Valid file types in mainframe, minicomputer, and PC versions of Focus are listed in Table 4.1.

TABLE 4.1 VALID FILE TYPES[a]

VM/CMS	PC/DOS	MVS/TSO
Program Files		
Program name FOCEXEC Disk-Id	Program name.FEX	USERID.FOCEXEC(Program name)
For example:		
SALES1 FOCEXEC A	SALES1.FEX	TSRRT1.FOCEXEC(SALES1)
Master File Description		
Filename MASTER Disk-Id	Filename.MAS	USERID.MASTER(Filename)
For example:		
STAFF MASTER A	STAFF.MAS	TSRRT1.MASTER(STAFF)
Focus Data Files		
Filename FOCUS Disk-Id	Filename.FOC	USERID.Filename.Focus
For example:		
STAFF FOCUS A	STAFF.FOC	TSRRT1.STAFF.Focus
External Files, Sequential Files, non-Focus Data Files[b]		
Filename DATA Disk ID	Filename.DAT	DATA.Filename
For example:		
INPUT DATA A	INPUT.DAT	DATA.INPUT

[a] These are recommended naming standards. However, most sites usually have specific naming standards and conventions that you must follow. Under the MVS/TSO, the general rule is that all files must be allocated before they can be used. With MVS/TSO, the best bet is to create a CLIST or ask someone to create a CLIST for you to preallocate all required files. An example of allocating a Focus data file from inside Focus is shown below:

```
>> Tso ALLOC F(STAFF) DA('TSRRT1.STAFF.FOCUS') SHR
                          └── This is the USERID or the
                              application ID
```

[b] The data files could have any valid file types. For example, INPUT EXTRACT A and PROD.OLD are both acceptable external filenames in Focus.

A program name can be up to a maximum of eight characters long and any combination of letters of the alphabet and/or numeric digits. However, at least one of the characters in the program name must be alphabetic. To start the coding process, type TED followed by the name of the program you are writing (e.g., if it is the first employee listing that you are creating, you could call it TED EMPLIST1). When you invoke TED to write a program, TED will automatically append the file type of FOCEXEC (FEX in PC/Focus) to your program name. EMPLIST1 will be created as EMPLIST1 FOCEXEC in VM/CMS Focus and as EMPLIST1.FEX in PC/Focus and most minicomputer versions of Focus. Under MVS/TSO it will probably be called something like TSRRT1.FOCEXEC (EMPLIST1) or TSRRT1.FOCEXEC.DATA(EMPLIST1). TSRRT1 is the user identification or the application identification. FOCEXEC identifies this MVS/

TSO library as a FOCEXEC type library. EMPLIST1 is the name of a member, i.e., a program in this library.

If you use another editor, remember to add the file type to your program name when you create it. In other words, if you are creating the EMPLIST1 TABLE request in the mainframe and are using the Xedit or the ISPF editor, you should name it EMPLIST1 FOCEXEC. If you are using a PC word processor to create a PC/Focus program, you should call it EMPLIST1.FEX. Any other program name (e.g., EMPLIST1 or EMPLIST1.PRG or EMPLIST1 PROGRAM) will be rejected by Focus.

After invoking TED, you will be presented with the TED data entry screen. You should first type the ADD command on the TED command line to expand the data entry area to, say, 22 lines. This, you will remember, is accomplished by typing "add 22" on the TED command line and pressing the Enter key. You could then start typing your program from the top of the screen. To go to the top, just press the Tab key twice and the cursor will be located at the top ready for data entry. You should then type your program by following the rules we discussed before (i.e., 30 to 40 characters per line). The last line should contain the END statement.

The following TABLE request is an example of a program created with TED.

```
00000 * * * TOP OF FILE * * *
00001 -*********************************************
00002 -* EMPLIST1
00003 -* THIS PROGRAM WILL PRODUCE THE LIST OF ALL EMPLOYEES
00004 -* IN THE MARKETING DEPARTMENT.
00005 -* AUTHOR: RICHARD R. TAHA
00006 -* VERSION 1.1
00007 -* 10/12/91.
00008 -*********************************************
00009 TABLE FILE STAFF
00010 PRINT DEPRTMNT_ID AND DEPT_NAME
00011 AND LAST_NAME AND FIRST_NAME
00012 IF DEPT_NAME EQ MARKETING
00013 END
00014 * * * END OF FILE * * *


===>                                                      EDIT MODE
```

As you can see, we have added several lines of comments to this program. It is always a good idea to identify the program name, the author, the date it was written, and the reason for the report request. Comment lines start with −* in Focus. On some computers you should only use * to start a comment line. Focus will ignore comment lines at execution time. You could abandon the program at any point, prior to saving it, by typing "QQUIT" or "QQ" on the TED command line.

After completing your program, you will have two options. One choice is to store your program and execute it later. In that case you should move your cursor to the TED command line, type "FILE," and press the Enter key. Alternatively, you could execute your program from the TED command line by typing "RUN" and pressing the Enter key. In this case the RUN command will first store your program on disk and will next execute it. If your program does not execute successfully, you could type the word "TED" in response to the Focus error message.

```
ERROR AT OR NEAR LINE 11 IN PROCEDURE E:EMPLIST1.FEX

(FOC003) THE FIELD NAME IS NOT IN THE DICTIONARY : NAME
 BYPASSING TO END OF COMMAND

(FOC009) INCOMPLETE REQUEST STATEMENT
```

>> ← You should respond by typing "TED" here to return to TED to correct the error.

Focus will return you back to the TED data entry screen. The first line of suspected error will be highlighted at the top of the screen.

```
E:EMPLIST1.FEX                 SIZE=14  LINE=11

00011 AND LAST NAME AND FIRST_NAME    ← This is the line with the error.
00012 IF DEPT_NAME EQ MARKETING         There is a missing underscore
00013 END                               (_) between LAST and NAME.
00014
00015 * * * END OF FILE * * *




===>     ← After correcting the error, type "RUN" and press the Enter key to
           execute your request.
```

To execute a previously stored program from the Focus > prompt, you should type "EX" followed by the name of the program (e.g., EX EMPLIST1). For the VM/CMS mainframe version:

```
>     ← Focus > prompt







EX EMPLIST1     ← The Exec command
```

For the PC version:

```
>> EX EMPLIST1
```

For the MVS/TSO version

```
> > EX EMPLIST1
```

Retype Command

The Retype command will redisplay the last report executed on your terminal. After you execute a TABLE request, you will have the opportunity to scroll through the executed report and view the contents. You would eventually get to the end of the report and will be returned to the Focus > prompt. If you then decide to review the report again, you could either reexecute the request or type "Retype" at the Focus > prompt. Reexecuting a request will consume additional computer resources. It will take extra time because Focus will have to reaccess the data file and its Master File Description and execute your report. It is much faster to use the Retype command and redisplay the report, which is still in the computer's main storage. You can execute the Retype command as often as you would like. However, if you have issued another Focus command since executing your report, the report will no longer be available in the main storage of the computer and the Retype command will not work. Instead, Focus will display the following message:

```
(FOCO26) REPORT NOT AVAILABLE FOR RETYPING
```

Example of Retype:

```
Ex EMPLIST1
```

Focus will display the report.

```
Retype
```

Focus will display the report again.

Online and Offline Commands

The default for displaying your requested reports is your terminal's display screen. In all the commands that we have reviewed so far, the resulting reports would have been displayed on your terminal's display screen. To redirect a report to your system's printer, you should type the Offline command—from the Focus > prompt—prior to executing the program that you are planning to run. See the following example.

```
Offline
```

```
Ex EMPLIST1
```

This will print the report on your system's printer instead of displaying it on the terminal. Next we can enter the following:

```
Ex Describe Staff
```

This time the hierarchical chart of the STAFF file will be sent to your system's printer. Offline will remain in effect until you change it to Online. To change to the Online mode, just type the word Online at the Focus > prompt.

You can easily move between Online and Offline modes while executing the same program. This is a useful feature because you can develop your program in the Online mode, display your report, and make repeated modifications. When you are satisfied that the report is working as it should be, you could switch to the Offline mode and print the final report on your printer. The following scenario illustrates how you could switch between the two modes.

```
Ex EMPLIST1
```

Since the default is Online, the resulting report will be displayed on the terminal.

```
Offline
```

Now you have moved into the Offline mode.

```
Retype
```

This will reprint the same report on the system's printer. No report will be displayed on your terminal.

```
Online
```

```
Retype
```

The same report will now be displayed on your terminal. Since you are now back in the Online mode, all your future programs will be displayed on the terminal unless you change the direction by typing another Offline command.

TABLE REQUEST VERBS

A verb is an action word. It tells Focus to do something specific. There are only four action words or verbs in the TABLE command:

```
LIST
PRINT
SUM  (ADD or WRITE are also acceptable)
COUNT
```

PRINT and SUM are the two most widely used of the four action words.

LIST

LIST is an action word that tells Focus to print an itemized list of your requested fields. For example, the command

```
TABLE FILE STAFF
LIST LAST_NAME AND FIRST_NAME
END
```

will produce an itemized listing of the last names of employees in the STAFF file.

```
PAGE      1


LIST    LAST_NAME           FIRST_NAME
----    ---------           ----------
   1    TURPIN              BENTON
   2    BORGIA              CESARE
   3    FREEMAN             DIANE
   4    HUNT                CHARLES
   5    TRENT               RICHARD
   6    TAYLOR              JUANITA
   7    COLE                ROBERT
   8    MORALES             CARLOS
   9    DUXBURY             JILLIAN
  10    ANDERSEN            CHRISTINE
  11    GREENSTREET         JAMES
  12    BOCHARD             ROBERT
  13    TAHANIEV            RICHARD
  14    CAMPOS              CARLOS
  15    ZARKOV              WILLIAM
  16    JAMESON             CARLA
```

PRINT

The PRINT command is very much like the LIST command. It reads the Focus database and will print the fields requested. It does not itemize the report. The entry

```
TABLE FILE STAFF
PRINT DEPT_NAME AND SECTION_NAME
AND LAST_NAME
END
```

will produce the following report:

```
PAGE     1


DEPT_NAME              SECTION_NAME            LAST_NAME
---------             ------------            ---------
FINANCE               PAYABLES                TURPIN
FINANCE               PAYABLES                BORGIA
FINANCE               COLLECTIONS             FREEMAN
OPERATIONS            ENGINEERING             HUNT
OPERATIONS            CUSTOMER SERVICES       TRENT
OPERATIONS            CUSTOMER SERVICES       TAYLOR
MARKETING             SALES                   COLE
MARKETING             SALES                   MORALES
ADMINISTRATION        EXECUTIVE               DUXBURY
ADMINISTRATION        EXECUTIVE               ANDERSEN
MIS                   DEVELOPMENT             GREENSTREET
MIS                   DEVELOPMENT             BOCHARD
MIS                   OPERATIONS              TAHANIEV
MIS                   OPERATIONS              CAMPOS
MARKETING             SALES                   ZARKOV
MARKETING             SALES                   JAMESON
```

The purpose of the PRINT verb is to (1) access the Focus file, (2) retrieve the information requested, and (3) display them on the screen. There are a few points worth remembering about the PRINT command. These points are also valid for other Focus action words.

　　1. Column titles are printed automatically. They are given the same names as their respective field names in the Master File Description. Thus the column with employee identification data will have the title "EMPLOYEE_ID." Similarly, the department name column will be titled "DEPT_NAME."

　　2. All column titles are underlined automatically by Focus.

　　3. You could always display a file's field names if you are coding a TABLE request interactively on the terminal. This is a useful feature, since you may forget a field name after having already keyed in several lines of code. To display the names of the fields, type a question mark followed immediately by the letter "F" at the Focus > prompt and then press the Enter key (i.e., > ?F). Remember that there should be no spaces between the ? and F. You could enter the ?F on any line after the TABLE statement.

```
>> TABLE FILE STAFF
>> ?F


 FILENAME=  STAFF
* DEPRTMNT_ID    DEPT_NAME
* SECTION_ID     SECTION_NAME
* EMPLOYEE_ID    LAST_NAME     FIRST_NAME   JOB_TITLE      STREET
  CITY           STATE         ZIP_CODE     TELEPHONE_NO   DATE_BIRTH
  DATE_HIRE      SALARY        PCT_INC      VACATION

>> PRINT DEPRTMNT_ID AND DEPT_NAME AND LAST_NAME          ←You can
>> END                                                   continue with the
                                                          rest of your
                                                          request.
```

4. The width of report column is dictated by its field format and field name. For example, if you look at the Master File Description for the STAFF file, you will notice that the format of the LAST_NAME field is A20. This means that any name up to 20 characters long could be contained in this field. The name of this field is, of course, LAST_NAME, which is only nine characters long. In this case Focus will allocate the higher number on the report. Therefore, the column width for the employee last name will be 20 characters wide. Similarly, the STREET field is 30 characters long, but the field name STREET is only six characters long, so Focus will reserve 30 characters on the report. On the other hand, the SECTION_ID field is six characters long, but the field name, SECTION_ID, is 10 characters long. In this case Focus will allocate 10 characters on the report. So the width of each report column is decided by the size of the field name and its format. The larger value will determine the column width. There are other ways to change the default column title and size on Focus reports. We discuss these advanced features in a later chapter.

5. The maximum width of a report is 256 characters. Most computer printers in use today can print only 132 characters across a page. This is enough for most business reports. Occasionally, you may be required to create a wider report. In that case you will need to use the panel feature of Focus. By setting the panel to increments of 80, Focus will divide each page into two or more pages which will be printed one after the other. The pages will be numbered 1.1, 1.2, 2.1, 2.2, and so on. The Set feature will be discussed later.

6. To improve readability, Focus allocates two blank spaces between each column of a report. The blank space between the columns could be modified by other, more advanced Focus features.

7. If the requested fields are key fields (i.e., the segment type has been selected as S1), the fields are printed in their logical order of entry.

8. Page numbers will be printed automatically on the upper left-hand side of every page of the report.

9. The word "AND" is an optional connector. You do not have to use it, but it helps with documenting the program and making it easier to understand.

10. Fields will be printed in the order with which they were coded in the print statement. In the example above, DEPRTMNT_ID will be the first column printed, followed by DEPT_NAME and LAST_NAME.

11. Aliases could be used instead of field names. Aliases could also be mixed with full field names in a TABLE request. For example, both of the following requests are valid and will produce identical reports.

```
TABLE FILE STAFF
PRINT LAST_NAME AND FIRST_NAME AND SALARY
END
```

is the same as

```
TABLE FILE STAFF
PRINT LN AND FN AND SALARY
END
```

12. Truncated field names are acceptable as long as they are unique. In the STAFF file, LAS is acceptable instead of LAST_NAME, but ST is not acceptable for STREET because it could also be the truncated field name for STATE. If you attempt to use nonunique truncated fields, Focus will reject your statement and will issue the following FOC error message:

```
(FOC016)  THE TRUNCATED NAME DESCRIBES MORE THAN ONE FIELD: ST
REPLY :>
```

If you type a question mark (?) in response to the REPLY :> prompt, you will get the following message:

```
The truncated set of characters used instead of the full
fieldname or field alias is not unique. For example,
if two fields are named 'COST' and 'COMPANY,' the repre-
sentation by the letters 'CO' is ambiguous. 'COS' and
'COM' would suffice.
REPLY :>
```

You will have the opportunity to correct the field name by typing "STR" or abandoning your TABLE request by typing "QUIT."

13. It is permissible to mix field names, aliases, and truncated field names in the same print statement.

14. If you want to refer to all fields within one segment, you have two choices. You could refer to each field individually in your TABLE request or, alternatively, you could issue a PRINT SEGMENT command as follows:

```
TABLE FILE STAFF
PRINT DEPRTMNT_ID AND DEPT_NAME
END
```

is the same as

```
TABLE FILE STAFF
PRINT SEG.DEPRTMNT
END
```

15. In later versions of Focus (release 6.0 and above on the mainframe and 4.00 and above on PC/Focus), you could use an asterisk (*) to print every field in a single-path file. Figure 4.2 shows the differences between a single-path and a multipath file.

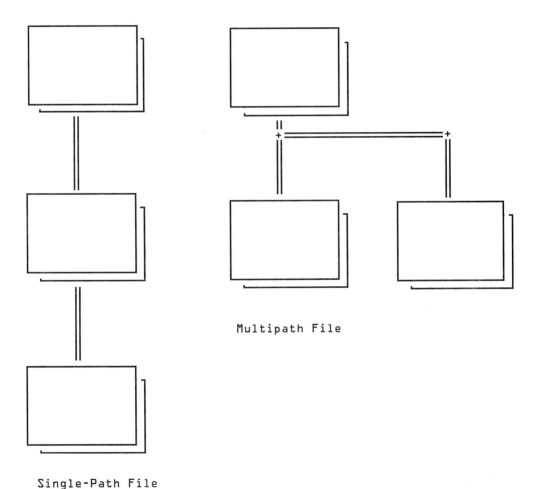

Multipath File

Single-Path File

Figure 4.2 Single-path and multipath files.

The following TABLE request

```
TABLE FILE STAFF
PRINT *
END
```

will print every field in the STAFF file. If you try this TABLE request on a multipath file, you will get the following message from Focus:

```
01010(FOC757)  WARNING : YOU REQUESTED A PRINT * FOR A MULTIPATH
FILE
```

Unfortunately, Focus does not stop there. It will continue to print the file, but only the leftmost path of the file is printed. The explanation for the FOC757 error message is printed below:

```
The PRINT * command causes the leftmost path in a file
to be printed. If the file has more than one path, data
that are not part of the leftmost path are not printed.
```

COUNT

The COUNT action word will add the occurrences of one or several fields within a file. The fields being counted could be alphanumeric or numeric.

```
TABLE FILE STAFF
COUNT DEPT_NAME AND SECTION_NAME AND LAST_NAME
END
```

The request above will count every occurrence of the DEPT_NAME, SECTION _NAME, and LAST_NAME fields in the STAFF file. It will produce the following report:

```
PAGE     1

DEPT_NAME    SECTION_NAME    LAST_NAME
COUNT        COUNT           COUNT
---------    ------------    ---------
       7             10             16
```

As the report above shows, there were seven occurrences of department names, 10 section names, and 16 employees in the STAFF file.

Almost all the rules discussed above for the PRINT command also apply to the COUNT, SUM, and LIST commands. You could count one or many fields in the same request. The fields being counted could be in different segments.

SUM

The SUM action word will add the values of individual fields that you have indicated in your TABLE request. In the STAFF file, the request SUM SALARY will add the salaries of all the employees in the company. As you know, we cannot add alphanumeric fields to each other. In most programming languages, any such request will probably stop your program dead in its tracks. In computer jargon this is known as a program *abending* or *bombing out*. In Focus, your program will not die. Instead, Focus will display the value of the last field that it encountered while trying to add alphanumeric fields. Therefore, the request SUM LAST_NAME will just print the last name in the file. An example of a SUM action word and the report that it will produce follows.

```
TABLE FILE STAFF
SUM SALARY AND VACATION
END


   PAGE     1

   SALARY        VACATION
   --------      --------
   855,050.00         982
```

SUM reserves one or more areas in the computer memory to store the result of adding together the values of the fields requested. We call these areas accumulators since they will be used to accumulate the values of the fields. These areas are usually the same size as the fields that are being added together. In the example above, the SALARY field is nine characters long, including the decimal point and the two decimal places. Therefore, the largest number that Focus could store in the accumulator area will be 999999.99. If we hired additional employees or gave increases to our current employees, the sum of all the salaries will exceed the size of the accumulator. In that case, Focus will still go ahead and print your report but will put several asterisks under the fields that exceeded the specified size:

```
PAGE     1

SALARY        VACATION
--------      --------
********           982
```

The number of asterisks corresponds to the number of characters in the field (e.g., if a field is eight characters long, you will see eight asterisks). There are several ways that this kind of error can be corrected.

1. You can change the format of the Master File Description and increase the size of the salary field to 12 or 14 or more. This is an acceptable solution, but you still do not know how large the company will grow or what will happen in the future. Also, every time that you make a change in the Master File Description, you must reorganize the Focus data file. Another problem is that by increasing the size of the field you are carrying empty characters in the computer storage and are processing them without reason. To explain this further: If the maximum size of a salary field is nine characters, it will accommodate a salary of $999,999.99. If you increase the format to, say, 14 characters, you will be able to accommodate $99,999,999,999.00. This might help you with the SUM action word, but you are increasing the size of your field and therefore your file unnecessarily and are affecting the performance of the computer.

2. The next option is using the DEFINE statement. DEFINE enables you to increase the size of a field temporarily and avoid the problems mentioned above. We discuss DEFINE in Chapter 9.

3. The third option is to change the value of the accumulator field on the fly. You do this by assigning a new value to the field in your TABLE request as you code the program. The following TABLE request demonstrates this technique:

```
TABLE FILE STAFF
SUM SALARY/D12.2
END
```

The slash character (/) following the field name will indicate to Focus that the field will have a new size during this operation. The new format follows the slash character. Therefore, the statement above instructs Focus to increase the size of the accumulator to 12 characters, including a decimal point and two decimal places. The largest value displayed will be $999,999,999.99.

You could also use this technique temporarily to reduce the size of an accumulator or a field. The following example shows how we can print only the first initial of employees' first names by using this method.

```
TABLE FILE STAFF
PRINT FIRST_NAME/A1 AND LAST_NAME
END
    PAGE    1


FIRST_NAME   LAST_NAME
----------   --------
    B        TURPIN
    C        BORGIA
    D        FREEMAN
    C        HUNT
    R        TRENT
    J        TAYLOR
    R        COLE
    C        MORALES
    W        ZARKOV
    C        JAMESON
```

```
     J              DUXBURY
     C              ANDERSEN
     J              GREENSTREET
     R              BOCHARD
     R              TAHANIEV
     C              CAMPOS
```

HOT SCREEN FACILITY

Hot Screen was introduced a few years ago to assist users in navigating through displayed reports. When you execute a TABLE request, the report is usually displayed on your terminal's CRT screen. A CRT screen is generally only 80 characters wide and up to 25 lines long. If your report is more than 25 lines long or more than 80 characters wide (and most reports are), you can just display one screen at a time by pressing the Enter key. Also, you can only go forward—and sideways to the right—in your report. In a wide report, Focus may divide the report into several sections vertically. You will see page 1.1 first followed by the middle part of the report, which will be page 1.2, and the rightmost part of the report, which will be page 1.3. The rest of pages of the report will follow the same pattern. It will not be possible to go back or save any of the information for later use. With Hot Screen, you can now achieve quite a few items that are still impossible under other system development tools, such as COBOL or Assembler or PL/I. To activate the Hot Screen editor, you will need to press the PF1 key (F1 on PCs) as soon as the first page of your report is displayed on the terminal's CRT screen. If you press the PF1 key, PC/Focus and most minicomputer versions of Focus will display the following help line at the bottom of your screen:

```
PAGE       1


DEPT_NAME               SECTION_NAME            LAST_NAME
----------              ------------            ---------
FINANCE                 PAYABLES                TURPIN
FINANCE                 PAYABLES                BORGIA
FINANCE                 COLLECTIONS             FREEMAN
OPERATIONS              ENGINEERING             HUNT
OPERATIONS              CUSTOMER SERVICES       TRENT
OPERATIONS              CUSTOMER SERVICES       TAYLOR
MARKETING               SALES                   COLE
MARKETING               SALES                   MORALES
ADMINISTRATION          EXECUTIVE               DUXBURY
ADMINISTRATION          EXECUTIVE               ANDERSEN
MIS                     DEVELOPMENT             GREENSTREET
MIS                     DEVELOPMENT             BOCHARD
MIS                     OPERATIONS              TAHANIEV
MIS                     OPERATIONS              CAMPOS
MARKETING               SALES                   ZARKOV
MARKETING               SALES                   JAMESON

KEYS: 1HELP 2FENCE 3END 4OFFLINE 5LOCAT 6SAVE 7BACK 8FORW 9LEFT 10RIGHT
```

The mainframe Focus help line is

```
KEYS: 1=HELP 2=FENCE 3=END 4=OFFL 5=LOCA 6=SAVE 7=BACK 8=FORW 10=LEFT 11=RIGHT
```

The help line in other versions of Focus is very similar to one of the versions displayed above. The help commands are pretty self-explanatory.

Hot Screen Function Keys

PF1 = Help key. If you press this key, Focus will display a screen of information about the other PF keys on the Hot Screen help line.

PF2 = Fence key. This key will let you freeze (fence) one column on the report and scroll through the rest of the screen columns to the right without losing sight of that column. Most PC spreadsheets have commands similar to this one. When reports are more than 80 characters wide, you may want to fix your leftmost field and scroll all the way to the rightmost field to review the rest of information. To use this key, press the PF2 (or F2) key once. In PC/Focus an arrow will appear at the bottom line of the screen. Use your cursor keys to move the arrow to the position that you desire and press the PF2 key or the Enter key once. You do not have to fix your position at the end of a column. You can freeze a column or part of a column; for example, you could just freeze the first five letters of the LAST_NAME field. After you freeze or fix your desired column, you can scroll to the right by using the PF11 (F10 in the PC) function key. To cancel the freeze or fence, press the PF2 (or F2) one more time. On the mainframe Focus, when you initially press the PF2 key, instead of an arrow you get the following message at the bottom of your screen:

```
Move cursor to right limit of fixed area; hit PF02 again
```

The message does not sound very user friendly. However, there is really no difference between the two versions. So, instead of the arrow, you will have to move your cursor to the desired location. Next, you press the PF2 key one more time to freeze the column. The rest of the operation is similar to the PC/Focus version reviewed above.

PF3 = End key. This key will immediately cancel the report on the screen and return you to the Focus > prompt.

PF4 = Offline key. This is equivalent to issuing the Offline command. If you press this key, you will get the following message at the bottom of your screen:

The cursor will be
positioned here.⌐

```
Select: 1-Print entire report 2-Print this page 3-Cancel 4-Hold –
```

This message seems self-explanatory. However, in this case the cursor is at the rightmost end of the line and the numbers 1, 2, 3, and 4 do not refer to PF keys. You must select a number, enter it, and press the Enter key to activate it. If you enter 1, Focus will send a copy of your report to your system's printer. If you type in number 4 and press the Enter key, Focus will create a HOLD file and place the information from the report in that file. Focus will also create a Master File Description for the HOLD file. You can access the HOLD file and use the Table commands to print reports from the HOLD file just like any other Focus file. We will learn more about HOLD files in a later chapter.

PF5 = Locate key.   This key will help you search for and locate any field on the report. PF5 is self-prompting; when you press the key, the cursor will move to the bottom of the screen and will prompt you to enter a string of characters (e.g., a last name such as Turpin). If it finds the string on any page, it will highlight it for you. PF5 only searches forward.

PF6 = Save key.   This key will save a line of report on a disk file. You simply position your cursor on the line that you want saved and press the PF6 key. The record will be saved in the standard sequential format, so it will be readable by other software packages and word processors.

PF7 and PF8 = Backward and Forward keys.   These two keys perform the functions of scrolling up and down the report. PF7 scrolls upward (i.e., you go toward the beginning of the report). PF8 will scroll downward. These are powerful commands, especially if you are reviewing a long report.

PF10 and PF11 = Scroll keys.   These keys will let you scroll to the right and left of a report. This is really useful if your report is wider than 80 characters across (most reports are). In PC/Focus, F9 and F10 perform the same functions as PF10 and PF11 on the mainframe. This is because most PCs have 10 function keys only.

Finally, you could also issue other TED-type commands with Hot Screen. If you have a long report, you could type the words "BOTTOM" or "TOP" at the bottom line of the screen to go to the end or beginning of the report, respectively. Hot Screen is a very useful facility and should be used to navigate through reports online.

STORING REPORTS ON A DISK FILE

By now, you should know how to display a Focus report on the terminal or print it offline on your system's printer. You could also store reports directly on a disk file. This is really an extension of the Focus Offline command. The trick here is to direct the output of your report to a disk file instead of the system's printer. There are several advantages to saving output files on disk instead of printing them directly.

1. The reports could be printed later. You could schedule your reports to run late at night or early in the morning, when the computing costs are lower. You could then have the reports printed later in the morning or on request, if needed. In many organizations, the needs for reports are not constantly evaluated. So you may find that many long reports are printed day after day for years and are no longer being used by the requesting departments. This happens because the users who requested the original reports are no longer there or the requirements for the reports have disappeared. If you save a report on a disk file and print it only on request by the user, you will at least save the cost of printing useless reports if the users are no longer interested in them.

2. A report displayed on the terminal is lost after it is displayed. A printed report could be misplaced. If you save your report on disk, it will be there as long as you need it.

3. You could make several copies of a report by printing it from a disk file. If you do not store your report on disk, you could still print more than one copy of a report by going offline and directing your printer to print several copies of the report. But you usually have to specify the number of copies ahead of time. If a report is stored on a disk file, you can make as many copies as you would like as often as you like.

4. A report stored on disk could be used by other mainframe and PC products. It could be accessed by system editors such as the ISPF/PDF editor or Xedit or by a word processor. It could also be edited and included as part of another report. For example, a Focus program could generate a report of sales by regions of the country for the entire company. This report could then be merged into the president's letter to all stockholders. The letter will probably be produced using a word processing package. The Focus report is easily retrieved from the disk file, where it was stored, and is integrated into the president's letter.

5. A report stored on disk is available for online viewing by many users. You must remember that an online report is just like any other computer file. You could view it with TED or system editors such as the ISPF/PDF editor and Xedit. Therefore, you have all the facilities of the editor available to you. You could search for and locate a particular account number or name or date. You could even modify the information on the report. It would be much faster to locate items online than shuffling through pages and pages of paper. Also, several users in different physical locations could view a report online concurrently.

How do we store our report on a disk? This is one of those areas where you are really dependent on your operating system and the standards in the data center. You should first ask the site coordinator for the shop standards. However, the general procedure for storing data on disk files is discussed below.

You will have to define or allocate the file that will be used to receive the report in place of the system's printer. You must issue commands to replace your printer with this file every time that you issue an Offline command. First, you will have to tell the operating system the name of the file that you are going to use or create. You could write on an already existing file or could create one for the report. In PC/Focus and VM/CMS Focus you could define the file from inside Focus by using the FILEDEF command. In TSO under MVS, you could use the Allocate command to allocate a file for your output. Some examples of defining an output file to the operating system follow.

VM/CMS focus

>

OFFLINE CLOSE   ← This command will make sure that any
                    previously opened output file is closed.

CMS FILEDEF OFFLINE DISK OUTLIST1 REPORT A

followed by:

OFFLINE

followed by the TABLE request.

PC/focus

>> FILEDEF OFFLINE DISK C:OUTLIST1.REP

followed by:

OFFLINE

followed by the TABLE request.

MVS focus

> > TSO ALLOCATE F(OFFLINE) DA(OUTLIST1.REP) SPACE(5 2) TRACKS SHR −
RECFM(F) LRECL(132)

followed by:

OFFLINE

followed by the TABLE request.

In all cases the report created by your program will be directed to a disk file and will be stored on disk. In VM/CMS it will be known as OUTLIST1 RE-PORT. In PC/Focus and MVS/TSO it will be stored as OUTLIST1.REP. After you complete your Focus session, you could view the file and print it directly or search online for items that are of interest to you.

FILEDEF stands for "file definition." In the case above, you are defining OFFLINE as the name of a file that is also named OUTLIST1 REPORT A. When you issue the Offline command prior to a Table request, the output will be directed to the Offline file, which is now a disk file called OUTLIST1 REPORT A instead of the system's printer. TSO ALLOCATE is a similar command that allocates or assigns a disk file name to the Offline report file.

TABLETALK

In concept, TableTalk is very similar to the FileTalk facility that we discussed in Chapter 3. It consists of a series of intelligent windows or pop-up menus that will assist you in developing your Table request. You can invoke the TableTalk feature from the > prompt by typing TableTalk. On some Focus versions, there is a main menu to allow you to select the TableTalk menu.

```
                   Menu Presentation of FOCUS facilities

   ┌──────────────────────────────────────────────────────────────────┐
   │ What would you like to do?                                         │
   │ ──────────────────────────                                         │
   │ TableTalk      Build column-oriented report                        │
   │ PlotTalk       Build a graph                                       │
   │ FileTalk       Describe a new database file                        │
   │ ModifyTalk     Build a MODIFY Procedure                            │
   │ Painters       Build free-format reports or screens                │
   │ Ted            Create/edit a file                                  │
   │ Scan           Browse/update a database file                       │
   │ Link           Communicate with other computers                    │
   │ System         Issue a DOS command                                 │
   │ Windows        Create, maintain & run WINDOWS                       │
   │ Exec           Create, maintain & run FOCEXECS                      │
   │ Help           Display HELP information                            │
   │ Other          FOCUS utilities (QUERY, JOIN, etc.)                 │
   │ Commands       Issue interactive FOCUS commands                    │
   │ Exit           Leave FOCUS and return DOS                          │
   └──────────────────────────────────────────────────────────────────┘

     Select options with ↑ ↓ and ENTER .. or ESC to back up
```

The first TableTalk menu consists of a listing of the names of Focus data files that are accessible to you. You select your file by moving the cursor bar to it and pressing the Enter key.

```
   ┌──────────────────────────────────────────────────────────────────┐
   │ INSTRUCTIONS :   1-Move cursor to name of file with ↑ ↓ arrow keys │
   │                  2-Depress  ENTER to Select file                   │
   │                  3-ESC key to QUIT                                 │
   └──────────────────────────────────────────────────────────────────┘


        ┌──────────────────────────────────────────────┐
        │ Select one of these files:          ↓        │
        │ ─────────────────────────                     │
        │ STAFF                                         │
        │ EMPLOYEE - Revise last request                │
        │ CAR                                           │
        │ EXPERSON                                      │
        │ AIRLINE                                       │
        │ EDUCFILE                                      │
        │ EMPLOYEE                                      │
        │ FINANCE                                       │
        │ JOBFILE                                       │
        │ LEDGER                                        │
        │ PROPERTY                                      │
        │ REGION                                        │
        └──────────────────────────────────────────────┘


              P C / F O C U S   T A B L E T A L K
```

The next menu is the main TableTalk menu. It follows the same concept as FileTalk. It presents you with successive windows and displays the program code as you progress through your selections. The TableTalk's main menu is almost identical in all versions of Focus.

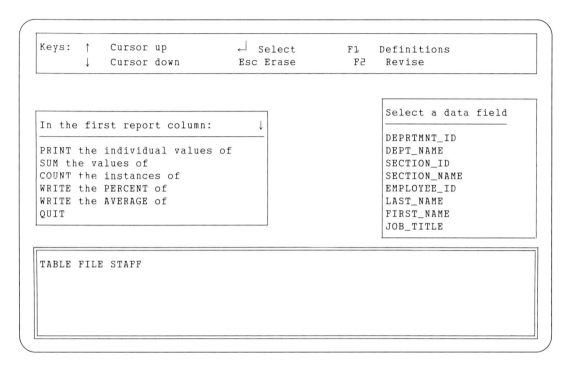

```
Keys:   ↑   Cursor up          ↵ Select       F1   Definitions
        ↓   Cursor down        Esc Erase       F2   Revise


                                              Select a data field
                                              ─────────────────────
In the first report column:        ↓          DEPRTMNT_ID
─────────────────────────────────────         DEPT_NAME
PRINT the individual values of                SECTION_ID
SUM the values of                             SECTION_NAME
COUNT the instances of                        EMPLOYEE_ID
WRITE the PERCENT of                          LAST_NAME
WRITE the AVERAGE of                          FIRST_NAME
QUIT                                          JOB_TITLE


TABLE FILE STAFF
```

Just like FileTalk, TableTalk will display the code that it develops at the bottom half of the screen. Although TableTalk is a sophisticated program, it is generally useful for simple programs only. For more complex programs, you will need to use the Define statement to create new fields and perform relational tests. Under these circumstances, TableTalk is not that effective. We will describe all forms of the Define commands in detail in Chapter 9.

TABLEF

TABLEF is a Focus command that is not properly understood by many people and as such is not used that often. The difference between the TABLE and TABLEF commands is as follows:

1. The TABLE command will retrieve data from a Focus file in the order in which it was entered in the Focus file. TABLEF will retrieve the data in its logical order. Therefore, if the segment data have a key, they will retrieve it by that key. The following two examples will demonstrate.

The first request is a straightforward TABLE request. Notice that we do not request data sorting. In a future chapter we will learn how to sort the data. In any case the data from this file are actually printed in the order in which they were entered.

```
TABLE FILE STAFF
PRINT DEPRTMNT_ID
AND DEPT_NAME AND LAST_NAME
END
```

```
PAGE    1

                    TABLE   EXAMPLE

DEPRTMNT_ID   DEPT_NAME              LAST_NAME
-----------   ---------              ---------
    12        FINANCE                TURPIN
    12        FINANCE                BORGIA
    12        FINANCE                FREEMAN
    15        OPERATIONS             HUNT
    15        OPERATIONS             TRENT
    15        OPERATIONS             TAYLOR
    20        MARKETING              COLE
    20        MARKETING              MORALES
    20        MARKETING              ZARKOV
    20        MARKETING              JAMESON
    10        ADMINISTRATION         DUXBURY
    10        ADMINISTRATION         ANDERSEN
    14        MIS                    GREENSTREET
    14        MIS                    BOCHARD
    14        MIS                    TAHANIEV
    14        MIS                    CAMPOS
```

In the following example I used TABLEF against the same file. TABLEF printed the information in the logical order of data that was established at the time I created my Master File Description. Because the DEPRTMNT_ID field is a key field, the information is printed in that order, not the physical order of entry as was the case with the TABLE command.

```
TABLEF FILE STAFF
PRINT DEPRTMNT_ID
AND DEPT_NAME AND LAST_NAME
END
```

TABLEF   EXAMPLE

DEPRTMNT_ID	DEPT_NAME	LAST_NAME
10	ADMINISTRATION	DUXBURY
10	ADMINISTRATION	ANDERSEN
12	FINANCE	TURPIN
12	FINANCE	BORGIA
12	FINANCE	FREEMAN
14	MIS	GREENSTREET
14	MIS	BOCHARD
14	MIS	TAHANIEV
14	MIS	CAMPOS
15	OPERATIONS	HUNT
15	OPERATIONS	TRENT
15	OPERATIONS	TAYLOR
20	MARKETING	COLE
20	MARKETING	MORALES
20	MARKETING	ZARKOV
20	MARKETING	JAMESON

The only problem is that if you use the TABLEF command, you cannot sort the records by using any of the Focus BY commands. The BY command, as we shall see in Chapter 5, is used to sequence a Focus file for reporting purposes. For example, in the STAFF file you could use the BY command to cause the report to be printed in last-name sequence. With the TABLEF command, you can still use the BY sort command to create a control break, but no sorting will take place. Use of the other Focus sort command, ACROSS, is also not allowed in TABLEF.

2. The Retype command that we discussed earlier in this chapter does not work with the TABLEF command.

3. On TABLE commands, you could issue the HOLD and SAVE commands to create extract files even after the report has been printed. On TABLEF you could only issue the HOLD and SAVE commands as part of the TABLEF request, so you could still create extract files. We will discuss HOLD and SAVE in Chapter 10. However, the HOLD and SAVE commands allow you to store the result of your Table requests on disk. The information that is stored as such could be used by other applications at a later time.

4. Multiple verbs are not allowed in TABLEF. We also discuss multiple Focus verbs in a later chapter.

The TABLEF command is definitely faster for printing data if you are not planning to sort your data or the existing logical order of data is acceptable.

The following figure displays the reports produced by the TABLE and TABLEF requests side-by-side.

TABLEF EXAMPLE   TABLE   EXAMPLE

DEPRTMNT_ID	DEPT_NAME	LAST_NAME	DEPRTMNT_ID	DEPT_NAME	LAST_NAME
10	ADMINISTRATION	DUXBURY	12	FINANCE	TURPIN
10	ADMINISTRATION	ANDERSEN	12	FINANCE	BORGIA
12	FINANCE	TURPIN	12	FINANCE	FREEMAN
12	FINANCE	BORGIA	15	OPERATIONS	HUNT
12	FINANCE	FREEMAN	15	OPERATIONS	TRENT
14	MIS	GREENSTREET	15	OPERATIONS	TAYLOR
14	MIS	BOCHARD	20	MARKETING	COLE
14	MIS	TAHANIEV	20	MARKETING	MORALES
14	MIS	CAMPOS	20	MARKETING	ZARKOV
15	OPERATIONS	HUNT	20	MARKETING	JAMESON
15	OPERATIONS	TRENT	10	ADMINISTRATION	DUXBURY
15	OPERATIONS	TAYLOR	10	ADMINISTRATION	ANDERSEN
20	MARKETING	COLE	14	MIS	GREENSTREET
20	MARKETING	MORALES	14	MIS	BOCHARD
20	MARKETING	ZARKOV	14	MIS	TAHANIEV
20	MARKETING	JAMESON	14	MIS	CAMPOS

SUMMARY

The TABLE environment is probably the most widely used Focus feature. You can use the TABLE command to print reports from Focus and non-Focus files. With Focus you could easily access VSAM, IMS, and DB2 and dBase files. In later chapters we expand on the TABLE command and introduce other features that will enable you to create complex reports. In this chapter we covered the following topics:

1. Using the Check File and Describe utilities to check Focus files and to obtain a record description
2. Getting in and out of the TABLE environment and Focus by using QUIT, QQUIT, END, RUN, and FIN
3. Coding simple Focus programs interactively
4. Executing Focus TABLE requests
5. Error-handling techniques
6. Using TED to code a Focus TABLE request
7. The four Focus action words: LIST, PRINT, COUNT, and SUM
8. The Retype command
9. Online and Offline commands
10. The Hot Screen facility
11. Storing Focus reports on a disk file for future use
12. TableTalk
13. TABLEF command

CHAPTER 5

SORTING, GROUP TOTALING, CONTROL BREAKS, AND SUMMARIZING DATA

MAIN TOPICS:

- Sorting
- Ranking
- Group Totals
- Control Breaks
- Summarizing

TABLE requests can produce reports that are sorted into almost any order. Reports are sorted by using one or both of the key phrases "BY" and "ACROSS." For example, a mailing list could be printed in ascending order of last names and/or zip codes. You could even perform a sort within a sort by sorting your file in zip code order, and then within each zip code, sorting the names in alphabetical order. BY is the more widely used sort command and we discuss it first.

THE BY PHRASE OR VERTICAL SORTING

The BY command is used to sort or sequence one or more fields in a Focus or non-Focus file. Since it sequences records that it reads, it is also called a BY sequencer. The BY command sorts records of the requested file vertically in rows down the report—hence the term *vertical sort*. The BY command could be used with any of the four TABLE action words. The general format of the BY phrase is as follows:

```
TABLE FILE filename
PRINT     ⎫
LIST      ⎬  BY field name
SUM       ⎪
COUNT     ⎭
END
```

PRINT and the BY Command

The PRINT verb, in conjunction with the BY command, produces a list of records sorted in order of the sort control field requested. The following example illustrates a simple TABLE request with the BY command:

```
TABLE FILE STAFF
PRINT LAST_NAME AND FIRST_NAME
BY SALARY          ← SALARY is the sort control
END                  field.
```

The TABLE request above will produce a report from the STAFF file in the ascending order of salaries, as the following report illustrates.

```
PAGE      1


     SALARY   LAST_NAME          FIRST_NAME
     ------   ---------          ----------
  22,500.00   TRENT              RICHARD
  26,550.00   TAYLOR             JUANITA
  32,000.00   ANDERSEN           CHRISTINE
              CAMPOS             CARLOS
  34,500.00   FREEMAN            DIANE
  35,000.00   BOCHARD            ROBERT
  36,700.00   JAMESON            CARLA
  39,000.00   COLE               ROBERT
  39,400.00   MORALES            CARLOS
  45,600.00   GREENSTREET        JAMES
  47,000.00   ZARKOV             WILLIAM
  55,400.00   TAHANIEV           RICHARD
  57,000.00   HUNT               CHARLES
  65,400.00   TURPIN             BENTON
 102,000.00   BORGIA             CESARE
 185,000.00   DUXBURY            JILLIAN
```

The following points are worth noting:

1. The first field being sorted is the first field to be printed. This field is known as the *sort field* or *sort control field* or *sort key*. If two or more sort fields are present, the first field will appear first, followed by the second, the third, and so on. The remainder of the fields will appear, after the sort fields are printed, from left to right in the order in which they were written in the TABLE request. The first sort key is usually referred to as the *major sort key*. Other sort keys are known as *secondary* or *minor sort keys*.

2. If there are duplicate or repeating values in the sort fields, they will not be printed. Instead, blank spaces will appear in the report column below the first value printed. This feature is known as *print suppression*. It is also known as *group printing,* because a field is printed only at the beginning of a duplicate group of fields. In the example above, both Christine Andersen and Carlos Campos earn a salary of $32,000.00 a year; therefore, Focus will not print the duplicate or redundant information about the second salary. This is a very useful feature of Focus because it can neatly identify control breaks on a report. A control break occurs any time that the value of a sort key changes (e.g., from department 14 to department 15). If there are many duplicate field values and they overflow from one page of the report to the next, Focus will print the duplicate value at the beginning of each new page. In most other languages, you will have to write your own code to suppress printing of repeating values.

3. The default in sorting is from the lowest value to the highest value. In other words, fields are sequenced from 0 to 9 in numeric fields and from A to Z in alphabetic fields. The order of sorting could be reversed by adding the word "HIGHEST" after the BY command. If we had used the phrase "BY HIGHEST SALARY" in the request above, the name and the salary of the person with the highest salary would have been printed first.

4. BY or ACROSS fields could be followed by other BY and/or ACROSS fields, but they cannot be followed by fields that are not being sorted. Therefore, in your TABLE request, you must place all the fields that are not being sorted ahead of the first BY or ACROSS field. For example, the following TABLE request is correct and will produce a report as follows:

```
TABLE FILE STAFF
PRINT SALARY AND PCT_INC AND VACATION          ← These fields are
BY DEPT_NAME BY LAST_NAME                          correctly placed before
END                                                the first BY command.
```

```
PAGE    1


DEPT_NAME               LAST_NAME          SALARY  PCT_INC VACATION
---------               ---------          -------  ------  -------
ADMINISTRATION          ANDERSEN        32,000.00     .07       35
                        DUXBURY        185,000.00     .05      110
FINANCE                 BORGIA         102,000.00     .06       15
                        FREEMAN         34,500.00     .00       99
                        TURPIN          65,400.00     .05      120
MARKETING               COLE            39,000.00     .04       43
                        JAMESON         36,700.00     .10       22
                        MORALES         39,400.00     .06       80
                        ZARKOV          47,000.00     .11       63
MIS                     BOCHARD         35,000.00     .09       40
                        CAMPOS          32,000.00     .08       60
                        GREENSTREET     45,600.00     .06       10
                        TAHANIEV        55,400.00     .09       85
OPERATIONS              HUNT            57,000.00     .11      140
                        TAYLOR          26,550.00     .10       10
                        TRENT           22,500.00     .08       50
```

The BY Phrase or Vertical Sorting

The following TABLE request is also correct:

```
TABLE FILE STAFF
PRINT SALARY BY DEPT_NAME BY LAST_NAME
BY PCT_INC BY VACATION
END
```

whereas the following TABLE request will not work:

```
TABLE FILE STAFF
PRINT SALARY BY DEPT_NAME BY LAST_NAME
AND PCT_INC AND VACATION        ← These fields are not sort
END                               control fields and cannot
                                  follow sort control fields.
```

5. Several BY phrases could be coded in a TABLE request. This is also known as *multiple sorting*. The sort field names should be valid field names or aliases or truncations of field names.

6. The maximum number of BY commands is 32. In practice, any report with more than five or six sort fields would be too confusing to understand. The following TABLE request has two sort keys. It creates a list of employee names within a company in alphabetical order of department names (i.e., Administration before Finance) and the highest salaries within those departments. It is important to note that in multiple sorting, the first sort key—in this case the DEPT_NAME—is sorted first. Then the secondary fields are sorted within the first sort field (i.e., SALARY within each DEPT_NAME).

```
TABLE FILE STAFF
PRINT LAST_NAME AND FIRST_NAME
BY DEPT_NAME
BY HIGHEST SALARY
END
```

```
PAGE     1
```

DEPT_NAME	SALARY	LAST_NAME	FIRST_NAME
ADMINISTRATION	185,000.00	DUXBURY	JILLIAN
	32,000.00	ANDERSEN	CHRISTINE
FINANCE	102,000.00	BORGIA	CESARE
	65,400.00	TURPIN	BENTON
	34,500.00	FREEMAN	DIANE
MARKETING	47,000.00	ZARKOV	WILLIAM
	39,400.00	MORALES	CARLOS
	39,000.00	COLE	ROBERT
	36,700.00	JAMESON	CARLA

```
MIS                         55,400.00   TAHANIEV      RICHARD
                            45,600.00   GREENSTREET   JAMES
                            35,000.00   BOCHARD       ROBERT
                            32,000.00   CAMPOS        CARLOS
OPERATIONS                  57,000.00   HUNT          CHARLES
                            26,550.00   TAYLOR        JUANITA
                            22,500.00   TRENT         RICHARD
```

In the report above, the department name (DEPT_NAME) is sorted from lowest value to highest value. The employee salary (SALARY) field is sorted from the highest value within each department to the lowest value. Also, notice how the repeating values for the department name (DEPT_NAME) have been suppressed. This is a simplified report, but it is similar to the types of reports that many organizations regularly produce to help them meet regulatory and audit requirements.

LIST and the BY Command

As we said before, the LIST verb is similar to the PRINT verb. When the same TABLE request as above is executed with LIST in place of PRINT, a similar report with a somewhat different flavor is produced.

```
TABLE FILE STAFF
LIST LAST_NAME AND FIRST_NAME
BY DEPT_NAME
BY HIGHEST SALARY
END


    PAGE     1


DEPT_NAME                 SALARY LIST   LAST_NAME     FIRST_NAME
---------                 ------ ----   ---------     ----------
  ADMINISTRATION       185,000.00   1   DUXBURY       JILLIAN
                        32,000.00   2   ANDERSEN      CHRISTINE
  FINANCE              102,000.00   1   BORGIA        CESARE
                        65,400.00   2   TURPIN        BENTON
                        34,500.00   3   FREEMAN       DIANE
  MARKETING             47,000.00   1   ZARKOV        WILLIAM
                        39,400.00   2   MORALES       CARLOS
                        39,000.00   3   COLE          ROBERT
                        36,700.00   4   JAMESON       CARLA
  MIS                   55,400.00   1   TAHANIEV      RICHARD
                        45,600.00   2   GREENSTREET   JAMES
                        35,000.00   3   BOCHARD       ROBERT
                        32,000.00   4   CAMPOS        CARLOS
  OPERATIONS            57,000.00   1   HUNT          CHARLES
                        26,550.00   2   TAYLOR        JUANITA
                        22,500.00   3   TRENT         RICHARD
```

Note that every time the value of a sort field changes, the LIST counter is reset to 1. Since this is an itemized list, you may find it easy to look up certain information. For example, you could see that there are four employees in the marketing department and that Carla Jameson is the lowest-paid employee in that department.

COUNT and the BY Command

The COUNT verb will add up the number of times a sort control field is read by the request. In the first report below, the PRINT verb is used to list the last name of employees in each section within each department.

```
TABLE FILE STAFF
PRINT LAST_NAME
BY DEPT_NAME
BY SECTION_NAME
END
```

```
   PAGE     1

   DEPT_NAME                SECTION_NAME            LAST_NAME
   ---------                ------------            ---------
   ADMINISTRATION           EXECUTIVE               DUXBURY
                                                    ANDERSEN
   FINANCE                  COLLECTIONS             FREEMAN
                            PAYABLES                TURPIN
                                                    BORGIA
   MARKETING                SALES                   COLE
                                                    MORALES
                                                    ZARKOV
                                                    JAMESON
   MIS                      DEVELOPMENT             GREENSTREET
                                                    BOCHARD
                            OPERATIONS              TAHANIEV
                                                    CAMPOS
   OPERATIONS               CUSTOMER SERVICES       TRENT
                                                    TAYLOR
                            ENGINEERING             HUNT
```

In the second request, the number of employees is counted in each section of each department. Note that the word "COUNT" is automatically placed in the column heading directly beneath the sort control field name.

```
TABLE FILE STAFF
COUNT LAST_NAME
BY DEPT_NAME
BY SECTION_NAME
END
```

```
                                        LAST_NAME
DEPT_NAME            SECTION_NAME        COUNT
---------           ------------        ---------
ADMINISTRATION      EXECUTIVE                   2
FINANCE             COLLECTIONS                 1
                    PAYABLES                    2
MARKETING           SALES                       4
MIS                 DEVELOPMENT                 2
                    OPERATIONS                  2
OPERATIONS          CUSTOMER SERVICES           2
                    ENGINEERING                 1
```

SUM and the BY Command

SUM adds the values of the numeric sort fields together, thereby creating a total for those fields.

```
TABLE FILE STAFF
SUM SALARY BY DEPT_NAME
BY SECTION_NAME
END
```

```
DEPT_NAME               SECTION_NAME             SALARY
---------               ------------             ------
ADMINISTRATION          EXECUTIVE           217,000.00
FINANCE                 COLLECTIONS          34,500.00
                        PAYABLES            167,400.00
MARKETING               SALES               162,100.00
MIS                     DEVELOPMENT          80,600.00
                        OPERATIONS           87,400.00
OPERATIONS              CUSTOMER SERVICES    49,050.00
                        ENGINEERING          57,000.00
```

In the report above, the salary of each section is added together and displayed. If we had coded our TABLE request to say

```
TABLE FILE STAFF
SUM SALARY BY DEPT_NAME
END
```

Focus would have only added the values of the salary fields in each department, as the following report shows.

```
DEPT_NAME                       SALARY
---------                       ------
ADMINISTRATION        217,000.00
FINANCE               201,900.00
MARKETING             162,100.00
MIS                   168,000.00
OPERATIONS            106,050.00
```

If SUM is used with an alphabetic or alphanumeric field, only the last value read is displayed. In the following report, we have used the SUM verb against an alphanumeric field.

```
TABLE FILE STAFF
SUM LAST_NAME AND FIRST_NAME
BY DEPT_NAME
END
```

```
   PAGE      1
```

```
DEPT_NAME                LAST_NAME              FIRST_NAME
---------                ---------              ----------
ADMINISTRATION           ANDERSEN               CHRISTINE
FINANCE                  FREEMAN                DIANE
MARKETING                JAMESON                CARLA
MIS                      CAMPOS                 CARLOS
OPERATIONS               TAYLOR                 JUANITA
```

The interesting fact about this report is that we have managed to print the last employee name in each department. You will find this feature useful in some applications.

ACROSS PHRASE OR HORIZONTAL SORTING

The ACROSS phrase is another command used by Focus programs to perform sorting of Focus and non-Focus data files. The general format of the ACROSS command is as follows:

```
TABLE FILE filename
PRINT
LIST
SUM              ACROSS field name
COUNT
END
```

The following is an example of a TABLE request with the ACROSS command.

```
TABLE FILE STAFF
SUM SALARY ACROSS DEPT_NAME
END
```

There are three main differences between the BY and ACROSS commands.

1. The ACROSS command places the sorted control field(s) horizontally across the width of the report. In other words, it sorts the information by rows.

2. The ACROSS command is best used with the SUM and COUNT verbs. It does not make much sense to use it with the PRINT verb. This has to do with the limitation of the width of printed paper. Just imagine if you had a TABLE request that instructed the computer to: PRINT LAST_NAME AND SALARY ACROSS DEPT_NAME. There could be tens or hundreds or even thousands of employees in a department. Even if Focus allowed it, the report would be thousands of characters wide and there is no printer in existence to print such a report. What is more, there are not many people around who could read and comprehend a 10-foot-wide report. However, the same request with the BY command would make sense, because the names and salaries would be printed vertically in columns, page after page, and there is no limitation on the number of pages in a printed report.

3. There is a maximum limit of five ACROSS phrases in each TABLE request. In practice, even five may be too many, since a business report is usually 132 characters wide, even though Focus allows a maximum report size of 256 characters. Usually, the output of a TABLE request with two or three ACROSS commands fills the width of the widest commercial computer paper, $14\frac{7}{8}$ inches. On the other hand, 32 BY fields could be issued in one TABLE request. An example of a TABLE request with the ACROSS command follows:

```
TABLE FILE STAFF
SUM SALARY ACROSS DEPT_NAME
END
```

The report is shown in Fig. 5.1.

Note: when you use a single ACROSS phrase, Focus does not place the name of the field on the report. So the report shown in Fig. 5.1 does not display the name of the sort key, which is SALARY. If you use two or more fields with the ACROSS command, all fields mentioned in the request will be displayed on the report, as you can see in the following TABLE request.

```
TABLE FILE STAFF
SUM SALARY AND VACATION
ACROSS DEPT_NAME
END
```

The report is shown in Fig. 5.2.

PAGE   1

| DEPT_NAME | | | | |
ADMINISTRATION	FINANCE	MARKETING	MIS	OPERATIONS
217,000.00	201,900.00	162,100.00	168,000.00	106,050.00

Figure 5.1

PAGE   1

| DEPT_NAME | | | | | | | | | |
| ADMINISTRATION | | FINANCE | | MARKETING | | MIS | | OPERATIONS | |
SALARY	VACATION	SALARY	VACATION	SALARY	VACATION	SALARY	VACATION	SALARY	VACATION
217,000.00	145	201,900.00	234	162,100.00	208	168,000.00	195	106,050.00	200

Figure 5.2

OTHER FOCUS SORT FEATURES

Matrix Reports

By combining the two commands of BY and ACROSS, we could produce a matrix-type report. This is like a two-dimensional report with values horizontally across and vertically down the report. These reports are usually very easy to review and understand and users, especially in financial applications, find them informative.

```
TABLE FILE STAFF
SUM SALARY ACROSS DEPT_NAME
BY SECTION_NAME
END
```

The report is shown in Fig. 5.3.

You could use multiple sort keys of BY and ACROSS subject to the limitations of five ACROSSes and 32 BYs in a TABLE request.

```
TABLE FILE STAFF
SUM SALARY AND VACATION
ACROSS DEPT_NAME
BY SECTION_NAME
END
```

The report is shown in Fig. 5.4. The dots indicate that no data are present in the file for those fields. For example, the administration department does not have a collections section or a customer services section. Therefore, there are no employees or salaries or accrued vacation hours for those fields under the administration department.

RANK

This command, which is used in conjunction with the BY command, ranks the numerical fields in a file by highest or lowest values. Also, you could use RANK to print a limited number of records from a file based on their relative standing or ranking. For example, in a marketing organization, you could request a listing of the top five salespersons in each region. In our hypothetical company, you could request a report of the five highest-paid employees in the company. The following example shows a report using the RANK command.

```
TABLE FILE STAFF
PRINT JOB_TITLE AND LAST_NAME
BY DEPRTMNT_ID
RANKED BY HIGHEST SALARY
END
```

DEPRTMNT_ID	RANK	SALARY	JOB_TITLE	LAST_NAME
10	1	185,000.00	PRESIDENT	DUXBURY
	2	32,000.00	EXECUTIVE ASSISTANT	ANDERSEN
12	1	102,000.00	LIAISON OFFICER	BORGIA
	2	65,400.00	HEAD ACCOUNTANT	TURPIN
	3	34,500.00	SUPERVISOR	FREEMAN
14	1	55,400.00	MANAGER, DATA CENTER	TAHANIEV
	2	45,600.00	SENIOR PROGRAMMER	GREENSTREET
	3	35,000.00	OPERATOR	BOCHARD
	4	32,000.00	OPERATOR	CAMPOS
15	1	57,000.00	MANAGER	HUNT
	2	26,550.00	SERVICE REP.	TAYLOR
	3	22,500.00	SERVICE REP.	TRENT
20	1	47,000.00	SALES REPRESENTATIVE	ZARKOV
	2	39,400.00	SALES REPRESENTATIVE	MORALES
	3	39,000.00	SALES REPRESENTATIVE	COLE
	4	36,700.00	SALES REPRESENTATIVE	JAMESON

The following TABLE request prints a list of the five highest-paid employees in the company.

```
TABLE FILE STAFF
PRINT LAST_NAME AND FIRST_NAME AND DEPT_NAME
RANKED BY TOP 5 SALARY
END
```

PAGE   1

RANK	SALARY	LAST_NAME	FIRST_NAME	DEPT_NAME
1	185,000.00	DUXBURY	JILLIAN	ADMINISTRATION
2	102,000.00	BORGIA	CESARE	FINANCE
3	65,400.00	TURPIN	BENTON	FINANCE
4	57,000.00	HUNT	CHARLES	OPERATIONS
5	55,400.00	TAHANIEV	RICHARD	MIS

You could also use the word "LOWEST" instead of "TOP" or "HIGHEST" with the RANK command.

Figure 5.3

| | DEPT_NAME | | | | |
SECTION_NAME	ADMINISTRATION	FINANCE	MARKETING	MIS	OPERATIONS
COLLECTIONS		34,500.00			
CUSTOMER SERVICES					49,050.00
DEVELOPMENT				80,600.00	
ENGINEERING					57,000.00
EXECUTIVE	217,000.00				
OPERATIONS				87,400.00	
PAYABLES		167,400.00			
SALES			162,100.00		

Figure 5.3

| | DEPT_NAME | | | | | | | | | |
| | ADMINISTRATION | | FINANCE | | MARKETING | | MIS | | OPERATIONS | |
SECTION_NAME	SALARY	VACATION	SALARY	VACATION	SALARY	VACATION	SALARY	VACATION	SALARY	VACATION
COLLECTIONS			34,500.00	99						
CUSTOMER SERVICES									49,050.00	60
DEVELOPMENT							80,600.00	50		
ENGINEERING									57,000.00	140
EXECUTIVE	217,000.00	145								
OPERATIONS							87,400.00	145		
PAYABLES			167,400.00	135						
SALES					162,100.00	208				

Figure 5.4

111

The IN-GROUPS-OF phrase allows you to group your records within a range selected by you or by your users. You could also select a top limit for your report. This command is useful in situations where you would want to compare sales results between regions or salary ranges within different departments of a company. The general format of this command is as follows:

```
TABLE FILE filename
PRINT    ⎫
SUM      ⎪  BY
COUNT    ⎬  ACROSS   field name IN-GROUPS-OF value [TOP limit]
LIST     ⎭
END
```

The following TABLE request will produce a report of salaries in groups of 5000.

```
TABLE FILE STAFF
COUNT EMPLOYEE_ID BY SALARY
IN-GROUPS-OF 5000 TOP 180000
END
```

PAGE   1

SALARY	EMPLOYEE_ID COUNT
20,000.00	1
25,000.00	1
30,000.00	3
35,000.00	4
45,000.00	2
55,000.00	2
65,000.00	1
100,000.00	1
180,000.00	1

The report above states that there are three employees whose salaries are within $5000 of $30,000, two employees whose salaries are within $5000 of $55,000, and so on. The maximum salary range it will print is $180,000.

The following rules apply to the IN-GROUPS-OF phrase:

1. Sort control fields must be numeric. Focus will not allow you to group alphanumeric fields, since it would be illogical.
2. IN-GROUPS-OF can only be used with the BY and ACROSS commands.

TOTALING ROWS AND COLUMNS IN A REPORT

So far, we have produced reports using various Focus commands and verbs. The reports have been useful, but it would have been better to have column totals and row totals for certain numeric fields. For example, if we print a report of all the employees and their respective salaries in the company, we should also print a line showing the grand total of all the salaries.

COLUMN-TOTAL is a Focus command that allows you to add numbers in columns and print a row of totals at the end of the report. ROW-TOTAL sums numeric fields across each row and prints a column of totals for the rows at the rightmost end of the report. The following request demonstrates the first feature.

```
TABLE FILE STAFF
SUM SALARY AND VACATION
AND COLUMN-TOTAL
BY DEPT_NAME BY SECTION_NAME
END
```

```
    PAGE     1


    DEPT_NAME              SECTION_NAME              SALARY    VACATION
    ---------             ------------             ------    --------
    ADMINISTRATION        EXECUTIVE               217,000.00      145
    FINANCE               COLLECTIONS              34,500.00       99
                          PAYABLES                167,400.00      135
    MARKETING             SALES                   162,100.00      208
    MIS                   DEVELOPMENT              80,600.00       50
                          OPERATIONS               87,400.00      145
    OPERATIONS            CUSTOMER SERVICES        49,050.00       60
                          ENGINEERING              57,000.00      140

    TOTAL                                         855,050.00      982
```

In this report, in addition to printing the total salaries and accrued vacation hours for each section within each department, the grand total of all the salaries and accrued vacation hours within the company are produced. Focus will also print the word "TOTAL" at the end of the report.

The following TABLE command will produce a report with the ROW-TOTAL command.

```
TABLE FILE STAFF
SUM SALARY ACROSS DEPT_NAME
AND ROW-TOTAL
END
```

The report is shown in Fig. 5.5.

| DEPT_NAME | | | | | |
ADMINISTRATION	FINANCE	MARKETING	MIS	OPERATIONS	TOTAL
217,000.00	201,900.00	162,100.00	168,000.00	106,050.00	855,050.00

Figure 5.5

| | DEPT_NAME | | | | | |
SECTION_NAME	ADMINISTRATION	FINANCE	MARKETING	MIS	OPERATIONS	TOTAL
COLLECTIONS	.	34,500.00	.	.	.	34,500.00
CUSTOMER SERVICES	.	.	.	.	49,050.00	49,050.00
DEVELOPMENT	.	.	.	80,600.00	.	80,600.00
ENGINEERING	.	.	.	.	57,000.00	57,000.00
EXECUTIVE	217,000.00	.	.	.	.	217,000.00
OPERATIONS	.	.	.	87,400.00	.	87,400.00
PAYABLES	.	167,400.00	.	.	.	167,400.00
SALES	.	.	162,100.00	.	.	162,100.00
TOTAL	217,000.00	201,900.00	162,100.00	168,000.00	106,050.00	855,050.00

Figure 5.6

114

COLUMN-TOTAL and ROW-TOTAL could be combined in matrix reports with BY and ACROSS as follows:

```
TABLE FILE STAFF
SUM SALARY AND ROW-TOTAL AND COLUMN-TOTAL
ACROSS DEPT_NAME
BY SECTION_NAME
END
```

The report is shown in Fig. 5.6.

Finally, if you do not need to specify which fields to column total or row total, you could use the ON TABLE syntax as follows:

```
TABLE FILE STAFF
SUM SALARY AND VACATION
BY DEPT_NAME
BY SECTION_NAME
ON TABLE COLUMN-TOTAL
END
```

The ON TABLE command will only total your numeric fields; alphabetic and alphanumeric fields will be left alone. It is not necessary to use the COLUMN-TOTAL and ROW-TOTAL with the BY or ACROSS commands exclusively. They could be used with regular Focus TABLE verbs such as PRINT and SUM. The following TABLE request and report show the combination of the PRINT and COLUMN-TOTAL commands.

```
TABLE FILE STAFF
PRINT LAST_NAME AND FIRST_NAME AND SALARY
AND VACATION
AND COLUMN-TOTAL
END
```

PAGE   1

LAST_NAME	FIRST_NAME	SALARY	VACATION
TURPIN	BENTON	65,400.00	120
BORGIA	CESARE	102,000.00	15
FREEMAN	DIANE	34,500.00	99
HUNT	CHARLES	57,000.00	140
TRENT	RICHARD	22,500.00	50
TAYLOR	JUANITA	26,550.00	10
COLE	ROBERT	39,000.00	43
MORALES	CARLOS	39,400.00	80
ZARKOV	WILLIAM	47,000.00	63
JAMESON	CARLA	36,700.00	22

```
DUXBURY            JILLIAN      185,000.00    '      110
ANDERSEN           CHRISTINE     32,000.00            35
GREENSTREET        JAMES         45,600.00            10
BOCHARD            ROBERT        35,000.00            40
TAHANIEV           RICHARD       55,400.00            85
CAMPOS             CARLOS        32,000.00            60

TOTAL
                                855,050.00           982
```

SUMMARY

Focus has very strong sorting capabilities. You can sort a file and create a report within a few minutes. Focus allows you to sort records two ways by using the BY and/or ACROSS commands. The BY command is used extensively in report creation to sort files and to display control breaks when field values change.

We also discussed the ACROSS command. This is a useful command, but you will have to be careful in using it because you are limited by the width of the print area of most computer printers. The combination of the BY and ACROSS commands creates fancy-looking reports. Again, you have to be careful that the report being prepared is meaningful and not just pretty. COLUMN-TOTAL and ROW-TOTAL are commands that could be used with or without BY and ACROSS to produce grand totals or row totals.

CHAPTER 6

DATA SELECTION
AND FILTERING

MAIN TOPICS:

- IF STATEMENT
- WHERE CLAUSE
- MULTIPLE RECORD SCREENING AND SELECTION

Information can be retrieved selectively by the use of one or more IF statements or WHERE clauses. IF or WHERE are used to select only the information that passes the screening conditions. Focus allows you to make several kinds of comparison. We will review the following in this chapter:

> Value comparison
> Multiple compound selection with "OR"
> Multiple IF statements
> Range checking
> Substring comparison
> Masked value comparison
> SIMILAR operator
> RECORDLIMIT option
> IF TOTAL and WHERE TOTAL

We review the IF statement first. The WHERE clause is similar to IF, but it is not currently available on all versions of Focus. We discuss the differences between IF and WHERE later in this chapter.

VALUE COMPARISON

Value comparison is the simplest and most commonly used screening test in Focus and indeed in most other languages. The value comparison uses the relation words EQ or IS (both of which mean "equal to") or NE or IS-NOT (meaning "not equal to"). The general format of the IF command is as follows:

```
IF field name RELATION test value
```

For example:

```
IF DEPT_NAME EQ 'MIS'
```

In this case, the field name is DEPT_NAME, the relation is EQ, and the test value is MIS.

Valid relation tests for comparing values in Focus are listed in Table 6.1. Some examples of the value comparison follow:

```
IF LAST_NAME NE 'TURPIN'
```

The record being tested by the statement above will be accepted only if the employee's last name is not Turpin.

```
IF SALARY EQ 55000
```

The tested field and therefore the record will be accepted only if the salary of the employee is exactly $55,000.

Value comparison rules

1. EQ and IS are identical and could be used interchangeably.
2. NE or IS-NOT are identical and could be used interchangeably.
3. Value comparisons could be used with both alphanumeric and numeric fields.
4. Single quotation marks (') around alphanumeric test fields are optional. For example, you could either type 'TURPIN' or TURPIN for the test value name and both would be accepted by Focus. However, if a test field contains embedded spaces, such as San Francisco or New York, the single quotation marks are mandatory; those fields should be coded as 'NEW YORK' and 'SAN FRANCISCO'.
5. By convention, the IF statement follows the AND and the BY statements and is usually the last statement in a TABLE request. However, it is possible to code the IF statement before the other statements in the TABLE request, but since it is seldom done, the resulting code could be confusing to other programmers and users.

TABLE 6.1 VALUE COMPARISON TESTS

Relation	Meaning
IS or EQ	If the field that you are testing is equal to the test value that follows the characters IS or EQ, the screening test is true and the record will be accepted. See below for examples.
IS-NOT or NE	If the field that you are testing is not equal to the test value that follows the relation (NE or IS-NOT), the test is true (i.e., the record will be accepted).

Examples of IF with value comparison

```
TABLE FILE STAFF
PRINT LAST_NAME AND FIRST_NAME AND CITY
BY DEPT_NAME
IF CITY EQ ANAHEIM
END
```

```
PAGE      1
```

LAST_NAME	FIRST_NAME	CITY
ZARKOV	WILLIAM	ANAHEIM
ANDERSEN	CHRISTINE	ANAHEIM

```
TABLE FILE STAFF
PRINT LAST_NAME AND FIRST_NAME
BY DEPT_NAME
IF DEPT_NAME IS-NOT FINANCE
END
```

```
PAGE      1
```

DEPT_NAME	LAST_NAME	FIRST_NAME
ADMINISTRATION	DUXBURY	JILLIAN
	ANDERSEN	CHRISTINE
MARKETING	COLE	ROBERT
	MORALES	CARLOS
	ZARKOV	WILLIAM
	JAMESON	CARLA
MIS	GREENSTREET	JAMES
	BOCHARD	ROBERT
	TAHANIEV	RICHARD
	CAMPOS	CARLOS
OPERATIONS	HUNT	CHARLES
	TRENT	RICHARD
	TAYLOR	JUANITA

In the example above, the employees in the finance department are excluded from the selection.

Multiple IF Selections

You could screen the field that you are testing against more than one test value. To do this, you should use the conjunction OR. This is also known as a compound condition. Observe the following:

```
TABLE FILE STAFF
PRINT LAST_NAME AND SALARY
BY DEPT_NAME
IF DEPT_NAME EQ 'MIS' OR 'FINANCE'
ON TABLE COLUMN-TOTAL
END


    PAGE    1


DEPT_NAME               LAST_NAME                      SALARY
---------               ---------                      ------
FINANCE                 TURPIN                      65,400.00
                        BORGIA                     102,000.00
                        FREEMAN                     34,500.00
MIS             ,       GREENSTREET                 45,600.00
                        BOCHARD                     35,000.00
                        TAHANIEV                    55,400.00
                        CAMPOS                      32,000.00


    TOTAL                                          369,900.00
```

In the request above, the test will be true and Focus will print the values of the last name and salary fields if the DEPT_NAME field of a record contains either MIS or FINANCE. You may sometimes need to satisfy more than one condition before accepting a record. In that case you should use multiple IF statements, one after another, as shown below.

```
TABLE FILE STAFF
PRINT LAST_NAME AND JOB_TITLE
BY SECTION_NAME
IF DEPT_NAME EQ 'MIS'
IF STATE EQ 'CA'
IF CITY NE 'LOS ANGELES'
END


    PAGE    1


SECTION_NAME            LAST_NAME              JOB_TITLE
------------            ---------              ---------
DEVELOPMENT             GREENSTREET            SENIOR PROGRAMMER
                        BOCHARD                OPERATOR
OPERATIONS              TAHANIEV               MANAGER, DATA CENTER
                        CAMPOS                 OPERATOR
```

The IF statements in the TABLE request above are translated by Focus to mean:

```
If department name equals MIS AND the state equals CA
AND the city is not equal to Los Angeles, then select an
employee record for further processing.
```

You could also combine the OR and multiple IF statements together as follows:

```
TABLE FILE STAFF
PRINT EMPLOYEE_ID AND LAST_NAME
AND SECTION_NAME
BY DEPT_NAME
IF DEPT_NAME EQ 'MIS' OR 'OPERATIONS'
IF CITY NE 'LOS ANGELES'
IF SECTION_NAME EQ 'ENGINEERING' OR 'DEVELOPMENT'
END
```

```
   PAGE     1

   DEPT_NAME             EMPLOYEE_ID   LAST_NAME      SECTION_NAME
   ---------             -----------   ---------      ------------
   MIS                   392345782     GREENSTREET    DEVELOPMENT
                         621893221     BOCHARD        DEVELOPMENT
   OPERATIONS            213456682     HUNT           ENGINEERING
```

Some pitfalls

1. The IF statement with OR can only be used to test one field at a time. In the example above, the statement IF DEPT_NAME EQ 'MIS' OR 'OPERA-TIONS' will test the value of the DEPT_NAME field of every record that it reads for MIS or OPERATIONS. If Focus finds either of the two values, it accepts the record and passes it on to the next screening statement, which checks the value of the city field in the record. We could even have several OR relations, such as IF DEPT_NAME EQ 'MIS' OR 'MARKETING' OR 'OPERATIONS'. However, you could not use OR to check more than one field in each IF statement. As an example, the statement IF DEPT_NAME EQ 'MIS' OR CITY EQ 'ANAHEIM', while logically accurate, is not acceptable to Focus as an IF statement and will be rejected. In this case you have tried to test two fields in one IF statement. It is still possible to make this kind of comparison in Focus, but you will need to use either the DEFINE statement (which we cover in a later chapter) or the WHERE clause.

2. You should not attempt to compare two fields of the same file against each other. For example, the following TABLE request is incorrect:

```
TABLE FILE CAR
PRINT COUNTRY AND MODEL
IF RETAIL_COST EQ DEALER_COST
END
```

The RETAIL_COST and DEALER_COST fields are in the same Focus file; therefore, Focus will reject the TABLE request. Again, the TABLE request above could be made to work by adding a DEFINE statement in the beginning or by substituting the WHERE clause for the IF statement.

RANGE COMPARISON OR RANGE TESTING

In range testing, the value of a field of information in the file is checked to see if it is within a requested range. Many times during the course of writing a Focus TABLE request, you will need to make a determination to see if the value of a numerical field such as salary is less than, say, $45,000. At other times, you may need to print all the employee last names that start with the letter "T" and the remaining letters of the alphabet. Focus has a number of relation tests that you could use to see if a field is within a certain range. The range relations and their meanings are itemized in Table 6.2.

Notes about range checking

1. The relations LT, GE, LE, and GT should only be used in the abbreviated forms shown below. You cannot use the greater-than sign (>) or the less-than sign (<).

2. The relations should not be spelled out fully, so "LESS THAN" is not acceptable as a substitute for LT.

TABLE 6.2 RANGE COMPARISON TESTS

Relation	Meaning
LT or IS-LESS-THAN	If the value in the field that is being tested is less than the test value specified in the TABLE request, the test is true. For example, the statement "IF SALARY LT 30000" will accept only records of employees whose salaries are less than $30,000. Therefore, 29999 will be acceptable but 30000 will be rejected.
GE	If the value in the field of the record that is being screened is equal to or greater than the test value specified in the TABLE request, that record will be accepted. For example, the statement "IF SALARY GE 30000" will accept only records of employees whose salaries are $30,000 and above.
LE	If the value in the field of the record being tested is less than or equal to the test value specified in the IF statement, that record will be accepted by the TABLE request. For example, the statement "IF SALARY LE 30000" will only accept records of employees whose salaries are exactly $30,000 or less.
GT or IS-MORE-THAN or EXCEEDS	This is the opposite of the LT relation. Any value greater than the test value stated in the IF statement will be acceptable.

3. Values with decimal points and places such as 10.5 and 145.02 are acceptable and should be entered with the decimal point and the decimal places. It is important to make a note of this because the decimal point in Focus is not assumed as it is in many other languages. In Focus it is hard coded as part of the value.

4. Range testing could be performed on both numeric and alphanumeric fields.

Examples of range testing

```
TABLE FILE STAFF
PRINT LAST_NAME AND SALARY
BY DEPT_NAME
IF SALARY LE 38000
END
```

```
    PAGE    1


    DEPT_NAME               LAST_NAME                   SALARY
    ---------               ---------                   ------
    ADMINISTRATION          ANDERSEN                 32,000.00
    FINANCE                 FREEMAN                  34,500.00
    MARKETING               JAMESON                  36,700.00
    MIS                     BOCHARD                  35,000.00
                            CAMPOS                   32,000.00
    OPERATIONS              TRENT                    22,500.00
                            TAYLOR                   26,550.00
```

```
TABLE FILE STAFF
PRINT FIRST_NAME BY DEPT_NAME
BY LAST_NAME
IF LAST_NAME GE 'F'
END
```

```
    PAGE    1


    DEPT_NAME               LAST_NAME               FIRST_NAME
    ---------               ---------               ----------
    FINANCE                 FREEMAN                 DIANE
                            TURPIN                  BENTON
    MARKETING               JAMESON                 CARLA
                            MORALES                 CARLOS
                            ZARKOV                  WILLIAM
    MIS                     GREENSTREET             JAMES
                            TAHANIEV                RICHARD
    OPERATIONS              HUNT                    CHARLES
                            TAYLOR                  JUANITA
                            TRENT                   RICHARD
```

Some pointers on range testing. If you already know the maximum and minimum values that you are selecting, you have two methods of using the IF statement to test a range of values:

1. You could use two IF statements (i.e., multiple IFs):

```
TABLE FILE STAFF
PRINT LAST_NAME AND EMPLOYEE_ID
BY DEPT_NAME
BY SALARY
IF SALARY GE 30000
IF SALARY LE 80000
END
```

2. Alternatively, you could use the FROM value-to-value relation:

```
TABLE FILE STAFF
PRINT LAST_NAME AND EMPLOYEE_ID
BY DEPT_NAME
BY SALARY
IF SALARY FROM 30000 TO 80000
END
```

Both of the TABLE requests above will select employee records with salaries in the range $30,000 to $80,000. See the following report:

```
PAGE      1


DEPT_NAME                 SALARY   LAST_NAME        EMPLOYEE_ID
---------                 ------   ---------        -----------
ADMINISTRATION         32,000.00   ANDERSEN           515478922
FINANCE                34,500.00   FREEMAN            504234521
                       65,400.00   TURPIN             294728305
MARKETING              36,700.00   JAMESON            413267891
                       39,000.00   COLE               293245178
                       39,400.00   MORALES            297748301
                       47,000.00   ZARKOV             312781122
MIS                    32,000.00   CAMPOS             432568023
                       35,000.00   BOCHARD            621893221
                       45,600.00   GREENSTREET        392345782
                       55,400.00   TAHANIEV           295738307
OPERATIONS             57,000.00   HUNT               213456682
```

Multiple IF statements and the FROM option could also be mixed together as shown below.

```
TABLE FILE STAFF
PRINT LAST_NAME AND DEPT_NAME
```

```
BY PCT_INC
BY SALARY
IF PCT_INC GE .01
IF SALARY FROM 20000 TO 32000 OR 46000 TO 85000
END
```

```
     PAGE     1


     PCT_INC        SALARY   LAST_NAME          DEPT_NAME
     -------        ------   ---------          ---------
         .05     65,400.00   TURPIN             FINANCE
         .07     32,000.00   ANDERSEN           ADMINISTRATION
         .08     22,500.00   TRENT              OPERATIONS
                 32,000.00   CAMPOS             MIS
         .09     55,400.00   TAHANIEV           MIS
         .10     26,550.00   TAYLOR             OPERATIONS
         .11     47,000.00   ZARKOV             MARKETING
                 57,000.00   HUNT               OPERATIONS
```

The negative form of the FROM relation is NOT-FROM.

SUBSTRING COMPARISON

This is one of the most powerful features of Focus. Basically, Focus checks the entire field to find an exact match to the character or characters that you have coded in the test value of the IF statement. Then, depending on whether the CONTAINS or the OMITS relation was used, it will either accept that record or ignore it and proceed to the next record. The test value that you supply could be any character or a string of characters. Table 6.3 shows the two relations and their meanings.

TABLE 6.3 SUBSTRING COMPARISON TESTS

Relation	Meaning
CONTAINS	If the test character or characters that you specified in your IF statement could be found anywhere in the field being checked, the field and its associated record will pass the IF screen and be accepted. For example, the statement ''IF LAST_NAME CONTAINS 'T' '' will accept any employee record that has the letter T anywhere in the last-name field. Therefore, Turpin, Hunt, Taylor, Tahaniev, Trent, and Greenstreet will all be accepted by the IF statement.
OMITS	If the test character or characters that you specified in your IF statement could not be found anywhere in the field being checked, that field and its associated record will pass the check as acceptable by the TABLE request. Therefore, the statement ''IF LAST_NAME OMITS 'T' '' will reject Tahaniev, Turpin, Hunt, Greenstreet, Trent, and Taylor.

Examples of CONTAINS and OMITS

```
TABLE FILE STAFF
PRINT LAST_NAME AND JOB_TITLE
IF LAST_NAME CONTAINS 'T'
END


    PAGE    1


   LAST_NAME             JOB_TITLE
   ---------             ---------
   TURPIN                HEAD ACCOUNTANT
   HUNT                  MANAGER
   TRENT                 SERVICE REP.
   TAYLOR                SERVICE REP.
   GREENSTREET           SENIOR PROGRAMMER
   TAHANIEV              MANAGER, DATA CENTER

TABLE FILE STAFF
PRINT LAST_NAME AND JOB_TITLE AND TELEPHONE_NO
IF JOB_TITLE CONTAINS 'MANAGER' OR 'HEAD'
OR 'PRESIDENT' OR 'SUPERVISOR'
IF TELEPHONE_NO CONTAINS '213' OR '714' OR '212'
END


    PAGE    1


   LAST_NAME             JOB_TITLE             TELEPHONE_NO
   ---------             ---------             ------------
   TURPIN                HEAD ACCOUNTANT       2135551232
   BORGIA                LIAISON MANAGER       2125554666
   FREEMAN               SUPERVISOR            7145551234
   HUNT                  MANAGER               7145558428
   DUXBURY               PRESIDENT             7145551020
   TAHANIEV              MANAGER, DATA CENTER  7145557893
```

Note how Focus searched the entire JOB_TITLE field to find a match for the test field. In one case—BORGIA—the word manager was the second word in the JOB_TITLE field, yet Focus still managed to retrieve it for you.

```
TABLE FILE STAFF
PRINT LAST_NAME AND FIRST_NAME
BY JOB_TITLE
BY SALARY
IF JOB_TITLE OMITS 'MANAGER' OR 'HEAD'
```

```
OR 'PRESIDENT'
END


    PAGE    1


    JOB_TITLE                  SALARY   LAST_NAME        FIRST_NAME
    ---------                  ------   ---------        ----------
    EXECUTIVE ASSISTANT        32,000.00  ANDERSEN       CHRISTINE
    OPERATOR                   32,000.00  CAMPOS         CARLOS
                               35,000.00  BOCHARD        ROBERT
    SALES REPRESENTATIVE       36,700.00  JAMESON        CARLA
                               39,000.00  COLE           ROBERT
                               39,400.00  MORALES        CARLOS
                               47,000.00  ZARKOV         WILLIAM
    SENIOR PROGRAMMER          45,600.00  GREENSTREET    JAMES
    SERVICE REP.               22,500.00  TRENT          RICHARD
                               26,550.00  TAYLOR         JUANITA
    SUPERVISOR                 34,500.00  FREEMAN        DIANE
```

Notice that we did not ask Focus to omit supervisors. CONTAINS is very useful for tracking and locating hard-to-find characters within a field. For example, if you had a VEHICLES file, you could produce a list of the most likely suspects in a hit-and-run accident even if you only had part of the license plate number of the car.

```
TABLE FILE VEHICLE
PRINT OWNER_NAME AND STREET AND CITY
AND TELEPHONE_NO
IF COLOR IS 'BLUE'
IF LICENSE CONTAINS 'TW1'
END
```

The request above would search every vehicle record in the file and look for the characters TW1 anywhere in a license plate of all the blue cars in the state.

The CONTAINS and OMITS clauses work on alphanumeric fields only. As you can see, there is a lot that could be done with alphanumeric fields that could not be done with numeric fields. You could, of course, redefine some numeric fields as alphanumeric fields and then use CONTAINS and OMITS. We will learn how to redefine fields when we discuss the DEFINE statement in Chapter 9. It is, however, best to define as alphanumeric every field that will not be part of an arithmetic operation. Therefore, taxes, salaries, insurance rates, percentages, amounts, balances, and similar items should always be defined as numeric. Other fields such as telephone numbers, social security numbers, and department numbers could and should be defined as alphanumeric. We reviewed the process of creating a Master File Description and defining fields and formats in Chapter 3. However, sometimes you do not have the opportunity to define a field, because you are dealing with a file that is already in existence and you will have to do your best with what you have at your disposal.

If the exact position of one or more characters within a field is known, you could then use the masked value test instead of CONTAINS or OMITS to screen your fields. Remember that CONTAINS and OMITS find the value anywhere within a field.

A *mask* is a string of characters like a mold or a template. The value of a field that is being checked is compared against the mask. The test value must always be enclosed in single quotation marks. The dollar sign ($) and the asterisk (*) play an important part in creating masks for field testing.

1. The dollar sign is used within the test value to instruct Focus, when it is screening a field, that it should ignore the characters that are in the same locations as the $ signs. For example, in the statement

```
IF LAST_NAME EQ 'T$$$$$$$$$$$$$$$$$'
```

we tell Focus that any last name starting with T should be selected. It does not matter what characters follow T. The $ is instructing Focus to ignore the rest of the characters in the field. In our STAFF file, Tahaniev, Trent, Taylor, and Turpin would be selected as a result of this statement. If you had used CONTAINS, you would have picked up all last names with T anywhere in the field, so Hunt and Greenstreet would also have been included. Depending on your business requirements, you may or may not have wanted to do that.

2. If you have a long string of characters such as the one above, you could use a $ and an * instead of a number of $ signs to tell Focus that the rest of characters should be ignored. The statement above could also be written as follows:

```
IF LAST_NAME EQ 'T$*'
```

The following example will select car records that start with the letter "T" and beyond.

```
TABLE FILE CAR
PRINT CAR AND MODEL
AND BODYTYPE BY COUNTRY
IF CAR GE 'T$*'
END
```

```
    PAGE      1
```

COUNTRY	CAR	MODEL	BODYTYPE
ENGLAND	TRIUMPH	TR7	HARDTOP
JAPAN	TOYOTA	COROLLA 4 DOOR DLX AUTO	SEDAN
SWEDEN	VOLVO	200 AUTO XJ	SEDAN

Any character position within the field that is going to be part of the screening process should be represented by the actual character that is being tested. The following example will explain this concept better.

```
IF TELEPHONE_NO EQ '213$$$$$$$'
```

This statement tells Focus to select only fields with the number 213 in the area code position. It does not matter what the rest of the numbers look like. The characters being selected could be located anywhere within the field. The following example will demonstrate the concept.

```
TABLE FILE STAFF
PRINT FIRST_NAME AND TELEPHONE_NO
AND DEPT_NAME
BY LAST_NAME
IF TELEPHONE_NO EQ '$$$555$$$$'
END
```

PAGE   1

LAST_NAME	FIRST_NAME	TELEPHONE_NO	DEPT_NAME
ANDERSEN	CHRISTINE	7145553894	ADMINISTRATION
BOCHARD	ROBERT	7145550212	MIS
BORGIA	CESARE	2125554666	FINANCE
CAMPOS	CARLOS	7145558812	MIS
COLE	ROBERT	7145550123	MARKETING
DUXBURY	JILLIAN	7145551020	ADMINISTRATION
FREEMAN	DIANE	7145551234	FINANCE
GREENSTREET	JAMES	2135553451	MIS
HUNT	CHARLES	7145558428	OPERATIONS
JAMESON	CARLA	7145555897	MARKETING
MORALES	CARLOS	7145557173	MARKETING
TAHANIEV	RICHARD	7145557893	MIS
TAYLOR	JUANITA	8185554771	OPERATIONS
TRENT	RICHARD	2135552911	OPERATIONS
TURPIN	BENTON	2135551232	FINANCE
ZARKOV	WILLIAM	7145554210	MARKETING

Masked value comparison has certain advantages over the CONTAINS and OMITS relations. If you know the exact location of the characters in the field, it is better to use the masked value comparison. CONTAINS and/or OMITS take longer to process, because they search the entire field character by character. However, if you do not know the location of a character or characters within a field, CONTAINS and/or OMITS are your best bets.

Use masked values for locating part numbers, stock numbers, phone numbers, zip codes, and street addresses. In short, use it whenever the general format and position of certain characters within a field are well known and are unlikely to change, such as area codes and prefix numbers of your telephone number. For example, most telephone numbers in southern California start with 213, 818, or 714. In San Francisco, the area code is always 415, and in parts of New York City it is 212. These values could be used in a mask either to accept or screen out a field and its associated record.

SIMILAR OPERATOR

SIMILAR relation testing is unlike other relations that we have discussed. When you issue an IF statement with SIMILAR, Focus looks for values in the field that have a pattern similar to that of the test value. The following TABLE request demonstrates the point.

```
TABLE FILE STAFF
PRINT LAST_NAME AND FIRST_NAME AND JOB_TITLE
IF FIRST_NAME SIMILAR 'CAR'
END
```

```
    PAGE     1


    LAST_NAME              FIRST_NAME   JOB_TITLE
    ---------             ----------   ---------
    BORGIA                CESARE       LIAISON MANAGER
    HUNT                  CHARLES      MANAGER
    TRENT                 RICHARD      SERVICE REP.
    MORALES               CARLOS       SALES REPRESENTATIVE
    JAMESON               CARLA        SALES REPRESENTATIVE
    TAHANIEV              RICHARD      MANAGER, DATA CENTER
    CAMPOS                CARLOS       OPERATOR
```

You will notice that all the first names selected have a similar pattern. For example, Charles and Carlos and parts of Richard and Cesare have a similarity to "CAR."

Note about SIMILAR. SIMILAR is not currently available on all versions of Focus. Check the availability before using this relation. You could always check the availability of a command or relation by writing a very small TABLE request for that command or relation. In this case you could try the following:

```
TABLE FILE EMPLOYEE
PRINT LAST_NAME AND FIRST_NAME
IF FIRST_NAME SIMILAR 'AR' OR 'CAR'
END
```

```
LAST_NAME           FIRST_NAME
---------           ----------
SMITH               MARY
SMITH               RICHARD
GREENSPAN           MARY
```

You will either get the report above or a Focus error message telling you that it did not recognize the word "SIMILAR."

WHERE CLAUSE

As mentioned earlier, WHERE and IF are similar in many respects. You could use WHERE with most of the relations that we have discussed so far in this chapter. Additionally, WHERE could perform two functions that the IF statement by itself could not perform. The first of these functions is the field-to-field comparison. You may recall that you could not compare two fields in the same file against each other using the IF statement. The other is the ability to perform complex calculations within the conditional statement. You could achieve both of the foregoing objectives by using the WHERE clause.

```
TABLE FILE CAR
PRINT CAR AND MODEL
AND DEALER_COST AND RETAIL_COST
WHERE DEALER_COST * 1.2 LT RETAIL_COST
IF COUNTRY NE 'W GERMANY'
END
```

```
PAGE     1
```

```
COUNTRY     CAR          MODEL                DEALER_COST   RETAIL_COST
-------     ---          -----                -----------   -----------
ENGLAND     JAGUAR       XJ12L AUTO               11,194        13,491
FRANCE      PEUGEOT      504 4 DOOR                4,631         5,610
ITALY       ALPHA ROMEO  2000 GT VELOCE            5,660         6,820
            ALPHA ROMEO  2000 SPIDER VELOCE        5,660         6,820
            ALPHA ROMEO  2000 4 DOOR BERLINA       4,195         5,925
            MASERATI     DORA 2 DOOR              25,000        31,000
```

This report lists the information requested about each car, only if the retail cost (i.e., the markup) is more than 20 percent over the dealer cost. Note that (1) we have compared two fields (DEALER_COST and RETAIL_COST) in the same file, and (2) we have performed calculations, on the fly, on one of the fields.

Following is an example of comparing two fields against two different values. Remember, this could not be done with the IF statement. The use of quotation marks around alphanumeric test values is not optional with the WHERE clause.

```
TABLE FILE STAFF
PRINT LAST_NAME AND DEPT_NAME AND CITY
WHERE DEPT_NAME CONTAINS 'MARKETING'
OR CITY CONTAINS 'ANAHEIM'
END
```

```
    PAGE    1
```

LAST_NAME	FIRST_NAME	DEPT_NAME	CITY
COLE	ROBERT	MARKETING	GARDEN GROVE
MORALES	CARLOS	MARKETING	LONG BEACH
ZARKOV	WILLIAM	MARKETING	ANAHEIM
JAMESON	CARLA	MARKETING	FOUNTAIN VALLEY
ANDERSEN	CHRISTINE	ADMINISTRATION	ANAHEIM

Here is another example of a compound WHERE relation. This time we used the AND conjunction to test two different fields for different values.

```
TABLE FILE STAFF
PRINT LAST_NAME AND DEPT_NAME AND CITY
WHERE DEPT_NAME CONTAINS 'MARKETING'
AND CITY CONTAINS 'ANAHEIM'
END
```

```
    PAGE    1
```

LAST_NAME	FIRST_NAME	DEPT_NAME	CITY
ZARKOV	WILLIAM	MARKETING	ANAHEIM

Notes about WHERE.   The WHERE clause is not currently available on PC/ Focus and the minicomputer versions of Focus. Check the availability before starting to write a program. The WHERE clause does not work with FROM and NOT-FROM relations. You could always use two or more WHERE statements with LT or GT relations instead. Remember, if your test value is not numeric, you must enclose it within quotation marks.

LIMITING THE NUMBER OF RECORDS SELECTED (THE IF RECORDLIMIT OR WHERE RECORDLIMIT RELATION)

If you are trying to create a new report from a huge file, you would not want to tie up your computing resources for long periods of time—sometimes 20 to 30 minutes—while you are conducting a test to see if your report is working. The RECORDLIMIT relation allows you to perform your test on a small subset of the real production file. In the following example we have requested a list of last names and the first names of all the employees who live in an area served by the 714 area code. In other words, these employees live in Orange County in California and all share the same area code for their phone number. Depending on our requirements, we could have requested 212 for New York City or 216 for the greater Cleveland area or 214 for the greater Dallas area. The report lists everybody with the area code requested.

```
TABLE FILE STAFF
PRINT LAST_NAME AND FIRST_NAME
AND TELEPHONE_NO
IF TELEPHONE_NO EQ '714$*'
END

    PAGE    1


    LAST_NAME                FIRST_NAME   TELEPHONE_NO
    ---------                ----------   ------------
    FREEMAN                  DIANE        7145551234
    HUNT                     CHARLES      7145558428
    COLE                     ROBERT       7145550123
    MORALES                  CARLOS       7145557173
    ZARKOV                   WILLIAM      7145554210
    JAMESON                  CARLA        7145555897
    DUXBURY                  JILLIAN      7145551020
    ANDERSEN                 CHRISTINE    7145553894
    BOCHARD                  ROBERT       7145550212
    TAHANIEV                 RICHARD      7145557893
    CAMPOS                   CARLOS       7145558812
```

In the second example below, the TABLE request was almost the same, except that we asked for a maximum of four records that met the condition requested. The report shows the first four successful records that had an area code of 714. Note that we did not ask for the first four records read by Focus, rather the first four records that met our first screening condition, which was the area code. The RECORDLIMIT relation will restrict the number of successful reads to the value that follows the EQ relation.

```
TABLE FILE STAFF
PRINT LAST_NAME AND FIRST_NAME
AND TELEPHONE_NO
```

```
IF TELEPHONE_NO EQ '714$*'
IF RECORDLIMIT EQ 4
END


    PAGE     1


    LAST_NAME                   FIRST_NAME   TELEPHONE_NO
    ---------                   ----------   ------------
    FREEMAN                     DIANE        7145551234
    HUNT                        CHARLES      7145558428
    COLE                        ROBERT       7145550123
    MORALES                     CARLOS       7145557173
```

As a matter of interest, if we had wanted to print the first four records read by Focus, we would have executed the following TABLE request:

```
TABLE FILE STAFF
PRINT LAST_NAME AND FIRST_NAME
AND TELEPHONE_NO
IF RECORDLIMIT EQ 4
END


    PAGE     1


    LAST_NAME                   FIRST_NAME   TELEPHONE_NO
    ---------                   ----------   ------------
    TURPIN                      BENTON       2135551232
    BORGIA                      CESARE       2125554666
    FREEMAN                     DIANE        7145551234
    HUNT                        CHARLES      7145558428
```

IF TOTAL AND WHERE TOTAL

Sometimes you may want to prepare a report that is selected based on the total values of all the fields in a file. Generally, whenever you use an IF statement or a WHERE clause, the record selection and screening take place at the time that the record is being retrieved by Focus from the data file. Sometimes, you may want to make a selection at the summary level. This would mean adding the values of the field together first and then making a decision as to whether to screen the summary value. For example, you may want to print the department names and the total salaries of each department only if the total salary for the department is greater than $165,000. The following examples will demonstrate the use of the IF or WHERE TOTAL commands.

The first TABLE request prints the salaries and the percentage salary increase by department name.

```
TABLE FILE STAFF
PRINT LAST_NAME AND SALARY AND PCT_INC
BY DEPT_NAME
END

    PAGE    1


    DEPT_NAME              LAST_NAME                    SALARY    PCT_INC
    ---------             ---------                    ------    -------
    ADMINISTRATION        DUXBURY                  185,000.00       .05
                          ANDERSEN                  32,000.00       .07
    FINANCE               TURPIN                    65,400.00       .05
                          BORGIA                   102,000.00       .06
                          FREEMAN                   34,500.00       .00
    MARKETING             COLE                      39,000.00       .04
                          MORALES                   39,400.00       .06
                          ZARKOV                    47,000.00       .11
                          JAMESON                   36,700.00       .10
    MIS                   GREENSTREET               45,600.00       .06
                          BOCHARD                   35,000.00       .09
                          TAHANIEV                  55,400.00       .09
                          CAMPOS                    32,000.00       .08
    OPERATIONS            HUNT                      57,000.00       .11
                          TRENT                     22,500.00       .08
                          TAYLOR                    26,550.00       .10
```

The second TABLE request uses the same sort criteria as the first TABLE request, except that it only selects employees whose salaries are greater than $40,000.

```
TABLE FILE STAFF
PRINT LAST_NAME AND SALARY AND PCT_INC
BY DEPT_NAME
IF SALARY GT 40000 END


    PAGE    1


    DEPT_NAME              LAST_NAME                    SALARY    PCT_INC
    ---------             ---------                    ------    -------
    ADMINISTRATION        DUXBURY                  185,000.00       .05
    FINANCE               TURPIN                    65,400.00       .05
                          BORGIA                   102,000.00       .06
    MARKETING             ZARKOV                    47,000.00       .11
    MIS                   GREENSTREET               45,600.00       .06
                          TAHANIEV                  55,400.00       .09
    OPERATIONS            HUNT                      57,000.00       .11
```

IF Total and WHERE Total   135

The third TABLE request uses the IF TOTAL command. Here we asked Focus to total the salaries of employees in each department first and then if the total salary in a department is greater than $165,000, select it for display or printing.

```
TABLE FILE STAFF
SUM SALARY BY DEPT_NAME
IF TOTAL SALARY GT 165000
END
```

```
    PAGE     1

    DEPT_NAME                 SALARY
    ---------                 ------
    ADMINISTRATION        217,000.00
    FINANCE               201,900.00
    MIS                   168,000.00
```

As you can see, the TABLE request above handles an operation that normally would have taken two programs to handle.

SUMMARY

IF and WHERE are very useful everyday statements in Focus. The WHERE clause is newer. It has more power than IF and could be used successfully in place of the IF statement in most situations. In some cases only IF could handle the file manipulation that is necessary to produce a report. Most of these instances fall into the category of more esoteric applications.

We discussed the following in this chapter.

1. Value comparison using IF to see if values in the fields in the records are equal or not equal to the test value we coded in our TABLE request.
2. Range testing. We reviewed the relations LT, GE, LE, and GT and the FROM option.
3. Compound IF conditions. These include the OR and multiple IF statements.
4. Masked values for testing fields where the specific locations of test characters are known, such as area codes and zip codes.
5. CONTAINS and/or OMITS. These relations enable us to search an entire field for one or more test characters.
6. RECORDLIMIT. This keyword is used to make developing and testing of Focus TABLE requests or programs easier by limiting the number of records that have to be retrieved from a file.
7. The WHERE clause. It is not currently available on all versions of Focus, but it is powerful and versatile.
8. SIMILAR. This is a new relation and will help you search alphanumeric fields that have similar patterns.
9. IF TOTAL and WHERE TOTAL. These commands provide record selection at the summary level.

CHAPTER 7

DESIGNING AND CREATING REPORT HEADINGS, FOOTINGS, AND LABELS

MAIN TOPICS:

- PAGE HEADING
- COLUMN HEADING
- PAGE FOOTING
- VARIABLES IN FOCUS
- SUBHEAD AND SUBFOOT
- GENERATING LABELS IN FOCUS
- GENERATING CUSTOMIZED LETTERS IN FOCUS

So far, we have coded and printed many reports using the BY, ACROSS, IF, WHERE, and other features of Focus. In all these reports, Focus had automatically placed the field names as the column titles. The only thing missing was the report heading. In this chapter we learn how to prepare reports with page headings and footings. In the next chapter we will also learn how to change the default column titles and to reposition the column locations on a report.

SOME TERMS USED IN REPORT PREPARATION

Refer to the following page from a computer-generated report while reviewing the discussion below.

Page headings or heading lines. These are descriptive titles that the programmers and/or the users assign to reports to distinguish one report from another. Page number, date, and time are also considered part of page headings. Headings could occupy one or more lines of text in the report. Additionally, most companies have certain standards and rules regarding page headings. For example, one company may decide that on every report the extreme upper left-hand

HRS032-23 } Page headings or heading lines

CONFIDENTIAL

EMPLOYEE BIWEEKLY SALARY AND SUGGESTED INCREASE
REPORT BY DEPARTMENT

} Page headings or heading lines

DEPARTMENT	EMPLOYEE NAME	BIWEEKLY PAY	PERCENT INCREASE	NEW SALARY	EMPLOYEE ID
ADMINISTRATION	C.ANDERSEN	1,230.77	7.00	1,316.92	515478922
	J.DUXBURY	7,115.38	5.00	7,471.15	291345672
	C.BORGIA	3,923.08	6.00	4,158.46	513724567
FINANCE	D.FREEMAN	1,326.92	.00	1,326.92	504234521
	B.TURPIN	2,515.38	5.00	2,641.15	294728305
MARKETING	R.COLE	1,500.00	4.00	1,560.00	293245178
	C.JAMESON	1,411.54	10.00	1,552.69	413267891
	C.MORALES	1,515.38	6.00	1,606.31	297748301
	W.ZARKOV	1,807.69	11.00	2,006.54	312781122
MIS	R.BOCHARD	1,346.15	9.00	1,467.31	621893221
	C.CAMPOS	1,230.77	8.00	1,329.23	432568023
	J.GREENSTREET	1,753.85	6.00	1,859.08	392345782
	R.TAHANIEV	2,130.77	9.00	2,322.54	295738307
OPERATIONS	C.HUNT	2,192.31	11.00	2,433.46	213456682
	J.TAYLOR	1,021.15	10.00	1,123.27	314562134
	R.TRENT	865.38	8.00	934.62	312562345
TOTAL		32,886.54		35,109.65	

Column titles or column headings

Data or information or detail lines

} ← Column total

THIS REPORT WAS PREPARED BY HUMAN RESOURCES DEPARTMENT
ON 02/09/91 AT 14.19.55 } ← Page footing

corner will contain the application name and the report number. You may come across a report with "HRS032-023" at the top corner of every page. This would mean that this report is part of the Human Resources Systems. The name of the program creating this report is HRS032. Also, this is the twenty-third report in the Human Resources System. There may also be other standards regarding placement of the page numbers and dates on each page of the report.

Column titles or column headings or titles. Titles identify the information that appears in the columns on a report. As you have seen so far, the column title is automatically generated by Focus. The title selected by Focus (the default) is the field name that appears in the Master File Description. Therefore, the column title of the field containing the last name of employees in our hypothetical company will be LAST_NAME. Later in this chapter I will show you how to change the default column titles.

Column totals, subtotals, and report totals. If your report has any type of numeric data, such as amounts, salaries, and balances, chances are that you will be requested to total those fields and print one or more summary lines. The total value may be for the entire organization or you may have to print a subtotal at the end of each department as well as a grand total for the entire organization.

PAGE HEADINGS AND FOOTINGS

In a TABLE request, the word "HEADING" is usually the first line of code right after the "TABLE FILE filename" line. To instruct Focus to print a page heading, the keyword "HEADING" should be placed on a line by itself. This must be followed by one or more lines of text that will describe the contents of the report. Text lines must be enclosed in double quotation marks ("). If one line of text is not enough, you could add more lines. Always enclose each heading line in a pair of double quotation marks as shown in the TABLE request below. When you finish with page headings, you could continue with the rest of the program, which usually starts with an action word such as "SUM" or "PRINT." Page heading text could include every letter of the alphabet and/or special symbols, except the double quotation marks.

```
TABLE FILE STAFF
HEADING
"LIST OF EMPLOYEES: FIRST NAME, LAST NAME "
"SORTED BY DEPARTMENT"
PRINT LAST_NAME AND FIRST_NAME
BY DEPT_NAME
END

  PAGE     1

  LIST OF EMPLOYEES: FIRST NAME, LAST NAME
  SORTED BY DEPARTMENT
```

```
DEPT_NAME            LAST_NAME            FIRST_NAME
---------            ---------            ----------
ADMINISTRATION       DUXBURY              JILLIAN
                     ANDERSEN             CHRISTINE
FINANCE              TURPIN               BENTON
                     BORGIA               CESARE
                     FREEMAN              DIANE
MARKETING            COLE                 ROBERT
                     MORALES              CARLOS
                     ZARKOV               WILLIAM
                     JAMESON              CARLA
MIS                  GREENSTREET          JAMES
                     BOCHARD              ROBERT
                     TAHANIEV             RICHARD
                     CAMPOS               CARLOS
OPERATIONS           HUNT                 CHARLES
                     TRENT                RICHARD
                     TAYLOR               JUANITA
```

The report above is a listing of company employees with a simple heading. Notice that the heading does not look very elegant. It starts way to the left of the page and there is no symmetry between the first and second heading lines. We could take a number of steps to improve the appearance of this report and display additional information for users. The following points should help you in creating better-looking, more meaningful reports.

1. Once you define a page heading, it will be repeated at the top of every page of the report, right below the automatic page number that is generated by Focus. You can have up to 57 heading lines in a TABLE request.

2. You could always center the page headings. Centering could be accomplished in one of two ways. One way is to use a sheet of quadrille or similar graph paper to format your report and determine the position of text and blank spaces on each heading line. You could then count the blank spaces on either side of the text and embed them in the heading:

```
"          NAME OF EMPLOYEES: FIRST NAME, LAST NAME          "
```

You could also let Focus handle the centering by adding the word ''CENTER'' immediately after ''HEADING'' in the Table request.

```
HEADING CENTER
"NAME OF EMPLOYEES: FIRST NAME, LAST NAME"
"SORTED BY DEPARTMENT"
```

Focus will automatically make sure that all page headings are centered at print time.

3. By skipping lines you could generate up to 57 blank lines between each heading line and between the last heading line and the first column title. You could accomplish this in two different ways.

    a. You could create blank headings by coding one or more heading lines with no text (i.e., spaces only):

```
"   "
```

The line above will cause the program to skip one line at print time. If you need to skip more than one line, you could repeat the line as many times as you would like.

```
TABLE FILE STAFF
"LIST OF EMPLOYEES: FIRST NAME, LAST NAME"
"   "
"   "
"   "
PRINT LAST_NAME
END
```

The TABLE request above will skip three lines after printing the first heading line and before printing the first column heading.

    b. Another method of skipping is to use a left caret or less-than sign (<), followed by a blank space, followed by a slash (/), followed by the number of lines that you want Focus to skip. The following TABLE request is identical to the preceding one except that it uses the alternate method.

```
TABLE FILE STAFF
"LIST OF EMPLOYEES: FIRST NAME, LAST NAME"
"< /3"
PRINT LAST_NAME
END
```

    4. Sometimes it is a good idea to have a footing on a report. A footing is just like a heading except that it appears at the bottom of the page. Footings are usually used to convey special messages or warnings to users. They could also be used to display the name of the programmer and the date and time of report execution. Like headings, footings can be centered. Footings are usually printed at the end of every page, immediately following the last line of data. You could move the footing text to the physical bottom of each page by adding the word ''BOTTOM'' at the end of the footing statement.

    Examples of footing with or without the footing bottom follow.

```
TABLE FILE STAFF
HEADING CENTER
"Example of FOOTING CENTER without the BOTTOM option"
"  "
SUM SALARY AND VACATION
BY DEPT_NAME
BY SECTION_NAME
ON TABLE COLUMN-TOTAL
FOOTING CENTER
"PREPARED BY SOMNER HOPKINS"
END
```

```
PAGE      1

          Example of FOOTING CENTER without the BOTTOM option

    DEPT_NAME              SECTION_NAME             SALARY   VACATION
    ---------             ------------             ------   --------

    ADMINISTRATION        EXECUTIVE            217,000.00        145
    FINANCE               COLLECTIONS           34,500.00         99
                          PAYABLES             167,400.00        135
    MARKETING             SALES                162,100.00        208
    MIS                   DEVELOPMENT           80,600.00         50
                          OPERATIONS            87,400.00        145
    OPERATIONS            CUSTOMER SERVICES     49,050.00         60
                          ENGINEERING           57,000.00        140


    TOTAL                                      855,050.00        982

              PREPARED BY SOMNER HOPKINS
```

Note that in the request above, the footing message or text appears right after the last line of data, not at the bottom of the page.

```
TABLE FILE STAFF
HEADING CENTER
"Example of FOOTING CENTER with the BOTTOM option"
"  "
SUM SALARY AND VACATION
BY DEPT_NAME
BY SECTION_NAME
ON TABLE COLUMN-TOTAL
FOOTING CENTER BOTTOM
"PREPARED BY SOMNER HOPKINS"
END
```

Example of FOOTING CENTER with the BOTTOM option

DEPT_NAME	SECTION_NAME	SALARY	VACATION
ADMINISTRATION	EXECUTIVE	217,000.00	145
FINANCE	COLLECTIONS	34,500.00	99
	PAYABLES	167,400.00	135
MARKETING	SALES	162,100.00	208
MIS	DEVELOPMENT	80,600.00	50
	OPERATIONS	87,400.00	145
OPERATIONS	CUSTOMER SERVICES	49,050.00	60
	ENGINEERING	57,000.00	140
TOTAL		855,050.00	982

PREPARED BY SOMNER HOPKINS

In the TABLE request above, the footing text is printed at the physical end of the page.

The following TABLE request combines some the features that we have reviewed so far. It uses page heading, page footing, line skipping, and the CENTER command.

```
TABLE FILE STAFF
HEADING CENTER
"NAME OF EMPLOYEES AND DEPARTMENTS"
"   "
"BY DATE OF HIRE"
" < /2 "
PRINT LAST_NAME AND FIRST_NAME AND DEPT_NAME
BY DATE_HIRE
FOOTING CENTER
"CREATED BY MIS DEPARTMENT.  PLEASE CALL THE PROGRAMMER"
"AT EXTENSION 2345 TO REPORT ANY PROBLEMS"
END
```

NAME OF EMPLOYEES AND DEPARTMENTS

BY DATE OF HIRE

DATE_HIRE	LAST_NAME	FIRST_NAME	DEPT_NAME
78/10/12	TURPIN	BENTON	FINANCE
79/12/08	FREEMAN	DIANE	FINANCE
82/08/07	GREENSTREET	JAMES	MIS
82/10/12	TRENT	RICHARD	OPERATIONS
82/12/15	JAMESON	CARLA	MARKETING
	BOCHARD	ROBERT	MIS
84/09/15	TAYLOR	JUANITA	OPERATIONS
84/11/11	BORGIA	CESARE	FINANCE
85/08/09	TAHANIEV	RICHARD	MIS
87/03/23	CAMPOS	CARLOS	MIS
87/07/13	HUNT	CHARLES	OPERATIONS
87/08/15	COLE	ROBERT	MARKETING
88/01/07	ANDERSEN	CHRISTINE	ADMINISTRATION
88/05/02	ZARKOV	WILLIAM	MARKETING
88/11/18	MORALES	CARLOS	MARKETING
88/12/10	DUXBURY	JILLIAN	ADMINISTRATION

CREATED BY THE MIS DEPARTMENT. PLEASE CALL THE PROGRAMMER
AT EXTENSION 2345 TO REPORT ANY PROBLEMS

Other Report Features

You could also insert other information from the file or the system in a page heading and/or page footing. For example, the current date is an item of information that could be obtained from your computer and placed in the heading along with your text. Names of departments or sections or employees could also be accessed. The symbol used to tell Focus that it should obtain the value of a field from a file and insert it in the report is the left caret sign (<). It is also known as a less-than sign and a spot marker. Whatever its name, when Focus sees the < in a heading or footing line at execution time, it will retrieve from the Focus file that is being accessed the value of the field name that follows the < sign and display it on the heading line or footing line at the location indicated by the <. The < is not printed in the report.

```
TABLE FILE STAFF
HEADING CENTER
"LIST OF EMPLOYEES BY DEPARTMENT: <DEPT_NAME "
PRINT LAST_NAME AND FIRST_NAME
BY DEPT_NAME
END
```

LIST OF EMPLOYEES BY DEPARTMENT: OPERATIONS

DEPT_NAME	LAST_NAME	FIRST_NAME
OPERATIONS	HUNT	CHARLES
	TRENT	RICHARD
	TAYLOR	JUANITA
MIS	GREENSTREET	JAMES
	BOCHARD	ROBERT
	TAHANIEV	RICHARD
	CAMPOS	CARLOS
MARKETING	COLE	ROBERT
	MORALES	CARLOS
	ZARKOV	WILLIAM
	JAMESON	CARLA
FINANCE	TURPIN	BENTON
	BORGIA	CESARE
	FREEMAN	DIANE
ADMINISTRATION	DUXBURY	JILLIAN
	ANDERSEN	CHRISTINE

PAGE   2

LIST OF EMPLOYEES BY DEPARTMENT: FINANCE

DEPT_NAME	LAST_NAME	FIRST_NAME
FINANCE	FREEMAN	DIANE
ADMINISTRATION	DUXBURY	JILLIAN

Focus will place the value of the first department name that it reads in the heading line. Obviously, department names change, so a new department name will be printed on the next page. This feature was not very useful in the example above because the size of test file in this book is very small. However, in a real business environment where there are many employees in each department, it could prove to be useful. If you have large departments and are printing information about the employees in these departments, you could just print the department name in the heading instead of printing it 55 or more times in a column on a report.

However, you will still need to sort the report by department names. Therefore, we must sort the information in a file by a field and, at the same time, suppress the printing of data from that field on a column on the report. As you know, we must use the BY or ACROSS commands to sort a Focus file. To suppress the printing of a field, we will use a new command called NOPRINT or SUP-PRINT. The only function of NOPRINT is to suppress the printing of a column. In other words, the column and the information that would have appeared in that column would simply vanish from the report. NOPRINT does not affect the requested sorting of the information by that field. In the following TABLE request we will sort the records by department name as requested, but will not display the department name column on the screen or print it on the printer. Instead, we show only the name of the department in the heading on each page.

```
TABLE FILE STAFF
HEADING CENTER
" "
"LIST OF EMPLOYEES BY DEPARTMENT: <DEPT_NAME"
" "
PRINT LAST_NAME AND FIRST_NAME
BY DEPT_NAME NOPRINT
IF DEPT_NAME EQ MARKETING
END


  PAGE     1


  LIST OF EMPLOYEES BY DEPARTMENT: MARKETING

  LAST_NAME            FIRST_NAME
  ---------           ----------
  COLE                ROBERT
  MORALES             CARLOS
  ZARKOV              WILLIAM
  JAMESON             CARLA
```

You could use NOPRINT almost anywhere to sort a record by one or more fields and not be forced to display or print your sort keys.

You could use the right caret (>) in heading lines to enclose a field such as <CITY> or <DEPT_NAME>. If you use both the left caret (<) and the right caret (>) to enclose a field name in a heading line to display a value from the file, Focus will reserve at the location indicated in the heading line the exact number of characters that were defined in the Master File Description. So if a city field is defined as being 16 characters long in the Master File Description, 16 spaces will be reserved for the field in the heading even if the actual length of the field being printed is only six characters. For example, "San Francisco" is 13 characters long (including the space in the middle), whereas city of "Orange" is only six characters long. Focus will reserve 16 characters for both of them on the heading line. If you do not want this to happen, you should not use the right caret at the end of the field name in the heading line. In that case the size of the displayed field is automatically adjusted to the actual value of the field that is being read, and if there is a field following the first field, that field will start closer to the first field. In the following two examples I demonstrate the effect of the right caret.

```
TABLE FILE STAFF
HEADING
"EMPLOYEE NAME AND ADDRESS"
"    "
"DEPARTMENT:<DEPT_NAME   SECTION:<SECN"
"    "
"STREET:<STREET "
"    "
"CITY: <CITY   PHONE:<TELEPHONE_NO "
"    "
PRINT LAST_NAME AND FIRST_NAME AND SALARY
IF SECTION_NAME IS ENGINEERING
END


   PAGE     1

  EMPLOYEE NAME AND ADDRESS

  DEPARTMENT:OPERATIONS   SECTION:ENGINEERING

  STREET:87A NEWTON

  CITY: ORANGE   PHONE:7145558428

  LAST_NAME              FIRST_NAME        SALARY
  ---------             ----------       ------
  HUNT                   CHARLES          57,000.00
```

Notice in the TABLE request above that we did not place a right caret after the DEPT_NAME and CITY fields. As a result, on the second heading line, the word ''SECTION'' and the value of the SECTION_NAME (ENGINEERING) field immediately followed the department name, which in this case was OPERATIONS. On the fourth heading line, the word ''PHONE'' and the actual TELEPHONE_NO field of the employee followed the employee's city name, ORANGE.

```
TABLE FILE STAFF
HEADING
"EMPLOYEE NAME AND ADDRESS"
"    "
"DEPARTMENT:<DEPT_NAME> SECTION:<SECN"
"    "
"STREET:<STREET>"
"    "
"CITY: <CITY> PHONE:<TELEPHONE_NO>"
"    "
PRINT LAST_NAME AND FIRST_NAME AND SALARY
IF SECTION_NAME IS ENGINEERING
END
```

```
PAGE     1

EMPLOYEE NAME AND ADDRESS

DEPARTMENT:OPERATIONS                    SECTION:ENGINEERING

STREET:87A NEWTON

CITY: ORANGE              PHONE:7145558428

LAST_NAME              FIRST_NAME        SALARY
---------             ----------        ------
  HUNT                  CHARLES         57,000.00
```

In the TABLE request above, we placed right carets after DEPT_NAME and CITY; Focus reserved the full 20 positions for the department and the full 16 words for the city name. Therefore, the next words started way to the right, after the end of the trailing blanks of the DEPT_NAME and CITY fields.

The following two TABLE requests demonstrate the same techniques. Here we have also shown how the value embedded in the heading is the first value that Focus encounters and changes only when the change of page occurs. However, if you use footing in your request, the value of the last sort field that Focus reads for that page is printed at the bottom of the page.

```
TABLE FILE STAFF
HEADING CENTER
"LIST OF DEPARTMENTS: <DEPT_NAME AND SECTIONS: <SECTION_NAME"
"  "
PRINT DEPT_NAME AND SECTION_NAME
FOOTING CENTER
"LAST DEPARTMENT ON THIS PAGE: <DEPT_NAME"
"LAST SECTION ON THIS PAGE:    <SECTION_NAME"
END

   PAGE     1

LIST OF DEPARTMENTS: FINANCE AND SECTIONS: PAYABLES
  DEPT_NAME              SECTION_NAME
  ---------             ------------
  FINANCE               PAYABLES
  FINANCE               COLLECTIONS
  OPERATIONS            ENGINEERING
  OPERATIONS            CUSTOMER SERVICES
  MARKETING             SALES
  ADMINISTRATION        EXECUTIVE
  MIS                   DEVELOPMENT
  MIS                   OPERATIONS

    LAST DEPARTMENT ON THIS PAGE: MIS
   LAST SECTION ON THIS PAGE:    OPERATIONS
```

```
TABLE FILE STAFF
HEADING CENTER
"LIST OF DEPARTMENTS: <DEPT_NAME> AND SECTIONS: <SECTION_NAME"
" "
PRINT DEPT_NAME AND SECTION_NAME
FOOTING CENTER
"LAST DEPARTMENT ON THIS PAGE: <DEPT_NAME"
"LAST SECTION ON THIS PAGE:    <SECTION_NAME"
END



    PAGE      1


LIST OF DEPARTMENTS: FINANCE              AND SECTIONS: PAYABLES


    DEPT_NAME              SECTION_NAME
    ---------             ------------
    FINANCE               PAYABLES
    FINANCE               COLLECTIONS
    OPERATIONS            ENGINEERING
    OPERATIONS            CUSTOMER SERVICES
    MARKETING             SALES
    ADMINISTRATION        EXECUTIVE
    MIS                   DEVELOPMENT
    MIS                   OPERATIONS


      LAST DEPARTMENT ON THIS PAGE: MIS
      LAST SECTION ON THIS PAGE:    OPERATIONS
```

Positioning Text on Headings

Generally speaking, Focus will place the text on the heading line in the position indicated in the TABLE request. So if the word "DEPARTMENT" starts in column 34 of the program, Focus will print it on the thirty-fourth column of the screen or the printer. Focus has facilities to change the print position by letting you mark the column in which you would want to start your text. This is why the < is also called a spot marker. We will use the right and left carets to position a page heading. Table 7.1 shows the various options that we could use to position text in page headings.

TABLE 7.1 COMMANDS FOR TEXT POSITIONING

Focus command	Example	Meaning
"< n" or "< n >"	"< 38 Department"	The word "Department" will be printed starting in column 38 of the heading line. The < and the number 38 will not be printed.
	"< 38 <DEPT_NAME"	The value of DEPT_NAME field (i.e., FINANCE) will be printed starting from column 38 of the heading line. The < and the number 38 will not be displayed on the screen or printed on the printer.
"< +n" or "< +n>"	"< +6"	The next character to be printed will start six columns to the right of this position. For example, "EMPLOYEE NAME< +6<CITY" means that the words "EMPLOYEE NAME" will appear first, followed by six blank spaces, followed by the value of the CITY field for that employee.
"< −n" or "< −n>"	"< −6"	The next character to be printed will start six columns to the left of the current position. For example, "<SALARY <−9 ****<LN <FN" will overlay all the salary field with asterisks and parts of an employee's last name.
"< /n" or "< /n>"	"< /4"	This command will instruct Focus to skip four lines before starting a new heading line. If this command is the last heading line, the spaces skipped will be between the last heading line and the column title line.

Following are some positioning examples.

```
TABLE FILE STAFF
HEADING
"<10 LIST OF EMPLOYEES IN THE <DEPT_NAME DEPARTMENT"
"< /2>"
PRINT FIRST_NAME AND LAST_NAME
AND TELEPHONE_NO
BY EMPLOYEE_ID
IF DEPT_NAME EQ MARKETING
END
```

```
              LIST OF EMPLOYEES IN THE MARKETING DEPARTMENT


EMPLOYEE_ID    FIRST_NAME    LAST_NAME              TELEPHONE_NO
-----------    ----------    ---------              ------------
 293245178     ROBERT        COLE                   7145550123
 297748301     CARLOS        MORALES                7145557173
 312781122     WILLIAM       ZARKOV                 7145554210
 413267891     CARLA         JAMESON                7145555897
```

In the TABLE request above, we have made use of spot markers to achieve two objectives. The first spot marker positioned the first character of our heading text—the letter "L" in "LIST"—on column 10 of the printer or screen. The second spot marker told Focus to extract the value of the field for DEPT_NAME and place it in the heading in the position that the spot marker indicated. We also used the skip line option "< /2" to skip two lines between the heading and the first column title line. Also note that by including the value of DEPT_NAME as part of the heading, we avoided having to create a column for DEPT_NAME and having to print it on every line for every employee.

The following example illustrates the use of spot markers to position the first letter of the department name six characters to the right of the colon in the heading. This is known as *relative positioning*.

```
TABLE FILE STAFF
HEADING
"<4 SALARY OF EMPLOYEES IN DEPARTMENT: < +6 <DEPT_NAME"
"       "
PRINT FIRST_NAME AND LAST_NAME
AND VACATION
BY DATE_HIRE
IF DATE_HIRE GT  870101
IF DEPT_NAME EQ MARKETING
END
  PAGE     1

    SALARY OF EMPLOYEES IN DEPARTMENT:      MARKETING

DATE_HIRE    FIRST_NAME    LAST_NAME            VACATION
---------    ----------    ---------            --------
 87/08/15    ROBERT        COLE                      43
 88/05/02    WILLIAM       ZARKOV                    63
 88/11/18    CARLOS        MORALES                   80
```

Including the Date and Time of Execution on the Report

Focus allows you to include the date and time of report preparation on the heading. You could place the date and time on separate lines by themselves or include them with one of the heading lines. Focus can pick up the value of the current system date and the current system time (time of day) from your operating system. These values are known as *variables*. There are other variables that Focus could access for you to use. They vary on different operating systems. The most common ones are the various formats of date and the time of day.

There are several types of variables in Focus: local, global, and system variables. *System variables* are available through your particular operating system (i.e., VM, MVS, DOS, etc.). The system date is an example of a system variable. *Local variables* are values that are used by the TABLE commands during the current TABLE request only. They disappear afterward. *Global variables* stay on until the end of the Focus session, so you could use them in several programs. Variables are identified to Focus by the ampersand (&) sign. Local variables are preceded by one ampersand. Global variables are preceded by double ampersands (i.e., &&).

Some examples of variables are (1) &DATE for the current system date, and (2) &CITY for a local variable assigned by you or the user. &&CITY and &&DEPT_NAME are global variables. To tell Focus that you are using a variable, you should precede your field name with an ampersand sign:

```
TABLE FILE STAFF
PRINT LAST_NAME AND SALARY
IF CITY EQ '&CITY'
END
```

or

```
TABLE FILE STAFF
HEADING
"DATE: &DATE"
"LIST OF EMPLOYEES BY DEPARTMENT AND DATE OF HIRE"
PRINT LAST_NAME
BY DEPT_NAME
BY DATE_HIRE
END
```

In the first example, Focus will expect you to enter the value of the city at execution time. We will see how very shortly. In the second example, Focus will automatically pick up the current date from the computer system and place it on the heading. You cannot use the variables in interactive Focus programming. They must be part of stored TABLE requests.

The following report makes use of Local and System variables in different ways. System variables such as &DATE are directly accessed by Focus, so there is no need for you to enter them physically at execution time. For other variables, you will need to supply a value to Focus.

There are two ways to enter values for variables. One method is to execute the TABLE request in the normal way (i.e., EX STAFFSAL). If you do that, Focus will respond by asking you to provide the value of the variable as shown in the following example.

```
> EX STAFFSAL        ← Your entry on Focus command line.

PLEASE SUPPLY VALUES REQUESTED   ← Focus's response.

CITY=       ← You must enter a value here, for example ANAHEIM.
```

In response, you must enter the value of the field that you need and press the Enter key. In this case, I entered "ANAHEIM."

The other method of supplying variables would be to include it (or them if you have more than one variable) as part of your execution command. In that case, you should say

```
> EX STAFFSAL CITY=ANAHEIM.
```

Focus will substitute the value of ANAHEIM for &CITY and will execute the program.

```
TABLE FILE STAFF
HEADING
"<4 SALARY AND VACATION REPORT FOR: &CITY ON: &DATE"
"    "
PRINT FIRST_NAME AND LAST_NAME
AND VACATION AND CITY
BY DATE_HIRE
IF CITY EQ '&CITY'
FOOTING
"<10 THIS REPORT WAS PREPARED AT: &TOD"
END


    PAGE    1

    SALARY AND VACATION REPORT FOR: ANAHEIM ON: 08/28/91

    DATE_HIRE   FIRST_NAME   LAST_NAME              VACATION  CITY
    ---------   ----------   ---------              --------  ----
    88/01/07    CHRISTINE    ANDERSEN                     35  ANAHEIM
    88/05/02    WILLIAM      ZARKOV                       63  ANAHEIM

         THIS REPORT WAS PREPARED AT: 12.54.04
```

Note: &DATE will access and provide the current system date in the MM/DD/YY (i.e., Month/Day/Year) format. You could request other date variables, such as YY/MM/DD (&YMD) or DD/MM/YY (&DMY). The time of execution (&TOD) is displayed in 24-hour format with minutes and seconds. Also note that in the TABLE request, the variable &CITY was enclosed in single quotation marks. This is necessary because the values that you are supplying could contain embedded blanks such as "Los Angeles," "New York," and "New Orleans."

SUBHEAD AND SUBFOOT

In this section we deal with two commands that will allow us to create mailing labels and/or customized letters from Focus and non-Focus files. SUBHEAD and SUBFOOT are similar to HEADING and FOOTING. A subhead text is usually, but not always, placed before the sort keys. The subfoot text is placed after the sort keys.

The following example illustrates the use of SUBHEAD for printing labels.

```
SET PAGE=NOPAGE
TABLE FILE STAFF
BY LAST_NAME NOPRINT
SUBHEAD
"< /4>"
"<FIRST_NAME  <LAST_NAME"
"< STREET"
"<CITY  <STATE <ZIP_CODE"
IF RECORDLIMIT EQ 8
END
```

Note the following about this TABLE request.

1. The first line issues the command "SET PAGE=NOPAGE." We are trying to create labels in this request; therefore, page break and page numbering must be suppressed. This is the command to do it. In some instances you may also need to issue a SET LINES (i.e., SET LINES= 22) command to change the system's line setting. This command could follow the SET PAGE and should be on a line by itself.

2. We have decided on three lines of text per label. We could have coded more if we needed to.

3. Look at the statement "BY LAST_NAME NOPRINT." Here we use the sort feature of Focus to print labels alphabetically in last-name sequence, but we do not want to print the last name by itself separately. If we do not code the NOPRINT command, the term "LAST_NAME" will appear as a column heading on the first label.

4. We allocated four lines between each label. This was to make sure that the TABLE request met specifications of the labels that we had in stock at the time. You should adjust the number of lines to meet your requirements.

5. We specified a RECORDLIMIT of 8. In the business world, you should start with a small subset such as 8 or 10 and test the program with the available labels before removing the "IF RECORD-LIMIT" statement.

The labels follow:

```
CESARE  BORGIA
347 SOUTH ROMA AVENUE
NEW YORK  NY 10001




ROBERT  COLE
37 EXETER DRIVE
GARDEN GROVE  CA 93110




DIANE  FREEMAN
22 SOUTH DEAN DRIVE
CANTON  CA 94107




CHARLES  HUNT
87A NEWTON
ORANGE  CA 93199




CARLOS  MORALES
883 MANNER DRIVE
LONG BEACH  CA 91230




JUANITA  TAYLOR
1901 LAKE AVE. #132
SANTA MONICA  CA 93127




RICHARD  TRENT
93 LA CIENEGA BLVD
LOS ANGELES  CA 91287
```

Subhead and Subfoot

```
BENTON   TURPIN
121 LA CIENEGA BLVD.
LOS ANGELES  CA 91345
```

Now that we have used the subhead feature of Focus to produce labels for our employees, I will show you how to use this feature to create customized letters.

Designing and Printing Customized Letters

Our Human Resources Department has requested us to prepare a letter that will be sent to employees whose accrued vacation hours have exceeded 100 hours. We should inform them that unless they use their vacation hours within the next 90 days, they could lose their excess vacation time. In each letter we should state the following information:

- The maximum vacation time each employee can carry forward from one year to the next is 100 hours.
- Each employee has 90 days in which to take his or her vacation hours.
- If the manager needs the services of such an employee during the next 90 days, the employee should inform the Human Resources representative.

The TABLE request for this application is as follows:

```
SET PAGE=OFF
SET LINES=66
SET PAPER=66
TABLE FILE STAFF
BY LAST_NAME NOPRINT PAGE-BREAK
SUBHEAD
" </4 "
" < 56 &DATE "
" </3 "
"      <FN <LN>   "
"      <STREET            "
"      <CITY <STATE <ZIP_CODE>        "
"    </1 "
"<8 Dear Employee,"
"  "
"<8 Your outstanding vacation as of &DATE stands at<VACATION "
"<8 hours."
"  "
"<8 It is our company's policy that each employee should not"
"<8 accrue more than 100 hours of vacation."
"  "
"<8 You are hereby requested to take all your outstanding"
```

```
"<8 vacation in excess of 100 hours within the next 90 days. "
"     "
"<8 If, due to a request by your direct manager, you are unable"
"<8 to take the excess accrued time during the 90-day period,"
"<8 please inform your Human Resources representative as soon "
"<8 possible."
"  </2    "
"<8 Sincerely "
"  </3    "
"<8 Vice President "
"<8 Human Resources "
"         "
IF VACATION GT 100
END
```

Note the following features.

- SET PAGE=OFF. Normally, in letter reports we do not want to print the page number. This command will suppress printing of page numbers.
- SET LINES=66. Most letters are written on $8\frac{1}{2}$- by 11-inch paper. The maximum number of lines that most printers can print on that kind of paper is 66 lines per page.
- SET PAPER=66. This tells Focus that the paper that we are using is also 66 lines long.
- &DATE. This is the system variable that will access and print the current date (i.e., today's date) on the letter. &DATE is also a local variable and will only be available during this program. Notice that we did not use the left caret sign (<) for system variables. System variables do not need the <.
- The rest of this TABLE request is self-explanatory. Note that I started every line with ''<8'' to set the left margin of the letter to 8 spaces.
- We made liberal use of other editing symbols to format the rest of the letter and make it look neat and attractive.

After you execute this TABLE request, the following letter report will be printed. The letter will look better with your company's logo at the top.

```
                                            01/02/91

JILLIAN DUXBURY
1020 JEFFRIES
IRVINE CA 93321



Dear Employee,

Your outstanding vacation as of 01/02/91 stands at 110
hours.

It is our company's policy that each employee should not
accrue more than 100 hours of vacation.
```

```
You are hereby requested to take all your outstanding
vacation in excess of 100 hours within the next 90 days.

If, due to a request by your direct manager, you are unable
to take the excess accrued time during the 90-day period,
please inform your Human Resources representative as soon
possible.



Sincerely



Vice President
Human Resources
```

SUBHEAD and SUBFOOT could be used in many similar instances to produce
text reports.

Designing and Creating Report Headings

Another good feature of the SUBHEAD command is that it enables you to prepare report headings. Report headings are printed on the first page of the report
by themselves. They are very much like report covers. They are not employed
often but are very useful. Since the SUBHEAD text is the only information on
that page, you could use report headings for covering confidential reports, routing
instructions, or even describing the contents of the fields in the report. To create
a report heading, type the following command at the end of the Table request just
before END. Note that you must use the word "AND" between the PAGE-
BREAK and SUBHEAD commands as shown below:

```
ON TABLE PAGE-BREAK AND SUBHEAD
"TEXT"
END
```

The following example illustrates this feature.

```
TABLE FILE STAFF
HEADING CENTER
"CONFIDENTIAL LIST OF EMPLOYEES EARNING"
"MORE THAN $60,000 PER YEAR"
"  "
PRINT LAST_NAME AND SALARY AND PCT_INC
BY DEPT_NAME
IF SALARY GT 65000
ON TABLE PAGE-BREAK AND SUBHEAD
" < /8 "
" < 22 THIS IS A CONFIDENTIAL REPORT "
"  "
" < 23 FOR COMPANY MANAGEMENT ONLY"
END
```

PAGE   1

              THIS IS A CONFIDENTIAL REPORT

              FOR COMPANY MANAGEMENT ONLY

PAGE   2

          CONFIDENTIAL LIST OF EMPLOYEES EARNING
                MORE THAN $60,000 PER YEAR

DEPT_NAME	LAST_NAME	SALARY	PCT_INC
ADMINISTRATION	DUXBURY	185,000.00	.05
FINANCE	TURPIN	65,400.00	.05
	BORGIA	102,000.00	.06

SUMMARY

I devoted most of this chapter to page heading and footing commands. I emphasized the following key topics in particular:

1. Terminology of various parts of a report
2. Page headings
3. Page footings
4. Embedding field values from Focus files in page headings and footings
5. Inserting system variables—mainly date and time of execution—in page headings and footings
6. Local and global variables
7. Use of < and > symbols to position text, field, and system values on headings and footings
8. SUBHEAD and SUBFOOT
9. Creating mailing labels and letters with Focus with the Subhead command
10. Using the SUBHEAD command to create report headings

CHAPTER 8

CUSTOMIZING REPORTS

MAIN TOPICS:

- CHANGING THE DEFAULT COLUMN TITLES
- PAGE BREAK, SKIPPING AND UNDERLINING
- MULTIPLE FOCUS VERBS
- PREFIXES OR DIRECT OPERATORS

So far I have dissected the page heading and page footing and have explained how to improve the appearance as well as the contents of heading and footing text lines. In this chapter I discuss the changes that we could make to column titles and the actual detail lines (data) that are being accessed and printed by Focus. I also show you how to use multiple verbs in TABLE requests and how to use Direct Operators or Prefixes to make reports even more meaningful.

CHANGING THE DEFAULT COLUMN TITLES

I said previously that column titles or column headings or titles could be changed from the default value assigned by Focus. You will remember that the default column titles printed by Focus are actually the field names from the Master File Description. To assign a new name to a column title, use the word "AS" followed by the new title that you would like to have. In the following example, we are replacing four default column titles with new values.

```
TABLE FILE STAFF
HEADING CENTER
"  "
"REPORT SHOWING HOW TO SUBSTITUTE OR MODIFY"
"THE DEFAULT COLUMN TITLES"
"  "
PRINT LAST_NAME AS  'EMPLOYEE LAST NAME'
AND SALARY AS 'YEARLY SALARY'
AND EMPLOYEE_ID AS 'EMPLOYEE,IDENTIFICATION,NUMBER'
BY DATE_HIRE AS 'DATE,OF,HIRE     '
IF DATE_HIRE LT 850101
END
```

```
              REPORT SHOWING HOW TO SUBSTITUTE OR MODIFY
                    THE DEFAULT COLUMN TITLES
DATE                                        EMPLOYEE
OF                                          IDENTIFICATION
HIRE        EMPLOYEE LAST NAME   YEARLY SALARY  NUMBER
--------    ------------------   -------------  ---------------
78/10/12    TURPIN                   65,400.00  294728305
79/12/08    FREEMAN                  34,500.00  504234521
82/08/07    GREENSTREET              45,600.00  392345782
82/10/12    TRENT                    22,500.00  312562345
82/12/15    JAMESON                  36,700.00  413267891
            BOCHARD                  35,000.00  621893221
84/09/15    TAYLOR                   26,550.00  314562134
84/11/11    BORGIA                  102,000.00  513724567
```

Note the following:

1. The new values that will replace default column titles must be enclosed in a pair of single quotation marks (').

2. Each new value should be preceded by the word "AS."

3. Use commas to separate title lines that will be stacked on top of each other. Notice how we stacked titles for the date of hire and employee identification number columns.

4. You could have up to five lines of column titles stacked on top of each other. We stacked our titles only three lines deep in the example above.

5. The Master File Description allows up to 12 characters for each field name. You can override that number while printing and have a longer or shorter title as long as you enclose it in single quotation marks. Notice how we increased the size of the salary column to "YEARLY SALARY," which is 13 characters long. The new titles will be temporary and will not affect the Master File Description or your Focus data file. Remember that if you increase the width of the column title, the corresponding column width will also increase and you will have a wider column. However, if you reduce the width of the title—to less than the length of the field that was assigned in the Master File Description—the column width will not decrease, because that could cause truncation of data (loss of some characters or numbers in the field) in that column.

6. You could insert blanks between various words on the title as long as the title is enclosed in a pair of single quotation marks.

7. You can customize the appearance of new titles by adding blank spaces in the beginning, middle, and/or end of the title within the single quotation marks (e.g., 'DATE,OF,HIRE   '). You may need to make this kind of adjustment to make the column titles line up better. I had to do that to line up the date of hire title with the column of dates below it.

8. You can delete a column title completely by placing two single quotation marks next to each other as the new title (i.e., PRINT LAST_NAME AS ' ') will print a column of last names without a column title. The following TABLE request demonstrates how to suppress printing of column titles.

```
TABLE FILE STAFF
HEADING CENTER
"    "
"REPORT SHOWING HOW TO SUPPRESS COLUMN TITLES"
"    "
PRINT LAST_NAME AS ''
AND SALARY AS ''
BY DEPT_NAME AS ''
IF RECORDLIMIT EQ 4
END
```

```
    PAGE     1


            REPORT SHOWING HOW TO SUPPRESS COLUMN TITLES

    FINANCE             TURPIN              65,400.00
                        BORGIA             102,000.00
                        FREEMAN             34,500.00
    OPERATIONS          HUNT                57,000.00
```

9. If you really need to reduce the actual length of a field to less than what has been assigned in the Master File Description, you could modify each field, on the fly, by following it with a slash and the new length. This modification will only last during that one TABLE request and will not affect the Focus data file. In the following TABLE request, we have reduced the length of two fields. The employee last-name field has been reduced to four characters, while the salary field has been reduced to five figures. The resulting report follows the TABLE request.

```
TABLE FILE STAFF
HEADING CENTER
"    "
"REPORT SHOWING HOW TO TRUNCATE FIELDS"
"    "
PRINT LAST_NAME/A4
AND SALARY/D5
BY DEPT_NAME
IF DEPT_NAME EQ 'FINANCE'
END
```

```
    PAGE     1


    REPORT SHOWING HOW TO TRUNCATE FIELDS
```

```
DEPT_NAME              LAST_NAME  SALARY
----------             ---------  ------
FINANCE                TURP       65,400
                       BORG       ******
                       FREE       34,500
```

Note that with numeric fields there is no truncation. The field is filled with asterisks to let you know that an error has occurred.

PAGE-BREAK HANDLING

The PAGE-BREAK command tells Focus to start a new page when the value of the sort field mentioned in the statement is changed. Say that you are printing a list of salaries for each department. Normally, information about departments will print down the length of the page one entry after another. The normal Focus page break will occur at around the fifty-fifth line of each printed page. A new department name may start anywhere on the page. Under these circumstances, you or the operator or somebody else will have to look at every page and separate the departments with a pair of scissors. Obviously, this is not a good solution. Focus provides you with the PAGE-BREAK command. You will use the PAGE-BREAK command to tell Focus to skip to a new page every time a sort value—such as a DEPT_NAME—changes. The following example will clarify this concept.

```
TABLE FILE STAFF
HEADING CENTER
" "
"REPORT SHOWING HOW TO PAGE BREAK          "
" "
PRINT LAST_NAME AS  'LAST NAME'
AND SALARY
BY DEPT_NAME AS 'DEPARTMENT' PAGE-BREAK
END

    PAGE     1


        REPORT SHOWING HOW TO PAGE BREAK

DEPARTMENT             LAST NAME                SALARY
----------             ---------                ------
ADMINISTRATION         DUXBURY               185,000.00
                       ANDERSEN               32,000.00
```

```
            REPORT SHOWING HOW TO PAGE BREAK

DEPARTMENT              LAST NAME               SALARY
----------             ----------              ------
FINANCE                TURPIN                 65,400.00
                       BORGIA                102,000.00
                       FREEMAN                34,500.00
```

```
            REPORT SHOWING HOW TO PAGE BREAK

DEPARTMENT              LAST NAME               SALARY
----------             ----------              ------
MARKETING              COLE                   39,000.00
                       MORALES                39,400.00
                       ZARKOV                 47,000.00
                       JAMESON                36,700.00
```

```
            REPORT SHOWING HOW TO PAGE BREAK

DEPARTMENT              LAST NAME               SALARY
----------             ----------              ------
MIS                    GREENSTREET            45,600.00
                       BOCHARD                35,000.00
                       TAHANIEV               55,400.00
                       CAMPOS                 32,000.00
```

```
            REPORT SHOWING HOW TO PAGE BREAK

DEPARTMENT              LAST NAME               SALARY
----------             ----------              ------
OPERATIONS             HUNT                   57,000.00
                       TRENT                  22,500.00
                       TAYLOR                 26,550.00
```

The following TABLE request prints a statement of salary and the most recent percentage salary increase for each employee. Notice how we used the PAGE-BREAK command to ensure that each employee statement is printed on a separate page. Also note the use of a new command called REPAGE. When you issue this command in your TABLE request, Focus will start every new page with page number one. The following TABLE request, with some modifications, could be used to produce payroll statements, simple bills, and other types of statements.

```
TABLE FILE STAFF
HEADING CENTER
" "
"CONFIDENTIAL"
" "
"EMPLOYEE PERSONAL INFORMATION STATEMENT AS OF &DATE"
" "
"DEPARTMENT: <DEPT _NAME"
PRINT EMPLOYEE_ID AS 'EMPLOYEE,NUMBER'
AND LAST_NAME AS 'LAST NAME'
AND FIRST_NAME AS 'FIRST NAME'
AND SALARY
AND PCT_INC AS 'PERCENT,SALARY,INCREASE'
BY LAST_NAME PAGE-BREAK REPAGE NOPRINT
END
```

PAGE   1

CONFIDENTIAL

EMPLOYEE PERSONAL INFORMATION STATEMENT AS OF 10/30/91

DEPARTMENT: ADMINISTRATION

EMPLOYEE NUMBER	LAST NAME	FIRST NAME	SALARY	PERCENT SALARY INCREASE
---------	---------	----------	------	--------
515478922	ANDERSEN	CHRISTINE	32,000.00	.07

PAGE   1

CONFIDENTIAL

EMPLOYEE PERSONAL INFORMATION STATEMENT AS OF 10/30/91

DEPARTMENT: MIS

EMPLOYEE NUMBER	LAST NAME	FIRST NAME	SALARY	PERCENT SALARY INCREASE
--------	---------	----------	------	--------
621893221	BOCHARD	ROBERT	35,000.00	.09

```
                          CONFIDENTIAL

       EMPLOYEE PERSONAL INFORMATION STATEMENT AS OF 10/30/91

                       DEPARTMENT: FINANCE
                                                    PERCENT
                                                    SALARY
       EMPLOYEE
       NUMBER     LAST NAME          FIRST NAME    SALARY   INCREASE
       --------   --------           ----------    ------   --------
       513724567  BORGIA             CESARE        102,000.00   .06
```

PAGE   1

```
                          CONFIDENTIAL

       EMPLOYEE PERSONAL INFORMATION STATEMENT AS OF 10/30/91

                        DEPARTMENT: MIS
                                                    PERCENT
                                                    SALARY
       EMPLOYEE
       NUMBER     LAST NAME          FIRST NAME    SALARY   INCREASE
       --------   --------           ----------    ------   --------
       432568023  CAMPOS             CARLOS        32,000.00    .08
```

In the TABLE request above, we could have used the SET PAGE=OFF command to suppress printing of the page number altogether. Place the SET PAGE=OFF on a line by itself right before the TABLE FILE statement:

```
SET PAGE=OFF
TABLE FILE STAFF
```

Another useful Focus command is the SET PAGE=NOPAGE. This command will suppress the regular page break function of Focus. As a result, your report will be printed as one long report.

SKIPPING LINES AND UNDERLINING TEXT

SKIP-LINE is often used to highlight the information on the report. The function of SKIP-LINE is to double-space the report, on the lines requested by you, and make it easier to read. The SKIP-LINE command could be used with Focus verbs as well as with BY and ON commands.

```
TABLE FILE STAFF
HEADING CENTER
"    "
"EXAMPLE OF SKIP-LINE IN A REPORT"
"    "
PRINT EMPLOYEE_ID AS 'EMPLOYEE,NUMBER'
AND LAST_NAME AS 'LAST NAME'
AND FIRST_NAME AS 'FIRST NAME'
BY DEPT_NAME SKIP-LINE
END
```

```
   PAGE     1


              EXAMPLE OF SKIP-LINE IN A REPORT

                      EMPLOYEE
DEPT_NAME             NUMBER      LAST NAME        FIRST NAME
---------             --------    ---------        ----------


ADMINISTRATION        291345672   DUXBURY          JILLIAN
                      515478922   ANDERSEN         CHRISTINE


FINANCE               294728305   TURPIN           BENTON
                      513724567   BORGIA           CESARE
                      504234521   FREEMAN          DIANE


MARKETING             293245178   COLE             ROBERT
                      297748301   MORALES          CARLOS
                      312781122   ZARKOV           WILLIAM
                      413267891   JAMESON          CARLA


MIS                   392345782   GREENSTREET      JAMES
                      621893221   BOCHARD          ROBERT
                      295738307   TAHANIEV         RICHARD
                      432568023   CAMPOS           CARLOS


OPERATIONS            213456682   HUNT             CHARLES
                      312562345   TRENT            RICHARD
                      314562134   TAYLOR           JUANITA
```

You can only use one SKIP-LINE in each TABLE request.
     Following is an example of using SKIP-LINE to double-space every line of a report.

```
TABLE FILE STAFF
HEADING CENTER
"    "
"EXAMPLE OF DOUBLE SPACING EVERY LINE"
"    "
```

```
PRINT EMPLOYEE_ID AS 'EMPLOYEE,NUMBER'
AND LAST_NAME AS 'LAST NAME'
AND FIRST_NAME AS 'FIRST NAME'
SKIP-LINE
IF RECORDLIMIT EQ 4
END
```

```
    PAGE     1


    EXAMPLE OF DOUBLE SPACING EVERY LINE

 EMPLOYEE
 NUMBER        LAST NAME         FIRST NAME
 _____      _____         _____

 294728305    TURPIN            DENTON

 513724567    BORGIA            CESARE

 504234521    FREEMAN           DIANE

 213456682    HUNT              CHARLES
```

UNDER-LINE is somewhat similar to SKIP-LINE. It could be used with the BY command. The UNDER-LINE command draws a line across the field requested. The following TABLE request is almost identical to the one above, except that it uses the UNDER-LINE command.

```
TABLE FILE STAFF
HEADING CENTER
"  "
"EXAMPLE OF THE UNDER-LINE COMMAND IN A REPORT"
"  "
PRINT EMPLOYEE_ID AS 'EMPLOYEE,NUMBER'
AND LAST_NAME AS 'LAST NAME'
AND FIRST_NAME AS 'FIRST NAME'
BY DEPT_NAME UNDER-LINE
END
```

```
                    EXAMPLE OF THE UNDER-LINE COMMAND IN A REPORT

                        EMPLOYEE
DEPT_NAME               NUMBER       LAST NAME            FIRST NAME
---------               --------     ---------            ----------
ADMINISTRATION          291345672    DUXBURY              JILLIAN
                        515478922    ANDERSEN             CHRISTINE
--------------------------------------------------------------------
FINANCE                 294728305    TURPIN               BENTON
                        513724567    BORGIA               CESARE
                        504234521    FREEMAN              DIANE
--------------------------------------------------------------------
MARKETING               293245178    COLE                 ROBERT
                        297748301    MORALES              CARLOS
                        312781122    ZARKOV               WILLIAM
                        413267891    JAMESON              CARLA
--------------------------------------------------------------------
MIS                     392345782    GREENSTREET          JAMES
                        621893221    BOCHARD              ROBERT
                        295738307    TAHANIEV             RICHARD
                        432568023    CAMPOS               CARLOS
--------------------------------------------------------------------
OPERATIONS              213456682    HUNT                 CHARLES
                        312562345    TRENT                RICHARD
                        314562134    TAYLOR               JUANITA
--------------------------------------------------------------------
```

SKIP-LINE and UNDER-LINE could be combined. In that case you will get both an underline and a double space. The double spacing will always follow the underlining.

```
TABLE FILE CAR
HEADING CENTER
"  "
"LIST OF CARS AND THEIR PRICES BY COUNTRY"
"  "
SUM DEALER_COST AND RETAIL_COST
BY COUNTRY
BY CAR SKIP-LINE UNDER-LINE
END
```

```
                LIST OF CARS AND THEIR PRICES BY COUNTRY

     COUNTRY      CAR              DEALER_COST      RETAIL_COST
     -------      ---              -----------      -----------

     ENGLAND      JAGUAR             18,621           22,369
     -----------------------------------------------------------

                  JENSEN             14,940           17,850
     -----------------------------------------------------------

                  TRIUMPH             4,292            5,100
     -----------------------------------------------------------

     FRANCE       PEUGEOT             4,631            5,610
     -----------------------------------------------------------

     ITALY        ALFA ROMEO         18,235           19,565
     -----------------------------------------------------------

                  MASERATI           25,000           31,500
     -----------------------------------------------------------

     JAPAN        DATSUN              2,626            3,139
     -----------------------------------------------------------

                  TOYOTA              2,886            3,339
     -----------------------------------------------------------

     SWEDEN       VOLVO                   0                0
     -----------------------------------------------------------

     W GERMANY    AUDI                5,063            5,970
     -----------------------------------------------------------

                  BMW                50,500           58,762
     -----------------------------------------------------------
```

FOLDING TEXT LINES WITH OVER AND FOLD-LINE COMMANDS

The OVER command allows you to decrease the width of a report by printing one field name over another.

```
TABLE FILE STAFF
HEADING CENTER
"  "
```

```
"USING OVER TO DECREASE REPORT WIDTH"
PRINT FIRST_NAME AND LAST__NAME
OVER STREET
OVER STATE
OVER CITY
OVER ZIP_CODE
BY LAST_NAME SKIP-LINE UNDER-LINE NOPRINT
IF RECORDLIMIT EQ 4
END


    PAGE    1

              USING OVER TO DECREASE REPORT WIDTH

 FIRST_NAME  CESARE      LAST_NAME  BORGIA
 STREET  347 SOUTH ROMA AVENUE
 CITY   NEW YORK
 STATE  NY
 ZIP_CODE  10001
------------------------------------------------------------

 FIRST_NAME  DIANE       LAST_NAME  FREEMAN
 STREET  22 SOUTH DEAN DRIVE
 CITY   CANTON
 STATE  CA
 ZIP_CODE  94107
------------------------------------------------------------

 FIRST_NAME  CHARLES     LAST_NAME  HUNT
 STREET  87A NEWTON
 CITY   ORANGE
 STATE  CA
 ZIP_CODE  93199
------------------------------------------------------------

 FIRST_NAME  BENTON      LAST_NAME  TURPIN
 STREET  121 LA CIENEGA BLVD.
 CITY   LOS ANGELES
 STATE  CA
 ZIP_CODE  91345
------------------------------------------------------------
```

As you can see, we managed to print a large amount of information in a small area by using OVER to decrease the width of the report. The following request uses column positioning and OVER to print a neat, yet meaningful report. Later in this chapter I will show you how to use column positioning. For now, just concentrate on the use of OVER in this TABLE request.

```
TABLE FILE CAR
HEADING CENTER
```

```
"   "
"LIST OF CARS, MODEL TYPE, DEALER COST AND RETAIL COST"
"   "
"BY COUNTRY"
"   "
PRINT CAR IN 20 OVER MODEL IN 20
OVER DEALER_COST IN 20 OVER RETAIL_COST IN 20
BY COUNTRY IN 10 BY CAR NOPRINT UNDER-LINE
IF RECORDLIMIT EQ 6
END


   PAGE    1


        LIST OF CARS, MODEL TYPE, DEALER COST AND RETAIL COST

                          BY COUNTRY


            COUNTRY
            -------
            ENGLAND   CAR         JAGUAR
                      MODEL       V12XKE AUTO
                      DEALER_COST                     7,427
                      RETAIL_COST                     8,878
                      CAR         JAGUAR
                      MODEL       XJ12L AUTO
                      DEALER_COST                    11,194
                      RETAIL_COST                    13,491
        ---------------------------------------------------------
                      CAR         JENSEN
                      MODEL       INTERCEPTOR III
                      DEALER_COST                    14,940
                      RETAIL_COST                    17,850
        ---------------------------------------------------------
                      CAR         TRIUMPH
                      MODEL       TR7
                      DEALER_COST                     4,292
                      RETAIL_COST                     5,100
        ---------------------------------------------------------
            FRANCE    CAR         PEUGEOT
                      MODEL       504 4 DOOR
                      DEALER_COST                     4,631
                      RETAIL_COST                     5,610
        ---------------------------------------------------------
            ITALY     CAR         ALFA ROMEO
                      MODEL       2000 4 DOOR BERLINA
                      DEALER_COST                     6,915
                      RETAIL_COST                     5,925
        ---------------------------------------------------------
```

Following is an example of producing labels with the OVER command.

```
SET PAGE=OFF
TABLE FILE STAFF
PRINT FIRST_NAME AS ' ' AND LAST_NAME  AS ' '
OVER STREET  AS ' '
OVER CITY   AS ' '
OVER STATE   AS ' '  AND ZIP_CODE  AS  ' '
BY LAST_NAME SKIP-LINE NOPRINT
IF DEPT_NAME EQ MARKETING
END
```

```
      ROBERT         COLE
      37 EXETER DRIVE
      GARDEN GROVE
      CA     93110


      CARLA          JAMESON
      727 STROMBRG ROAD
      FOUNTAIN VALLEY
      CA     91205


      CARLOS         MORALES
      883 MANNER DRIVE
      LONG BEACH
      CA     91230


      WILLIAM        ZARKOV
      544 E. KATELLA  #4
      ANAHEIM
      CA     91422
```

FOLD-LINE is similar to OVER. However, it works on sort fields only. As you will remember from the example above, the field names following the OVER command were not sort fields.

```
TABLE FILE STAFF
HEADING CENTER
"  "
"USING FOLD-LINE TO DECREASE REPORT WIDTH "
"  "
PRINT LAST_NAME FIRST_NAME
JOB_TITLE
BY DEPT FOLD-LINE SKIP-LINE UNDER-LINE
BY LAST_NAME NOPRINT
IF RECORDLIMIT EQ 8
END
```

```
       USING FOLD-LINE TO DECREASE REPORT WIDTH

DEPT_NAME
---------
   LAST_NAME              FIRST_NAME  JOB_TITLE
   ---------              ----------  ---------

FINANCE
   BORGIA                 CESARE      LIAISON MANAGER
   FREEMAN                DIANE       SUPERVISOR
   TURPIN                 BENTON      HEAD ACCOUNTANT
-----------------------------------------------------------

MARKETING
   COLE                   ROBERT      SALES REPRESENTATIVE
   MORALES                CARLOS      SALES REPRESENTATIVE
-----------------------------------------------------------

OPERATIONS
   HUNT                   CHARLES     MANAGER
   TAYLOR                 JUANITA     SERVICE REP.
   TRENT                  RICHARD     SERVICE REP.
-----------------------------------------------------------
```

You will notice that the field name and the title that are being followed by FOLD-LINE are offset two spaces to the left of other fields and titles to make them easier to read.

COLUMN POSITIONING

So far, all the reports that we have produced have followed the standard Focus order. In other words, fields sorted by the BY command were always printed first in the order that they were typed in on the TABLE request. This was followed by the other fields (i.e., AND fields), which were printed in the order that you had written them in the TABLE request. If you code the statement "PRINT LAST_NAME AND FIRST_NAME," the last-name field is always printed first. You can actually override this order and print your fields anywhere on the report by using the column-positioning word *IN*. You will use IN to position your column—even the sort field columns—anywhere on the report. This is a very powerful feature of Focus and together with FOLD-LINE could help you produce all kinds of complex reports.

```
TABLE FILE STAFF
HEADING
"   "
```

```
"USING THE POSITIONING COMMAND: 'IN' TO CHANGE THE DEFAULT"
"               PRINT COLUMN"
" "
PRINT LAST_NAME IN 1
JOB_TITLE IN 43
BY DEPT_NAME IN 23 UNDER-LINE SKIP-LINE
BY LAST_NAME NOPRINT
END
```

PAGE   1

USING THE POSITIONING COMMAND: 'IN' TO CHANGE THE DEFAULT
                PRINT COLUMN

LAST_NAME	DEPT_NAME	JOB_TITLE
ANDERSEN DUXBURY	ADMINISTRATION	EXECUTIVE ASSISTANT PRESIDENT
BORGIA FREEMAN TURPIN	FINANCE	LIAISON MANAGER SUPERVISOR HEAD ACCOUNTANT
COLE JAMESON MORALES ZARKOV	MARKETING	SALES REPRESENTATIVE SALES REPRESENTATIVE SALES REPRESENTATIVE SALES REPRESENTATIVE
BOCHARD CAMPOS GREENSTREET TAHANIEV	MIS	OPERATOR OPERATOR SENIOR PROGRAMMER MANAGER, DATA CENTER
HUNT TAYLOR TRENT	OPERATIONS	MANAGER SERVICE REP. SERVICE REP.

SUMMARIZING (TOTALING) FIELD VALUES ON FOCUS REPORTS

We have already seen that you could use the COLUMN-TOTAL and ROW-TOTAL commands to produce meaningful summary lines or columns for Focus reports. Focus has several other commands to add field values. These commands produce subtotals and grand totals. They are somewhat similar but have different uses. The subtotal commands are as follows:

```
SUBTOTAL
SUB-TOTAL
RECOMPUTE
SUMMARIZE
RECAP
COMPUTE
```

At this time, we will review the SUBTOTAL and SUB-TOTAL. These commands work on sort fields (BY and ACROSS) and with the ON command only.
    The SUBTOTAL command adds the values of fields and displays a subtotal of the numeric fields every time that the value of the specified sort field (i.e., BY field) changes. In the following TABLE request, we are requesting a subtotal of employee salaries by SECTION_NAME. The report does exactly that. It does not subtotal the employee salaries at the DEPT_NAME level, which is part of the TABLE request at a higher level (i.e., the first sort field is not totaled).

```
TABLE FILE STAFF
HEADING CENTER
"  "
"USING THE SUBTOTAL SUMMARIZING COMMANDS "
" TO TOTAL FIELDS "
"  "
PRINT LAST_NAME IN 45 AND SALARY IN 55
BY DEPT_NAME
BY SECTION_NAME SUBTOTAL
END
```

```
    PAGE     1


           USING THE SUBTOTAL SUMMARIZING COMMANDS

               TO TOTAL FIELDS

    DEPT_NAME           SECTION_NAME       LAST_NAME      SALARY
    ---------           ------------       ---------      ------

    ADMINISTRATION      EXECUTIVE          DUXBURY     185,000.00
                                           ANDERSEN     32,000.00


    *TOTAL SECTION_NAME EXECUTIVE                       217,000.00
```

```
FINANCE                COLLECTIONS           FREEMAN    34,500.00

*TOTAL SECTION_NAME COLLECTIONS                         34,500.00

                       PAYABLES              TURPIN     65,400.00
                                             BORGIA    102,000.00

*TOTAL SECTION_NAME PAYABLES                           167,400.00

MARKETING              SALES                 COLE       39,000.00
                                             MORALES    39,400.00
                                             ZARKOV     47,000.00
                                             JAMESON    36,700.00

*TOTAL SECTION_NAME SALES                              162,100.00

MIS                    DEVELOPMENT           GREENSTREET45,600.00
                                             BOCHARD    35,000.00

*TOTAL SECTION_NAME DEVELOPMENT                         80,600.00

                       OPERATIONS            TAHANIEV   55,400.00
                                             CAMPOS     32,000.00

*TOTAL SECTION_NAME OPERATIONS                          87,400.00

OPERATIONS             CUSTOMER SERVICES     TRENT      22,500.00
                                             TAYLOR     26,550.00

*TOTAL SECTION_NAME CUSTOMER SERVICES                   49,050.00

                       ENGINEERING           HUNT       57,000.00

*TOTAL SECTION_NAME ENGINEERING                         57,000.00

TOTAL                                                  855,050.00
```

The following TABLE request uses the SUB-TOTAL command. Notice that the two requests are otherwise identical. However, the resulting report sub-totals the employee salaries at both the section and department name levels. So SUB-TOTAL is similar to SUBTOTAL except that it also subtotals the values of the fields at all the higher-level sort fields.

```
TABLE FILE STAFF
HEADING CENTER
"   "
"USING THE SUB-TOTAL SUMMARIZING COMMANDS "
" TO TOTAL FIELDS "
"   "
PRINT LAST_NAME IN 45 AND SALARY IN 55
```

```
BY DEPT_NAME
BY SECTION_NAME SUB-TOTAL
END
```

PAGE   1

USING THE SUB-TOTAL SUMMARIZING COMMANDS
TO TOTAL FIELDS

DEPT_NAME	SECTION_NAME	LAST_NAME	SALARY
ADMINISTRATION	EXECUTIVE	DUXBURY	185,000.00
		ANDERSEN	32,000.00

```
*TOTAL SECTION_NAME EXECUTIVE                  217,000.00
*TOTAL DEPT_NAME ADMINISTRATION                217,000.00
```

| FINANCE | COLLECTIONS | FREEMAN | 34,500.00 |

```
*TOTAL SECTION_NAME COLLECTIONS                 34,500.00
```

| | PAYABLES | TURPIN | 65,400.00 |
| | | BORGIA | 102,000.00 |

```
*TOTAL SECTION_NAME PAYABLES                   167,400.00
*TOTAL DEPT_NAME FINANCE                       201,900.00
```

MARKETING	SALES	COLE	39,000.00
		MORALES	39,400.00
		ZARKOV	47,000.00
		JAMESON	36,700.00

```
*TOTAL SECTION_NAME SALES                      162,100.00
*TOTAL DEPT_NAME MARKETING                     162,100.00
```

| MIS | DEVELOPMENT | GREENSTREET | 45,600.00 |
| | | BOCHARD | 35,000.00 |

```
*TOTAL SECTION_NAME DEVELOPMENT                 80,600.00
```

| | OPERATIONS | TAHANIEV | 55,400.00 |
| | | CAMPOS | 32,000.00 |

```
*TOTAL SECTION_NAME OPERATIONS                  87,400.00
*TOTAL DEPT_NAME MIS                           168,000.00
```

| OPERATIONS | CUSTOMER SERVICES | TRENT | 22,500.00 |
| | | TAYLOR | 26,550.00 |

```
*TOTAL SECTION_NAME CUSTOMER SERVICES                49,050.00

                ENGINEERING            HUNT        57,000.00

*TOTAL SECTION_NAME ENGINEERING                     57,000.00
*TOTAL DEPT_NAME OPERATIONS                        106,050.00


TOTAL                                              855,050.00
```

In both cases the TABLE request will automatically produce a grand total of all the numeric fields at the end of the report. To suppress printing of the grand total, use the NO TOTAL command at the end of the TABLE request.

```
ON TABLE NOTOTAL
END
```

Both subtotal commands produce totals by sort fields of all the numeric sort fields. In the following TABLE request, ''BY SECTION_NAME SUB-TOTAL'' will subtotal the salary and the vacation fields.

```
TABLE FILE STAFF
PRINT LAST_NAME AND SALARY AND VACATION
BY SECTION_NAME SUB-TOTAL
END
```

To subtotal a specific field or fields, you list the field name or field names that you want subtotaled after the word ''SUB-TOTAL.'' So the statement above must be changed to ''BY SECTION_NAME SUB-TOTAL SALARY.''

```
TABLE FILE STAFF
PRINT LAST_NAME AND SALARY AND VACATION
BY SECTION_NAME SUB-TOTAL SALARY
END
```

CHANGING THE FOCUS DEFAULT PAGE NUMBER

So far we have let Focus handle the page numbering of reports. For most reports, that is just fine. However, should the need arise, you could move the location of the page number block to other parts of the report. The command used to place the page number anywhere else on the report is TABPAGENO. The following TABLE request shows how we moved the page number text and the page number itself to the extreme right-hand side of the report.

```
TABLE FILE STAFF
HEADING
"DATE: &DATE < 53 PAGE NO: <TABPAGENO"
"        "
```

```
"         "          CHANGING THE DEFAULT POSITION OF PAGE NO."
"  "
PRINT LAST_NAME IN 45 AND SALARY IN 56
BY DEPT_NAME FOLD-LINE
BY SECTION_NAME SKIP-LINE
IF DEPT_NAME EQ MIS OR FINANCE
END
```

```
DATE: 02/01/91                              PAGE NO:      1

              CHANGING THE DEFAULT POSITION OF PAGE NO.

    DEPT_NAME
    ---------
       SECTION_NAME                    LAST_NAME      SALARY
       ------------                    ---------      ------

FINANCE
       COLLECTIONS                     FREEMAN      34,500.00
       PAYABLES                        TURPIN       65,400.00
                                       BORGIA      102,000.00

    MIS
       DEVELOPMENT                     GREENSTREET  45,600.00
                                       BOCHARD      35,000.00

       OPERATIONS                      TAHANIEV     55,400.00
                                       CAMPOS       32,000.00
```

If your user is interested in printing the page number at the bottom of the page, you could oblige by putting "TABPAGENO" at the bottom by using the footing statement:

```
TABLE FILE STAFF
HEADING
"DATE: &DATE"
"       "
"         MOVING THE PAGE NUMBER TO THE BOTTOM OF THE PAGE"
"  "
PRINT LAST_NAME IN 45 AND SALARY IN 56
BY DEPT_NAME FOLD-LINE
BY SECTION_NAME SKIP-LINE
IF DEPT_NAME EQ MIS OR FINANCE
FOOTING CENTER
"PAGE NO: <TABPAGENO"
END
```

PRINTING VERY WIDE REPORTS

Focus gives you the ability to produce very wide reports. As you know, the display screen on your terminal is only 80 characters wide. To make a wide report you should make use of the left and right carets (< and >). The following example illustrates the code for a wide report.

```
TABLE FILE STAFF
HEADING
"                                        "
"     "
"<10 THIS IS A VERY WIDE REPORT: <60 LAST_NAME <85 FIRST_NAME
 < 105 SALARY AND VACATION BY DEPARTMENT NAME AND SECTION NAME"
"   "
PRINT LAST_NAME AND FIRST_NAME AND SALARY AND VACATION
BY DEPT_NAME
BY SECTION_NAME SKIP-LINE
IF DEPT_NAME EQ MIS OR FINANCE
END
```

REPORT GENERATION WITH MULTIPLE FOCUS VERBS

All the reports that we have produced so far have included only one Focus verb (i.e., PRINT, LIST, SUM, and COUNT). We could use more than one verb in a TABLE request to produce complex reports. There are certain restrictions in using multiple verbs in TABLE requests. First an example.

```
TABLE FILE STAFF
HEADING CENTER
"   "
"EXAMPLE OF USING MULTIPLE VERBS IN FOCUS"
"   "
"INDIVIDUAL AND TOTAL SALARIES FOR EACH DEPARTMENT"
"   "
SUM SALARY AS 'TOTAL,DEPARTMENT,SALARY' BY DEPT_NAME
LIST EID AS 'EMPLOYEE,ID'
AND LAST BY DEPT_NAME BY HIGHEST SALARY
END
```

```
                    EXAMPLE OF USING MULTIPLE VERBS IN FOCUS

                 INDIVIDUAL AND TOTAL SALARIES FOR EACH DEPARTMENT

                      TOTAL
                      DEPARTMENT               EMPLOYEE
DEPT_NAME             SALARY       SALARY  LIST ID        LAST_NAME
---------             ------       ------  ---- -------   ---------
ADMINISTRATION 217,000.00     185,000.00  1    291345672 DUXBURY
                                32,000.00  2    515478922 ANDERSEN
FINANCE          201,900.00    102,000.00  1    513724567 BORGIA
                                65,400.00  2    294728305 TURPIN
                                34,500.00  3    504234521 FREEMAN
MARKETING        162,100.00     47,000.00  1    312781122 ZARKOV
                                39,400.00  2    297748301 MORALES
                                39,000.00  3    293245178 COLE
                                36,700.00  4    413267891 JAMESON
MIS              168,000.00     55,400.00  1    295738307 TAHANIEV
                                45,600.00  2    392345782 GREENSTREET
                                35,000.00  3    621893221 BOCHARD
                                32,000.00  4    432568023 CAMPOS
OPERATIONS       106,050.00     57,000.00  1    213456682 HUNT
                                26,550.00  2    314562134 TAYLOR
                                22,500.00  3    312562345 TRENT
```

As you can see, the first verb, SUM, was followed by another verb, LIST. The verb SUM sorted the file in department name sequence. The list verb sorted by department name as well as by highest salary. The rules are simple:

1. The first verb must be either SUM or COUNT.

2. PRINT or LIST can only be the last verb in the TABLE request. You can only use either PRINT or LIST.

3. SUM or COUNT can be repeated as many times as necessary within the TABLE request, but cannot follow PRINT or LIST.

4. All subsequent verbs must follow the same sort sequence and pattern as the first verb. However, remember that if you use LIST or PRINT once, you cannot use those verbs or another verb again in that TABLE request.

Examples of correct and incorrect multiple verbs

```
TABLE FILE STAFF
SUM SALARY BY DEPT_NAME
PRINT LAST_NAME BY DEPT_NAME BY SALARY
```

The entry above is correct because the second verb follows the same sort order as the first verb.

```
TABLE FILE STAFF
SUM SALARY BY DEPT_NAME BY SECTION_NAME
COUNT LAST_NAME BY DEPT_NAME
```

This is not correct, because the second and each subsequent verb must follow the same sort sequence as those of the preceding verbs. You could add additional sort fields after satisfying this requirement. To correct the statement above you should change the code as follows:

```
COUNT LAST_NAME BY DEPT_NAME BY SECTION_NAME
```

The following statements are also technically correct, though not very good Focus code.

```
TABLE FILE TEST1
SUM FIELD1 BY A BY B
COUNT FIELD2 BY A BY B BY C
SUM FIELD3 BY A BY B BY C
PRINT FIELD4 BY A BY B BY C BY D
END
```

However, the following is not acceptable because the last statement has fewer sort keys than the ones preceding it.

```
TABLE FILE TEST1
SUM FIELD1 BY A BY B
COUNT FIELD2 BY A BY B BY C
SUM FIELD3 BY A BY B BY C
PRINT FIELD4 BY A BY B
END
```

Using ROW-TOTAL and COLUMN-TOTAL with Multiple Verbs

The following TABLE request is an example of using COLUMN-TOTAL with a TABLE request.

```
TABLE FILE STAFF
HEADING CENTER
"  "
"EXAMPLE OF USING MULTIPLE VERBS IN FOCUS"
"  "
"USING COLUMN-TOTAL WITH MULTIPLE VERBS"
"  "
"EMPLOYEE SALARY AND VACATION HOURS FOR"
"  "
" <DEPT_NAME DEPARTMENT"
```

```
"  _____"
"  "
SUM SALARY AS 'DEPARTMENT,SALARY'
BY DEPT_NAME PAGE-BREAK NOPRINT
LIST LAST_NAME AS 'LAST,NAME'
AND VACATION AS 'VACATION,HOURS'
BY DEPT_NAME
BY HIGHEST SALARY AS 'EMPLOYEE,SALARY'
ON TABLE COLUMN-TOTAL
IF RECORDLIMIT EQ 8
END
```

```
        PAGE      1

                    EXAMPLE OF USING MULTIPLE VERBS IN FOCUS

                      USING COLUMN-TOTAL WITH MULTIPLE VERBS

                    EMPLOYEE SALARY AND VACATION HOURS FOR

                        ADMINISTRATION DEPARTMENT
                        _____

    DEPARTMENT     EMPLOYEE              LAST            VACATION
    SALARY         SALARY      LIST     NAME            HOURS
    _____     _____    ____     ____            _____

    217,000.00   185,000.00       1     DUXBURY             110
                  32,000.00       2     ANDERSEN             35


        PAGE      2

                    EXAMPLE OF USING MULTIPLE VERBS IN FOCUS

                      USING COLUMN-TOTAL WITH MULTIPLE VERBS

                    EMPLOYEE SALARY AND VACATION HOURS FOR

                          FINANCE DEPARTMENT
                        _____

    DEPARTMENT     EMPLOYEE              LAST            VACATION
    SALARY         SALARY      LIST     NAME            HOURS
    _____     _____    ____     ____            _____

    201,900.00   102,000.00       1     BORGIA              15
                  65,400.00       2     TURPIN             120
                  34,500.00       3     FREEMAN             99
```

EXAMPLE OF USING MULTIPLE VERBS IN FOCUS

USING COLUMN-TOTAL WITH MULTIPLE VERBS

EMPLOYEE SALARY AND VACATION HOURS FOR

MARKETING DEPARTMENT

DEPARTMENT SALARY	EMPLOYEE SALARY	LIST	LAST NAME	VACATION HOURS
162,100.00	47,000.00	1	ZARKOV	63
	39,400.00	2	MORALES	80
	39,000.00	3	COLE	43
	36,700.00	4	JAMESON	22

EXAMPLE OF USING MULTIPLE VERBS IN FOCUS

USING COLUMN-TOTAL WITH MULTIPLE VERBS

EMPLOYEE SALARY AND VACATION HOURS FOR

MIS DEPARTMENT

DEPARTMENT SALARY	EMPLOYEE SALARY	LIST	LAST NAME	VACATION HOURS
168,000.00	55,400.00	1	TAHANIEV	85
	45,600.00	2	GREENSTREET	10
	35,000.00	3	BOCHARD	40
	32,000.00	4	CAMPOS	60

EXAMPLE OF USING MULTIPLE VERBS IN FOCUS

USING COLUMN-TOTAL WITH MULTIPLE VERBS

EMPLOYEE SALARY AND VACATION HOURS FOR

OPERATIONS DEPARTMENT

```
DEPARTMENT      EMPLOYEE            LAST                 VACATION
SALARY          SALARY      LIST    NAME                 HOURS
----------      --------    ----    ----                 --------
106,050.00      57,000.00     1     HUNT                      140
                26,550.00     2     TAYLOR                     10
                22,500.00     3     TRENT                      50
    PAGE     6
```

```
          EXAMPLE OF USING MULTIPLE VERBS IN FOCUS

           USING COLUMN-TOTAL WITH MULTIPLE VERBS

           EMPLOYEE SALARY AND VACATION HOURS FOR

                         DEPARTMENT
                ---------------------------
```

```
DEPARTMENT      EMPLOYEE            LAST                 VACATION
SALARY          SALARY      LIST    NAME                 HOURS
----------      --------    ----    ----                 --------
TOTAL
855,050.00                                                   982
```

The IF Clause and Multiple Verbs

The IF clause is applied to all the records regardless of where they appear in a multiple-verb TABLE request. So if the IF or WHERE clause is the last statement in the request following a verb, the IF will apply to all the verbs preceding that verb.

PREFIXES OR DIRECT OPERATORS

Prefixes or direct operators could act directly on any field that follows a Focus verb. Each prefix is attached, with a period, to one field only (e.g., TOT. SALARY). The prefix is the word "TOT," which means total of salaries. Prefixes allow you to supplement the normal action of the verb and compute other values for the fields in the request. Prefixes should be used only with SUM and COUNT verbs. They are not effective with PRINT and the LIST verbs. You cannot directly sort the result of a prefix command by using the BY or ACROSS commands. You must first create a HOLD file to store the results of your TABLE request and then sort the fields in the HOLD file. A HOLD file is just like a Focus file which is created automatically by Focus at your command. We discuss HOLD file creation and processing in a later chapter.

When using prefixes, you could issue the following command:

```
SUM MIN.SALARY BY DEPT_NAME.
```

You could not, however, issue the following command:

```
BY DEPT_NAME SUM.SALARY
```

The second Focus statement is in error, because you are trying to sort the result of a prefix command.

The following TABLE request is an example of TOT, which is one of the Focus prefixes. The function of TOT is to total the values of all the occurrences of the field that is attached to it.

```
TABLE FILE STAFF
HEADING
"< 1  DATE: &DATE                              "
"    "
"                LIST DEPARTMENTS IN THE COMPANY  "
"    "
"          TOTAL SALARY FOR THE COMPANY IS: $<TOT.SAL "
"    "
"    TOTAL VACATION HOURS ACCRUED IN COMPANY IS: <TOT.VAC HOURS"
"    "
SUM SALARY AND VACATION
BY DEPT_NAME
BY SECTION_NAME
FOOTING CENTER
"PAGE NO: <TABPAGENO"
END
```

```
    DATE: 02/03/91


            LIST DEPARTMENTS IN THE COMPANY

        TOTAL SALARY FOR THE COMPANY IS: $855,050.00

    TOTAL VACATION HOURS ACCRUED IN COMPANY IS: 982 HOURS

    DEPT_NAME          SECTION_NAME          SALARY  VACATION
    ---------          ------------          ------  --------

    ADMINISTRATION     EXECUTIVE           217,000.00      145
    FINANCE            COLLECTIONS          34,500.00       99
                       PAYABLES            167,400.00      135
    MARKETING          SALES               162,100.00      208
    MIS                DEVELOPMENT          80,600.00       50
                       OPERATIONS           87,400.00      145
    OPERATIONS         CUSTOMER SERVICES    49,050.00       60
                       ENGINEERING          57,000.00      140

                    PAGE NO:    1
```

TABLE 8.1 PREFIXES

Prefix	Meaning
AVE.	Average of values of the fields being processed in the request. For example, SUM AVG. SALARY BY DEPT_NAME will show the average salary for each department.
TOT.	Total of all the values of the requested fields in the file. For example, SUM TOT.SALARY, will total the value of the salary field for all the file.
PCT.	Percentage of the values in the group will be computed. For example, SUM SALARY AND PCT.SALARY BY DEPT_NAME will display the total department salary as a percentage of the total company salary. This action is equivalent to the following formula:

$$\left.\begin{array}{l} \text{PCT.SALARY} \\ \text{BY} \\ \text{DEPARTMENT} \end{array}\right\} = (\text{DEPARTMENT SALARY / TOTAL SALARY}) \times 100$$

MIN.	Minimum value of the group being evaluated will be displayed. SUM MIN.SALARY BY DEPT_NAME will display the lowest salary within each department.
MAX.	This is the opposite of the MIN. prefix. It will find and display the maximum value of the field requested.
CNT.	Will count the values of the field being evaluated. For example, CNT.EID will count the number of times EID (EMPLOYEE_ID) field is read in the TABLE request.
SUM.	Will total (sum) the values of the field being evaluated. SUM.SALARY BY DEPT_NAME will add the values of salaries in each department.
FST.	Will show the first occurrence of the field in the group that is being evaluated. For example, SUM SALARY AND FST.SALARY BY DEPT will show the total salary by department and also the value of the first salary field in each department. FST. is not the same as MIN. It will display the first, not the smallest.
LST.	This will show the value of the last field in the group being evaluated. LST. is not the same as MAX.

The TOT.SALARY and TOT.VAC fields added the values of all the salary fields and vacation fields in the company and printed it where we had requested, as part of a heading line. Note that unlike other values in the heading lines, TOT.SALARY and TOT.VACATION are not changed when the department values change. Table 8.1 lists the other important prefixes.

In the following TABLE request, we used several of the prefixes described in the table.

```
TABLE FILE STAFF
HEADING
"< 1  DATE: &DATE                              "
"     "
"     REPORT SHOWING MINIMUM, MAXIMUM AND AVERAGE SALARY"
"     "
"        TOTAL SALARY FOR THE COMPANY IS: $<TOT.SAL "
"     "
 "     TOTAL VACATION HOURS ACCRUED IN COMPANY IS: <TOT.VAC
HOURS"
"     "
```

```
SUM SALARY AS 'TOTAL,DEPARTMENT,SALARY'
AND MAX.SAL AS 'HIGHEST,SALARY,IN,DEPARTMENT'
AND MIN.SAL AS 'LOWEST,SALARY,IN,DEPARTMENT'
AND AVE.SAL AS 'AVERAGE,SALARY,IN,DEPARTMENT'
BY DEPT_NAME AS 'DEPARTMENT'
FOOTING CENTER
"PAGE NO: <TABPAGENO"
END
```

```
    DATE: 12/03/91


        REPORT SHOWING MINIMUM, MAXIMUM AND AVERAGE SALARY

          TOTAL SALARY FOR THE COMPANY IS: $855,050.00

      TOTAL VACATION HOURS ACCRUED IN COMPANY IS: 982 HOURS

                              HIGHEST      LOWEST
                   TOTAL      SALARY       SALARY       AVERAGE
                   DEPARTMENT IN           IN           SALARY
                                                        IN
    DEPARTMENT     SALARY     DEPARTMENT   DEPARTMENT   DEPARTMENT
    ----------     ----------  ----------   ----------   ----------
    ADMINISTRATION 217,000.00 185,000.00   32,000.00   108,500.00
    FINANCE        201,900.00 102,000.00   34,500.00    67,300.00
    MARKETING      162,100.00  47,000.00   36,700.00    40,525.00
    MIS            168,000.00  55,400.00   32,000.00    42,000.00
    OPERATIONS     106,050.00  57,000.00   22,500.00    35,350.00


                    PAGE NO:     1
```

In the example above, we have used four Prefixes. We used TOT. to calculate the total salaries and accrued vacation hours of all the employees and placed them strategically in the heading lines. We used MAX. to calculate the maximum salary in each department. We used MIN. to calculate the minimum salary in each department. To find the average salary in each department, we used the prefix AVE.

In the following TABLE request, we will use PCT., FST., and LST. The PCT.SAL calculates the salary of departments as the percentage of the company's total salary cost. We will find out that the administration department's total salary cost is 25.38 percent of that of the entire company.

```
TABLE FILE STAFF
HEADING
"< 1  DATE: &DATE                         "
"      "
"         REPORT SHOWING VALUE OF EACH DEPARTMENT SALARY"
"      "
"         AS A PERCENTAGE OF TOTAL COMPANY SALARY "
"      "
```

```
"      TOTAL SALARY FOR THE COMPANY IS: $<TOT.SAL "
"     "
SUM SALARY AS 'TOTAL,DEPARTMENT,SALARY'
AND PCT.SAL AS 'AS,PERCENTAGE,OF,THE COMPANY'
AND FST.SAL AS 'FIRST,SALARY,IN,DEPARTMENT'
AND LST.SAL AS 'LAST,SALARY,IN,DEPARTMENT'
BY DEPT_NAME AS 'DEPARTMENT'
ON TABLE COLUMN-TOTAL SALARY PCT.SAL
FOOTING CENTER
"PAGE NO: <TABPAGENO"
END
```

```
     DATE: 12/04/91


           REPORT SHOWING VALUE OF EACH DEPARTMENT SALARY

              AS A PERCENTAGE OF TOTAL COMPANY SALARY

           TOTAL SALARY FOR THE COMPANY IS: $855,050.00
```

| | TOTAL
DEPARTMENT | AS
PERCENTAGE
OF | FIRST
SALARY
IN | LAST
SALARY
IN |
DEPARTMENT	SALARY	THE COMPANY	DEPARTMENT	DEPARTMENT
ADMINISTRATION	217,000.00	25.38	185,000.00	32,000.00
FINANCE	201,900.00	23.61	65,400.00	34,500.00
MARKETING	162,100.00	18.96	39,000.00	36,700.00
MIS	168,000.00	19.65	45,600.00	32,000.00
OPERATIONS	106,050.00	12.40	57,000.00	26,550.00
TOTAL	855,050.00	100.00		

```
                        PAGE NO:    1
```

The following TABLE request shows the combination of COUNT with
SUM. As you will see, the effect is like using both the COUNT and SUM verbs to
add all the salaries and count the number of employees in each department. The
combination of SUM and CNT. or COUNT and SUM. is very useful in TABLE
requests.

```
TABLE FILE STAFF
HEADING
"< 1  DATE: &DATE                                "
"     "
"       REPORT SHOWING COMBINATION OF COUNT WITH SUM."
"     "
"     "
COUNT EID AS 'EMPLOYEE,COUNT'
AND SUM.SALARY AS 'TOTAL,DEPARTMENT,SALARY'
```

```
BY DEPT_NAME AS 'DEPARTMENT'
ON TABLE COLUMN-TOTAL
FOOTING CENTER
"PAGE NO: <TABPAGENO"
END
```

```
    DATE: 11/04/91

        REPORT SHOWING COMBINATION OF COUNT WITH SUM.


                                    TOTAL
                         EMPLOYEE   DEPARTMENT
    DEPARTMENT           COUNT      SALARY
    ----------          --------   ----------
    ADMINISTRATION              2   217,000.00
    FINANCE                     3   201,900.00
    MARKETING                   4   162,100.00
    MIS                         4   168,000.00
    OPERATIONS                  3   106,050.00

    TOTAL                      16   855,050.00

            PAGE NO:     1
```

In the TABLE request above we could have substituted

```
SUM SALARY AND CNT.EID BY DEPT_NAME
```

instead of

```
COUNT EID AND SUM.SALARY BY DEPT_NAME
```

The results would have been almost identical, the only difference being that the salary column would have been displayed before the employee count column.

The following report is another example of the prefixes. This time we have mixed the COUNT with AVE. to get an employee count per department as well as the average salary in each department.

```
TABLE FILE STAFF
HEADING
"< 1  DATE: &DATE                            "
"     "
"                    NUMBER OF EMPLOYEES "
"     "
"        AND THE AVERAGE SALARY IN EACH DEPARTMENT "
"     "
COUNT EID AS 'EMPLOYEE,COUNT'
```

```
AND AVE.SAL
BY DEPT_NAME
FOOTING CENTER
"PAGE NO: <TABPAGENO"
END
```

```
   DATE: 12/04/91

            NUMBER OF EMPLOYEES

     AND THE AVERAGE SALARY IN EACH DEPARTMENT

                      EMPLOYEE      AVE
   DEPT_NAME          COUNT         SALARY
   ---------          --------      ------

   ADMINISTRATION            2   108,500.00
   FINANCE                   3    67,300.00
   MARKETING                 4    40,525.00
   MIS                       4    42,000.00
   OPERATIONS                3    35,350.00


           PAGE NO:     1
```

SUMMARY

In this chapter we discussed the remaining techniques in preparing and customizing reports. Between these two chapters, you have learned most of the commands and methods that you are ever likely to need for formatting reports. The following items were discussed.

1. Techniques for customizing the default column titles
2. Increasing the number of lines of column titles from one line to five lines
3. Positioning columns of data anywhere on the report
4. Report format modifiers:
   a. PAGE-BREAK
   b. SKIP-LINE
   c. UNDER-LINE
5. OVER and FOLD-LINE to help in producing narrow reports and creating special statements in payroll and billing applications
6. Changing the default page number position
7. Using SUBTOTAL and SUB-TOTAL for totaling sorted fields
8. Multiple verbs
9. Prefixes or direct operators

CHAPTER 9

CREATING WORK FIELDS
IN FOCUS®:
DEFINE AND COMPUTE

MAIN TOPICS:

- Performing Arithmetic Functions and EDIT Functions
- Joining Fields Together: Decoding and Encoding
  Fields
- Logical Conditions
- Date Manipulation
- Compute Statement
- Special Focus Supplied Functions
- Summarizing

DEFINE

Define comes in several forms and is one the most powerful Focus commands used in writing report requests. Basically, Define allows the user to perform the following feats:

- Create new fields for the duration of the Focus request.
- Introduce literals (numeric or alphanumeric constants) such as tax rates into your Focus program.
- Perform simple and complex arithmetic operations.
- Perform extensive editing on a field.
- Join several fields together to create a new field.
- Perform simple and complex logical decision-making tasks such as IF, THEN, ELSE and compound logical statements such as IF with AND and/or OR.
- Decode and encode fields.
- Perform date conversions such as converting Julian dates to Gregorian dates and month/day/year (MDY) format to year/month/day (YMD) format.

- Convert numeric fields to alphanumeric fields, and vice versa.
- Perform other tasks such as locating the preceding occurrence of certain record types.

The DEFINE command is an instruction to Focus to perform certain functions that are not readily available under the native TABLE commands. The DEFINE commands are always placed before the TABLE commands since they create the new fields and perform computations that the TABLE commands will rely upon. The fields created by the DEFINE command are treated by the TABLE commands just like any other real fields from a Focus or external (non-Focus) file. Therefore, you can use the new fields as key fields for sorting the records in the file.

DEFINE SYNTAX

The general syntax of the DEFINE command is as follows:

```
DEFINE FILE filename [CLEAR or ADD]
                          ┌─Action that must be performed
                          ↓
New Field/format = Expression ;
END
```

The actions may be one expression or a combination of several expressions, one building upon another or totally independent of each other, as we shall shortly see. Note that each expression in the DEFINE command must end with a semicolon (;). You can also only use up to 12 characters as the new field name (the left-hand side of the expression statement).

The TABLE command immediately follows the DEFINE command. For example:

```
DEFINE FILE STAFF    ← The DEFINE command identifies
                         the appropriate file.

NEWSALARY/D12.2=(SALARY*1.08) ;   ← A DEFINE expression. Notice the ;.
END              ← The END must follow the last DEFINE expression.
TABLE FILE STAFF
HEADING CENTER
" "
"LIST OF ANNUAL SALARY INCREASE FOR EACH EMPLOYEE"
"IN THE MIS AND ADMINISTRATION DEPARTMENTS"
" "
PRINT LAST_NAME
AND SALARY AND NEWSALARY AS 'NEW,SALARY'
BY DEPT_NAME
IF DEPT_NAME EQ 'MIS' OR 'ADMINISTRATION'
END
```

In the request above, we have created a new field called NEWSALARY. This field has a format of D12.2 and is used to hold the result of product of employee salary multiplied by 1.08. Note that the NEWSALARY field is created before the TABLE request has been initiated. Also, remember that like all DEFINE fields, this field is temporary and will disappear at the end of the Focus session.

```
PAGE    1


            LIST OF ANNUAL SALARY INCREASE FOR EACH EMPLOYEE
                IN THE MIS OR ADMINISTRATION DEPARTMENTS


                                                           NEW
DEPT_NAME               LAST_NAME           SALARY        SALARY
---------               ---------           ------        ------
ADMINISTRATION          DUXBURY          185,000.00    199,800.00
                        ANDERSEN          32,000.00     34,560.00
MIS                     GREENSTREET       45,600.00     49,248.00
                        BOCHARD           35,000.00     37,800.00
                        TAHANIEV          55,400.00     59,832.00
                        CAMPOS            32,000.00     34,560.00
```

Basic rules for the DEFINE command

1. New field names could be up to 12 characters long.
2. Fields must be uppercase only.
3. New fields must start with the letters A through Z.
4. Numbers 0 through 9 are allowed as part of the new field name.
5. An underscore (_) is allowed as part of the new field name.
6. Avoid special characters.
7. The new field name should be followed by a / and the format (type and size) of the field (e.g., BONUS/D11.2 or NEW_NAME/A20). If you do not put in the format of the new field, Focus will assume a format of D12.2 for the new field. So, make sure that you state your format correctly.
8. You can stack DEFINE commands one after the other. There is no need to define each expression with a new DEFINE command.
9. A DEFINE command is generally available until the end of the Focus session.

The DEFINE CLEAR command will cancel any existing DEFINE commands from previous TABLE requests. In the following example, the DEFINE command will clear all the previous DEFINEs that may have existed in the system.

```
DEFINE FILE STAFF CLEAR
F_SURTAX/D9.2=(SALARY*.01) ;
EMERG_TAX/D9.2=(SALARY*.005) ;
END
```

To add completely new DEFINE commands without erasing the previous ones, use the ADD option after each new DEFINE statement.

```
-*CHAPT9
-*CHAP9-27
DEFINE FILE STAFF
FEDTAX/D9.2= (50000-SALARY) *.28;
SSTAX/D9.2=(SALARY/12) * .0702;
END
DEFINE FILE STAFF ADD          ← Note the ADD option here.
BONUS_VAC/I4 WITH VACATION=8 ;
TOT_VAC/I4=BONUS_VAC+VACATION ;
END
TABLE FILE STAFF
PRINT LAST_NAME/A10
AND SALARY AND FEDTAX AS 'FEDERAL,TAXES'
AND SSTAX AS 'SOCIAL,SECURITY,TAX'
AND BONUS_VAC AS 'BONUS,VACATION,HOURS'
AND TOT_VAC AS 'TOTAL,VACATION,HOURS'
IF DEPT_NAME EQ  'MARKETING'
END
```

```
     PAGE      1


                                       SOCIAL     BONUS     TOTAL
                             FEDERAL   SECURITY   VACATION  VACATION
     LAST_NAME    SALARY     TAXES     TAX        HOURS     HOURS
     ---------    ------     -------   --------   --------  --------
     COLE         39,000.00  3,080.00    228.15         8        51
     MORALES      39,400.00  2,968.00    230.49         8        88
     ZARKOV       47,000.00    840.00    274.95         8        71
     JAMESON      36,700.00  3,724.00    214.69         8        30
```

If you do not use the DEFINE with ADD, the second DEFINE will erase the first DEFINE.

You can always check to see if you have any DEFINEs left in the memory by typing the ? (question mark) DEFINE from the Focus prompt >.

```
? DEFINE


FILE      FIELD NAME   FORMAT   FIELDNO   SEGNO      ADDR    VIEW     TYPE
STAFF     FEDTAX       D9.2        20        3     780E0400
STAFF     SSTAX        D9.2        21        3     780F0400
STAFF     BONUS_VAC    I4          22        3     78100400
STAFF     TOT_VAC      I4          23        3     38110400
```

Mathematical Functions

This is probably one of the easiest DEFINE commands to understand. As you have noticed, the TABLE environment allows you to perform certain arithmetic functions. These functions are generally limited to totaling numeric fields (SUB-TOTAL, SUB-TOTAL, COLUMN-TOTAL, and ROW-TOTAL). However, in many Focus programs you will be required to perform arithmetic tasks beyond the capabilities of the TABLE commands. In the following TABLE request, we are requesting Focus to perform a simple arithmetic operation.

```
DEFINE FILE STAFF
INCREASE/D10.2=(PCT_INC*SALARY) ;
END
TABLE FILE STAFF
HEADING CENTER
" "
"DOLLAR AMOUNT OF SALARY INCREASE FOR EACH EMPLOYEE"
"IN THE ADMINISTRATION AND FINANCE DEPARTMENTS"
" "
PRINT LAST_NAME
AND SALARY AND
INCREASE
BY DEPT_NAME
IF DEPT_NAME EQ 'ADMINISTRATION' OR 'FINANCE'
ON DEPT_NAME SUB-TOTAL
ON DEPT_NAME PAGE-BREAK
END
```

PAGE   1

DOLLAR AMOUNT OF SALARY INCREASE FOR EACH EMPLOYEE
IN THE ADMINISTRATION AND FINANCE DEPARTMENTS

DEPT_NAME	LAST_NAME	SALARY	INCREASE
ADMINISTRATION	DUXBURY	185,000.00	9,250.00
	ANDERSEN	32,000.00	2,240.00
*TOTAL ADMINISTRATION		217,000.00	11,490.00

PAGE   2

DOLLAR AMOUNT OF SALARY INCREASE FOR EACH EMPLOYEE
IN THE ADMINISTRATION AND FINANCE DEPARTMENTS

DEPT_NAME	LAST_NAME	SALARY	INCREASE
---------	---------	------	--------
FINANCE	TURPIN	65,400.00	3,270.00
	BORGIA	102,000.00	6,120.00
	FREEMAN	34,500.00	.00
*TOTAL FINANCE			
		201,900.00	9,390.00

PAGE   3

DOLLAR AMOUNT OF SALARY INCREASE FOR EACH EMPLOYEE
IN THE ADMINISTRATION AND FINANCE DEPARTMENTS

DEPT_NAME	LAST_NAME	SALARY	INCREASE
---------	---------	------	--------
TOTAL		418,900.00	20,880.00

Basic symbols used in arithmetic operations. In any computer language, you must learn a few of the arithmetic symbols that are used to instruct the computer to perform mathematical operations. Some of the basic symbols are different from what we usually use in everyday life. All the Focus arithmetic operators are described in Table 9.1.

Basic order of execution in arithmetic operations. You must also follow the standard order of evaluation of arithmetic expressions as established by the operating system. The order of evaluation and execution in Focus and most other languages is as follows:

1. ( ) Parentheses
2. ** Exponentiation (or raising to a power of)
3. * Multiplication
4. / Division
5. + Addition
6. − Subtraction

TABLE 9.1 ARITHMETIC OPERATION SYMBOLS

Symbol	Meaning
+	Perform addition of two fields.
−	Perform subtraction of one field from another.
*	Multiply one field by another. (*Note:* This is equivalent to the multiplication sign ×.)
/	Divide one field by another.
**	Raise one field to the power indicated following the double-asterisk ** symbol. For example, 2**3 means raise 2 to the power of 3, or multiply 2 three times by itself (i.e., $2 \times 2 \times 2$ or $2^3 = 8$).

Define Syntax

This means that in any mathematical expression, the value of the figures inside parentheses will be calculated first. If there are several sets of parentheses embedded within each other, the innermost set will be resolved first. Numbers that need to be raised to a power will be calculated next. This is followed by any multiplication, division, addition, and subtraction, in that order.

You must be very explicit in describing an expression. Implicit operations will not be accepted by Focus. For example, $2(A+B)(A-B)$ is perfectly acceptable to human beings but is not acceptable to Focus. The correct format is $2*(A+B)*(A-B)$.

The multiplication and division operations are commutative. In other words, they produce the same result, regardless of the order of execution. The same is true for addition and subtraction. Therefore, $(A*B/C)$ will produce the same result whether you multiply A by B first and then divide the answer by C or divide B by C and then multiply the answer by A. Similarly, $(4+5-3)$ is the same as $(4-3+5)$. However, if you mix multiplication or division operations with addition and/or subtraction operations, the order of execution will determine the result that you are going to get. For example, let's take $(4*5-3)$. If we multiply 4 by 5 and then subtract 3 from the result, we will have 17. On the other hand, if we subtract 3 from 5 and then multiply the result by 4, we will get 8. The following examples should clarify our discussions so far.

1. $(12+5-4*3/4) ** 2$. This expression, as computed by Focus, is equal to 196. First the computer will multiply -4 by 3, which will, as calculated by Focus, result in -12. Next, -12 is divided by 4, which will result in -3. Next, 12 and 5 are added together. This will give 17. The result of $17-3$ is equal to 14, and 14 to the power of 2 is equal to $14 \times 14 = 196$.

$$-4 \ * \ 3 = -12$$
$$-12 \ / \ 4 = \ -3$$
$$12 \ + \ 5 = \ 17$$
$$17 \ - \ 3 = \ 14$$
$$14 \ * \ 14 = \ 196$$

If we had just started performing calculations from left to right, without paying attention to the order of execution, our result would have been 95.0625.

$$12 \quad + 5 \quad = 17$$
$$17 \quad - 4 \quad = 13$$
$$13 \quad * 3 \quad = 39$$
$$39 \quad / 4 \quad = \ 9.75$$
$$9.75 \ * \ 9.75 = 95.0625$$

This is not what Focus will do. Focus will perform the calculation as shown in the previous paragraph and will produce a result of 196. If it is your intention to force Focus to follow your method of calculation, you must construct your expression with parentheses to direct the flow of calculations. If you really wanted Focus to follow the above method strictly and perform calculations from left to right, you would use the following method to describe the action that you wanted to Focus.

$$((((12+5)-4)*3)/4) ** 2 = 95.0625$$

2. $12+5-4*3/4 ** 2$. This expression is equal to 16.25. Remember that there are no parentheses here. So the exponentiation, or raising to the power, will occur first. 4 to the power of 2 is $4 \times 4 = 16$. Next, -4 is multiplied by 3, giving us -12. Next, -12 is divided by 16, which will give us -0.75. Finally, 12 and 5 are added to each other and -0.75 is subtracted from that total to produce a final total of 16.25.

$$
\begin{array}{rcl}
4 ** 2 & = & 16 \\
-4 * 3 & = & -12 \\
-12 / 16 & = & -0.75 \\
12 + 5 & = & 17 \\
17 - 0.75 & = & 16.25
\end{array}
$$

3. $12+(5-4*3)/4 ** 2$. This expression is equal to 11.5625.

$$
\begin{array}{rcl}
-4 * 3 & = & -12 \\
5 - 12 & = & -7 \\
4 * 4 & = & 16 \\
-7 / 16 & = & -0.4375 \\
12 - 0.4375 & = & 11.5625
\end{array}
$$

So, when in doubt, use parentheses. You can always use parentheses to direct the way calculations are performed.

You can also perform complex arithmetic operations. For example, in the following program we must first calculate the amount of increase for each employee by multiplying current salary by the percentage of increase field (PCT_INC). The next several statements are directed to determining the deductions, both compulsory and voluntary, that each employee has to make. Finally, each employee's new annual and monthly increase is calculated. The TABLE request, which follows the DEFINE command, prints the result of all these calculated fields. It also performs a sort on the INCREASE field, which is a defined field. As you can see, DEFINEd fields are treated just like real fields in Focus.

```
DEFINE FILE STAFF
INCREASE/D10.2=(PCT_INC*SALARY) ;
NEW_SAL/D12.2=(SALARY+INCREASE) ;
EXTRA_SSN/D10.2=(INCREASE * .072) ;
EXTRA_FTAX/D10.2=(INCREASE * .28) ;
EXTRA_STAX/D10.2=(INCREASE * .09) ;
HEALTH/D10.2=(INCREASE *.01) ;
OTHER_DED/I2= 20 ;
NET_INCRS/D8.2=
(INCREASE-((EXTRA_SSN+EXTRA_FTAX+EXTRA_STAX)+(HEALTH+OTHER_DED)));
NET_MONTH/D6.2=NET_INCRS / 12 ;
END
TABLE FILE STAFF
HEADING CENTER
"    "
"NET MONTHLY TAKE HOME PAY PER PERSON AFTER DEDUCTION OF"
"ALL FEDERAL, STATE, SOCIAL SECURITY TAXES, AND OTHER DEDUCTIONS"
"    "
```

```
PRINT LAST_NAME/A12
AND SALARY AS 'CURRENT,SALARY' AND NEW_SAL AS 'NEW,SALARY'
AND INCREASE AS 'GROSS,YEARLY,INCREASE'
AND NET_INCRS AS 'NET,MONTHLY,INCREASE'
AND NET_MONTH AS 'NET,MONTHLY,INCREASE'
BY HIGHEST INCREASE NOPRINT
IF INCREASE GT 0
END
```

Also note the following:

1. I wanted to see the entire report on the screen without scrolling to the left and to the right. I therefore reduced the LAST_NAME field to 12 characters at print time. See my code above.

2. One of the employees did not receive a salary increase. However, since we had a fixed deduction of $20.00, the net increase for that employee would have been displayed as a negative figure. I used the statement IF INCREASE GT 0 to exclude that record from printing. Later I will show you how to screen a record before the calculation begins.

I cannot overemphasize the importance of putting parentheses in correctly. If you remove any of the parentheses in the NET_INCRS expression, you will almost certainly get a different result. Always check your calculations manually with a few records before moving your program into production.

PAGE   1

NET MONTHLY TAKE HOME PAY PER PERSON AFTER DEDUCTION OF
ALL FEDERAL, STATE, SOCIAL SECURITY TAXES, AND OTHER DEDUCTIONS

LAST_NAME	CURRENT SALARY	NEW SALARY	GROSS YEARLY INCREASE	NET YEARLY INCREASE	NET MONTHLY INCREASE
DUXBURY	185,000.00	194,250.00	9,250.00	5,049.00	420.75
HUNT	57,000.00	63,270.00	6,270.00	3,415.96	284.66
BORGIA	102,000.00	108,120.00	6,120.00	3,333.76	277.81
ZARKOV	47,000.00	52,170.00	5,170.00	2,813.16	234.43
TAHANIEV	55,400.00	60,386.00	4,986.00	2,712.33	226.03
JAMESON	36,700.00	40,370.00	3,670.00	1,991.16	165.93
TURPIN	65,400.00	68,670.00	3,270.00	1,771.96	147.66
BOCHARD	35,000.00	38,150.00	3,150.00	1,706.20	142.18
GREENSTREET	45,600.00	48,336.00	2,736.00	1,479.33	123.28
TAYLOR	26,550.00	29,205.00	2,655.00	1,434.94	119.58
CAMPOS	32,000.00	34,560.00	2,560.00	1,382.88	115.24
MORALES	39,400.00	41,764.00	2,364.00	1,275.47	106.29
ANDERSEN	32,000.00	34,240.00	2,240.00	1,207.52	100.63
TRENT	22,500.00	24,300.00	1,800.00	966.40	80.53
COLE	39,000.00	40,560.00	1,560.00	834.88	69.57

I will now show you another complex DEFINE command. This time, we will perform the compound interest calculation. The formula for compound interest calculation is as follows:

$$S = P(1 + i)^n$$

where S = compound amount, or the principal and interest at the end of the nth period
P = original principal
i = interest rate in each period
n = number of periods

As an example, let us take $10,000 and invest it in a money market fund. We could invest it at a bank that will compound interest monthly for a year at an interest rate of 12 percent. At the end of 1 year we should have $11,268.25 in our account.

$$S = 10,000 \times (1 + (0.12/12))^{12} = \$11,268.25$$

If the interest was compounded daily for 365 days, the formula is the same. The result is somewhat higher.

$$S = 10,000 \times (1 + (0.12/365))^{365} = \$11,274.75$$

We are using the same formula in the following TABLE request. Let us assume that our organization paid the salary increases in one lump sum at the beginning of the year—without any deductions—and our employees had a choice of investing the amounts at two different banks. Both banks were offering 12 percent interest on deposits. However, one was advertising a daily compounding of interest, whereas the other was compounding monthly. The following DEFINE commands and the TABLE request compute the amount of principal and interest that each employee would have after 12 months, depending on the two different compounding techniques.

```
DEFINE FILE STAFF
INCREASE/D10.2= (SALARY*PIN)  ;
S/D10.2=  INCREASE*(1+(.12/12)) ** 12 ;
S1/D10.2=  INCREASE*(1+(.12/365)) ** 365 ;
END
TABLE FILE STAFF
HEADING CENTER
"  "
"EFFECT OF MONTHLY AND DAILY COMPOUNDING OF INTEREST"
"AFTER ONE YEAR ON A DEPOSIT"
"  "
"THE INTEREST RATE IS 12 PERCENT"
"  "
PRINT LAST_NAME AND INCREASE AS 'INITIAL,DEPOSIT'
AND S AS 'PRINCIPAL AND,INTEREST:,WITH,MONTHLY,COMPOUNDING'
AND S1 AS 'PRINCIPAL AND,INTEREST:,WITH,DAILY,COMPOUNDING'
BY HIGHEST INCREASE NOPRINT
IF INCREASE GT 0
END
```

EFFECT OF MONTHLY AND DAILY COMPOUNDING OF INTEREST
AFTER ONE YEAR ON A DEPOSIT

THE INTEREST RATE IS 12 PERCENT

LAST_NAME	INITIAL DEPOSIT	PRINCIPAL AND INTEREST: WITH MONTHLY COMPOUNDING	PRINCIPAL AND INTEREST: WITH DAILY COMPOUNDING
DUXBURY	9,250.00	10,423.13	10,429.14
HUNT	6,270.00	7,065.19	7,069.27
BORGIA	6,120.00	6,896.17	6,900.14
ZARKOV	5,170.00	5,825.69	5,829.04
TAHANIEV	4,986.00	5,618.35	5,621.59
JAMESON	3,670.00	4,135.45	4,137.83
TURPIN	3,270.00	3,684.72	3,686.84
BOCHARD	3,150.00	3,549.50	3,551.55
GREENSTREET	2,736.00	3,082.99	3,084.77
TAYLOR	2,655.00	2,991.72	2,993.45
CAMPOS	2,560.00	2,884.67	2,886.34
MORALES	2,364.00	2,663.81	2,665.35
ANDERSEN	2,240.00	2,524.09	2,525.54
TRENT	1,800.00	2,028.29	2,029.45
COLE	1,560.00	1,757.85	1,758.86

As you can see, the effect of compounding is not that dramatic for smaller amounts over a short period of time. However, you will get far better results if you compound interest over a longer period of time. Try the same TABLE request with other periods, such as 20 years or more, and see the results.

Normally, all DEFINE expressions are related to real fields. For example, in BONUS/D10.2=(SALARY*1.08), the salary field is a real field. However, you may want to create a field that has no relation to the real fields in your file. In this case you must link this field with another real field or DEFINEd field with the WITH statement. For example, IRA/D10.2 WITH SALARY = 2000. This is just a temporary association and will not affect your file.

```
DEFINE FILE STAFF
IRA/D10.2 WITH SALARY = 2000 ;
END
TABLE FILE STAFF
PRINT LAST_NAME AND SALARY AND IRA
IF SALARY LT 45000
END
```

```
LAST_NAME                     SALARY            IRA
---------                     ------            ---
FREEMAN                    34,500.00       2,000.00
TRENT                      22,500.00       2,000.00
TAYLOR                     26,550.00       2,000.00
COLE                       39,000.00       2,000.00
MORALES                    39,400.00       2,000.00
JAMESON                    36,700.00       2,000.00
ANDERSEN                   32,000.00       2,000.00
BOCHARD                    35,000.00       2,000.00
CAMPOS                     32,000.00       2,000.00
```

EDIT Function

This is a very versatile function. The EDIT function has two basic subfunctions. The first subfunction is conversion. With this function we could convert alphanumeric data to integer data, and vice versa. For example, the following statement converts the employee identification (EMPLOYEE_ID) field from alphanumeric (A type) to numeric (I type).

```
DEFINE FILE STAFF
NUMERIC_ID/I9=EDIT(EMPLOYEE_ID) ;
END
TABLE FILE STAFF
PRINT EMPLOYEE_ID AND NUMERIC_ID
BY LAST_NAME
END
```

PAGE   1

```
LAST_NAME            EMPLOYEE_ID   NUMERIC_ID
---------            -----------   ----------
ANDERSEN             515478922     515478922
BOCHARD              621893221     621893221
BORGIA               513724567     513724567
CAMPOS               432568023     432568023
COLE                 293245178     293245178
DUXBURY              291345672     291345672
FREEMAN              504234521     504234521
GREENSTREET          392345782     392345782
HUNT                 213456682     213456682
JAMESON              413267891     413267891
MORALES              297748301     297748301
TAHANIEV             295738307     295738307
TAYLOR               314562134     314562134
```

```
TRENT                     312562345        312562345
TURPIN                    294728305        294728305
ZARKOV                    312781122        312781122
```

You can now perform mathematical operations on the NUMERIC_ID field.

The following statement converts a numeric field (DATE_HIRE) to an alphanumeric field.

```
DEFINE FILE STAFF
ALPHA_DOH/A6=EDIT(DATE_HIRE) ;
END
TABLE FILE STAFF
PRINT LAST_NAME
AND DATE_HIRE BY ALPHA_DOH AS 'ALPHA,DATE OF,HIRE'
END
```

The ALPHA_DOH has been defined as an alphanumeric field.

```
PAGE      1


ALPHA
DATE OF
HIRE        LAST_NAME                  DATE_HIRE
-------     ----------                 ---------
781012      TURPIN                     78/10/12
791208      FREEMAN                    79/12/08
820807      GREENSTREET                82/08/07
821012      TRENT                      82/10/12
821215      JAMESON                    82/12/15
            BOCHARD                    82/12/15
840915      TAYLOR                     84/09/15
841111      BORGIA                     84/11/11
850809      TAHANIEV                   85/08/09
870323      CAMPOS                     87/03/23
870713      HUNT                       87/07/13
870815      COLE                       87/08/15
880107      ANDERSEN                   88/01/07
880502      ZARKOV                     88/05/02
881118      MORALES                    88/11/18
881210      DUXBURY                    88/12/10
```

Note that you could convert alphanumeric fields to the I type, and vice versa. You cannot, however, convert D- or P-type fields to alphanumeric, and vice versa. If you want to do that, you must first convert them to the I type as follows:

```
DEFINE FILE STAFF
NUMERIC_ID/I9=EDIT(EMPLOYEE_ID) ;
```

```
DECIM_ID/D9=NUMERIC_ID ;
END
TABLE FILE STAFF
PRINT LAST_NAME/A12 AND
EMPLOYEE_ID AND NUMERIC_ID AND DECIM_ID
END
```

PAGE   1

LAST_NAME	EMPLOYEE_ID	NUMERIC_ID	DECIM_ID
TURPIN	294728305	294728305	294,728,305
BORGIA	513724567	513724567	513,724,567
FREEMAN	504234521	504234521	504,234,521
HUNT	213456682	213456682	213,456,682
TRENT	312562345	312562345	312,562,345
TAYLOR	314562134	314562134	314,562,134
COLE	293245178	293245178	293,245,178
MORALES	297748301	297748301	297,748,301
ZARKOV	312781122	312781122	312,781,122
JAMESON	413267891	413267891	413,267,891
DUXBURY	291345672	291345672	291,345,672
ANDERSEN	515478922	515478922	515,478,922
GREENSTREET	392345782	392345782	392,345,782
BOCHARD	621893221	621893221	621,893,221
TAHANIEV	295738307	295738307	295,738,307
CAMPOS	432568023	432568023	432,568,023

Note that to convert a numeric field from one type to another (e.g., I to D) you should not use the word "EDIT" on the right-hand side of the expression. Therefore, in the example above, the correct format, as illustrated, was DEC_ID/D9=NUMERIC_ID.

In the following example, we are converting a decimal (D-type) field to an integer (I-type) field. The integer field is then converted to an alphanumeric field.

```
DEFINE FILE STAFF
I_SALARY/I9=SALARY ;
ALPHA_SALARY/A9=EDIT(I_SALARY) ;
END
TABLE FILE STAFF
PRINT LAST_NAME AND SALARY
I_SALARY AS 'INTEGER,SALARY'
AND ALPHA_SALARY AS 'ALPHA,SALARY'
END
```

```
                                        INTEGER   ALPHA
LAST_NAME                     SALARY     SALARY    SALARY
---------                     ------    -------    ------
TURPIN                     65,400.00      65400    000065400
BORGIA                    102,000.00     102000    000102000
FREEMAN                    34,500.00      34500    000034500
HUNT                       57,000.00      57000    000057000
TRENT                      22,500.00      22500    000022500
TAYLOR                     26,550.00      26550    000026550
COLE                       39,000.00      39000    000039000
MORALES                    39,400.00      39400    000039400
ZARKOV                     47,000.00      47000    000047000
JAMESON                    36,700.00      36700    000036700
DUXBURY                   185,000.00     185000    000185000
ANDERSEN                   32,000.00      32000    000032000
GREENSTREET                45,600.00      45600    000045600
BOCHARD                    35,000.00      35000    000035000
TAHANIEV                   55,400.00      55400    000055400
CAMPOS                     32,000.00      32000    000032000
```

EDIT under mask function. Masking is another form of editing. Masking allows you to insert blanks or special characters within a field. You can also use masking to discard parts of a field at print time. Masking will work only on alphanumeric (A-type) fields. Therefore, to use it on fields with other formats, you must first convert them to alphanumeric format, as I have shown you previously. In using a mask, you will use several characters in a specific way. These characters and their meaning are explained in Table 9.2.

TABLE 9.2 MASK CHARACTERS

Character	Meaning
9	Select the character that is in the same position as the 9 in the mask and print it.
$	Ignore the character that is in the same position as $ in the field.
– or / or any other character	Insert this character in the field in the same position as indicated on the mask.

The following examples will clarify all concepts discussed above.

```
DEFINE FILE STAFF
SSN/A11=EDIT(EMPLOYEE_ID, '999-99-9999') ;
END
TABLE FILE STAFF
PRINT LAST_NAME AND EMPLOYEE_ID AND
```

```
SSN AS 'SOCIAL,SECURITY,NUMBER'
BY LAST_NAME NOPRINT
IF RECORDLIMIT EQ 6
END
```

In this TABLE request we converted EMPLOYEE_ID to the social security format by using the EDIT function. The new field and its format are entered on the left-hand side of the equal sign. On the right-hand side of the equal sign, the word "EDIT" is entered first, followed by the field that is used for masking, followed by a comma, followed by the mask enclosed in single quotation marks. The real field and the mask are enclosed in parentheses. Also, notice that the size of the new field, SSN, has been increased by 2, to 11, to accommodate the hyphens that we have inserted in the EMPLOYEE_ID field.

```
     PAGE      1



                                            SOCIAL
                                            SECURITY
     LAST_NAME            EMPLOYEE_ID        NUMBER
     ---------            -----------        --------
     BORGIA              513724567          513-72-4567
     FREEMAN             504234521          504-23-4521
     HUNT                213456682          213-45-6682
     TAYLOR              314562134          314-56-2134
     TRENT               312562345          312-56-2345
     TURPIN              294728305          294-72-8305
```

In the following example, I used the masking features to separate the area code of a telephone number from the rest of the field. Additionally, to make the phone number more readable, I reformatted the phone number by inserting a hyphen between the prefix and the extension number.

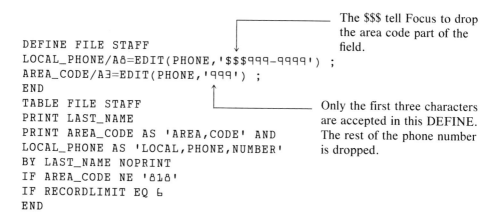

```
DEFINE FILE STAFF
LOCAL_PHONE/A8=EDIT(PHONE,'$$$999-9999') ;
AREA_CODE/A3=EDIT(PHONE,'999') ;
END
TABLE FILE STAFF
PRINT LAST_NAME
PRINT AREA_CODE AS 'AREA,CODE' AND
LOCAL_PHONE AS 'LOCAL,PHONE,NUMBER'
BY LAST_NAME NOPRINT
IF AREA_CODE NE '818'
IF RECORDLIMIT EQ 6
END
```

The $$$ tell Focus to drop the area code part of the field.

Only the first three characters are accepted in this DEFINE. The rest of the phone number is dropped.

Define Syntax

LAST_NAME	AREA CODE	LOCAL PHONE NUMBER
---------	---	-----
BORGIA	212	555-4666
COLE	714	555-0123
FREEMAN	714	555-1234
HUNT	714	555-8428
TRENT	213	555-2911
TURPIN	213	555-1232

In the following example we have used the masking features to join the first initial of the employee name to the last name. Notice how we added a dot after the first initial to make the result more readable. Note that we also used the column-positioning command IN to move the last-name field next to the first-initial field.

```
DEFINE FILE STAFF
FIRST_INIT/A2=EDIT(FIRST_NAME, '9.') ;
END
TABLE FILE STAFF
PRINT FIRST_INIT AS '' AND
LAST_NAME AS 'EMPLOYEE,NAMES'  IN 3
BY LAST_NAME NOPRINT
IF RECORDLIMIT EQ 6
END
```

PAGE   1

EMPLOYEE NAMES

C.BORGIA
D.FREEMAN
C.HUNT
J.TAYLOR
R.TRENT
B.TURPIN

In the following example, we have changed the way that the values of date fields are being printed by adding embedded dashes.

```
DEFINE FILE STAFF
NDOH/A8=EDIT(DOH, '99-99-99') ;
```

```
END
TABLE FILE STAFF
PRINT LAST_NAME AND NDOH AS 'DATE,OF,HIRE'
BY LAST_NAME NOPRINT
IF RECORDLIMIT EQ 6
END


     PAGE     1


                         DATE
                         OF
     LAST_NAME           HIRE
     ---------           ----
     BORGIA              84-11-11
     FREEMAN             79-12-08
     HUNT                87-07-13
     TAYLOR              84-09-15
     TRENT               82-10-12
     TURPIN              78-10-12
```

Concatenation Function

Concatenation, in Focus, is the joining of two or more alphanumeric fields to create a new field. The concatenation symbol is the vertical bar. It will look either like a ¦ in the PC or | in the mainframe environment.

If you create a new field from the combination of two or more fields, you must remember that the length of the new field must be at least as long as the total length of the fields being concatenated. For example, in the DEFINE command

```
DEFINE FILE STAFF
FULLNAME/A30=FN¦LN ;
END
```

the new field called FULLNAME is 30 characters long. This is equal to 10 characters for the first name and 20 characters for the last name.

Additional characters, such as a comma, may be inserted between concatenated fields to help with readability. However, you must enclose them in a pair of single quotation marks.

```
DEFINE FILE STAFF
EMPNAME/A30=FN¦','¦LN ;
END
```

For example:

```
DEFINE FILE STAFF
EMPNAME/A31=FN¦','¦LN  ;
```

```
END
TABLE FILE STAFF
PRINT EMPNAME AS 'EMPLOYEE  NAME'
AND DEPT_NAME AS 'DEPARTMENT,NAME'
IF RECORDLIMIT EQ 6
END


    PAGE     1


                                    DEPARTMENT
    EMPLOYEE  NAME                  NAME
    ---------------                 ----------
    BENTON     ,TURPIN              FINANCE
    CESARE     ,BORGIA              FINANCE
    DIANE      ,FREEMAN             FINANCE
    CHARLES    ,HUNT                OPERATIONS
    RICHARD    ,TRENT               OPERATIONS
    JUANITA    ,TAYLOR              OPERATIONS
```

You could use two vertical bars ¦ ¦ to eliminate the trailing blanks between the two fields.

```
        FULLNAME/A31=FN¦¦(' '¦LN) ;
```

In the following example, I have used a double bar to concatenate the first-name field and the last-name field without the trailing blanks. I have also shown you how to concatenate more than two fields.

```
-*CHAPT9
-*CHAP9-14
DEFINE FILE STAFF
EMPNAME/A31=FN¦¦ (' ' ¦LN) ;
EMPNAME2/A53=DEPT_NAME¦¦': '¦¦FN¦¦','¦¦LN  ;
END
TABLE FILE STAFF
PRINT EMPNAME AS 'EMPLOYEE  NAME'
AND EMPNAME2 AS  'DEPARTMENT,AND,EMPLOYEE NAME'
IF RECORDLIMIT EQ 6
END
```

```
PAGE     1


                                    DEPARTMENT
                                    AND
    EMPLOYEE   NAME                 EMPLOYEE NAME
    --------------                  --------------
    BENTON TURPIN                   FINANCE:BENTON,TURPIN
    CESARE BORGIA                   FINANCE:CESARE,BORGIA
    DIANE FREEMAN                   FINANCE:DIANE,FREEMAN
    CHARLES HUNT                    OPERATIONS:CHARLES,HUNT
    RICHARD TRENT                   OPERATIONS:RICHARD,TRENT
    JUANITA TAYLOR                  OPERATIONS:JUANITA,TAYLOR
```

As I said earlier, concatenation is only available for alphanumeric fields (A type). If you would like to concatenate numeric fields, you should first convert them to A type by using the DEFINE EDIT function.

LAST Function

The LAST function in DEFINE will refer to the last occurrence of the value of a field. This function could only be used on actual Focus data file fields. You could not use it on numbers or on the result of calculations.

```
DEFINE FILE CAR
PREV_MODEL/A24=LAST MODEL ;
END
TABLE FILE CAR
PRINT CAR AND MODEL AND PREV_MODEL
BY COUNTRY
END


    PAGE     1



COUNTRY      CAR          MODEL                   PREV_MODEL
-------      ---          -----                   ----------
ENGLAND      JAGUAR       V12XKE AUTO
             JAGUAR       XJ12L AUTO              V12XKE AUTO
             JENSEN       INTERCEPTOR III         XJ12L AUTO
             TRIUMPH      TR7                     INTERCEPTOR III
FRANCE       PEUGEOT      504 4 DOOR              TR7
ITALY        ALFA ROMEO   2000 4 DOOR BERLINA     504 4 DOOR
             ALFA ROMEO   2000 GT VELOCE          2000 4 DOOR BERLINA
             ALFA ROMEO   2000 SPIDER VELOCE      2000 GT VELOCE
             MASERATI     DORA 2 DOOR             2000 SPIDER VELOCE
JAPAN        DATSUN       B210 2 DOOR AUTO        DORA 2 DOOR
```

Note that the first PREV_MODEL column does not have a value, since there is no value before the first record is read.

DECODE Function

Sometimes, it is necessary to store one- or two-character abbreviations instead of whole field values. This is usually done for the following reasons:

1. To make the information on forms and applications more meaningful to the user
2. To make the data entry easier by reducing the number of key entries
3. To conserve disk storage and speed up transfer time to and from the disk units

For example, a field called VETERAN STATUS on an employee application form may be followed by a little box and instructions to enter either Y or N in that box. This design satisfies all of the requirements above. It is very easy for the person filling the form. It will conserve disk storage, and therefore fewer data will need to be transferred between the disk and the central processing unit. Finally, it is easier for the data entry operator, since all he or she has to input is either the letter Y or the letter N. Another example is the SEX field in a record. It is usually entered as M or F. Another widely used example is the months in the year. In many instances, the people who are filling the form are only required to enter the month number instead of the entire month name. The end user of data may decide that he or she would want to see the month name spelled out (e.g., February instead of 2).

Focus provides the DECODE function to translate or interpret these codes into more meaningful words at report time. It is necessary to pay attention to the general format of the DECODE function, which follows:

```
DEFINE NEWFIELD/FORMAT= DECODE FIELD NAME(Code1'Result1'
                        Code2'result2'
                        Code3'result3'
                        Else 'Default') ;
```

- The field name that is being decoded could be either alphanumeric or numeric.
- Code is the value in the field that the DECODE will search for.
- Result is the value that will replace the Code value.
- The default or action following ELSE will take place only if the search for the stated codes has not been successful. If the ELSE clause is omitted, Focus will assign either a zero or a blank to replace the value of any code that does not match the specified codes.
- The list of DECODE and the result can be up to a maximum of 40 pairs long.

In the following program, I have used the DECODE function to print the words "SENIOR STAFF" every time that it comes across the word "MANAGER" and "MIDDLE MANAGEMENT" for "supervisors." Other members of staff are treated as nonmanagers.

```
DEFINE FILE STAFF
POSITION/A19=DECODE TITLE(MANAGER 'SENIOR STAFF'
PRESIDENT 'SENIOR STAFF'
SUPERVISOR 'MIDDLE MANAGEMENT' ELSE 'NONMANAGERIAL') ;
END
TABLE FILE STAFF
PRINT LAST_NAME AND TITLE AND POSITION
IF RECORDLIMIT EQ 6
END
```

```
   PAGE     1


   LAST_NAME               JOB_TITLE               POSITION
   ---------               ---------               --------
   TURPIN                  HEAD ACCOUNTANT         NONMANAGERIAL
   BORGIA                  LIAISON MANAGER         NONMANAGERIAL
   FREEMAN                 SUPERVISOR              MIDDLE MANAGEMENT
   HUNT                    MANAGER                 SENIOR STAFF
   TRENT                   SERVICE REP.            NONMANAGERIAL
   TAYLOR                  SERVICE REP.            NONMANAGERIAL
```

In the following example, I have made rather extensive use of Edit and the DECODE commands. First, I changed the date of hire (DATE_HIRE), which is integer type (I) to alphanumeric type (A type). Next, I used the masking function of the DEFINE EDIT command to separate the year from the month and day. Next, I used the DECODE function to translate month numbers to month names. Finally, I used the concatenation function to attach the month name to the day and the year.

In the TABLE request that follows the DEFINE command, I selected the employee last-name field and the new date field (ALPHA_DOH) for printing. Also notice that I sorted the report by the DATE_HIRE field to make sure that the employees are printed in order of date of hire. However, it was not necessary to print this field as well, so I suppressed its printing.

```
DEFINE FILE STAFF
TEMPDATE/A6=EDIT(DATE_HIRE,'999999') ;
TEMPYEAR/A2=EDIT(TEMPDATE,'99$$$$') ;
TEMPMONTH/A2=EDIT(TEMPDATE,'$$99$$') ;
TEMPDAY/A2=EDIT(TEMPDATE,'$$$$99') ;
ALPHAMONTH/A9=DECODE TEMPMONTH(01 'JANUARY' 02 'FEBRUARY'
03 'MARCH' 04 'APRIL' 05 'MAY' 06 'JUNE' 07 'JULY'
08 'AUGUST' 09 'SEPTEMBER' 10 'OCTOBER' 11 'NOVEMBER'
12 'DECEMBER' ELSE 'ERROR') ;
ALPHA_DOH/A20=
ALPHAMONTH¦ ' ' ¦TEMPDAY¦ ',' ¦ ' ' ¦ TEMPYEAR ;
END
TABLE FILE STAFF
PRINT LAST_NAME AND ALPHA_DOH AS 'DATE OF HIRE'
```

```
BY DATE_HIRE NOPRINT
IF RECORDLIMIT EQ 8
END


  PAGE    1


LAST_NAME                DATE OF HIRE
---------                ------------
  TURPIN                 OCTOBER   12, 78
  FREEMAN                DECEMBER  08, 79
  TRENT                  OCTOBER   12, 82
  TAYLOR                 SEPTEMBER 15, 84
  BORGIA                 NOVEMBER  11, 84
  HUNT                   JULY      13, 87
  COLE                   AUGUST    15, 87
  MORALES                NOVEMBER  18, 88
```

The following example is important in the sense that the DECODE function has been used to encode longer functional names into numbers from 1 to 5. I used the new field that I created (DEPT_CODE) to sort the file. I deliberately did not encode the section name, to show you the difference in the amount of space that would be saved by using codes.

```
DEFINE FILE STAFF
DEPT_CODE/A1=DECODE DEPT_NAME (ADMINISTRATION '1'
OPERATIONS '2' MIS '3' MARKETING '4' FINANCE '5' ELSE '6') ;
END
TABLE FILE STAFF
PRINT SECTION_NAME AS 'SECTION,NAME'
AND LAST_NAME AS 'EMPLOYEE,LAST,NAME'
BY DEPT_CODE AS 'DEPARTMENT,CODE'
END

  PAGE    1


                                       EMPLOYEE
DEPARTMENT   SECTION                   LAST
CODE         NAME                      NAME
----------   -------                   --------
  1          EXECUTIVE                 DUXBURY
             EXECUTIVE                 ANDERSEN
  2          ENGINEERING               HUNT
             CUSTOMER SERVICES         TRENT
             CUSTOMER SERVICES         TAYLOR
  3          DEVELOPMENT               GREENSTREET
             DEVELOPMENT               BOCHARD
             OPERATIONS                TAHANIEV
```

```
          OPERATIONS              CAMPOS
  4       SALES                   COLE
          SALES                   MORALES
          SALES                   ZARKOV
          SALES                   JAMESON
  5       PAYABLES                TURPIN
          PAYABLES                BORGIA
          COLLECTIONS             FREEMAN
```

Finally, the DECODE list could be stored in a separate file and accessed by Focus at execution time. In this way, without touching your program you could create a file and allow the user to modify the contents as the need arises. The syntax of this type of DECODE is as follows:

```
DECODE field name (filename ELSE default) ;
```

The filename is the name of the file that holds the list of pairs that could be up to 40. This file must be defined to Focus before execution by either the FILEDEF command or the ALLOCATE command.

In the following example, I first created a file called MFILE and keyed in the DECODE pairs as shown.

```
01 'JANUARY'
02 'FEBRUARY'
03 'MARCH'
04 'APRIL'
05 'MAY'
06 'JUNE'
07 'JULY'
08 'AUGUST'
09 'SEPTEMBER'
10 'OCTOBER'
11 'NOVEMBER'
12 'DECEMBER'
```

Next, I modified one of the previous programs in this chapter that translated the numbers of month into month names, and pointed it to that file.

```
-*CHAPT9
-*CHAP9-19
DEFINE FILE STAFF
TEMPDATE/A6=EDIT(DATE_HIRE,'999999') ;
TEMPYEAR/A2=EDIT(TEMPDATE,'99$$$$') ;
TEMPMONTH/A2=EDIT(TEMPDATE,'$$99$$') ;
TEMPDAY/A2=EDIT(TEMPDATE,'$$$$99') ;
ALPHAMONTH/A9=
DECODE TEMPMONTH(MFILE ELSE 'ERROR') ;       ← This statement refers Focus to
                                                the MFILE, which contains
ALPHA_DOH/A20=                                  the DECODE pairs.
```

```
ALPHAMONTH¦ ' ' ¦TEMPDAY¦ ',' ¦ ' ' ¦ TEMPYEAR ;
END
TABLE FILE STAFF
PRINT LAST_NAME AND ALPHA_DOH AS 'DATE OF HIRE'
BY DATE_HIRE NOPRINT
IF RECORDLIMIT EQ 8
END
```

Before executing the program, you must allocate that file.

In the PC/Focus environment, you will code something as follows:

```
FILEDEF MFILE DISK MFILE.DAT
```

The VM/CMS equivalent would be

```
CMS FILEDEF MFILE DISK MFILE DATA A
```

The MVS/TSO equivalent would be

```
TSO ALLOCATE F(MFILE) DA('MFILE.DATA')SHR
```

Define Logical Conditions

This DEFINE is probably the most powerful of the DEFINE commands. In a way it is like a miniprogramming language within Focus. It allows you to use IF, THEN, and ELSE statements to perform simple or very complex logical and conditional tests.

1. Comparing two fields in the same file
2. Using Contains and Omits in the DEFINE to screen records prior to the Table request
3. Performing arithmetic operation within the DEFINE expression and screening the records based on the result of operations
4. Using compound IF statements (OR and AND) separately or together
5. Using the negated IF statement (e.g., IF NOT in the DEFINE command)
6. Using embedded IFs and IF, THEN, ELSE statements

Comparing two fields in the same file. As you may remember from a previous chapter, you cannot compare two fields in the same file with each other with the IF statement in the TABLE request. This deficiency has been rectified with the introduction of the WHERE clause in Focus. The WHERE clause may or may not be available at your site. Also, the WHERE clause was not available prior to 1989 and you may be required to maintain or modify those older programs for years to come. To compare two fields together with the IF statement, you use the DEFINE command as follows.

```
-*CHAP9.
-*CHAP9-20
```

```
DEFINE FILE CAR
PRICE_ERROR/A11=IF RETAIL_COST LT DEALER_COST
                THEN 'ERROR'
                ELSE ' ' ;
END
TABLE FILE CAR
PRINT CAR AND DEALER_COST AS 'DEALER,COST'
AND RETAIL_COST AS 'RETAIL,COST'
AND PRICE_ERROR AS 'COST,ERROR'
BY COUNTRY
IF RECORDLIMIT EQ 8
END
```

Remember that the CAR file at your installation may have different values from
those at my data center. Therefore, the result of your Table request may be
different from mine. However, the logic of this program is correct and will work
on any file.

```
    PAGE      1


                                  DEALER   RETAIL  COST
    COUNTRY     CAR               COST     COST    ERROR
    -------     ---               -----    ------  -----
    ENGLAND     JAGUAR            7,427     8,878
                JAGUAR           11,194    13,491
                JENSEN          14,940    17,850
                TRIUMPH          4,292     5,100
    FRANCE      PEUGEOT          4,631     5,610
    ITALY       ALFA ROMEO       6,915     5,925   ERROR
                ALFA ROMEO       5,660     6,820
                ALFA ROMEO       5,660     6,820
```

Using CONTAINS and OMITS.   You can use CONTAINS and OMITS to
screen records based on the value of one part or all of a field. In the following
example I have used the CONTAINS clause to select the titles president, manager, head, and supervisor anywhere in the job title field. Next, I issued two IF,
THEN, ELSE statements to make my first selection. Finally, in the TABLE
request part of the program, I sorted my report by the new field (POSITION). I
have, in effect, created a tabular organization chart with the staff in title order. I
could have refined this report further by making a selection by seniority (i.e.,
based on the date of hire) or salary. You can use this technique on any file.

```
-*CHAPT9
-*CHAP9-21
DEFINE FILE STAFF
POSITION/A19=IF TITLE CONTAINS 'MANAGER'
OR 'PRESIDENT'
THEN '1'
```

```
ELSE IF TITLE CONTAINS 'SUPERVISOR' OR 'HEAD'
THEN '2'
ELSE  '3' ;
END
TABLE FILE STAFF
PRINT LAST_NAME/A12 AS 'LAST NAME'
AND TITLE  AS 'JOB TITLE'
BY DEPT_NAME AS 'DEPARTMENT,NAME'
BY POSITION NOPRINT
END
```

```
PAGE     1


DEPARTMENT
NAME                    LAST NAME       JOB TITLE
----------              ----------      ----------
ADMINISTRATION          DUXBURY         PRESIDENT
                        ANDERSEN        EXECUTIVE ASSISTANT
FINANCE                 BORGIA          LIAISON MANAGER
                        TURPIN          HEAD ACCOUNTANT
                        FREEMAN         SUPERVISOR
MARKETING               COLE            SALES REPRESENTATIVE
                        MORALES         SALES REPRESENTATIVE
                        ZARKOV          SALES REPRESENTATIVE
                        JAMESON         SALES REPRESENTATIVE
MIS                     TAHANIEV        MANAGER, DATA CENTER
                        GREENSTREET     SENIOR PROGRAMMER
                        BOCHARD         OPERATOR
                        CAMPOS          OPERATOR
OPERATIONS              HUNT            MANAGER
                        TRENT           SERVICE REP.
                        TAYLOR          SERVICE REP.
```

In the following example, I have mixed numeric and alphanumeric fields together and used the IF, THEN, ELSE statement and the greater-than (GT) relation. Briefly, I wanted to select anybody who was making more than $45,000 or lived in the city of Los Angeles. The new field that I created under the DEFINE command is called FLAG. A FLAG is usually used to help distinguish one type of field or value from another. So I FLAGged a record, so to speak, if either the value of salary field was greater than $45,000 or the city field was equal to Los Angeles. In the TABLE request, I checked for the FLAG value and printed only records FLAGged as '1'.

```
-*CHAPT9
-*CHAP9-22
DEFINE FILE STAFF
FLAG/A1=IF SALARY GT  45000  OR
CITY EQ 'LOS ANGELES' THEN '1' ELSE '0' ;
END
```

```
TABLE FILE STAFF
PRINT LAST_NAME/A12 AS 'LAST NAME'
AND CITY AND SALARY
IF FLAG EQ '1'
END


    PAGE     1


    LAST NAME     CITY               SALARY
    ---------     ----               ------
    TURPIN        LOS ANGELES        65,400.00
    BORGIA        NEW YORK          102,000.00
    HUNT          ORANGE             57,000.00
    TRENT         LOS ANGELES        22,500.00
    ZARKOV        ANAHEIM            47,000.00
    DUXBURY       IRVINE            185,000.00
    GREENSTREET   LAKEWOOD           45,600.00
    TAHANIEV      SANTA ANA          55,400.00
```

Performing arithmetic operations within the DEFINE command. You can perform arithmetic operations as part of the DEFINE logical conditions command. The result of the arithmetic operations will determine the direction that you must take in your program. In the following program, in the first DEFINE command, I perform two arithmetic calculations within an IF statement. Based on the results of the calculations I set the FLAG field to either 1 or 0. In the second expression, I calculate the difference between the two salary increases. The third and fourth expressions were single-operation statements.

```
-*CHAPT9
-*CHAP9-22
DEFINE FILE STAFF
FLAG/A1=IF SALARY*PCT_INC LT SALARY*.08
THEN '1' ELSE '0' ;
DIFFERENCE/D10.2CR=SALARY*.08 - SALARY*PCT_INC ;
PLANNED_INC/D10.2=SALARY*PIN ;
SUGGEST_INC/D10.2=SALARY*.08 ;
END
TABLE FILE STAFF
HEADING CENTER
"  "
"EFFECT OF INCREASING ALL THE SALARIES BY 8 PERCENT INSTEAD OF"
"  "
"THE ORIGINALLY PLANNED INCREASE"
"  "
PRINT LAST_NAME/A12 AS 'LAST NAME'
AND SALARY AS 'CURRENT,SALARY'
AND PLANNED_INC AS 'PLANNED,INCREASE'
```

```
AND SUGGEST_INC AS 'SUGGESTED,INCREASE'
AND DIFFERENCE
AND COLUMN-TOTAL
IF FLAG EQ '1'
END
```

The resulting report lists the employees who were scheduled to receive less than an 8 percent increase and lets me know the effect on their salaries and the extra cost to the company if we increased their salaries by exactly 8 percent instead.

```
PAGE     1

EFFECT OF INCREASING ALL THE SALARIES BY 8 PERCENT INSTEAD OF

       THE ORIGINALLY PLANNED INCREASE


                    CURRENT      PLANNED     SUGGESTED
LAST NAME           SALARY       INCREASE    INCREASE     DIFFERENCE
---------           -------      --------    ---------    ----------
TURPIN              65,400.00    3,270.00    5,232.00     1,962.00
BORGIA             102,000.00    6,120.00    8,160.00     2,040.00
FREEMAN             34,500.00         .00    2,760.00     2,760.00
COLE                39,000.00    1,560.00    3,120.00     1,560.00
MORALES             39,400.00    2,364.00    3,152.00       788.00
DUXBURY            185,000.00    9,250.00   14,800.00     5,550.00
ANDERSEN            32,000.00    2,240.00    2,560.00       320.00
GREENSTREET         45,600.00    2,736.00    3,648.00       912.00

TOTAL
                   542,900.00   27,540.00   43,432.00    15,892.00
```

Using compound IF statements.   As you have seen so far, we have used the IF compound statement several times in our examples. You could use the AND and/or OR in any conditional statement. In the following example, I am using the IF statement with AND and OR in the same DEFINE expression. In this program, I am trying to select only employees who work for either the marketing department or the MIS department and have started working for the company since the first day of January 1983.

```
-*CHAPT9
-*CHAP9-24
DEFINE FILE STAFF
ELIG/A14= IF DATE_HIRE GE 830101
AND ( DEPT_NAME EQ 'MARKETING' OR  DEPT_NAME EQ 'MIS')
THEN 'ELIGIBLE'
ELSE 'NOT ELIGIBLE'  ;
END
```

```
TABLE FILE STAFF
PRINT LAST_NAME/A12 AS 'LAST,NAME'
AND DATE_HIRE AS 'DATE,OF HIRE'
AND ELIG AS 'ELIGIBILITY,STATUS'
BY DEPT_NAME AS 'DEPARTMENT,NAME'
END
```

```
PAGE      1


DEPARTMENT            LAST          DATE      ELIGIBILITY
NAME                 NAME          OF HIRE   STATUS
----------           ----          -------   -----------

ADMINISTRATION       DUXBURY       88/12/10  NOT ELIGIBLE
                     ANDERSEN      88/01/07  NOT ELIGIBLE
FINANCE              TURPIN        78/10/12  NOT ELIGIBLE
                     BORGIA        84/11/11  NOT ELIGIBLE
                     FREEMAN       79/12/08  NOT ELIGIBLE
MARKETING            COLE          87/08/15  ELIGIBLE
                     MORALES       88/11/18  ELIGIBLE
                     ZARKOV        88/05/02  ELIGIBLE
                     JAMESON       82/12/15  NOT ELIGIBLE
MIS                  GREENSTREET   82/08/07  NOT ELIGIBLE
                     BOCHARD       82/12/15  NOT ELIGIBLE
                     TAHANIEV      85/08/09  ELIGIBLE
                     CAMPOS        87/03/23  ELIGIBLE
OPERATIONS           HUNT          87/07/13  NOT ELIGIBLE
                     TRENT         82/10/12  NOT ELIGIBLE
                     TAYLOR        84/09/15  NOT ELIGIBLE
```

You could perform many complex calculations with the IF compound statement. However, please remember two items. The first thing is that your IFs should be explicit, not implicit. In other words, I could have said IF DEPT_NAME EQ MARKETING OR MIS instead of repeating the DEPT_ NAME again. Although this may be acceptable in other programming languages, it is not good Focus code. The other suggestion is to try to group your conditions in parentheses if you can. They clarify your intent, both for Focus and for the next person who may be trying to modify your program.

The following program contains another complex statement. The company has decided to lay off all the employees in California who are earning more than $45,000 per year. However, this decision does not apply to the president of the company, who is also a California resident.

```
-*CHAPT9
-*CHAP9-25
DEFINE FILE STAFF
LAYOFF/A10= IF STATE EQ 'CA' AND SALARY GT  45000
AND TITLE NE 'PRESIDENT' THEN 'LAYOFF'
ELSE ' '  ;
```

```
END
TABLE FILE STAFF
PRINT LAST_NAME/A12 AS 'LAST,NAME'
AND DATE_HIRE AS 'DATE,OF HIRE'
AND LAYOFF AS 'LAYOFF,STATUS'
BY DEPT_NAME AS 'DEPARTMENT,NAME'
END
```

PAGE   1

DEPARTMENT NAME	LAST NAME	DATE OF HIRE	LAYOFF STATUS
ADMINISTRATION	DUXBURY	88/12/10	
	ANDERSEN	88/01/07	
FINANCE	TURPIN	78/10/12	LAYOFF
	BORGIA	84/11/11	
	FREEMAN	79/12/08	
MARKETING	COLE	87/08/15	
	MORALES	88/11/18	
	ZARKOV	88/05/02	LAYOFF
	JAMESON	82/12/15	
MIS	GREENSTREET	82/08/07	LAYOFF
	BOCHARD	82/12/15	
	TAHANIEV	85/08/09	LAYOFF
	CAMPOS	87/03/23	
OPERATIONS	HUNT	87/07/13	LAYOFF
	TRENT	82/10/12	
	TAYLOR	84/09/15	

Using the negated IF statement. The negated IF is about the most confusing of the conditional statements. However, it is sometimes preferable to use this type of IF statement. However, most of the time you could use any of the other IF statements instead and get the same results. In the following example, if the department name is not equal to marketing or administration, the employees are targeted for relocation to Oregon.

```
-*CHAPT9
-*CHAP9-26
DEFINE FILE STAFF
RELOCATING/A10= IF NOT(DEPT_NAME EQ 'MARKETING'
OR DEPT_NAME EQ 'ADMINISTRATION') THEN 'RELOCATING'
ELSE 'NO'  ;
END
TABLE FILE STAFF
PRINT LAST_NAME/A12 AS 'LAST,NAME'
AND RELOCATING AS 'RELOCATING,TO,OREGON'
```

```
AND TITLE AS 'JOB,TITLE'
BY DEPT_NAME AS 'DEPARTMENT,NAME'
END


   PAGE     1



                                    RELOCATING
DEPARTMENT          LAST            TO              JOB
NAME                NAME            OREGON          TITLE
----------          ----            ----------      -----
ADMINISTRATION      DUXBURY         NO              PRESIDENT
                    ANDERSEN        NO              EXECUTIVE ASSISTANT
FINANCE             TURPIN          RELOCATING      HEAD ACCOUNTANT
                    BORGIA          RELOCATING      LIAISON MANAGER
                    FREEMAN         RELOCATING      SUPERVISOR
MARKETING           COLE            NO              SALES REPRESENTATIVE
                    MORALES         NO              SALES REPRESENTATIVE
                    ZARKOV          NO              SALES REPRESENTATIVE
                    JAMESON         NO              SALES REPRESENTATIVE
MIS                 GREENSTREET     RELOCATING      SENIOR PROGRAMMER
                    BOCHARD         RELOCATING      OPERATOR
                    TAHANIEV        RELOCATING      MANAGER, DATA CENTER
                    CAMPOS          RELOCATING      OPERATOR
OPERATIONS          HUNT            RELOCATING      MANAGER
                    TRENT           RELOCATING      SERVICE REP.
                    TAYLOR          RELOCATING      SERVICE REP.
```

IF, THEN, ELSE statement.   Several of our examples so far have included the IF, THEN, ELSE logical condition statement. In the following example I have used two IF, THEN, ELSE statements. The first one determines if an employee resides in California and is making more than $34,000 per year. The second logical selection is based on the results of the first DEFINE statement. If the employee meets those two requirements, he or she has a surtax (additional tax) of 5 percent levied on salary above $34,000.

```
-*CHAPT9
-*CHAP9-28
DEFINE FILE STAFF
SELECT/A12=IF STATE EQ 'CA' AND  SALARY GT 34000
          THEN 'EXTRATAX'
          ELSE 'NO EXTRATAX' ;
SURTAX/D10.2= IF SELECT EQ 'EXTRATAX'
          THEN (SALARY-34000)*.05
          ELSE  0 ;
END
TABLE FILE STAFF
PRINT LAST_NAME/A10
```

```
AND SALARY AND SELECT AND SALARY AND SURTAX
BY LAST_NAME NOPRINT
END
```

PAGE   1

LAST_NAME	SALARY	SELECT	SALARY	SURTAX
ANDERSEN	32,000.00	NO EXTRATAX	32,000.00	.00
BOCHARD	35,000.00	EXTRATAX	35,000.00	50.00
BORGIA	102,000.00	NO EXTRATAX	102,000.00	.00
CAMPOS	32,000.00	NO EXTRATAX	32,000.00	.00
COLE	39,000.00	EXTRATAX	39,000.00	250.00
DUXBURY	185,000.00	EXTRATAX	185,000.00	7,550.00
FREEMAN	34,500.00	EXTRATAX	34,500.00	25.00
GREENSTREET	45,600.00	EXTRATAX	45,600.00	580.00
HUNT	57,000.00	EXTRATAX	57,000.00	1,150.00
JAMESON	36,700.00	EXTRATAX	36,700.00	135.00
MORALES	39,400.00	EXTRATAX	39,400.00	270.00
TAHANIEV	55,400.00	EXTRATAX	55,400.00	1,070.00
TAYLOR	26,550.00	NO EXTRATAX	26,550.00	.00
TRENT	22,500.00	NO EXTRATAX	22,500.00	.00
TURPIN	65,400.00	EXTRATAX	65,400.00	1,570.00
ZARKOV	47,000.00	EXTRATAX	47,000.00	650.00

In the final example, I will use two IF, THEN, ELSE statements. Notice that one is embedded or nested within the other one. The logic is as follows: It is the annual bonus time at our company. If an employee is the president or a manager, he or she will get a lump-sum bonus, equivalent to one and a half times his or her annual salary. If the employee is a supervisor or department head, he or she will get only 1.2 times the annual salary. The rest of the employees get only 50 percent of their salaries as lump-sum bonuses. The report is sorted by the highest bonus amount payable to the employee.

```
-*CHAPT9
-*CHAP9-29
DEFINE FILE STAFF
BONUS/D12.2=IF (TITLE CONTAINS 'MANAGER' OR 'PRESIDENT')
        THEN 1.5*SALARY
        ELSE IF (TITLE CONTAINS 'HEAD' OR 'SUPERVISOR')
        THEN 1.2*SALARY
        ELSE .5*SALARY ;
END
TABLE FILE STAFF
PRINT LAST_NAME/A10 AS 'LAST,NAME'
AND SALARY AND BONUS AS 'ANNUAL,BONUS'
AND TITLE AS 'JOB,TITLE'
BY HIGHEST BONUS NOPRINT
END
```

LAST NAME	SALARY	ANNUAL BONUS	JOB TITLE
----	------	------	-----
DUXBURY	185,000.00	277,500.00	PRESIDENT
BORGIA	102,000.00	153,000.00	LIAISON MANAGER
HUNT	57,000.00	85,500.00	MANAGER
TAHANIEV	55,400.00	83,100.00	MANAGER, DATA CENTER
TURPIN	65,400.00	78,480.00	HEAD ACCOUNTANT
FREEMAN	34,500.00	41,400.00	SUPERVISOR
ZARKOV	47,000.00	23,500.00	SALES REPRESENTATIVE
GREENSTREET	45,600.00	22,800.00	SENIOR PROGRAMMER
MORALES	39,400.00	19,700.00	SALES REPRESENTATIVE
COLE	39,000.00	19,500.00	SALES REPRESENTATIVE
JAMESON	36,700.00	18,350.00	SALES REPRESENTATIVE
BOCHARD	35,000.00	17,500.00	OPERATOR
ANDERSEN	32,000.00	16,000.00	EXECUTIVE ASSISTANT
CAMPOS	32,000.00	16,000.00	OPERATOR
TAYLOR	26,550.00	13,275.00	SERVICE REP.
TRENT	22,500.00	11,250.00	SERVICE REP.

Date Manipulation

Focus has several ways of date manipulation. You could convert Gregorian dates (e.g., 91/01/22) to Julian dates (e.g., 91022), and vice versa. You could print the name of the days of the week and you could convert YYMMDD date formats to MMDDYY date formats, and vice versa. In the following example, regular Gregorian dates have been converted to Julian dates. Julian date is the actual number of days that have passed since the beginning of the year. For example, 91/01/01 is a Gregorian date. The Julian equivalent is 91001. Also, 90/03/21 in Gregorian is equal to 90080 in Julian. With Julian dates, sorting is much easier. Also, it is easier to find the difference, in the number of days, between two dates.

```
-*CHAPT9
-*CHAP9-30
DEFINE FILE STAFF
JULIDATE/I6=JULDAT(DOH,JULIDATE) ;
END
TABLE FILE STAFF
PRINT LAST_NAME/A12 AS 'LAST,NAME'
AND JULIDATE AS 'JULIAN,DATE OF,HIRE'
AND DOH AS 'GERGORIAN,DATE OF,HIRE'
AND TITLE AS 'JOB,TITLE'
end
```

```
                    JULIAN     GREGORIAN
LAST                DATE OF    DATE OF      JOB
NAME                HIRE       HIRE         TITLE
----                --------   ----------   -----
TURPIN                 78285   78/10/12     HEAD ACCOUNTANT
BORGIA                 84316   84/11/11     LIAISON MANAGER
FREEMAN                79342   79/12/08     SUPERVISOR
HUNT                   87194   87/07/13     MANAGER
TRENT                  82285   82/10/12     SERVICE REP.
TAYLOR                 84259   84/09/15     SERVICE REP.
COLE                   87227   87/08/15     SALES REPRESENTATIVE
MORALES                88323   88/11/18     SALES REPRESENTATIVE
ZARKOV                 88123   88/05/02     SALES REPRESENTATIVE
JAMESON                82349   82/12/15     SALES REPRESENTATIVE
DUXBURY                88345   88/12/10     PRESIDENT
ANDERSEN               88007   88/01/07     EXECUTIVE ASSISTANT
GREENSTREET            82219   82/08/07     SENIOR PROGRAMMER
BOCHARD                82349   82/12/15     OPERATOR
TAHANIEV               85221   85/08/09     MANAGER, DATA CENTER
CAMPOS                 87082   87/03/23     OPERATOR
```

YM.   YM could help you find the number of months between two different days. In the following TABLE request, I have used two ways of calculating the number of months between two dates. The first two DEFINE expressions display the first method. I first calculated the number of days between the date of hire (DOH) and the current system date (&YMD). Next, I divided the result by 30 to obtain the number of months between the two dates.

The second method of calculating the number of months between two dates involves using one of the built-in functions of the Focus DEFINE command. In this case I used the following expression to calculate the difference between the two dates in months:

```
DIFF3/I4=YM(DOH1,YM1,DIFF3) ;
```

However, to use this function, your dates must be either in YYYYMM (year and month, e.g., 199005) or YYMM (e.g., 9005) formats. Since our date of hire and the system date are both in the YMD (year, month, and day, e.g., 90/05/12) format we must first get rid of (truncate) the day's part of our dates and convert the dates to the YYMM format. To achieve this, we must divide the dates by the number 100. The results are the converted dates in YYMM format, which is then used in the expression to obtain the number of months between the date of hire and the current date. I have printed the result from both methods of date conversion side by side so you could see that there is no difference in the output.

```
-*CHAPT9
-*CHAP9-32
DEFINE FILE STAFF
```

```
DIFF1/I6=YMD(DOH,&YMD) ;
DIFF2/I4=DIFF1/30  ;
DOH1/I4=(DOH/100) ;
YM1/I4=(&YMD/100)  ;
DIFF3/I4=YM(DOH1,YM1,DIFF3) ;
END
TABLE FILE STAFF
HEADING CENTER
" "
"LIST OF EMPLOYEES WITH LESS THAN 2 YEARS OF SERVICE"
" "
PRINT LAST_NAME/A12 AS 'LAST,NAME'
AND DATE_HIRE AS 'DATE,OF,HIRE'
AND DIFF1 AS 'NUMBER,OF,DAYS,EMPLOYED'
AND DIFF2 AS 'NO,OF,MONTH,EMPLOYED'
AND DIFF3 AS 'NO,OF,MONTH,EMPLOYED'
IF DIFF1 LT 730
END
```

The number 730 in the TABLE request above is the sum of number of days in 2 years (365 × 2).

```
     PAGE     1


     LIST OF EMPLOYEES WITH LESS THAN 2 YEARS OF SERVICE

                         NUMBER    NO        NO
                  DATE   OF        OF        OF
     LAST         OF     DAYS      MONTH     MONTH
     NAME         HIRE   EMPLOYED  EMPLOYED  EMPLOYED
     ----         ----   --------  --------  --------

     MORALES      88/11/18    489        16        16
     ZARKOV       88/05/02    689        22        22
     DUXBURY      88/12/10    467        15        15
```

AYMD. AYMD allows you to add any number of days to a given date. This feature is specially useful to financial institutions for calculating the maturity dates of certificates of deposits (CDs) and Bonds. In the following example, I have actually used the AYMD function plus a few other DEFINE commands.

1. I added 90 days to the employee date of hire. The new field called DIFF will contain the employee's date of hire plus 90 days.

2. Next, I used the IF, THEN, ELSE statement with compound condition logic (OR) to create a special bonus field. The DEFINE logic in this statement gives an 8 percent bonus to employees who have been employees for less than 90 days or are over 40 years old. Everybody else gets a 4 percent bonus.

3. I calculated the age of each employee as of his or her last birthday, subtracting it from the current date. Note that I divided both the date of birth (DOB) and the current date (&YMD) by 10,000. This is done to get rid of the month and day part of the year.

```
-*CHAPT9
-*CHAP9-33
DEFINE FILE STAFF
DIFF/I6=AYMD(DOH,90,DIFF) ;
NEWDATE/A8=EDIT(DIFF,'99/99/99') ;
BONUS/D10.2=IF(DIFF GT &YMD OR AGE GE 40 )
                THEN (SALARY*.08)
                ELSE (SALARY*.04) ;
AGE/I2=(&YMD/10000)-(DOB/10000) ;

END
TABLE FILE STAFF
HEADING CENTER
" "
"LIST OF EMPLOYEES WHO GET A SPECIAL BONUS"
"AS OF: &DATE"
" "
PRINT LAST_NAME/A12 AS 'LAST,NAME'
AND DOB AS 'DATE,OF BIRTH'
AND AGE AS 'AGE,LAST,BIRTHDAY'
AND DOH AS 'DATE,OF HIRE' AND SALARY
AND BONUS
IF RECORDLIMIT EQ 4
END
```

```
    PAGE    1


            LIST OF EMPLOYEES WHO GET A SPECIAL BONUS
                      AS OF: 03/24/90


                      AGE
    LAST        DATE    LAST      DATE
    NAME      OF BIRTH  BIRTHDAY  OF HIRE    SALARY      BONUS
    ----      --------  --------  -------    ------      -----
    TURPIN    44/03/15      46    78/10/12   65,400.00   5,232.00
    BORGIA    57/07/08      32    84/11/11  102,000.00   4,080.00
    FREEMAN   52/09/06      37    79/12/08   34,500.00   1,380.00
    HUNT      43/09/09      46    87/07/13   57,000.00   4,560.00
```

AYM. This feature will allow you to add any number of months to a date and come up with the new year and month. For example, by adding 18 months to 91/04/15, you will get 92/10/15. In the following program, I used the DEFINE command and AYM to add 12 months to the date of hire. Note that I divided the

date of hire by 100 to remove the days' portion from the date. The date 91/05/12
divided by 100 will yield 91/05. I then added 12 to the number of months and
created the NEWDATE field.

```
-*CHAPT9
-*CHAP9-34
DEFINE FILE STAFF
NEWDATE/I4=AYM((DOH/100),12,NEWDATE) ;
END
TABLE FILE STAFF
HEADING CENTER
" "
"LISTING SHOWING THE EFFECT OF ADDING 12 MONTH"
"TO A DATE"
" "
PRINT LAST_NAME/A12 AS 'LAST,NAME'
AND DOH AS 'DATE,OF HIRE'
AND NEWDATE
IF RECORDLIMIT EQ 4
END

    PAGE     1


    LISTING SHOWING THE EFFECT OF ADDING 12 MONTH
               TO A DATE

    LAST            DATE
    NAME            OF HIRE  NEWDATE
    ----            -------  -------
    TURPIN          78/10/12    7910
    BORGIA          84/11/11    8511
    FREEMAN         79/12/08    8012
    HUNT            87/07/13    8807
```

Format conversion.   Focus also allows you to convert the format of dates
from YMD to MDY, and vice versa. The following DEFINE command will illustrate the ease of this conversion.

```
-*CHAPT9
-*CHAP9-35
DEFINE FILE STAFF
CONVMDY/MDY=DOH ;
CONVDMY/DMY=DOH ;
CONVYMD/YMD=CONVMDY ;
END
TABLE FILE STAFF
HEADING CENTER
" "
```

```
"REPORT SHOWING THE CONVERSION OF DATE FROM ONE"
"FORMAT TO ANOTHER"
" "
PRINT LAST_NAME/A12 AS 'LAST,NAME'
AND DOH AS 'DATE,OF HIRE'
AND CONVMDY AS 'DATE IN,STANDARD,FORMAT'
AND CONVDMY AS 'DATE IN,EUROPEAN,FORMAT'
AND CONVYMD AS 'DATE IN,YEAR MONTH DAY,FORMAT'
IF RECORDLIMIT EQ 6
END
```

As you will remember, the date-of-hire field (DATA_HIRE) is in the metric format. In the TABLE request above, I used the conversion formats MDY, DMY, and YMD to let Focus automatically convert the date of hire from metric to standard and to European format. Finally, I converted the date back to the metric format again to show how easy it is to perform the conversion.

```
    PAGE     1


            REPORT SHOWING THE CONVERSION OF DATE FROM ONE
                        FORMAT TO ANOTHER

                               DATE IN    DATE IN    DATE IN
           LAST        DATE    STANDARD   EUROPEAN   YEAR MONTH DAY
           NAME        OF HIRE FORMAT     FORMAT     FORMAT
           ----        ------- --------   --------   --------------
           TURPIN      78/10/12 10/12/78  12/10/78         78/10/12
           BORGIA      84/11/11 11/11/84  11/11/84         84/11/11
           FREEMAN     79/12/08 12/08/79  08/12/79         79/12/08
           HUNT        87/07/13 07/13/87  13/07/87         87/07/13
           TRENT       82/10/12 10/12/82  12/10/82         82/10/12
           TAYLOR      84/09/15 09/15/84  15/09/84         84/09/15
```

COMPUTE

The COMPUTE statement is very like the DEFINE command. You can use practically all the DEFINE functions that we have so far reviewed. The syntax for a COMPUTE statement is as follows:

```
COMPUTE
FIELD NAME/FORMAT=expression ;
```

Like the DEFINE command, you do not have to repeat the COMPUTE statement for each expression. The main difference between the COMPUTE statement and the DEFINE command is the point of execution. With DEFINE, you actually create fields that are treated just like regular Focus file or external file fields. That means that you could use them as a sort key for sorting your file. You could also

TABLE 9.3 COMPARISON OF DEFINE AND COMPUTE FIELDS

Define fields	Compute fields
Act like real fields within the file	Work on results of SUM, COUNT, LIST, and PRINT (i.e., after the commands have taken effect).
Can be used for sorting	Cannot be sorted; the only way to sort fields created by the Compute statement is to create a HOLD file at the end of the TABLE command and sort that HOLD file later
Are available for use by Focus until you leave Focus or clear them	Compute fields are known to Focus only during the life of the current TABLE request; you cannot use them in the following Focus TABLE requests without reentering them

use a DEFINE field in more than one TABLE request, as long as you do not clear it or leave the Focus session. On the other hand, COMPUTE is created, so to speak, at the time the report is about to be printed. In other words, it works on the results of the Focus TABLE verbs (PRINT, SUM, LIST, and COUNT). Therefore, it cannot be used as a sort key to sort your report by. Also, the COMPUTE statements are available only during execution of the current TABLE request. They disappear after the report is printed. The major differences between the COMPUTE statement and the DEFINE command are summarized in Table 9.3.

In the following TABLE request, I used the DEFINE command to reduce the size of the last-name field to 11. However, my purpose was to show that I could sort my report by this DEFINEd field. The COMPUTE statement is part of the TABLE request. As you will notice, it is very much like a DEFINE command. I have three IF, THEN, ELSE statements, and each has an arithmetic operation embedded in it. However, it is not possible to sort the report by the NEWSAL field, which is a COMPUTE field, although it is possible to sort the report by LAST1 field, because it is a DEFINEd field. This is because, unlike the DEFINE commands, which are executed before the TABLE request, the COMPUTE statements are executed, on the fly, just as the report is going to the printer. It is therefore not available for sorting. Of course, as soon as the report is finished, the NEWSAL and any value in it will disappear and will not be available for other reports. The only way to save the values created by COMPUTE fields is to use either the HOLD or SAVE command at the end of a TABLE request. We could then initiate another TABLE request with the HOLD file as the requested file and perform all the regular TABLE commands, such as printing and sorting, on the HOLD file. We review the HOLD and SAVE commands in Chapter 10.

```
-*CHAPT9
-*CHAP9-36
DEFINE FILE STAFF
LAST1/A11=EDIT(LN,'99999999999') ;
END
TABLE FILE STAFF
PRINT LAST1 AS 'LAST NAME' AND SAL AND COMPUTE
```

```
NEWSAL/P10.2C =
            IF DEPT_NAME EQ 'FINANCE'
            THEN SALARY*1.03
            ELSE
            IF DEPT_NAME EQ 'ADMINISTRATION'
            THEN SALARY*1.04
            ELSE
            IF DEPT_NAME EQ 'MIS'
            THEN SALARY*1.06
            ELSE SALARY*1.02 ;
BY DEPT_NAME
BY LAST1 NOPRINT
END
```

```
PAGE     1


DEPT_NAME               LAST NAME       SALARY          NEWSAL
---------               ---------       ------          ------
ADMINISTRATION          ANDERSEN        32,000.00       33,280.00
                        DUXBURY        185,000.00      192,400.00
FINANCE                 BORGIA         102,000.00      105,060.00
                        FREEMAN         34,500.00       35,535.00
                        TURPIN          65,400.00       67,362.00
MARKETING               COLE            39,000.00       39,780.00
                        JAMESON         36,700.00       37,434.00
                        MORALES         39,400.00       40,188.00
                        ZARKOV          47,000.00       47,940.00
MIS                     BOCHARD         35,000.00       37,100.00
                        CAMPOS          32,000.00       33,920.00
                        GREENSTREE      45,600.00       48,336.00
                        TAHANIEV        55,400.00       58,724.00
OPERATIONS              HUNT            57,000.00       58,140.00
                        TAYLOR          26,550.00       27,081.00
                        TRENT           22,500.00       22,950.00
```

Because COMPUTE executes at report time and does not create a new field, it can be used for certain tasks where DEFINE cannot be used. For example in the following TABLE request, the DEFINE command creates a new field called PRATIO1. Because this field is created at the DEFINE level, it is treated like a real field. As a result, the Focus TABLE command

```
DEFINE FILE CAR
PRATIO1/D6.2=(RETAIL_COST/DEALER_COST);
END
TABLE FILE CAR
SUM RETAIL_COST AS 'RETAIL,COST'
AND DEALER_COST AS 'DEALER,COST'
AND PRATIO1 AS 'DEFINED,PRICE,RATIO'
```

will calculate the PRATIO1 for each car by (1) dividing its retail cost by its dealer cost to obtain PRATIO1, and (2) adding all the PRATIO1's together. Remember, we are using the SUM command here. As a result, if you have more than one car in your inventory (as is the case with Alpha Romeo, BMW, and Jaguar), the result is wrong because it is a sum of ratios (PRATIO1) for every car category in your fleet. If, on the other hand, you had only one car in your fleet, the answer would obviously be correct and that is the case for Audi, Toyota, and a couple of others.

```
    PAGE     1


                                       DEFINED
                        RETAIL   DEALER PRICE
                        COST     COST   RATIO
    CAR
    ---                 ------   ------ -------
    ALFA ROMEO          19,565   18,235   3.27
    AUDI                 5,970    5,063   1.18
    BMW                 58,762   50,500   6.82
    DATSUN               3,139    2,626   1.20
    JAGUAR              22,369   18,621   2.40
    JENSEN              17,850   14,940   1.19
    MASERATI            31,500   25,000   1.26
    PEUGEOT              5,610    4,631   1.21
    TOYOTA               3,339    2,886   1.16
    TRIUMPH              5,100    4,292   1.19
    VOLVO                    0        0    .00
```

The only way to get a correct answer every time is to use the COMPUTE statement. COMPUTE will perform its assigned task—which is dividing the retail cost by dealer cost—at the final moment just before printing the line. Therefore, the sum of values of all the retail costs is divided by the sum of values of all the dealer costs for each car category, and the correct retail-to-dealer ratio is obtained regardless of the number of cars in the inventory.

```
-*CHAP9-37
DEFINE FILE CAR
PRATIO1/D6.2=(RETAIL_COST/DEALER_COST);
END
TABLE FILE CAR
HEADING CENTER
" "
"REPORT SHOWING THE DIFFERENCE BETWEEN USING"
"DEFINE AND COMPUTE IN CALCULATING RATIO"
"  "
SUM RETAIL_COST AS 'RETAIL,COST'
AND DEALER_COST AS 'DEALER,COST'
AND PRATIO1 AS 'DEFINED,PRICE,RATIO'
AND COMPUTE
PRATIO2/D6.2=(RETAIL_COST / DEALER_COST)  ;
```

```
AS 'CORRECT,PRICE,RATIO'
BY CAR
END


   PAGE   1


           REPORT SHOWING THE DIFFERENCE BETWEEN USING
            DEFINE AND COMPUTE IN CALCULATING RATIO
```

```
                                              ┌──────── This is wrong.
                                              │
                                              │
                                              ▼
                                   DEFINED   CORRECT
                        RETAIL    DEALER   PRICE     PRICE
          CAR           COST      COST     RATIO     RATIO
          ───           ──────    ──────   ───────   ───────
          ALFA ROMEO    19,565    18,235    3.27      1.07
          AUDI           5,970     5,063    1.18      1.18
          BMW           58,762    50,500    6.82      1.16
          DATSUN         3,139     2,626    1.20      1.20
          JAGUAR        22,369    18,621    2.40      1.20
          JENSEN        17,850    14,940    1.19      1.19
          MASERATI      31,500    25,000    1.26      1.26
          PEUGEOT        5,610     4,631    1.21      1.21
          TOYOTA         3,339     2,886    1.16      1.16
          TRIUMPH        5,100     4,292    1.19      1.19
          VOLVO              0         0     .00       .00
```

You can also use COMPUTE to create running totals. In the following Table request, I used COMPUTE to create a running serial number or sequence number for each employee. This is separate from the employee identification number (EMPLOYEE_ID). You could use this feature to print a report with running serial numbers. If you use the HOLD command to save the report as a file, you will end up with a new file with the serial number as a real field that could be used in other reports or calculations. Additionally, unlike the LIST command, the serial number does not reset itself to zero every time that a sort field such as department name changes.

```
-*CHAPT9
-*CHAP9-38
TABLE FILE STAFF
PRINT LAST_NAME/A12  AS 'LAST,NAME'
AND SALARY
AND COMPUTE
SERIAL_NO/I6=SERIAL+1 ;
AS 'SERIAL,NO' IN 1
BY DEPT_NAME IN 10
BY LAST_NAME NOPRINT
END
```

```
SERIAL                          LAST
NO         DEPT_NAME            NAME              SALARY
------     ---------            ----              ------
       1   ADMINISTRATION       ANDERSEN        32,000.00
       2                        DUXBURY        185,000.00
       3   FINANCE              BORGIA         102,000.00
       4                        FREEMAN         34,500.00
       5                        TURPIN          65,400.00
       6   MARKETING            COLE            39,000.00
       7                        JAMESON         36,700.00
       8                        MORALES         39,400.00
       9                        ZARKOV          47,000.00
      10   MIS                  BOCHARD         35,000.00
      11                        CAMPOS          32,000.00
      12                        GREENSTREET     45,600.00
      13                        TAHANIEV        55,400.00
      14   OPERATIONS           HUNT            57,000.00
      15                        TAYLOR          26,550.00
      16                        TRENT           22,500.00
```

Another feature that you could use with the COMPUTE statement is to use the column position to perform calculations. Sometimes, especially in reports generated by HOLD files, two columns may have the same title. By using the column position, you could direct your calculations without referring to field names. In the following example, I have summed the maximum and minimum salaries for each department and calculated the difference between the maximum and the minimum by using the COMPUTE statement and the column position. C1 is column 1 and C2 is column 2. Remember that the sort column (in this case the department name column) does not count as a column.

```
-*CHAP9
-*CHAP9-41
TABLE FILE STAFF
HEADING CENTER
" "
"REPORT SHOWING THE USE OF COLUMN NUMBERS"
"IN CALCULATIONS"
" "
SUM MAX.SALARY AND MIN.SALARY
AND COMPUTE
DIFFERENCE/D10.2= C1 - C2 ;
BY DEPT_NAME
END
```

```
            REPORT SHOWING THE USE OF COLUMN NUMBERS
                       IN CALCULATIONS

                         MAX           MIN
DEPT_NAME                SALARY        SALARY      DIFFERENCE
---------                ------        ------      ----------
ADMINISTRATION           185,000.00    32,000.00   153,000.00
FINANCE                  102,000.00    34,500.00    67,500.00
MARKETING                 47,000.00    36,700.00    10,300.00
MIS                       55,400.00    32,000.00    23,400.00
OPERATIONS                57,000.00    22,500.00    34,500.00
```

Using Multiple COMPUTE Statements

Focus allows you to use multiple COMPUTE statements within a Focus TABLE request. This is just like the DEFINE command, and the value of a field created by one COMPUTE statement is immediately usable by the following COMPUTE statements.

```
-*CHAP9
-*CHAP9-42
TABLE FILE STAFF
HEADING CENTER
" "
"REPORT SHOWING THE USE OF MULTIPLE COMPUTES"
" "
PRINT SALARY AND COMPUTE
INCREASE/D10.2=(SALARY*PCT_INC);
ADDED_TAX/D10.2=INCREASE*.28 ;  AS 'ADDITIONAL,TAXES'
BY DEPT_NAME AS 'DEPARTMENT,NAME'
END
```

```
            REPORT SHOWING THE USE OF MULTIPLE COMPUTES

                                                    ADDITIONAL
DEPARTMENT
NAME                     SALARY        INCREASE     TAXES
----------               ------        --------     ----------
ADMINISTRATION           185,000.00    9,250.00     2,590.00
                          32,000.00    2,240.00       627.20
FINANCE                   65,400.00    3,270.00       915.60
                         102,000.00    6,120.00     1,713.60
                          34,500.00        .00           .00
```

MARKETING	39,000.00	1,560.00	436.80
	39,400.00	2,364.00	661.92
	47,000.00	5,170.00	1,447.60
	36,700.00	3,670.00	1,027.60
MIS	45,600.00	2,736.00	766.08
	35,000.00	3,150.00	882.00
	55,400.00	4,986.00	1,396.08
	32,000.00	2,560.00	716.80
OPERATIONS	57,000.00	6,270.00	1,755.60
	22,500.00	1,800.00	504.00
	26,550.00	2,655.00	743.40

SPECIAL FOCUS SUPPLIED FUNCTIONS

Focus provides several additional, powerful functions that you could use in TABLE requests. They are listed below.

ABS	absolute value
INT	integer value (i.e., without decimal parts)
MAX	maximum value
MIN	minimum value
LOG	base e logarithm
SQRT	square root of a number or expression

The most useful of these functions in the business world are the ABS and INT. ABS obtains the absolute value of a number (i.e., without signs). So absolute values of −5 and +5 are the same. INT obtains the integer part of a number [e.g., 5.67 and 5.8 and 5.1 are the same to the integer (INT) function].

In the following TABLE request, you can see that the same number with the ABS function will give a value without signs.

```
-*CHAP9
-*CHAP9-39
DEFINE FILE STAFF
DIFF/P10=ABS(SALARY - (SALARY+SALARY*PIN)) ;
DIFF2/P10=(SALARY - (SALARY+SALARY*PIN)) ;
END
TABLE FILE STAFF
HEADING CENTER
" "
"REPORT SHOWING THE SAME VALUE WITH AND WITHOUT"
"THE ABS FUNCTION"
" "
PRINT LAST_NAME AS 'LAST,NAME'
AND DIFF AND DIFF2
IF RECORDLIMIT EQ 6
END
```

```
REPORT SHOWING THE SAME VALUE WITH AND WITHOUT
            THE ABS FUNCTION

LAST
NAME                        DIFF         DIFF2
----                        ----         -----
TURPIN                      3270         -3270
BORGIA                      6120         -6120
FREEMAN                        0             0
HUNT                        6270         -6270
TRENT                       1800         -1800
TAYLOR                      2655         -2655
```

The following program shows the use of the INT function. You will notice that the formats of both STATE_TAX1 and STATE_TAX2 are the same. The only difference between the two is the INT function. As shown on the report that follows the program, the result is that the DEFINE expression with the INT function will always truncate the decimal values following an integer value.

```
-*CHAP9-40
DEFINE FILE STAFF
STATE_TAX1/D10.2=INT(( SALARY-15000)*.0075);
STATE_TAX2/D10.2=(( SALARY-15000)*.0075) ;
END
TABLE FILE STAFF
HEADING CENTER
" "
"REPORT SHOWING THE SAME VALUE WITH AND WITHOUT"
"THE INT FUNCTION"
" "
PRINT LAST_NAME AS 'LAST,NAME'
AND STATE_TAX1 AND STATE_TAX2
IF RECORDLIMIT EQ 6
END
```

```
REPORT SHOWING THE SAME VALUE WITH AND WITHOUT
            THE INT FUNCTION
```

LAST NAME	STATE_TAX1	STATE_TAX2
----	----------	----------
TURPIN	378.00	378.00
BORGIA	652.00	652.50
FREEMAN	146.00	146.25
HUNT	315.00	315.00
TRENT	56.00	56.25
TAYLOR	86.00	86.63

RECOMPUTE AND SUMMARIZE COMMANDS

In a previous chapter I discussed the SUB-TOTAL and SUBTOTAL commands used to sum sort fields in a Table request. RECOMPUTE and SUMMARIZE are used to calculate totals for computed fields. RECOMPUTE is similar to SUBTOTAL. It will perform all the functions of SUBTOTAL. Additionally, it will calculate correct subtotals for all the computed fields created by the COMPUTE statements in a Table request. SUMMARIZE is similar to SUB-TOTAL. It will also calculate subtotals for the computed fields created by the COMPUTE statement.

The following program creates a ratio between the total amount of deductions from an employee's salary and his or her gross annual salary. As you will notice, the ratio is correct for each individual employee. However, if there are two or more employees in a section, the department level and the grand total level of the ratio are incorrect. This is because when performing the Sub-totaling function, Focus will add the values of all the fields together at each control break level. This will also include the computed fields (i.e., the DED_SALRATIO). The solution in the case of the SUBTOTAL command is the RECOMPUTE command, which will also recalculate ratios at group level.

```
-*SUBTOTAL  COMMAND
DEFINE FILE STAFF
FED_TAX/D9.2 = IF SALARY GT 45000
          THEN SALARY * .34
          ELSE SALARY * .28 ;
OTHER_DED/D9.2 = SALARY * .07 ;
TOTAL_DED/D9.2 = FED_TAX + OTHER_DED   ;
END
TABLE FILE STAFF
HEADING CENTER
"EXAMPLE OF THE SUBTOTAL SUBCOMMAND"
"   "
SUM SALARY AND TOTAL_DED
AND COMPUTE
DED_SALRATIO/D4.2 =TOTAL_DED/SALARY ;
AS 'DEDUCT,SALARY,RATIO'
BY DEPT_NAME AS 'DEPARTMENT'
BY SECTION_NAME
```

Recompute and Summarize Commands

```
BY HIGHEST TOTAL_DED  NOPRINT
ON SECTION_NAME SUBTOTAL AS 'SECTION: '
END
```

PAGE   1

EXAMPLE OF THE SUBTOTAL SUBCOMMAND

```
                                                    DEDUCT
                                                    SALARY
DEPARTMENT           SECTION_NAME       SALARY   TOTAL_DED RATIO
----------           ------------       ------   --------- ----
ADMINISTRATION       EXECUTIVE        185,000.00  75,850.00   .41
                                       32,000.00  11,200.00   .35


SECTION: EXECUTIVE                    217,000.00  87,050.00   .76}─

FINANCE              COLLECTIONS       34,500.00  12,075.00   .35

SECTION: COLLECTIONS                   34,500.00  12,075.00   .35

                     PAYABLES         102,000.00  41,820.00   .41
                                       65,400.00  26,814.00   .41

SECTION: PAYABLES                     167,400.00  68,634.00   .82}─

MARKETING            SALES             47,000.00  19,270.00   .41
                                       39,400.00  13,790.00   .35
                                       39,000.00  13,650.00   .35
                                       36,700.00  12,845.00   .35

SECTION: SALES                        162,100.00  59,555.00  1.46}─

MIS                  DEVELOPMENT       45,600.00  18,696.00   .41
                                       35,000.00  12,250.00   .35

SECTION: DEVELOPMENT                   80,600.00  30,946.00   .76}─

                     OPERATIONS        55,400.00  22,714.00   .41
                                       32,000.00  11,200.00   .35

SECTION: OPERATIONS                    87,400.00  33,914.00   .76}─

OPERATIONS           CUSTOMER SERVICES 26,550.00   9,292.50   .35
                                       22,500.00   7,875.00   .35

SECTION: CUSTOMER SERVICES             49,050.00  17,167.50   .70}─

                     ENGINEERING       57,000.00  23,370.00   .41

SECTION: ENGINEERING                   57,000.00  23,370.00   .41


TOTAL                                 855,050.00 332,711.50  6.02}─
```

All these
values are
incorrect

The following program is almost identical to the preceding program. The only difference is the use of SUB-TOTAL instead of SUBTOTAL. As you will notice, we now also have a total salary, total deduction, and deduction-to-salary ratio for the department field. In the preceding example, these summary lines were not created. However, notice that the ratio of deductions to salary is still inaccurate at the group level. Also, you will notice that in none of these two examples the BY field following the section name has been totaled.

```
-*SUB-TOTAL   COMMAND
DEFINE FILE STAFF
FED_TAX/D9.2 = IF SALARY GT 45000
              THEN SALARY * .34
              ELSE SALARY * .28 ;
OTHER_DED/D9.2 = SALARY * .07 ;
TOTAL_DED/D9.2 = FED_TAX + OTHER_DED   ;
END
TABLE FILE STAFF
HEADING CENTER
"EXAMPLE OF THE SUB-TOTAL SUBCOMMAND"
"  "
SUM SALARY AND TOTAL_DED
AND COMPUTE
DED_SALRATIO/D4.2 =TOTAL_DED/SALARY ;
AS 'DEDUCT,SALARY,RATIO'
BY DEPT_NAME AS 'DEPARTMENT'
BY SECTION_NAME
BY HIGHEST TOTAL_DED NOPRINT
ON SECTION_NAME SUB-TOTAL AS 'SECTION: '
END
```

PAGE   1

EXAMPLE OF THE SUB-TOTAL SUBCOMMAND

DEPARTMENT	SECTION_NAME	SALARY	TOTAL_DED	DEDUCT SALARY RATIO
----------	------------	------	---------	----
ADMINISTRATION	EXECUTIVE	185,000.00	75,850.00	.41
		32,000.00	11,200.00	.35
SECTION: EXECUTIVE		217,000.00	87,050.00	.76
*TOTAL DEPT_NAME ADMINISTRATION		217,000.00	87,050.00	.76
FINANCE	COLLECTIONS	34,500.00	12,075.00	.35
SECTION: COLLECTIONS		34,500.00	12,075.00	.35
	PAYABLES	102,000.00	41,820.00	.41
		65,400.00	26,814.00	.41

Recompute and Summarize Commands

243

```
SECTION: PAYABLES                          167,400.00   68,634.00    .82⎤─
*TOTAL DEPT_NAME FINANCE                    201,900.00   80,709.00   1.17⎦

MARKETING             SALES                 47,000.00   19,270.00    .41
                                            39,400.00   13,790.00    .35
                                            39,000.00   13,650.00    .35
                                            36,700.00   12,845.00    .35

SECTION: SALES                             162,100.00   59,555.00   1.46⎤
*TOTAL DEPT_NAME MARKETING                 162,100.00   59,555.00   1.46⎦

MIS                   DEVELOPMENT           45,600.00   18,696.00    .41 │ These values
                                            35,000.00   12,250.00    .35 │ are incorrect

SECTION: DEVELOPMENT                         80,600.00   30,946.00    .76⎤─

                      OPERATIONS             55,400.00   22,714.00    .41
                                             32,000.00   11,200.00    .35

SECTION: OPERATIONS                          87,400.00   33,914.00    .76⎤
*TOTAL DEPT_NAME MIS                        168,000.00   64,860.00   1.52⎦

OPERATIONS            CUSTOMER SERVICES      26,550.00    9,292.50    .35
                                             22,500.00    7,875.00    .35

SECTION: CUSTOMER SERVICES                   49,050.00   17,167.50    .70⎤─

                      ENGINEERING            57,000.00   23,370.00    .41

SECTION: ENGINEERING                         57,000.00   23,370.00    .41
*TOTAL DEPT_NAME OPERATIONS                 106,050.00   40,537.50   1.11

TOTAL                                       855,050.00  332,711.50   6.02⎤─
```

The RECOMPUTE command will recalculate the result of the computed field (in this case the ratio of TOTAL_DED to SALARY) at the group and grand total level. It is used instead of the SUBTOTAL command only.

```
-*RECOMPUTE  COMMAND
DEFINE FILE STAFF
FED_TAX/D9.2 = IF SALARY GT 45000
            THEN SALARY * .34
            ELSE SALARY * .28 ;
OTHER_DED/D9.2 = SALARY * .07 ;
TOTAL_DED/D9.2 = FED_TAX + OTHER_DED  ;
END
TABLE FILE STAFF
HEADING CENTER
```

```
"EXAMPLE OF THE RECOMPUTE SUBCOMMAND"
"  "
SUM SALARY AND TOTAL_DED
AND COMPUTE
DED_SALRATIO/D4.2 =TOTAL_DED/SALARY ;
AS 'DEDUCT,SALARY,RATIO'
BY DEPT_NAME AS 'DEPARTMENT'
BY SECTION_NAME
BY HIGHEST TOTAL_DED NOPRINT
ON SECTION_NAME RECOMPUTE AS 'SECTION: '
END
```

Note the use of RECOMPUTE
in place of SUBTOTAL.

PAGE   1

EXAMPLE OF THE RECOMPUTE SUBCOMMAND

DEPARTMENT	SECTION_NAME	SALARY	TOTAL_DED	DEDUCT SALARY RATIO
ADMINISTRATION	EXECUTIVE	185,000.00	75,850.00	.41
		32,000.00	11,200.00	.35
SECTION: EXECUTIVE		217,000.00	87,050.00	.40
FINANCE	COLLECTIONS	34,500.00	12,075.00	.35
SECTION: COLLECTIONS		34,500.00	12,075.00	.35
	PAYABLES	102,000.00	41,820.00	.41
		65,400.00	26,814.00	.41
SECTION: PAYABLES		167,400.00	68,634.00	.41
MARKETING	SALES	47,000.00	19,270.00	.41
		39,400.00	13,790.00	.35
		39,000.00	13,650.00	.35
		36,700.00	12,845.00	.35
SECTION: SALES		162,100.00	59,555.00	.37
MIS	DEVELOPMENT	45,600.00	18,696.00	.41
		35,000.00	12,250.00	.35
SECTION: DEVELOPMENT		80,600.00	30,946.00	.38
	OPERATIONS	55,400.00	22,714.00	.41
		32,000.00	11,200.00	.35
SECTION: OPERATIONS		87,400.00	33,914.00	.39

```
OPERATIONS              CUSTOMER SERVICES   26,550.00     9,292.50    .35
                                            22,500.00     7,875.00    .35


SECTION: CUSTOMER SERVICES                  49,050.00    17,167.50    .35

                        ENGINEERING         57,000.00    23,370.00    .41


SECTION: ENGINEERING                        57,000.00    23,370.00    .41



TOTAL                                      855,050.00   332,711.50    .39
```

Finally, SUMMARIZE is similar to RECOMPUTE, except that it replaces SUB-TOTAL to recalculate the group totals and the grand total correctly.

```
-*SUMMARIZE  COMMAND
DEFINE FILE STAFF
FED_TAX/D9.2 = IF SALARY GT 45000
            THEN SALARY * .34
            ELSE SALARY * .28 ;
OTHER_DED/D9.2 = SALARY * .07 ;
TOTAL_DED/D9.2 = FED_TAX + OTHER_DED   ;
END
TABLE FILE STAFF
HEADING CENTER
"EXAMPLE OF THE SUMMARIZE SUBCOMMAND"
"  "
SUM SALARY AND TOTAL_DED
AND COMPUTE
DED_SALRATIO/D4.2 =TOTAL_DED/SALARY ;
AS 'DEDUCT,SALARY,RATIO'
BY DEPT_NAME AS 'DEPARTMENT'
BY SECTION_NAME
BY HIGHEST TOTAL_DED NOPRINT
ON SECTION_NAME SUMMARIZE AS 'SECTION: '
END                       ↑
```
└──────Note the use of SUMMARIZE in place of SUB-TOTAL.

```
    PAGE     1
```

EXAMPLE OF THE SUMMARIZE SUBCOMMAND

```
                                                           DEDUCT
                                                           SALARY
DEPARTMENT          SECTION_NAME        SALARY   TOTAL_DED RATIO
----------          ------------        ------   --------- ----
ADMINISTRATION      EXECUTIVE         185,000.00  75,850.00  .41
                                       32,000.00  11,200.00  .35


SECTION: EXECUTIVE                    217,000.00  87,050.00  .40
*TOTAL DEPT_NAME ADMINISTRATION       217,000.00  87,050.00  .40
```

```
FINANCE                COLLECTIONS         34,500.00   12,075.00    .35

SECTION: COLLECTIONS                       34,500.00   12,075.00    .35

                       PAYABLES           102,000.00   41,820.00    .41
                                           65,400.00   26,814.00    .41

SECTION: PAYABLES                         167,400.00   68,634.00    .41
*TOTAL DEPT_NAME FINANCE                   201,900.00   80,709.00    .40

MARKETING              SALES               47,000.00   19,270.00    .41
                                           39,400.00   13,790.00    .35
                                           39,000.00   13,650.00    .35
                                           36,700.00   12,845.00    .35

SECTION: SALES                            162,100.00   59,555.00    .37
*TOTAL DEPT_NAME MARKETING                162,100.00   59,555.00    .37

MIS                    DEVELOPMENT         45,600.00   18,696.00    .41
                                           35,000.00   12,250.00    .35

SECTION: DEVELOPMENT                       80,600.00   30,946.00    .38

                       OPERATIONS          55,400.00   22,714.00    .41
                                           32,000.00   11,200.00    .35

SECTION: OPERATIONS                        87,400.00   33,914.00    .39
*TOTAL DEPT_NAME MIS                      168,000.00   64,860.00    .39

OPERATIONS             CUSTOMER SERVICES   26,550.00    9,292.50    .35
                                           22,500.00    7,875.00    .35

SECTION: CUSTOMER SERVICES                 49,050.00   17,167.50    .35

                       ENGINEERING         57,000.00   23,370.00    .41

SECTION: ENGINEERING                       57,000.00   23,370.00    .41
*TOTAL DEPT_NAME OPERATIONS               106,050.00   40,537.50    .38


TOTAL                                     855,050.00  332,711.50    .39
```

RECAP COMMAND

RECAP allows you to use subtotal values in a TABLE request calculation. In the following example, I have calculated the departmental net salary after all the deductions. The RECAP command allowed me to subtotal each department salary and total deduction and use them in my calculation without using the SUBTOTAL command. Also, as you will notice, the subtotal values are not printed. Only the DEPT_NET field is printed. You can also use the COMPUTE command instead of RECAP in the statement.

```
-*RECAP COMMAND
DEFINE FILE STAFF
FED_TAX/D9.2 = IF SALARY GT 45000
               THEN SALARY * .34
               ELSE SALARY * .28 ;
OTHER_DED/D9.2 = SALARY * .07 ;
TOTAL_DED/D9.2 = FED_TAX + OTHER_DED  ;
END
TABLE FILE STAFF
HEADING CENTER
"EXAMPLE OF THE RECAP SUBCOMMAND"
"  "
SUM SALARY AND TOTAL_DED
BY DEPT_NAME AS 'DEPARTMENT'
BY LAST_NAME
ON DEPT_NAME
UNDER-LINE RECAP DEPT_NET/D10.2 = SALARY - TOTAL_DED ;
END
```

```
    PAGE     1


               EXAMPLE OF THE RECAP SUBCOMMAND

   DEPARTMENT           LAST_NAME                 SALARY    TOTAL_DED
   ----------           ---------                 ------    ---------
   ADMINISTRATION       ANDERSEN              32,000.00    11,200.00
                        DUXBURY              185,000.00    75,850.00

   ** DEPT_NET                               129,950.00


   -----------------------------------------------------------------
   FINANCE              BORGIA               102,000.00    41,820.00
                        FREEMAN               34,500.00    12,075.00
                        TURPIN                65,400.00    26,814.00

   ** DEPT_NET                               121,191.00


   -----------------------------------------------------------------
   MARKETING            COLE                  39,000.00    13,650.00
                        JAMESON               36,700.00    12,845.00
                        MORALES               39,400.00    13,790.00
                        ZARKOV                47,000.00    19,270.00

   ** DEPT_NET                               102,545.00


   -----------------------------------------------------------------
```

MIS	BOCHARD	35,000.00	12,250.00
	CAMPOS	32,000.00	11,200.00
	GREENSTREET	45,600.00	18,696.00
	TAHANIEV	55,400.00	22,714.00
** DEPT_NET		103,140.00	

OPERATIONS	HUNT	57,000.00	23,370.00
	TAYLOR	26,550.00	9,292.50
	TRENT	22,500.00	7,875.00
** DEPT_NET		65,512.50	

SUMMARY

The DEFINE command is one of the most useful and powerful commands in Focus. There are many variations to this command. As you have noticed in this chapter, we can perform almost any operation with the DEFINE command. More specifically, we created new fields, performed complex arithmetic calculations, connected two separate fields together, performed complex logical operations, and decoded short field values into longer, more meaningful field values. You can also perform various date routines to calculate the elapsed time between two dates or convert one type of date to another.

The COMPUTE statement can perform the same tasks that the DEFINE command can perform. There are two main differences between the two commands. One is that since COMPUTEd fields operate at the result of fields just before printing, they cannot be sorted. The other difference is that DEFINEd fields are treated just like real field by Focus and when it comes to computing ratios and percentages, DEFINEd fields could produce inaccurate results because they accumulate the result of any calculation. On the other hand, COMPUTE acts on the result.

The other features discussed in this chapter were the special functions of Focus, such as ABS and INT. These features are not in everyday use in Focus programming but have specific powers that could save you time in some TABLE requests. Finally, we reviewed SUBTOTAL and SUB-TOTAL and introduced RECOMPUTE, SUMMARIZE, and RECAP.

CHAPTER 10

ADVANCED FEATURES
OF THE FOCUS®
REPORT WRITER

MAIN TOPICS:

- HOLD AND SAVE FILES
- JOINING FILES TOGETHER FOR REPORTING (JOIN AND MATCH)
- STATIC CROSS-REFERENCES
- ALTERNATE VIEWS OF FILE STRUCTURE

Note: Because of the complexity of some of the programs, almost all the important programs in the remaining chapters of this book are identified by a chapter number, i.e., CHAPT10 and a program ID number, i.e. CHAPT10-2. This is done to make it easier to refer to and find particular programs. Program ID numbers within a chapter are for identification and may not be in sequence.

HOLD FILES

In previous chapters we have several times referred to the HOLD file, which can be created by Focus as a by-product of the TABLE request. The syntax of the HOLD command is as follows:

```
HOLD [AS name] [FORMAT format]
```

The HOLD command creates another Focus file from a TABLE request. When you issue the HOLD command, Focus will (1) create a new Master File Description for the new file, and (2) create a Focus data file and store the data from the report in that file. The data file created by the HOLD command has all the data fields from the report. However, the headings, column titles, footings, or page numbers are not stored.

HOLD files are created at the end of the TABLE request program. A

HOLD file is a temporary file. However, you can save it as a permanent file by renaming it. Otherwise, the HOLD file will disappear at the end of the Focus session or as soon as another HOLD file is created. You could, of course, clear the HOLD file from the Focus memory by issuing the HOLD CLEAR command from the Focus prompt.

The following TABLE request will print the report as requested. However, after the report is printed, Focus will then stop at the prompt line with a message (see below) informing the user that the report file has now been saved temporarily and is available as a Focus file:

```
-*CHAPT10
-*CHAP10-2
TABLE FILE STAFF
PRINT EMPLOYEE_ID
AND LAST_NAME    AS 'LAST,NAME'
AND FIRST_NAME   AS 'FIRST,NAME'
IF RECORDLIMIT EQ 6
END
HOLD
```

```
        PAGE    1


                 LAST               FIRST
    EMPLOYEE_ID  NAME               NAME
    -----------  ----               -----
    294728305    TURPIN             BENTON
    513724567    BORGIA             CESARE
    504234521    FREEMAN            DIANE
    213456682    HUNT               CHARLES
    312562345    TRENT              RICHARD
    314562134    TAYLOR             JUANITA

HOLDING...
```

You can ignore the message and go on to other tasks. However, if you are interested in looking at the structure of the HOLD file, you could issue the following command at the Focus prompt:

```
? HOLD
```

Focus will respond with the definition of the file that is being kept in memory as a HOLD file for you.

```
DEFINITION OF CURRENT HOLD FILE

FIELDNAME        ALIAS          FORMAT

EMPLOYEE_ID      E01            A9
LAST_NAME        E02            A20
FIRST_NAME       E03            A10
```

If you want to view the actual Master File Description that was created by Focus for the HOLD file, you could look at it by issuing the TED HOLD.MAS (PC/Focus), TED HOLD MASTER (VM/CMS), or similar command in other operating systems. The result is shown below.

```
FILE=HOLD               ,SUFFIX=FIX
SEGNAME=HOLD
FIELDNAME    =EMPLOYEE_ID  ,E01        ,A9        ,A09       ,$
FIELDNAME    =LAST_NAME    ,E02        ,A20       ,A20       ,$
FIELDNAME    =FIRST_NAME   ,E03        ,A10       ,A10       ,$
```

You will notice that Focus has replaced the Aliases initially assigned by you with aliases starting with E01. Focus does that because sometimes two printed columns will have the same title but are really derived differently. This is especially true if you used the ACROSS phrase in your TABLE request. In these cases the only way to access the correct fields is by using the aliases that Focus has assigned to your HOLD file fields. Also, remember that DEFINE and COMPUTE fields do not have aliases, so Focus has to come up with a universal naming method for aliases.

You can now access the HOLD file just like other Focus files and issue all the usual Focus commands.

```
TABLE FILE HOLD
PRINT LAST_NAME
AND FIRST_NAME
BY E01
END
  PAGE     1
```

```
EMPLOYEE_ID    LAST_NAME           FIRST_NAME
-----------    ---------           ----------
213456682      HUNT                CHARLES
294728305      TURPIN              BENTON
312562345      TRENT               RICHARD
314562134      TAYLOR              JUANITA
504234521      FREEMAN             DIANE
513724567      BORGIA              CESARE
```

Notice that the mix of HOLD file aliases and the real field names is acceptable to Focus.

There are two ways of creating a HOLD file. The first is as shown above. You execute a TABLE request, print your file, and the HOLD file is created as a by-product of the TABLE request. The other way is to insert the HOLD statement before the END command. In that case the report printing is suppressed. However, the HOLD file is created as before.

```
TABLE FILE STAFF
PRINT EMPLOYEE_ID
AND LAST_NAME   AS 'LAST,NAME'
AND FIRST_NAME  AS 'FIRST,NAME'
IF RECORDLIMIT EQ 6
ON TABLE HOLD
END
```

There is no difference between the statement above and the first TABLE request except that the report is no longer printed.

You could also use the HOLD as a statement in the middle of your TABLE request.

```
TABLE FILE STAFF
PRINT EMPLOYEE_ID
AND LAST_NAME   AND HOLD
BY FIRST_NAME
END
```

This will produce a HOLD file similar to the previous HOLD file except that it is sorted by the first-name field.

If you decide to keep the HOLD file permanently, you could do so by giving it another name. In that case Focus will produce a Master File Description with your assigned name.

```
TABLE FILE STAFF
PRINT EMPLOYEE_ID
AND LAST_NAME   AS 'LAST,NAME'
AND FIRST_NAME  AS 'FIRST,NAME'
IF RECORDLIMIT EQ 6
ON TABLE HOLD AS EMPFILE
END
```

In the example above, a new file called EMPFILE is created. Again, it has all the attributes of a Focus file. It has a Master File Description and a data file. It is a permanent file and will not disappear after you leave the Focus session.

Advantages of the HOLD command

1. *Extraction of a subset of data from large files for future use.* For example, the following TABLE command will extract and create a file called MFILE with just six fields. You could then use this smaller file for other types of processing and/or archiving. It would require less storage and would be less expensive than keeping the original file for a long period of time. Of course, an extract file used for historical purposes has to be designed properly to store vital data.

In the following example, we will keep the EMPLOYEE_Id, the first name, the last name, the salary, and today's date in the new file. So the resulting file is much smaller than the original would have been. We called this the MFILE (short for "month file"). In some applications, we could have one historical file for each month of the year.

```
-*CHAPT10
-*CHAP10-5
DEFINE FILE STAFF
SAVE_DATE/I6=&YMD ;
END

TABLE FILE STAFF
PRINT EMPLOYEE_ID
AND LAST_NAME/A12
AND FIRST_NAME
AND SALARY
BY  SAVE_DATE
ON TABLE HOLD AS MFILE
END
```

You can always display the Master File Description of the HOLD file to examine its contents.

```
> TED HOLD MASTER A or similar command.

FILE=MFILE            ,SUFFIX=FIX
SEGNAME=HOLD
FIELDNAME   =SAVE_DATE    ,E01       ,I6       ,A06      ,$
FIELDNAME   =EMPLOYEE_ID  ,E02       ,A9       ,A09      ,$
FIELDNAME   =LAST_NAME    ,E03       ,A20      ,A20      ,$
FIELDNAME   =LAST_NAME    ,E04       ,A12      ,A12      ,$
FIELDNAME   =FIRST_NAME   ,E05       ,A10      ,A10      ,$
FIELDNAME   =SALARY       ,E06       ,D9.2C    ,A09      ,$
```

It is important to note that in this Master File Description, we have two fields with the same field name (LAST_NAME). In the TABLE request, I instructed Focus to print only 12 characters of the last-name field (LAST_NAME/A12). I did that because I wanted to keep my report narrow. However, the system will keep both the short version and the long version in the new file. Since they both have the same field name, the only way to access these fields for printing is through using aliases that were assigned by Focus to these fields (i.e., E03 and E04).

2. *Sorting of COMPUTEd fields.* As you will remember, COMPUTEd fields are generated at report time and therefore cannot be sorted in the TABLE request that created them. To sort COMPUTEd fields, you must create a HOLD file at the end of the TABLE request. The HOLD file will contain all the fields in that TABLE request, including the COMPUTEd fields. The next step would be to access that HOLD file just like any other Focus file and sort the file by requested fields.

```
-*CHAPT10
-*CHAP10-7
TABLE FILE STAFF
PRINT DEPT_NAME AND LAST_NAME AND SALARY
AND PIN AND COMPUTE
NEW_PAY/D10.2=(SALARY*PIN)+SALARY ;
ON TABLE HOLD
END
TABLE FILE HOLD
HEADING CENTER
" "
"LIST OF EMPLOYEES BY DEPARTMENT"
"BY HIGHEST SALARY AFTER INCREASE"
" "
PRINT LAST_NAME AS 'LAST,NAME'
BY DEPT_NAME AS 'DEPARTMENT,NAME'
BY HIGHEST NEW_PAY AS 'NEW,SALARY'
END
```

```
       PAGE      1


                 LIST OF EMPLOYEES BY DEPARTMENT
                 BY HIGHEST SALARY AFTER INCREASE

      DEPARTMENT              NEW       LAST
      NAME                    SALARY    NAME
      ----------              ------    ----
      ADMINISTRATION       194,250.00   DUXBURY
                            34,240.00   ANDERSEN
      FINANCE              108,120.00   BORGIA
                            68,670.00   TURPIN
                            34,500.00   FREEMAN
      MARKETING             52,170.00   ZARKOV
                            41,764.00   MORALES
                            40,560.00   COLE
                            40,370.00   JAMESON
      MIS                   60,386.00   TAHANIEV
                            48,336.00   GREENSTREET
                            38,150.00   BOCHARD
                            34,560.00   CAMPOS
      OPERATIONS            63,270.00   HUNT
                            29,205.00   TAYLOR
                            24,300.00   TRENT
```

3. *Sorting summed and counted fields.* Counting and adding happens during the execution phase of the TABLE request. Therefore, the results are not available for sorting. You can use a HOLD file to store the results of these requests and sort them afterward.

```
-*CHAPT10
-*CHAP10-6
TABLE FILE STAFF
SUM SALARY
AND VACATION
BY DEPT_NAME
END
HOLD
TABLE FILE HOLD
PRINT DEPT_NAME
AND VACATION
BY SALARY
END
```

```
    PAGE      1


    DEPT_NAME                      SALARY   VACATION
    ---------                      ------   --------
    ADMINISTRATION              217,000.00       145
    FINANCE                     201,900.00       234
    MARKETING                   162,100.00       208
    MIS                         168,000.00       195
    OPERATIONS                  106,050.00       200


    PAGE      1


       SALARY   DEPT_NAME              VACATION
       ------   ---------              --------
    106,050.00  OPERATIONS                  200
    162,100.00  MARKETING                   208
    168,000.00  MIS                         195
    201,900.00  FINANCE                     234
    217,000.00  ADMINISTRATION              145
```

Across and Hold

When the ACROSS phrase is used in a HOLD file, the columns are counted from left to right. This is the same way that they appear on the report.

```
-*CHAPT10
-*CHAP10-8
TABLE FILE STAFF
SUM SALARY AND VACATION ACROSS STATE
BY DEPT_NAME
END
```

PAGE   1

	STATE				
	CA			NY	
DEPT_NAME	SALARY	VACATION		SALARY	VACATION
--------------	----------	--------		----------	--------
ADMINISTRATION	217,000.00	145		.	.
FINANCE	99,900.00	219		102,000.00	15
MARKETING	162,100.00	208		.	.
MIS	168,000.00	195		.	.
OPERATIONS	106,050.00	200		.	.

Now, if you execute a HOLD command from the Focus > prompt, Focus will save this file in the HOLD format.

```
HOLD
```

Next, let us issue a query HOLD command to see the structure of this file.

```
?  HOLD
```

DEFINITION OF CURRENT HOLD FILE

FIELDNAME	ALIAS	FORMAT
DEPT_NAME	E01	A20
SALARY	E02	D9.2C
VACATION	E03	I4
SALARY	E04	D9.2C
VACATION	E05	I4

You will notice that both the salary and the vacation fields have the same field names but different aliases, since one set of values belongs to New York employees and the other set to California employees. The following TABLE request shows how we use the aliases to access the fields that we really want to access. Access by real field names in this instance would not have been very meaningful.

```
TABLE FILE HOLD
PRINT E01 AND E02 AND E03
END
```

Notice that because we did not choose E04 and E05, the information about New York was not included on the report.

```
PAGE      1


DEPT_NAME                    SALARY  VACATION
----------                   ------  --------
ADMINISTRATION             217,000.00     145
FINANCE                     99,900.00     219
MARKETING                  162,100.00     208
MIS                        168,000.00     195
OPERATIONS                 106,050.00     200
```

Various HOLD Formats

The HOLD file format has been improved over the years. Originally, the HOLD command would create a flat, single-segment Focus file. This is still the default for the HOLD command. However, depending on your system and the version of Focus that you are currently using, you can direct Focus to create any of the following types of files as the HOLD file:

$$
\text{ON TABLE HOLD AS new filename [Format}
\begin{cases}
\text{Focus} \\
\text{WP} \\
\text{Lotus} \\
\text{Alpha} \\
\text{DIF} \\
\text{CALC} \\
\text{SQL} \\
\text{SYLK} \\
\text{DB2} \\
\text{Teradata}
\end{cases}
\text{]}
$$

For example, you could save a HOLD file in the word-processing format, so that later you could manipulate it with using a word processor. The command for doing the above is as follows.

```
ON TABLE HOLD AS WORDFILE FORMAT WP
```

The options are described briefly in Table 10.1. Since they are different on different releases and implementations, you should consult with your site Focus coordinator about the available options.

SAVE FILES

The SAVE command is similar to the HOLD command. It comes in two flavors, SAVE and SAVB. The syntax is also similar to the HOLD command. The SAVE

TABLE 10.1 HOLD FILE OPTIONS

Option	Meaning
FOCUS	Converts the report output to a HOLD file in Focus format
WP	Converts the entire report to a word-processing format; the titles, headings, footings, and subtotals are also converted
Lotus	Converts the report request to a format that Lotus can access and manipulate
Alpha	Converts the HOLD data file to alphanumeric format
DIF	Converts the output into a format that could be accepted by most spreadsheet packages. This format also incorporates headings, footings, etc.
CALC	Creates a format acceptable to the Focus spreadsheet program FOCCALC
SQL	Creates an output in SQL/DS format
SYLK	Creates a file in the Microsoft's Multiplan format
DB2	Creates a file that is in the same format as DB2 tables
Teradata	Creates an output compatible with Teradata Tables

command extracts data from a Focus or non-Focus file and stores it in a flat sequential alphanumeric file. Unlike HOLD, it does not create a Master File Description. There are no headings or title lines or subtotals in a save file, just pure data. There are no spaces between the fields in the SAVE file. All this makes a file created by the SAVE command an ideal medium for extracting data and transferring to other non-Focus filing systems and databases. Since SAVE files are created in the standard ASCII or EBCDIC formats (depending on the operating system), they are acceptable to all other filing structures that operate under that operating system. For example, a SAVE file created under MVS could be used as a regular transaction file for updating a VSAM file or a DB2 database. In the following example, a report is created and saved as flat magnetic file on disk. The disk file is called OUTPUT1. It could be used as a transaction file to update another Focus or external non-Focus file in the same computer system. It could even be loaded (copied) on magnetic tape and sent to another organization as an input file to their system.

```
-* CHAP4=T10
-* CHAP10-9
TABLE FILE STAFF
PRINT LAST_NAME AND FIRST_NAME
AND SALARY
AND COMPUTE
SERIAL_NO/I4=SERIAL_NO+1 ;
BY EMPLOYEE_ID
ON TABLE SAVE AS OUTPUT1
END
```

After execution of this TABLE request, Focus will display the record layout of the saved file. The layouts will vary a little, depending on your operating system and Focus version, but will be similar to the following:

```
NUMBER OF RECORDS IN TABLE=    16    LINES=    16

ASCII RECORD NAMED OUTPUT1

FIELDNAME           ALIAS        FORMAT    LENGTH

EMPLOYEE_ID         EID          A9            9
LAST_NAME           LN           A20          20
FIRST_NAME          FN           A10          10
SALARY              INCOME       D9.2C         9
SERIAL_NO                        I4            4

TOTAL                                         52
```

You will need this record layout for accessing this file with other programming languages.

If you access this file (OUTPUT1) and print it on your printer or look at it on the terminal, it will look as follows:

```
213456682HUNT                  CHARLES      57000.00      1
291345672DUXBURY               JILLIAN     185000.00      2
293245178COLE                  ROBERT       39000.00      3
294728305TURPIN                BENTON       65400.00      4
295738307TAHANIEV              RICHARD      55400.00      5
297748301MORALES               CARLOS       39400.00      6
312562345TRENT                 RICHARD      22500.00      7
312781122ZARKOV                WILLIAM      47000.00      8
314562134TAYLOR                JUANITA      26550.00      9
392345782GREENSTREET           JAMES        45600.00     10
413267891JAMESON               CARLA        36700.00     11
432568023CAMPOS                CARLOS       32000.00     12
504234521FREEMAN               DIANE        34500.00     13
513724567BORGIA                CESARE      102000.00     14
515478922ANDERSEN              CHRISTINE    32000.00     15
621893221BOCHARD               ROBERT       35000.00     16
```

Before creating a SAVE file it is best to ALLOCATE or FILEDEF the file to the operating system. If you do not, Focus will create a default file name for the files that have been saved. Like HOLD, the SAVE command could be placed before the END command on the TABLE request or could immediately follow it.

A SAVB file is like a SAVE file except that it is created in the internal Focus format. Since it cannot be read by most other languages and access methods, it is usually used as a transaction file to a Focus database.

JOIN COMMAND

The JOIN command allows you to attach two or more Focus and/or Focus and non-Focus files and databases together and view them as a single file. JOIN is a dynamic command. In other words, it goes into effect as soon as it is issued to Focus and is cleared as soon as you leave your Focus session or issue the JOIN CLEAR * from the Focus > prompt. JOINed databases remain physically separate but are viewed as one database by Focus during the Focus session. You can join the following databases and files together in Focus.

```
FOCUS
FIX (QSAM or external sequential files)
ISAM
VSAM
IMS
SQL
DB2
MODEL 204
ADABAS
DATACOM/DB
IDMS
TOTAL
COMMA DELIMITED external files
```

The JOIN command syntax is as follows:

```
JOIN  field1 in file1 to [ALL] field2 in file2[as join name]
```

For example:

```
JOIN EMPLOYEE_ID IN STAFF TO SSN IN EMPHIST AS JOIN1
```

Up to 16 files and/or databases could be joined together at one time. Joined files could be part of other JOINS, or one file could be part of a JOIN more than once in the same JOIN.

When two databases are JOINed together, the first is called the *host file* and the second is referred to as the *cross-referenced file*. The files are accessed through the first file only. In other words, the cross-referenced file is considered an extension of the host file during the session.

The ALL option could be used if the cross-referenced file has more than one segment and the field you are referring to is in a segment that can have many occurrences. In that case if you do not use the ALL option, you can only access the first occurrence of that particular segment. With the ALL option all occurrences will become available to you during the TABLE request.

To join two files together, they must have two fields in common. The two fields do not have to share the same name but must have the same format in both Master File Descriptions. For example, EMPLOYEE_ID field could be joined to a field called SSN in another file. SSN must be alphanumeric (A type) and nine characters long. The receiving field in a JOIN statement—in this case SSN— must be declared as an indexed field in its Master File Description.

Before we try our first example, I must introduce a new Focus file. This file is called EMPHIST. The Master File Description for this file is shown below. Turn to Appendix A for the data file and program used to load this Focus file.

```
FILENAME=EMPHIST,SUFFIX=FOC
SEGNAME=ONE,SEGTYPE=S1
FIELDNAME=SSN,ALIAS=EID,FORMAT=A9,FIELDTYPE=I,$
FIELDNAME=MARITAL_STAT,ALIAS=MS,FORMAT=A1,$
FIELDNAME=SEX,ALIAS=SEX,FORMAT=A1,$
FIELDNAME=DEGREE,ALIAS=EDUCATION,FORMAT=A4,$
FIELDNAME=PREVIOUS_SAL,ALIAS=OLDSAL,FORMAT=D9.2C,$
```

EMPHIST contains historical and personal information about our employees. It has a key field called the SSN, which is short for the "social security number." This field is nine characters long, which is the same as the EMPLOYEE_ID field in the STAFF file. Also notice that this field is indexed (FIELDTYPE=I). All potential cross-referenced files should be created with a key field that is indexed.

Other fields in this file are self-explanatory. The MARITAL_STAT field will contain the following values:

```
S=SINGLE
M=MARRIED
D=DIVORCED
W=WIDOWED
```

The SEX field will contain either F for "female" or M for "male." The DEGREE field is almost a free-format field. It allows up to four characters of description, indicating the employees' highest level of education. For example, HS stands for high school, MBA for Master of Business Administration, and so on.

Finally, the PREVIOUS_SAL field contains the salary of the employee prior to last increase. For instance, the president of the company, Jillian Duxbury, is currently earning $185,000. Her previous salary was $142,000. The figure $142,000 will be in her record in the EMPHIST file.

In the following example I used the JOIN command to link the STAFF file to the EMPHIST file. This will create a new temporary file which is the combination of the two JOINed files. This file is known to Focus by the host filename, which is STAFF. Notice that I have used the DEFINE statement to decode the marital status field in this file. In the TABLE request that follows the DEFINE statement, I used fields from both files to create my report.

```
-*CHAP10
-*CHAP10-10
JOIN EMPLOYEE_ID IN STAFF TO SSN IN EMPHIST AS JOIN1
DEFINE FILE STAFF
MARIT_S/A8=DECODE MARITAL_STAT('M' MARRIED 'S' SINGLE
                              'D' DIVORCED
                              'W' WIDOWED
                               ELSE  ERROR) ;
END
TABLE FILE STAFF
HEADING CENTER
"  "
"EXAMPLE OF JOINING TWO FILES TOGETHER"
"  "
PRINT LAST_NAME/A12 AS 'LAST,NAME'
AND MARIT_S AS 'MARITAL,STATUS'
AND SEX AND DEGREE AND OLDSAL AS 'PREVIOUS,SALARY'
BY EMPLOYEE_ID AS 'EMPLOYEE,ID'
END
```

The JOIN name, which in this case is called JOIN1, does not play any part in JOINing two files together. Its only use is for disconnecting the linkage between the two files. So after you complete your program, you may want to clear the JOIN. In that case you would issue the JOIN CLEAR JOIN1 command from the Focus prompt. To clear all the other JOINs that may be in effect, issue JOIN CLEAR *. In any case, all the JOINs will be cleared automatically as soon as you leave the Focus session.

EXAMPLE OF JOINING TWO FILES TOGETHER

EMPLOYEE ID	LAST NAME	MARITAL STATUS	SEX	DEGREE	PREVIOUS SALARY
213456682	HUNT	MARRIED	M	MBA	50,500.00
291345672	DUXBURY	SINGLE	F	BS	142,000.00
293245178	COLE	SINGLE	M	HS	36,000.00
294728305	TURPIN	MARRIED	M	BA	49,000.00
295738307	TAHANIEV	MARRIED	M	MBA	51,300.00
297748301	MORALES	SINGLE	M	HS	37,600.00
312562345	TRENT	SINGLE	M	HS	18,000.00
312781122	ZARKOV	WIDOWED	M	PHD	42,000.00
314562134	TAYLOR	DIVORCED	F	HS	24,500.00
392345782	GREENSTREET	WIDOWED	M	BA	41,000.00
413267891	JAMESON	SINGLE	F	BA	34,000.00
432568023	CAMPOS	MARRIED	M	AA	30,000.00
504234521	FREEMAN	MARRIED	F	BS	28,000.00
513724567	BORGIA	WIDOWED	M	MA	95,000.00
515478922	ANDERSEN	SINGLE	F	AA	28,000.00
621893221	BOCHARD	MARRIED	M	HS	31,200.00

As I said earlier, a JOINed file is like a real file. So we can use all the Focus utility commands to check the structure and display a graphic picture of the file's hierarchy. The following command from the Focus prompt line will perform both functions.

```
CHECK FILE STAFF PICTURE


NUMBER OF ERRORS=        0
NUMBER OF SEGMENTS=      4     (REAL=    3   VIRTUAL=    1)
NUMBER OF FIELDS=       23     INDEXES=  1   FILES=      2)
TOTAL LENGTH OF ALL FIELDS= 228
```

The resulting graphic is shown in Fig. 10.1. As you will notice, the EMPHIST segment square is lined with dotted lines. Also, the word "KU" (meaning that this is a unique segment type and has a key field) is printed on top of the segment. The letter K instead of the letter S and the dotted square indicate that this is a virtual segment. The other segments are, of course, real.

There are two types of keyed virtual segments: KU (Keyed Unique) instances and KM (Keyed Multiple) instances. KM occurs when the cross-referenced file has multiple instances of the same segment. If your host file is linked to a virtual segment and it is also linked to its parent or child segments through the cross-referenced segment, the segment types KL (Keyed Linked) and KLU (Keyed Linked Unique) are specified.

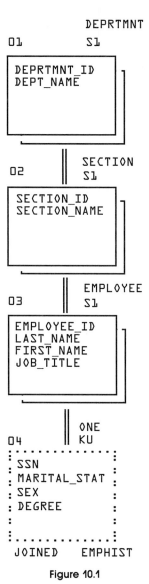

Figure 10.1

If you decide to keep the JOINed file permanently, you could create a new file by using the HOLD command as described previously. For example, the following program combines the STAFF file and the EMPHIST file and will create a new permanent Focus file called STAFHIST:

```
-*CHAP10
-*CHAP10-11
JOIN EMPLOYEE_ID IN STAFF TO SSN IN EMPHIST AS JOIN1
TABLE FILE STAFF
PRINT LAST_NAME
AND MARITAL_STAT
AND SEX AND DEGREE
AND SALARY AND OLDSAL
BY EMPLOYEE_ID
ON TABLE HOLD AS STAFHIST
END
```

Recursive JOINS

A Focus file can also be joined to itself to create a recursive structure. For example, a child segment may be joined to a parent segment, so that the parent becomes the descendent (child) of the descendent segment. This technique could be used in manufacturing for the bill of material processing systems. Remember that the cross-referenced segment, even if it is in the same file, must conform to JOIN rules. It must be indexed and the field being cross-referenced must have the same size and format as the host segment.

MATCH COMMAND

The MATCH command provides similar capabilities as the JOIN command. MATCH is not as easy to use as the JOIN command. However, it works on files where the cross-referenced field is not indexed or where using the JOIN command would not be possible. With match, you first access one file and select the fields that you want to match. Next you will select the other file and do the same thing with the fields in that file. Finally, you put both results in a HOLD file (which, by the way, could be renamed to a permanent file) and access the HOLD file, which will have information from both matched files.

The following program demonstrates the use of the MATCH command to produce the same report as we produced earlier with the JOIN command. As you will notice, the MATCH command is more cumbersome to use and its logic is not as easy to comprehend.

```
MATCH FILE STAFF
PRINT LAST_NAME
BY EMPLOYEE_ID
RUN              ← Use the RUN command here instead of END to let
                   Focus know that you want to continue processing.
FILE EMPHIST
PRINT MARITAL_STAT AND SEX AND DEGREE AND OLDSAL
BY SSN
AFTER MATCH HOLD OLD-AND-NEW
END
DEFINE FILE HOLD
```

```
MARIT_S/A8=DECODE MARITAL_STAT('M' MARRIED 'S' SINGLE
                                'D' DIVORCED
                                'W' WIDOWED
                                ELSE  ERROR) ;
END
TABLE FILE HOLD
PRINT EMPLOYEE_ID AS 'EMPLOYEE,ID'
AND LAST_NAME/A12 AS 'LAST,NAME'
AND MARIT_S AS 'MARITAL,STATUS'
AND SEX AND DEGREE AND PREVIOUS_SAL AS 'PREVIOUS,SALARY'
IF RECORDLIMIT EQ 6
END
```

EMPLOYEE ID	LAST NAME	MARITAL STATUS	SEX	DEGREE	PREVIOUS SALARY
213456682	HUNT	MARRIED	M	MBA	50,500.00
291345672	DUXBURY	SINGLE	F	BS	142,000.00
293245178	COLE	SINGLE	M	HS	36,000.00
294728305	TURPIN	MARRIED	M	BA	49,000.00
295738307	TAHANIEV	MARRIED	M	MBA	51,300.00
297748301	MORALES	SINGLE	M	HS	37,600.00

In the program above, I used the MATCH command to perform the following:

1. Select two fields from the STAFF file and keep the fields on hold. You will need at least one sort field (BY field) in the first MATCH request.
2. Select five fields from the EMPHIST file. Note that the selection was sorted by the SSN field.
3. Store all the selected field in a HOLD file.
4. Use a TABLE request against the HOLD file to print the requested report.

One of the restrictions of the MATCH command is that you cannot use the ACROSS phrase, IF Total, or Compute statement in your program. You can use the DEFINE command. However, you can only use it near the end as part of the HOLD command. Another problem is that you can only merge up to six files in one request. Recall that with JOIN you can link up to 16 files together. However, you can always match non-Focus files with the MATCH command.

We have used one type of MATCH combination in the example above. This was OLD-AND-NEW. The OLD-AND-NEW statement means records that appear in both the old and new files will become part of the HOLD file. Other combinations are possible are as follows:

```
                                                  ┌──────────  The default
                                                  ↓
                                         ⎧ OLD-OR-NEW  ⎫
                                         ⎪ OLD-NOT-NEW ⎪
AFTER MATCH HOLD [AS filename]           ⎨ NEW-NOT-OLD ⎬
                                         ⎪ OLD-NOR-NEW ⎪
                                         ⎪ OLD         ⎪
                                         ⎩ NEW         ⎭
```

For additional information on the above, use the reference manual for your particular system.

STATIC CROSS-REFERENCES

With a static cross-reference, the key field description of the cross-referenced segment is included in the host file's Master File Description. In this way, every time that the HOST file is accessed, the cross-referenced files will become available to Focus. This technique could only be used on Focus files.

In the following example, I created a new file called STAFFCR. This is just like the STAFF file except that in the last line of the Master File Description, there is reference to another segment in another file.

```
SEGNAME=ONE,SEGTYPE=KU,PARENT=EMPLOYEE,
CRFILE=EMPHIST,CRKEY=EID,$
```

The statement above establishes a virtual link to another file (EMPHIST) to which we want to cross-reference. Remember that a static cross-reference can only be used on Focus files (see Table 10.2). It is active as soon as you issue the TABLE request for the HOST file, in this case STAFFCR.

TABLE 10.2 SEGMENT ATTRIBUTES IN STATIC CROSS-REFERENCES

Cross reference	Meaning
SEGNAME	This is the name of the segment in the cross-referenced file. This segment may be a single-segment file or the parent or child of another segment in the cross-referenced file.
SEGTYPE	The segment type will be KU or KM or KLU or KL. The letter K indicates a virtual segment. A single segment file will be KU. KU means Keyed segment. The letter U means unique since there is only one occurrence of each record type in a single-segment file. KM refers to a segment that has many instances. This type of segment is usually a child of another segment. KLU and KL refer to situations where the HOST file is linked to a segment in the cross-referenced file and through that segment is also linked to other segments of that file.
PARENT	This field refers to the new parent segment of the cross-referenced field in the HOST file.
CRFILE	This is the name of the cross-reference file.
CRKEY	This is the name of the key field in the cross-referenced segment that will be linked to the HOST file.

A completed Master File Description with a static cross-reference follows:

```
FILENAME=STAFFCR,SUFFIX=FOC
SEGNAME=DEPRTMNT,SEGTYPE=S1
FIELDNAME=DEPRTMNT_ID,ALIAS=DID,FORMAT=A6,$
FIELDNAME=DEPT_NAME,ALIAS=DEPT,FORMAT=A20,$
SEGNAME=SECTION,PARENT=DEPRTMNT,SEGTYPE=S1
FIELDNAME=SECTION_ID,ALIAS=SECID,FORMAT=A6,$
FIELDNAME=SECTION_NAME,ALIAS=SECN,FORMAT=A20,$
SEGNAME=EMPLOYEE,PARENT=SECTION,SEGTYPE=S1
FIELDNAME=EMPLOYEE_ID,ALIAS=EID,FORMAT=A9,$
FIELDNAME=LAST_NAME,ALIAS=LN,FORMAT=A20,$
FIELDNAME=FIRST_NAME,ALIAS=FN,FORMAT=A10,$
FIELDNAME=JOB_TITLE,ALIAS=TITLE,FORMAT=A20,$
FIELDNAME=STREET,ALIAS=STR,FORMAT=A30,$
FIELDNAME=CITY,ALIAS=TOWN,FORMAT=A16,$
FIELDNAME=STATE,ALIAS=ST,FORMAT=A2,$
FIELDNAME=ZIP_CODE,ALIAS=ZIP,FORMAT=A5,$
FIELDNAME=TELEPHONE_NO,ALIAS=PHONE,FORMAT=A10,$
FIELDNAME=DATE_BIRTH,ALIAS=DOB,FORMAT=I6YMD,$
FIELDNAME=DATE_HIRE,ALIAS=DOH,FORMAT=I6YMD,$
FIELDNAME=SALARY,ALIAS=INCOME,FORMAT=D9.2C,$
FIELDNAME=PCT_INC,ALIAS=PIN,FORMAT=D5.2C,$
FIELDNAME=VACATION,ALIAS=VAC,FORMAT=I4,$
SEGNAME=ONE,SEGTYPE=KU,PARENT=EMPLOYEE,CRFILE=EMPHIST,
CRKEY=EID,$
```

The following TABLE request will produce exactly the same report as the previous reports produced by the JOIN and MATCH commands.

```
-*CHAP10
-*CHAP10-12
DEFINE FILE STAFFCR
MARIT_S/A8=DECODE MARITAL_STAT('M' MARRIED 'S' SINGLE
                               'D' DIVORCED
                               'W' WIDOWED
                                ELSE  ERROR) ;
END
TABLE FILE STAFFCR
HEADING CENTER
"  "
"EXAMPLE OF JOINING TWO FILES TOGETHER"
"  "
PRINT LAST_NAME/A12 AS 'LAST,NAME'
AND MARIT_S AS 'MARITAL,STATUS'
AND SEX AND DEGREE AND OLDSAL AS 'PREVIOUS,SALARY'
BY EMPLOYEE_ID AS 'EMPLOYEE,ID'
END
```

The main rule to remember is that cross-reference keys in both files must have the same format and the same field name or at least a common alias. In the JOIN command, both fields must have the same format, but they could have different field names or aliases.

Advantages and Disadvantages of JOIN, MATCH, and Static Cross-References

By far the easiest way of joining two files together is by using the JOIN command. However, in case of Focus files, the cross-referenced field must be indexed. Also, the JOIN command must be issued every time that you want to link two or more files together. In addition, when you use the JOIN command, you are accessing the entire structure of the cross-referenced file, and this may not be desirable or acceptable in certain circumstances.

MATCH is the older technology. It is heavily used by some programmers who learned Focus before the advent of the JOIN command. It can be used when the cross-referenced file is not indexed. However, it can handle only six files, and the logic of using this command is rather convoluted.

Static cross-referencing runs the fastest. The first time that you set up a static cross-reference, Focus will take extra time to set up the needed pointers between the files; this is also known as *resolving the pointers*. After that time, the link always remains active and therefore provides a faster method of accessing the data in both files. Another advantage of static cross-references, is that you do not have to link the HOST file to the entire structure of the cross-referenced file. You can actually select the segment or segments that you want to cross-reference. Static cross-references need proper planning and require some expertise in setting up correctly. The internal pointers that are set up by Focus will consume four additional characters of file space for each segment instance.

ALTERNATE VIEWS OF FILES

You can view the structure of a Focus file from different angles or viewpoints. For example, in the STAFF file, we seem to use the employee segment more often than the department or the section segments. You can access the file through the Employee segment and avoid going through the other two segments. To do so, you must add the name of the key field in the segment that you want to be your window into the structure after the filename in the TABLE command. In our case we will need to code the following:

```
TABLE FILE STAFF.EMPLOYEE_ID
```

This TABLE request will make Focus look at this file through the employee segment instead of the department segment. To see the graphical display of how the file will look to Focus, issue the CHECK FILE command from the Focus > prompt as shown below.

```
CHECK FILE STAFF.EMPLOYEE_ID PICTURE

NUMBER OF ERRORS=        0
NUMBER OF SEGMENTS=      3     (REAL=    1    VIRTUAL=    2   )
NUMBER OF FIELDS=       18     INDEXES=  0    FILES=      1
TOTAL LENGTH OF ALL FIELDS= 204
```

The resulting graphic is shown in Fig. 10.2. KLU (Keyed through Linkage Unique) means that this segment is a keyed segment that is virtually linked to the parent segment and it is unique. Notice that we have turned the structure upside down. Therefore, for each employee segment, there is one section segment and one department segment. Contrast that with the original structure of the STAFF file, where for each department there were many sections and for each section many employees.

You will notice that the employee segment has now become the root segment, and the section and department segments are now viewed as child segments. This method of accessing a file could be very useful, especially when you

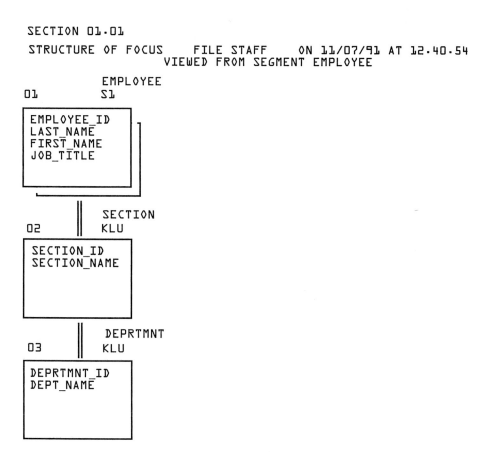

Figure 10.2

have several layers of segments that you do not normally access in your application. Also, in certain files, you may find that you have more instances of parent segments than of child segments. For example, there could be 20,000 occurrences of a parent segment but only 5000 instances of the child segment in a file. In other words, there are cases where the parent segments do not have any child segments. In these cases it is much better to access the file through a child segment since your program will only need to access, say, 5000 segments instead of 20,000 to get to the data that are needed.

Following is an example of accessing our STAFF file through the EMPLOYEE_ID field.

```
-*CHAP10
-*CHAP10-13
TABLE FILE STAFF.EMPLOYEE_ID
HEADING CENTER
" "
"EXAMPLE OF ACCESSING A FILE WITH AN ALTERNATE VIEW"
" "
PRINT LAST_NAME AS 'LAST NAME'
AND SALARY AND CITY
BY DATE_HIRE AS  'DATE,OF HIRE'
IF RECORDLIMIT EQ 6
END


    PAGE    1


      EXAMPLE OF ACCESSING A FILE WITH AN ALTERNATE VIEW

    DATE
    OF HIRE  LAST NAME                   SALARY  CITY
    -------  ---------                   ------  ----
    78/10/12  TURPIN                   65,400.00  LOS ANGELES
    79/12/08  FREEMAN                  34,500.00  CANTON
    82/10/12  TRENT                    22,500.00  LOS ANGELES
    84/09/15  TAYLOR                   26,550.00  SANTA MONICA
    84/11/11  BORGIA                  102,000.00  NEW YORK
    87/07/13  HUNT                     57,000.00  ORANGE
```

Please note that when you use the alternate view feature, the information retrieved from the child segment—which has now become the root segment—will be retrieved sequentially. You can, of course, use the BY phrase to sort the records in any order that you want to, and this is what we did with our example above.

You may find that in many cases, using the alternate view will speed up your processing time. However, you must be really familiar with your data before attempting to use alternate views. The field that you use for alternate viewing should ideally be indexed. Although this is not a requirement. The EMPLOYEE_ID field in our STAFF file is not indexed. Indexing will definitely speed up the processing and improve the efficiency of the program. You should also always run your program both ways, with and without alternate views, and compare the processing time before making a final commitment.

SUMMARY

In this chapter we looked at some advanced features of Focus. We discovered how we could use the HOLD command to save the result of Focus TABLE requests and use them in other TABLE requests. We learned that you can use HOLD to create another Focus or non-Focus external file and use these files later in other programs.

The SAVE command is in many ways similar to the HOLD command. However, it does not produce a Master File Description. The output of the SAVE command is a sequential file that can be transported and used by other IBM and non-IBM systems by programs written in other languages.

The linking of Focus and external files together was a major part of this chapter. We introduced three ways of reporting from linked or joined files. The JOIN command is by far the most powerful because it can be used as a relational tool to link many disparate filing structures together. The static cross-reference creates virtual segments that are available as soon as you access the real Focus file that is acting as host. MATCH is the original way of linking Focus files together. If your files are indexed, use the JOIN command instead of MATCH. If your files are not indexed, you can always use the Focus Rebuild utility to index the fields that need to be used in a JOIN command.

Alternate view is a feature of Focus that is not used as often as it should be. It could really cut down your processing time and improve your program efficiency. However, you must be comfortable with using Focus and familiar with your data before attempting to use them.

EXTERNAL FILE PROCESSING AND OTHER ADVANCED FEATURES OF FOCUS®

MAIN TOPICS:

- OTHER REPORT WRITER-RELATED TOPICS
- INTERNAL OPERATIONS OF FOCUS DURING THE TABLE REQUEST EXECUTION
- PLOTS AND GRAPHICS
- EXTERNAL FILES PROCESSING
- MISSING SEGMENTS

In this chapter we wrap up the remaining parts of the Focus report-writing section. The next section deals with Focus data base management and maintenance. Some of the items discussed in this chapter are applicable to all versions of Focus; others, such as External file handling, work somewhat differently on various Focus platforms. My objective in this chapter is to give you a very good overview of the remaining subjects. You can then refer to your site manual or reference book for specifics about the various items.

INTERNAL OPERATIONS OF FOCUS

Several times in previous chapters I have mentioned the fact that the COMPUTE statement acts on the results of fields at the time of execution. Other Focus commands are executed at different times. In the next few pages I review the internal operation of Focus as it reads a TABLE request and prepares to print a report. The Focus TABLE language is an interpretive language. In other words, the instructions are read one statement at a time and are executed in that order. Other languages such as COBOL are compiled languages. These languages are first run through a compiler that converts the code to machine language for later processing. The machine language programs are then executed. The Focus MODIFY programs that we review in the next section of this book could be either interpretive or compiled. The four steps in executing a TABLE request are summarized below:

Interpretation of TABLE Request Code

1. The Focus TABLE request program is read by Focus one line at a time.
2. Focus will check to see if the Master File Description is available. Note that depending on your operating system, the Master file may be in a library (MVS), a separate minidisk (VM/CMS) or another directory (PC).
3. Focus will look for the Focus data file that is referenced in the TABLE request. You will have to allocate this file by using the Allocate or FILEDEF commands prior to executing your Focus request.
4. Focus will substitute the variables (i.e., &DATE, &YMD, etc.) with actual data.
5. Focus will check the syntax of the TABLE request for correct Focus grammar.
6. Focus will select segments and fields that have been chosen in the TABLE request.

Retrieval of Data

1. Segments are read into the computer primary storage.
2. All IF commands within the TABLE request are performed to screen out unwanted records.
3. DEFINEd fields are created. In newer versions of Focus, the DEFINEd fields are immediately compiled into machine language and remain active. This will speed up processing if these commands are going to be repeated over and over.
4. All IF conditions within the DEFINEd statements are performed.

Processing of Data

1. All sorts (BY and ACROSS) are performed by Focus.
2. Focus will execute all SUM, PRINT, COUNT, and LIST commands.
3. Focus will allocate a working area on a disk unit for the TABLE request. This work area is called FOCSORT.
4. The steps for retrieving and processing are repeated until the end of the file is reached.

Output and Formatting of Data

1. Focus will execute the COMPUTE statements.
2. Focus will perform the IF TOTAL selection.
3. Headings, footings, and column totals are prepared for printing.
4. Focus will perform column positioning as follows:

```
AS
ACROSS
AND
OVER
NOPRINT
IN
```

5. Subtotals (i.e., SUBTOTALs, SUB-TOTALs, ROW-TOTALs, COLUMN-TOTALs) are computed by Focus.
6. Final formatting of the report is performed. These are SKIP-LINE, PAGE-BREAK, and UNDER-LINE.

PLOTS OR GRAPHICS IN FOCUS

Focus provides the added advantage of allowing users to produce graphs directly from Focus files. There are currently many graphics packages in the PC market. Some of them are very sophisticated and can produce tremendous-looking graphs. The mainframe and minicomputer markets do not have the same abundance of graphics software packages. One of the reasons is that mainframe systems require special monitors to produce plots, whereas almost any cheap PC monitor with a graphics card is capable of displaying graphs.

The quality of graphs produced by Focus is not as superior as some better dedicated graphics packages. After all, Focus is a data base management and reporting system and was not designed to compete with the hotshot PC graphics packages. However, one thing that Focus can do that none of the dedicated packages can do is to calculate and print graphs directly from the file. In other packages, you must first extract the data, manipulate them, and then invoke the graphics software program. Another advantage of Focus is that the Graph syntax and all the commands are identical to the TABLE request syntax and command. The only difference is that instead of invoking the TABLE environment with the TABLE FILE command, you must invoke the GRAPH environment with the GRAPH FILE command. The following are the main types of plots and graphs that could be handled by Focus.

Connected point graph or line plot. This type of graph is created by using the SUM command and the ACROSS phrase. In other words, by adding a numeric field across another numeric field you will obtain a connected point graph.

```
-*CHAPTER 11
-*CHA11-4
-* A CONNECTED POINT GRAPH.
GRAPH FILE STAFF
HEADING CENTER
" "
"EXAMPLE OF CONNECTED POINT GRAPH"
"A GRAPH SHOWING THE RELATION OF SALARY"
"AND THE PERCENTAGE INCREASE IN SALARY"
```

```
SUM SALARY  ACROSS PCT_INC
END
```

The resulting graph is shown in Fig. 11.1.

Histogram.   This type of graph is produced by using the SUM command and the ACROSS phrase. In this case, the ACROSS field must be alphanumeric to get the histogram.

```
-*CHAPTER 11
-*CHA11-1
-* A HISTOGRAM GRAPH.
JOIN EID IN STAFF TO SSN IN EMPHIST AS JJ
GRAPH FILE STAFF
HEADING CENTER
" "
"EXAMPLE OF HISTOGRAM"
"A HISTOGRAM OF PREVIOUS SALARY AND CURRENT SALARY BY"
"DEPARTMENT NAME"
SUM PREVIOUS_SAL AS 'PREVIOUS  SALARY'
AND SALARY AS 'CURRENT  SALARY'
ACROSS DEPT_NAME  AS 'DEPARTMENT NAME'
END
```

The resulting graph is shown in Fig. 11.2.

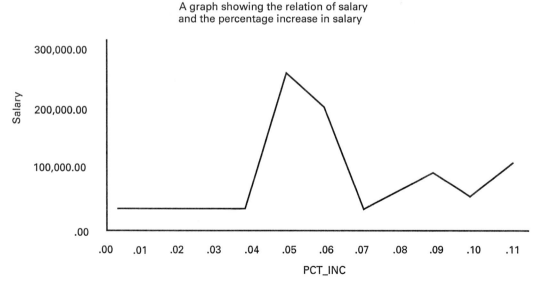

Figure 11.1 Connected point graph.

```
                    EXAMPLE OF HISTOGRAM
          A HISTOGRAM OF PREVIOUS SALARY AND CURRENT SALARY BY
                        DEPARTMENT NAME
          P   PREVIOUS   SALARY
          C   CURRENT    SALARY


300,000.00 +
           I
           I
           I             CCC
200,000.00 +             CCC        CCC
           I             PPPCCC     PPPCCC                  CCC
           I             PPPCCC     PPPCCC     PPPCCC       PPPCCC
           I             PPPCCC     PPPCCC     PPPCCC       PPPCCC     CCC
100,000.00 +             PPPCCC     PPPCCC     PPPCCC       PPPCCC     PPPCCC
           I             PPPCCC     PPPCCC     PPPCCC       PPPCCC     PPPCCC
           I             PPPCCC     PPPCCC     PPPCCC       PPPCCC     PPPCCC
           I             PPPCCC     PPPCCC     PPPCCC       PPPCCC     PPPCCC
     .00 +--------------------------------------------------------------------
                    ADMINISTRATION        MARKETING            OPERATIONS
                            FINANCE                   MIS


                            DEPARTMENT NAME
```

Figure 11.2 Histogram.

Bar chart.   A bar chart is produced by using the SUM or COUNT command and the BY phrase. The BY field may be numeric or alphanumeric.

```
-*CHAPTER 11
-*CHA11-2
-* A BAR CHART.
GRAPH FILE STAFF
HEADING CENTER
" "
"EXAMPLE OF BAR CHART"
"A BAR CHART OF SALARY OF EMPLOYEES BY DEPARMENT"
SUM SALARY BY DEPT_NAME AS 'DEPARTMENT NAME'
END
```

The graph is shown in Fig. 11.3.

```
                    EXAMPLE OF BAR CHART
           A BAR CHART OF SALARY OF EMPLOYEES BY DEPARMENT
DEPARTMENT NAME                      SALARY

           100,000.00      140,000.00      180,000.00      220,000.00
                  120,000.00      160,000.00      200,000.00
               +-------+-------+-------+-------+-------+-------+
ADMINISTRATION I======================================================
FINANCE        I==================================================
MARKETING      I=========================
MIS            I==========================
OPERATIONS     I=
```

Figure 11.3 Bar chart.

Scatter diagram. This type of graph is created by using the PRINT command and the BY or ACROSS phrases.

```
-*CHAPTER 11
-*CHA11-3
-* A SCATTER DIAGRAM.
GRAPH FILE STAFF
HEADING CENTER
" "
"EXAMPLE OF SCATTER DIAGRAM"
"DIAGRAM OF SALARIES BY DEPARTMENT"
PRINT SAL BY DEPT_NAME AS 'DEPARTMENT  NAME'
END
```

See Fig. 11.4.

```
                   EXAMPLE OF SCATTER DIAGRAM
                 DIAGRAM OF SALARIES BY DEPARTMENT
DEPARTMENT  NAME                      SALARY

          20,000.00 60,000.00100,000.00140,000.00180,000.00
                40,000.00 80,000.00120,000.00160,000.00200,000.00
               +----+----+----+----+----+----+----+----+----+
ADMINISTRATION I  1                                        1
FINANCE        I  1        1           1
MARKETING      I   3 1
MIS            I   2   1 1   ← Number of occurrence of field
OPERATIONS     11          1
```

Figure 11.4 Scatter diagram.

Pie chart. Most of the foregoing types of graphs could be displayed in pie chart format. However, you must have a monitor capable of displaying pie charts. To instruct Focus to print a graph in the pie chart format you must issue the SET PIE=ON prior to your plot request.

```
-*CHAPTER 11
-*CHA11-5
-* A PIE CHART GRPAH.
SET PIE=ON
GRAPH FILE STAFF
HEADING CENTER
" "
"EXAMPLE OF PIE CHART"
"A CHART OF TOTAL SALARIES BY EACH DEPARTMENT"
SUM SALARY AS 'CURRENT  SALARY'
ACROSS DEPT_NAME AS 'DEPARTMENT  NAME'
END
```

See Fig. 11.5.

There is a lot more to the Focus graphics capabilities. You could adjust the vertical and horizontal axes and you could specify printing on plotters. This is just an introduction to the GRAPH environment. If you need to use the graph commands for sophisticated applications, you should refer to your Focus manual for specific instructions.

A chart of total salaries by each department

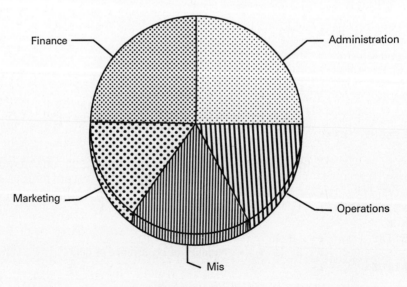

Figure 11.5 Pie chart.

ACCESSING EXTERNAL FILES

Focus provides a host of facilities for accessing non-Focus external files. You can use Focus to access the following types of files.

QSAM (fixed-format sequential files)
ISAM
VSAM
Dbase
DB2
IMS
IDMS
ADABAS
TOTAL
DATACOM/DB

The reason for accessing external files via Focus is the ease of programming and the power of the Focus TABLE commands. The usual alternative in commercial programming is COBOL. It will take several hours to write, compile, and test a simple COBOL report program. In most third-generation programming languages including COBOL, each report heading and column title must be described in the program in exact detail. Any simple mistake will cause either an aborted program or erroneous results. A three-page COBOL program to access a simple sequential file and print a report with headings, titles, and totals will take at least 4 hours to write, compile, test, and produce. The same report will take approximately 20 to 30 minutes to prepare in Focus. The other reason is the power of the TABLE commands. You can easily sort and add single or multiple control breaks to your program by using one or more BY or ACROSS phrases. You could even display your report in graph form. If you wanted to create a COBOL program with control breaks, you will need to add more development time for generating sort and control break logic.

Finally, Focus is very versatile. With Focus, you could easily join several external files to each other and create relational environments for reporting purposes. All you will need is a Master File Description for each file. You could then use the MATCH or the JOIN commands to link the files together. The only requirement for accessing any file is that it must have a Master File Description. Creating a Master File Description is easy. All you do is define the field names and formats just as we have done with Focus files. There are few minor differences. You only need to create a Master File Description once, for each external file. After that, you can just refer to that file and use the regular TABLE commands just as you would with a Focus file.

The following file is a sequential fixed-format file. It is called EXTFILE1. This file was created by a COBOL program. To access this file, you will need to create a Master File Description for it. The SUFFIX attribute for this file type must be defined as FIX. This will tell Focus that it is a sequential file. Also, each field needs an additional format attribute, which is called the ACTUAL or ACTUAL USAGE. The FORMAT attribute is the usage that Focus will use. The ACTUAL USAGE is the format of the field in its native form. Most of the time, the actual usage or format is described as A type. Its main purpose is to let Focus know the actual amount of space that each field is occupying. The main exceptions are the numeric decimal and packed decimal data. On the mainframe Focus they can be defined as Z type for zoned decimal or P type for packed decimal. On PCs and minicomputers, you should refer to the Focus user manual for that particular operating system to learn how numeric data need to be declared.

```
FILENAME=EXTFILE1,SUFFIX=FIX
SEGNAME=ONE,$
FIELDNAME=CUSTNO,ALIAS=CN,FORMAT=I6,ACTUAL=A6,$
FIELDNAME=CUST_NAME,ALIAS=CN,FORMAT=A20,ACTUAL=A20,$
FIELDNAME=STREET,ALIAS=STR,FORMAT=A24,ACTUAL=A24,$
FIELDNAME=CITY,ALIAS=CIT,FORMAT=A15,ACTUAL=A15,$
FIELDNAME=STATE,ALIAS=ST,FORMAT=A2,ACTUAL=A2,$
FIELDNAME=ZIP,ALIAS=ZIP,FORMAT=A5,ACTUAL=A5,$
FIELDNAME=BALANCE,ALIAS=BAL,USAGE=D9.2,ACTUAL=Z7.2,$
FIELDNAME=FILLER, ALIAS=FILLER, USAGE=A1,ACTUAL=A1,$
```

You can just about use any TABLE command and produce reports from an external file. It is treated by the TABLE environment just like a Focus file. The following TABLE request prints a simple report from EXTFILE1. As you will notice, the TABLE request commands and the report generated are similar to other requests that we have generated.

```
-*CHAPTER 11
-*CHA11-6
TABLE FILE EXTFILE1
HEADING CENTER
" "
"EXAMPLE OF AN EXTERNAL FILE ACCESSED BY FOCUS"
" "
PRINT CUST_NAME AS 'CUSTOMER,NAME'
AND CITY AND STATE
BY CUSTNO AS 'CUSTOMER,NUMBER'
END

  PAGE    1


     EXAMPLE OF AN EXTERNAL FILE ACCESSED BY FOCUS

CUSTOMER   CUSTOMER
NUMBER     NAME                         CITY            STATE
--------   --------                     ----            -----
  102558   BEN TURPIN                   LAGUNA NIGUEL   CA
  123454   AMANDA BARRY                 LAKEWOOD        CA
  123456   RICHARD TAHANIEV             SAN CARLOS      CA
  123457   JACK HOLMES                  BELMONT         NY
  123458   FRED CARSON                  CLEVELAND       OH
  123558   BRUCE TERN                   IRVINE          CA
```

You do not have to describe every field in your external file to Focus; just the fields that you are going to use are sufficient. The fields that are of no interest to you could be coded as filler fields. For example, if I did not need the customer street address, customer city, customer state, and the customer zip code, I could very easily have coded the following Master File Description:

```
FILENAME=EXTFILE1,SUFFIX=FIX
SEGNAME=ONE,$
FIELDNAME=CUSTNO,ALIAS=CN,FORMAT=I6,ACTUAL=A6,$
FIELDNAME=CUST_NAME,ALIAS=CN,FORMAT=A20,ACTUAL=A20,$
FIELDNAME=FILLER,ALIAS=FILL,FORMAT=A46,ACTUAL=A46,$
FIELDNAME=BALANCE,ALIAS=BAL,USAGE=D9.2  ,ACTUAL=Z7.2,$
FIELDNAME=FILLER, ALIAS=FILLER, USAGE=A1,ACTUAL=A1,$
```

Filler fields can contain up to 256 characters. If you need more, use several filler fields one after another.

The Master File Description above was created for a simple sequential file. There are other types of files and databases that could be accessed by Focus. The most common ones are sequential files with multiple data occurrence (i.e., repeating fields) and VSAM files. The concepts are all the same. The complexity and programming are a little different.

Valid Suffixes

Table 11.1 is a list of valid suffixes for external files. This list applies to IBM file types and databases. You should refer to your Focus User's Manual for other suffixes.

TABLE 11.1 SUFFIXES FOR EXTERNAL FILES

Type of file	Suffix
Fixed format	FIX
Free format	COM
Focus	FOC
IMS	IMS
SQL/DS	SQLDS
DB2	SQLDS
VSAM	VSAM
DATACOM	DATACOM
ADABAS	ADBSIN

You can also join two or more external files together. The following two files, TEMPO and TEMPO2, are external sequential files created by a COBOL program. I have created Master File Descriptions for both files, as shown below.

Following is the Master File Description for the first external file, called TEMPO.

```
FILENAME=TEMPO,SUFFIX=FIX
SEGNAME=TEMPO
```

```
FIELDNAME=TEMPLOYEE_ID,ALIAS=TEID,FORMAT=A9,ACTUAL=A9,$
FIELDNAME=TLAST_NAME,ALIAS=TLN,FORMAT=A20,ACTUAL=A20,$
FIELDNAME=TFIRST_NAME,ALIAS=TFN,FORMAT=A10,ACTUAL=A10,$
FIELDNAME=TSALARY,ALIAS=TINCOME,FORMAT=D9.2C,ACTUAL=A9,$
FIELDNAME=TDEPT_NAME,ALIAS=TDEPT,FORMAT=A20,ACTUAL=A20,$
```

Following is a file description for the second external file, called TEMPO2.

```
FILENAME=TEMPO2,SUFFIX=FIX
SEGNAME=TEMPO2
FIELDNAME=EMPLOYEE_ID,ALIAS=EID,FORMAT=A9,ACTUAL=A9,$
FIELDNAME=LAST_NAME,ALIAS=LN,FORMAT=A20,ACTUAL=A20,$
FIELDNAME=SECTION_NAME,ALIAS=SECN,FORMAT=A20,ACTUAL=A20,$
```

Following is the data file for the first external file. It is called TEMPO DATA.

```
213456682HUNT            CHARLES      57000.00OPERATIONS
291345672DUXBURY         JILLIAN     185000.00ADMINISTRATION
293245178COLE            ROBERT       39000.00MARKETING
294728305TURPIN          BENTON       65400.00FINANCE
295738307TAHANIEV        RICHARD      55400.00MIS
297748301MORALES         CARLOS       39400.00MARKETING
312562345TRENT           RICHARD      22500.00OPERATIONS
312781122ZARKOV          WILLIAM      47000.00MARKETING
314562134TAYLOR          JUANITA      26550.00OPERATIONS
392345782GREENSTREET     JAMES        45600.00MIS
413267891JAMESON         CARLA        36700.00MARKETING
432568023CAMPOS          CARLOS       32000.00MIS
504234521FREEMAN         DIANE        34500.00FINANCE
513724567BORGIA          CESARE      102000.00FINANCE
515478922ANDERSEN        CHRISTINE    32000.00ADMINISTRATION
621893221BOCHARD         ROBERT       35000.00MIS
```

Following is the data file for the sequential file, called TEMPO2 DATA.

```
213456682HUNT            ENGINEERING
291345672DUXBURY         EXECUTIVE
293245178COLE            SALES
294728305TURPIN          PAYABLES
295738307TAHANIEV        OPERATIONS
297748301MORALES         SALES
312562345TRENT           CUSTOMER SERVICES
312781122ZARKOV          SALES
314562134TAYLOR          CUSTOMER SERVICES
392345782GREENSTREET     DEVELOPMENT
413267891JAMESON         SALES
432568023CAMPOS          OPERATIONS
504234521FREEMAN         COLLECTIONS
```

```
513724567BORGIA              PAYABLES
515478922ANDERSEN            EXECUTIVE
621893221BOCHARD             DEVELOPMENT
```

Following is the Focus TABLE request to join the two external files and print a report from both data files. Note the FILEDEF commands to ensure that Focus can point to both files. This program was written in Focus under the VM/CMS operating system. Under other operating systems, there will be similar allocation commands.

```
-*TEMPO1
-*EXAMPLE OF JOIN OF 2 SEQUENTIAL FILES.
CMS FILEDEF TEMPO DISK TEMPO DATA A (PERM
CMS FILEDEF TEMPO2 DISK TEMPO2 DATA A (PERM
JOIN TEMPLOYEE_ID IN TEMPO TO EMPLOYEE_ID IN TEMPO2 AS JT1
TABLE FILE TEMPO
PRINT TLAST_NAME/A12 AS 'LAST,NAME'
AND TSALARY AS 'SALARY'
BY TDEPT AS 'DEPARTMENT' BY SECTION
END
```

```
PAGE    1


                                          LAST
DEPARTMENT         SECTION_NAME           NAME            SALARY
----------         ------------           ----            ------
ADMINISTRATION     EXECUTIVE              DUXBURY      185,000.00
                                          ANDERSEN      32,000.00
FINANCE            COLLECTIONS            FREEMAN       34,500.00
                   PAYABLES               TURPIN        65,400.00
                                          BORGIA       102,000.00
MARKETING          SALES                  COLE          39,000.00
                                          MORALES       39,400.00
                                          ZARKOV        47,000.00
                                          JAMESON       36,700.00
MIS                DEVELOPMENT            GREENSTREET   45,600.00
                                          BOCHARD       35,000.00
                   OPERATIONS             TAHANIEV      55,400.00
                                          CAMPOS        32,000.00
OPERATIONS         CUSTOMER SERVICES      TRENT         22,500.00
                                          TAYLOR        26,550.00
                   ENGINEERING            HUNT          57,000.00
```

VALUABLE HINTS FOR COBOL PROGRAMMERS

I have mentioned that it is very easy to read external files with Focus. However, files created by Cobol present a challenge to people who are not accustomed to bits and bytes of computer systems.

Basically, numeric data is stored in three different ways. These are: (1) the display format also known as Zoned Decimal, (2) the packed decimal format which is commonly known as Computational-3 or Comp-3 and (3) the pure binary format which is also known as Computational, Comp or Hex. I will not go into the reasons for the development of these different standards here. However, I will show you examples of each type of data and the Focus translation in the Master File Description. The following table will display examples of each class of data in its Cobol File Description (FD) usage and the way they have to be represented to Focus in the Master File Description.

Cobol		Focus	
File description usage		Actual format	Usage format
Display Usage:			
9(4)		Z4 or A4	A4 or D4
9(13)V99		Z15.2	D15.2
9(4)V9(4)		Z8.4	D9.4
S9(5)V9		Z6.1	P8.1
S99		Z2	P3
9(9)V99		Z11.2	A11 or P13.2
Packed Decimal Format:			
9(9)V99	COMP-3	P6	P9.2 or P10.2
S9(5)	COMP-3	P3	P5
S9(4)V999	COMP-3	P4	P8.3
S9(5)V9	COMP-3	P4	P7.1
S9(5)V99	COMP-3	P4	P8.2
S9(3)	COMP-3	P2	P3
S9V99	COMP-3	P2	P5.2
Binary Format			
S9(4)	COMP	I2	I4
S9(8)V9	COMP	I4	I9
S9(6)V999	COMP	I4	I9
S9	COMP	I2	I1
S9(5)	COMP	I4	I5
S9(9)	COMP	I4	I9

MISSING SEGMENTS

Sometimes, when you produce a report you will find that there are parent segments without any child (descendent) segments. There are a number of reasons for this phenomenon. The most likely reason is that a field is not appropriate for a particular report field. For example, in the following report each employee could work in one department only, and therefore there is a missing field value indicated in front of the employee's name in the other department.

```
-*CHAPTER 11
-*CHA11-7
TABLE FILE STAFF
HEADING CENTER
" "
"EXAMPLE OF MISSING DATA ON A REPORT"
" "
PRINT SALARY ACROSS DEPT_NAME AS 'DEPARTMENT'
BY LAST_NAME AS 'LAST,NAME'
IF DEPT_NAME EQ 'MIS' OR 'FINANCE'
END
```

```
    PAGE     1


              EXAMPLE OF MISSING DATA ON A REPORT

                          DEPARTMENT
                          FINANCE                MIS
        LAST
        NAME
        ----------------------------------------------------------
        BOCHARD                      .           35,000.00
        BORGIA            102,000.00                  .
        CAMPOS                       .           32,000.00
        FREEMAN            34,500.00                  .
        GREENSTREET                  .           45,600.00
        TAHANIEV                     .           55,400.00
        TURPIN             65,400.00                  .
```

The missing field values on reports are referred to as NODATA fields. They are usually represented by a period, as shown above. The period is the default. You could replace it with any other character string—up to 11 characters long—by using the SET command before the TABLE request. For example, the following SET commands are all valid:

```
SET NODATA = MISSING
```

or

```
SET NODATA = NONE
```

or

```
SET NODATA = ' '    ← This will leave a blank space instead of
                         a period.
```

Missing Segment Instances

Missing segments are more important and could be more troublesome than missing data fields on a report. Missing segments occur in multisegment files. Missing segments are caused when there are no actual child segments for a particular parent segment. For example, let us assume that in our hypothetical organization, we have set up two new departments. One is the human resources department and the other one is the production department. Each department has two sections. However, although these departments and sections have been approved, there are currently no employees in these departments. If we add these new segments to our Focus STAFF file, we will have one department segment for each department and two section segments under each department. At this time, there would be no employee segments. In these cases, the employee segments are said to be missing segments. The section segments and the department segments for these two departments are called *short paths* because they are not part of a complete set of segments.

Missing segments can affect the outcome of reports. For example, in a report request, if you request data from employee segments as well as the parent segments of the STAFF file, Focus will ignore the two departments and section segments with the missing child segments even though there is information in the department and section segments. To show you the effect of missing segments, I am going to add two new departments and two new segments within each department to our STAFF file. The new fields are as follows:

Deprtmnt_ID	DEPT_NAME	Section_ID	Section_Name
22	Human Resources	221	Policies
		222	Recruiting
24	Production	241	Inspection
		242	Assembly

I will first write a TABLE request to access this new file and just print the department and section information. You will notice that in this TABLE request, I am instructing Focus to print the values of the department name and the section name and the department ID. All this information is in the two parent segments. As you will see from the report following the TABLE request, both the production department and the human resources department and their respective sections are printed on the report.

```
-*CHAPTER 11
-*CHA11-8
TABLE FILE STAFF
HEADING CENTER
" "
"EXAMPLE OF MISSING SEGMENTS IN A FOCUS FILE"
"EXAMPLE NUMBER 1 WITH PARENT SEGMENTS ONLY"
" "
```

```
PRINT DEPT_NAME AS 'DEPARTMENT,NAME'
AND SECN AS 'SECTION,NAME'
BY DID AS 'DEPARTMENT,ID'
END
```

PAGE   1

     EXAMPLE OF MISSING SEGMENTS IN A FOCUS FILE
      EXAMPLE NUMBER 1 WITH PARENT SEGMENTS ONLY

DEPARTMENT ID	DEPARTMENT NAME	SECTION NAME
10	ADMINISTRATION	EXECUTIVE
12	FINANCE	PAYABLES
	FINANCE	COLLECTIONS
14	MIS	DEVELOPMENT
	MIS	OPERATIONS
15	OPERATIONS	ENGINEERING
	OPERATIONS	CUSTOMER SERVICES
20	MARKETING	SALES
22	HUMAN RESOURCES	POLICIES
	HUMAN RESOURCES	RECRUITING
24	PRODUCTION	INSPECTION
	PRODUCTION	ASSEMBLY

In the following TABLE request, I have added a new instruction to extract
data from the Employee segment also. In this case Focus will not even print the
data from the department and section segments of the two departments. Therefore, if you have a short path, the TABLE request will print information from the
parent segments if there is no mention of a field name from a missing segment.
Otherwise, if your TABLE request refers to any missing descendent segments,
information from parent segments of missing segments will also be omitted.

```
-*CHAPTER 11
-*CHA11-9
TABLE FILE STAFF
HEADING CENTER
"    "
"EXAMPLE OF MISSING SEGMENTS IN A FOCUS FILE"
"EXAMPLE NUMBER 2 WITH DESCENDENT SEGMENT"
"    "
PRINT DEPT_NAME AS 'DEPARTMENT,NAME'
AND SECN AS 'SECTION,NAME' AND LAST_NAME
BY DID AS 'DEPARTMENT,ID'
END
```

PAGE   1

```
                  EXAMPLE OF MISSING SEGMENTS IN A FOCUS FILE
                  EXAMPLE NUMBER 2 WITH DESCENDENT SEGMENT

DEPARTMENT    DEPARTMENT          SECTION
ID            NAME                NAME                 LAST_NAME
----------    ----------          -------              ---------
10            ADMINISTRATION      EXECUTIVE            DUXBURY
              ADMINISTRATION      EXECUTIVE            ANDERSEN
12            FINANCE             PAYABLES             TURPIN
              FINANCE             PAYABLES             BORGIA
              FINANCE             COLLECTIONS          FREEMAN
14            MIS                 DEVELOPMENT          GREENSTREET
              MIS                 DEVELOPMENT          BOCHARD
              MIS                 OPERATIONS           TAHANIEV
              MIS                 OPERATIONS           CAMPOS
15            OPERATIONS          ENGINEERING          HUNT
              OPERATIONS          CUSTOMER SERVICE     TRENT
              OPERATIONS          CUSTOMER SERVICE     TAYLOR
20            MARKETING           SALES                COLE
              MARKETING           SALES                MORALES
              MARKETING           SALES                ZARKOV
              MARKETING           SALES                JAMESON
```

If you need to include parent segments of missing descendent segments on a report, you must use the SET command before executing the TABLE request. There are three variations of the SET command.

SET ALL=OFF   ← This is default and will exclude parents of missing segments.

SET ALL=ON   ← This will include the parents of missing segments on a report. However, if you use an IF statement to screen any of the missing segment fields, the parent segments for those missing segments will also be excluded.

SET ALL=PASS   ← This will print parent instances of missing segments, even if an IF statement is used to screen a field in a descendent segment field.

The following program is a modified version of the program above. The only difference is the addition of the SET command.

```
-*CHAPTER 11
-*CHA11-10
SET ALL=PASS      ← Notice the SET command.
TABLE FILE STAFF
HEADING CENTER
"   "
```

```
"EXAMPLE OF MISSING SEGMENTS IN A FOCUS FILE"
"EXAMPLE NUMBER 3, USE OF SET ALL = PASS "
"  "
PRINT DEPT_NAME/A16 AS 'DEPARTMENT,NAME'
AND SECN/A16 AS 'SECTION,NAME'
AND LAST_NAME
BY DID AS 'DEPARTMENT,ID'
END
```

As you will notice, because of the new SET command (SET ALL=PASS), all instances of parents of missing segments are included in the report. The missing segments are identified with a period.

```
           EXAMPLE OF MISSING SEGMENTS IN A FOCUS FILE
             EXAMPLE NUMBER 3, USE OF SET ALL=PASS
```

DEPARTMENT ID	DEPARTMENT NAME	SECTION NAME	LAST_NAME
10	ADMINISTRATION	EXECUTIVE	DUXBURY
	ADMINISTRATION	EXECUTIVE	ANDERSEN
12	FINANCE	PAYABLES	TURPIN
	FINANCE	PAYABLES	BORGIA
	FINANCE	COLLECTIONS	FREEMAN
14	MIS	DEVELOPMENT	GREENSTREET
	MIS	DEVELOPMENT	BOCHARD
	MIS	OPERATIONS	TAHANIEV
	MIS	OPERATIONS	CAMPOS
15	OPERATIONS	ENGINEERING	HUNT
	OPERATIONS	CUSTOMER SERVICE	TRENT
	OPERATIONS	CUSTOMER SERVICE	TAYLOR
20	MARKETING	SALES	COLE
	MARKETING	SALES	MORALES
	MARKETING	SALES	ZARKOV
	MARKETING	SALES	JAMESON
22	HUMAN RESOURCES	POLICIES	.
	HUMAN RESOURCES	RECRUITING	.
24	PRODUCTION	INSPECTION	.
	PRODUCTION	ASSEMBLY	.

Finally, we can produce a report that prints only the parents instances of missing segments. In this case, we will use the SET ALL=PASS command again. However, in the following TABLE request, I have set an impossible condition for the IF statement. A last name can be both equal and not equal to spaces. As a result, all the employee segments with real data are excluded. This is an important TABLE request, because it will allow you to locate and perhaps fix missing segments in a file.

```
-*CHAPTER 11
-*CHA11-11
SET ALL=PASS
TABLE FILE STAFF
HEADING CENTER
" "
"EXAMPLE OF MISSING SEGMENTS IN A FOCUS FILE"
"EXAMPLE NUMBER 4, USE OF SET ALL = PASS "
"TO PRINT ONLY THE PARENTS OF MISSING SEGMENTS"
" "
PRINT DEPT_NAME/A16 AS 'DEPARTMENT,NAME'
AND SECN/A16 AS 'SECTION,NAME'
AND LAST_NAME
IF LAST_NAME EQ ' '
IF LAST_NAME NE ' '
BY DID AS 'DEPARTMENT,ID'
END
```

```
    PAGE      1


              EXAMPLE OF MISSING SEGMENTS IN A FOCUS FILE
                 EXAMPLE NUMBER 4, USE OF SET ALL=PASS
              TO PRINT ONLY THE PARENTS OF MISSING SEGMENTS

DEPARTMENT   DEPARTMENT        SECTION
ID           NAME              NAME            LAST_NAME
----------   ----------        -------         ---------
22           HUMAN RESOURCES   POLICIES          .
             HUMAN RESOURCES   RECRUITING        .
24           PRODUCTION        INSPECTION        .
             PRODUCTION        ASSEMBLY          .
```

SUMMARY

In this chapter we first discussed the internal operations of Focus while executing a TABLE request. A good understanding of how Focus prioritizes the execution of a TABLE request is very valuable to a programmer in designing a Focus program. It also helps in debugging a Focus program. If a program fails, you could debug it easier if you knew what actions Focus was performing on the TABLE request at the time of program failure.

Graphics and plots are becoming more and more important in the business world. Focus has managed to keep up with the competition and even improve the quality and sophistication of its graphs.

As a professional programmer, you will need to understand how to access external files with Focus TABLE commands. This is an exciting area and is constantly being enhanced by the makers of Focus. You can just about report from any file on IBM equipment. You could join external files, and what is more, you could convert external files to Focus format by using the HOLD command.

Missing segments could cause a nightmare for users and programmers alike. Sometimes, segments are legitimately missing. Other times parent segments have become redundant because a company may lay off the employees of a department or transfer them to another department without informing the data administration group. Therefore, the parent segments do not get deleted. The same situation will happen with mechanical components that are part of a manufactured assembly. The assembly may be obsolete and the company may not carry any of the parts, but someone has neglected to remove the parent segment of the particular assembly.

FILE MAINTENANCE
USING BATCH TRANSACTIONS

MAIN TOPICS:

- REVIEW OF MASTER FILE DESCRIPTION
- UPDATING FOCUS FILES USING FIXFORM AND FREEFORM
- START AND STOP

You may remember that in Chapter 3 we described the procedure for creating a Master File Description for a Focus file. As you know, a Focus file could be designed as a single-segment (relational) or multiple-segment hierarchical database. Hierarchical files could be designed as single path or multiple path. We can also join up to 16 Focus and/or non Focus external files for reporting purposes. Most other languages lack this relational feature of Focus.

ADDITIONAL ADVANCED FEATURES OF MASTER FILE DESCRIPTION ENTRIES

Define

By now, you should be very familiar with the various versions of the DEFINE command in the TABLE environment. You can also use the DEFINE attribute in the Master File Description to perform certain operations every time you access the file. DEFINE in Master File Description is just like DEFINE in the TABLE request. It does not change the nature of Focus data file. However, it modifies the output. The advantage of putting the DEFINE command in the Master File Description is that it does not have to be repeated every time in each TABLE request.

    In the following example, I have modified the original STAFF Master File Description. I added three new DEFINE statements at the end of the employee segment. The first entry computes the biweekly pay of each employee from the salary field. The second entry joins (concatenates) the first name and the last name of each employee to create a new field with both names. The third entry joins the city, state, and zip code fields together (this is a useful feature when you are printing mailing labels). From here on, I do not have to use any DEFINE statements in my TABLE requests to calculate or create those three fields. Also note the TITLE and DESCRIPTION attributes that I have included in this Master File Description. I will tell you more about them shortly.

```
FILENAME=STAFF,SUFFIX=FOC
SEGNAME=DEPRTMNT,SEGTYPE=S1
FIELDNAME=DEPRTMNT_ID,ALIAS=DID,FORMAT=A6,
DESC='DEPARTMENT IDENTIFICATION',$      ← The description field.
FIELDNAME=DEPT_NAME,ALIAS=DEPT,FORMAT=A20,$
SEGNAME=SECTION,PARENT=DEPRTMNT,SEGTYPE=S1
FIELDNAME=SECTION_ID,ALIAS=SECID,FORMAT=A6,$
$ 'SECTION IDENTIFICATION',$     ← Another way of adding comments
FIELDNAME=SECTION_NAME,ALIAS=SECN,FORMAT=A20,$       to a field.
SEGNAME=EMPLOYEE,PARENT=SECTION,SEGTYPE=S1
FIELDNAME=EMPLOYEE_ID,ALIAS=EID,FORMAT=A9,$
FIELDNAME=LAST_NAME,ALIAS=LN,FORMAT=A20,
TITLE='EMPLOYEE,LAST NAME',$            ← The TITLE attribute.
FIELDNAME=FIRST_NAME,ALIAS=FN,FORMAT=A10,$
FIELDNAME=JOB_TITLE,ALIAS=TITLE,FORMAT=A20,$
FIELDNAME=STREET,ALIAS=STR,FORMAT=A30,$
FIELDNAME=CITY,ALIAS=TOWN,FORMAT=A16,$
FIELDNAME=STATE,ALIAS=ST,FORMAT=A2,$
FIELDNAME=ZIP_CODE,ALIAS=ZIP,FORMAT=A5,$
FIELDNAME=TELEPHONE_NO,ALIAS=PHONE,FORMAT=A10,$
FIELDNAME=DATE_BIRTH,ALIAS=DOB,FORMAT=I6YMD,$
FIELDNAME=DATE_HIRE,ALIAS=DOH,FORMAT=I6YMD,$
FIELDNAME=SALARY,ALIAS=INCOME,FORMAT=D9.2C,$
FIELDNAME=PCT_INC,ALIAS=PIN,FORMAT=D5.2C,$
FIELDNAME=VACATION,ALIAS=VAC,FORMAT=I4,$
DEFINE BIWEEKLY/D7.2=SALARY/26;$            ← These three fields are all
DEFINE FULL_NAME/A31=FIRST_NAME ¦ LAST_NAME ;$     DEFINE statements
DEFINE ADDRESS/A26=CITY ¦  STATE ¦' '¦ ZIP; $      within the Master
                                                   File Description.
```

Examples of the DEFINE attribute in the Master File Description:

```
-*CHAPTER 12
-*CHA12-1
-*
TABLE FILE STAFF
HEADING CENTER
"  "
"EXAMPLE OF USING THE DEFINE IN THE "
"MASTER FILE DESCRIPTION "
"  "
PRINT FULL_NAME AS 'EMPLOYEE NAME'
AND BIWEEKLY AS 'BIWEEKLY,SALARY'
```

```
BY DEPT_NAME AS 'DEPARTMENT,NAME'
END

PAGE     1


          EXAMPLE OF USING THE DEFINE IN THE
               MASTER FILE DESCRIPTION

    DEPARTMENT                                      BIWEEKLY
    NAME                    EMPLOYEE NAME           SALARY
    ----------              --------------          --------

    ADMINISTRATION          JILLIAN   DUXBURY       7,115.38
                            CHRISTINE ANDERSEN      1,230.77
    FINANCE                 BENTON    TURPIN        2,515.38
                            CESARE    BORGIA        3,923.08
                            DIANE     FREEMAN       1,326.92
    MARKETING               ROBERT    COLE          1,500.00
                            CARLOS    MORALES       1,515.38
                            WILLIAM   ZARKOV        1,807.69
                            CARLA     JAMESON       1,411.54
    MIS                     JAMES     GREENSTREET   1,753.85
                            ROBERT    BOCHARD       1,346.15
                            RICHARD   TAHANIEV      2,130.77
                            CARLOS    CAMPOS        1,230.77
    OPERATIONS              CHARLES   HUNT          2,192.31
                            RICHARD   TRENT           865.38
                            JUANITA   TAYLOR        1,021.15


-*CHAPTER 12
-*CHA12-2
-*
TABLE FILE STAFF
HEADING CENTER
" "
"ANOTHER EXAMPLE OF USING THE DEFINE IN THE "
"MASTER FILE DESCRIPTION TO CREATE MAILING LABELS"
" "
PRINT FULL_NAME AS ' '
OVER STREET AS ' '
OVER ADDRESS AS ' '
BY LAST_NAME NOPRINT
ON ADDRESS SKIP-LINE
IF RECORDLIMIT EQ 5
END
```

```
     ANOTHER EXAMPLE OF USING THE DEFINE IN THE
MASTER FILE DESCRIPTION TO CREATE MAILING LABELS


     CESARE     BORGIA
     347 SOUTH ROMA AVENUE
     NEW YORK          NY   10001

     DIANE      FREEMAN
     22 SOUTH DEAN DRIVE
     CANTON          CA   94107

     CHARLES    HUNT
     87A NEWTON
     ORANGE          CA   93199

     RICHARD    TRENT
     93 LA CIENEGA BLVD
     LOS ANGELES     CA   91287

     BENTON     TURPIN
     121 LA CIENEGA BLVD.
     LOS ANGELES     CA   91345
```

TITLE

The TITLE attribute allows you to change the column title default on the report heading. As you have seen so far, the column title in every TABLE request is usually the field name. The column titles can be changed by using the AS phrase to override the field names. You could also create an alternate title by coding it directly in the Master File Description. The title can be up to 64 characters long and can be displayed or printed on up to five lines. Use commas to stack the title into separate lines. The following TABLE request and the ensuing report display the effect of the TITLE attribute.

```
-*CHAPTER 12
-*CHA12-3
-*
TABLE FILE STAFF
HEADING CENTER
"  "
"EXAMPLE OF USING THE TITLE IN THE "
"MASTER FILE DESCRIPTION "
"  "
PRINT LAST_NAME
BY DEPT_NAME
```

```
IF RECORDLIMIT EQ 5
END


   PAGE     1


      EXAMPLE OF USING THE TITLE IN THE
          MASTER FILE DESCRIPTION

                        EMPLOYEE
DEPT_NAME               LAST NAME
---------               ---------
FINANCE                 TURPIN
                        BORGIA
                        FREEMAN
OPERATIONS              HUNT
                        TRENT
```

The TITLE attribute overrides the field name at print time. If necessary, it can be overridden by the AS phrase.

LOCATION

The LOCATION attribute is used to physically separate a segment from its parent segment.

```
SEGNAME=INHIST,PARENT=STAFFHST,LOCATION=HISTORY
```

The statement above will cause the INHIST segment to be physically separated (i.e., on a separate disk unit) from its parent. This feature is useful when you may want to balance your load between various disk volumes. Also, each Focus file has a maximum physical file size of 256 megabytes. This is equivalent to 256 million characters of data or roughly 2,000 copies of this book stored on disk. You can remove the size constraint by placing some segments into other physical locations. The location attribute name can be up to eight characters long. You can use the LOCATION attribute to store your text fields in a separate file.

DESCRIPTION

The DESCRIPTION or DESC is an optional attribute that allows you to document each field. You are allowed up to 44 characters of information for each field name in your Master File Description. The description field is considered a comment line and is ignored during processing. Another method of adding comment to a field is to place a dollar sign ($) followed by a space on the line following the field name description. DESCRIPTION can contain any alphanumeric character. If you need to use a comma, remember to enclose the text within single quotation marks.

HELPMESSAGE

This attribute may not be available on some versions of Focus. The HELP-MESSAGE attribute enables you to include up to 78 characters of text (on one line only) in your Master File Description for any given field. The help message will be displayed—along with the regular Focus error messages—at the bottom of screen during data entry time in the Focus Modify CRTFORM environment.

If an error occurs during data entry, Focus will usually display its own message. However, Focus messages are generally vague and could be ambiguous to the data-entry clerk. This is because Focus cannot be application specific and has to generate a message that applies to most error situations. You can therefore add your own line of error or help message to the Focus-generated message. For example:

```
FIELDNAME=DATE_HIRE,ALIAS=DOH,FORMAT=I6YMD,$
HELPMESSAGE=THE FORMAT FOR DATE OF HIRE SHOULD BE I6YMD
```

If alphanumeric characters are entered into the DATE HIRE field during data-entry time, the following Focus error message will appear at the bottom of the screen.

```
FORMAT ERROR IN VALUE ENTRIES ON FIELD DATE_HIRE
```

This will be followed by your HELPMESSAGE entry.

```
THE FORMAT FOR DATE OF HIRE SHOULD BE I6YMD
```

During online data entry, you can display the help message for any field. This can be done by assigning one of your function keys (the PF keys or the F keys) to help messages. This is accomplished by using the SET command to assign one of your function keys to invoke the help functions:

```
SET PF10=HELP
```

The SET command must be executed before the MODIFY command. Thereafter, during data entry, you could place your cursor on any field on the screen and press PF10. This will cause the related help message to be displayed on the screen. If no help messages exist for a given field, the following message will appear on the screen instead.

```
NO HELP AVAILABLE FOR THIS FIELD
```

ACCEPT

The ACCEPT attribute allows you to screen incoming data and reject records that do not pass validation attribute. This feature is used to screen data during the online or batch data entry process. Each ACCEPT statement follows a related field.

```
ACCEPT = (CA or AZ or NY)
ACCEPT =  15,000 TO 240000
ACCEPT = FIND (FIELD or FILE)
```

The first statement will only allow the entry of any one of the three states. Other values, such as OH or NV or WA, will be rejected at data entry time. The second statement will perform a range test on the input fields and will only accept values that are between 15,000 and 240,000. Any other value will be rejected. For example, if this entry was related to an employee salary field, any other value would have been rejected. The third ACCEPT statement will search for a field in another file. We will learn more about the FIND command later.

The following example shows a partial listing of the STAFF Master File Description with the ACCEPT attributes.

```
FIELDNAME=CITY,ALIAS=TOWN,FORMAT=A16,$
FIELDNAME=STATE,ALIAS=ST,FORMAT=A2,$
ACCEPT= (CA OR AZ OR NY),$
FIELDNAME=ZIP_CODE,ALIAS=ZIP,FORMAT=A5,$
FIELDNAME=TELEPHONE_NO,ALIAS=PHONE,FORMAT=A10,$
FIELDNAME=DATE_BIRTH,ALIAS=DOB,FORMAT=I6YMD,$
FIELDNAME=DATE_HIRE,ALIAS=DOH,FORMAT=I6YMD,$
FIELDNAME=SALARY,ALIAS=INCOME,FORMAT=D9.2C,$
ACCEPT = 15000 TO 24000,$
FIELDNAME=PCT_INC,ALIAS=PIN,FORMAT=D5.2C,$
```

Remember: after completing the Master File Description, you must initialize it with the CREATE command. The function of the CREATE command is to create an empty Focus data file, rather like a shell, that could be used for data entry at a future time. CREATE is optional on some systems, but it is best to get into the habit of allocating and initializing your Focus data files on all versions of Focus. The CREATE command syntax is as follows:

```
CREATE FILE filename PICTURE
```

that is,

```
CREATE FILE STAFF PICTURE
```

UPDATING FOCUS FILES USING SEQUENTIAL TRANSACTIONS

There are several ways of updating a Focus file. Four of these methods use the MODIFY environment. The syntax of the MODIFY command is as follows:

```
                        ┌ ECHO  ┐
MODIFY FILE file name    
                        └ TRACE ┘
```

```
Modify statements (i.e., FIXFORM, CRTFORM, etc.)
```

```
DATA [ ON ddname (i.e., the file that contains the input data)]
END
```

The ECHO command invokes the ECHO facility, which will simply display the MODIFY request at execution time. The TRACE command invokes the TRACE facility which will display the name of each CASE paragraph that is executed. This applies if the request uses the Focus CASE logic, discussed in Chapter 13.

The other methods of updating a Focus file are the SCAN, FSCAN, or Host Language Interface (HLI) facilities. A brief description of each method follows.

FIXFORM

This method is widely used for updating Focus files with the information from a batch file. A batch file is a collection of records or transactions that have been recorded on a magnetic file such as disk pack or magnetic tape. The FIXFORM commands allow you to write a program to use these transactions to update a Focus data file. By updating, I mean adding new records to the data file, changing records, and deleting records. The updating function is also known as maintaining a file or modifying a file. The records in the transaction file must have a fixed format (i.e., all the identical fields must be the same length and must all start in the same location in each record). For example, if we are updating the STAFF file, all the records in the transaction file must have the same length, and all the fields, such as employee number or employee last name, must start in the same position in every record.

FREEFORM

The FREEFORM file maintenance commands are similar to the FIXFORM commands. The main use of FREEFORM is in processing comma-delimited files. These files are usually created by other programs, such as dBase and Lotus. The main difference between a fixed-format input file and a free-format input file is that free-format fields can be of variable length. In other words, identical fields do not always start on the same location in each record in the transaction file. The person coding a Focus update program must specify each field by giving it the field name prior to entering the data for that field. This is a cumbersome method of data entry, and although it has its specialized uses, it is not a common way of updating Focus data files.

PROMPT

The PROMPT command allows you to update selected fields of a Focus data file online. Updating is done one field at a time and the user is prompted each time a new field needs to be updated—hence the name PROMPT.

MODIFY CRTFORM Statement and FIDEL

The MODIFY CRTFORM invokes the FIDEL (Focus Interactive Data Entry Language) facility. FIDEL generates formatted screens for full-screen data entry. As a programmer, you must first create a screen with various fields of information for the user. The user enters the information in the designated areas of the screen and when completely satisfied, presses the Enter key to transmit the data from the terminal screen and update the Focus data file.

FSCAN and SCAN Facilities

You can also update a Focus data file directly by using either of these two facilities. The syntax is very simple.

```
SCAN FILE file name
```

that is,

```
SCAN FILE STAFF
```

or

```
FSCAN FILE filename
```

that is,

```
FSCAN FILE STAFF
```

The SCAN facility is self-prompting. You can actually add, change, or delete records one record at a time directly from the terminal. This is also the only way to change the value of segment key fields. You cannot change the value of key fields with the MODIFY command. For example, if you find out that the employee ID in the STAFF file is entered incorrectly you cannot just change it with the MODIFY command as you would a salary field. This is because the employee ID is a key field. To change a key field value under the MODIFY environment, you must first delete the entire segment and/or the record and then re-enter it with the new key value. This could be avoided by using either the SCAN or FSCAN facility. However, you must be careful in using these facilities because they do not leave an audit trail and also because you can accidentally change or delete entire sets of records. Finally, you cannot build data validation routines into SCAN and FSCAN facilities.

Host Language Interface (HLI) Facility

This feature allows you to maintain Focus data files by using second- and third-generation computer languages such as Assembler, COBOL, C, and FORTRAN.

FIXFORM FACILITY

As I said earlier, the FIXFORM subcommand describes the record layout (field size, field type, and relative location of each field) of an input file to Focus. If you have a large amount of input data, the FIXFORM is the main method for updating a Focus file. The FIXFORM subcommand can read data from files in external alphanumeric as well as internal Focus format. A file created in internal Focus format is usually the result of the SAVB command in a TABLE request.

Before attempting to update a Focus file, you should usually make sure that the file actually exists. This is usually done by a CMS Exec or Batch files in PC/DOS or TSO CLIST or similar command. A typical CMS Exec program to check for the existence of the STAFF file is shown below.

```
TRACE OFF
* THIS SIMPLE EXEC WILL CHECK FOR THE PRESENCE
* OF A FILE PRIOR TO TRYING TO EXECUTE A
* PROGRAM USING IT
STATE STAFF FOCUS A
&IF &RETCODE NE 0 &GOTO -BADRC
&STACK EXEC FOCUS
&STACK EX CHA15-16
&STACK FIN
-MESG &TYPE FOCUS JOB COMPLETED
&GOTO -EXIT

-BADRC     ← This paragraph will be performed if the file does not exist.
&TYPE 'FILE NOT AVAILABLE'

-EXIT    ← This will cause the processing to stop.
&TYPE    'END OF RUN'
EXIT
```

&RETCODE is a CMS system variable that will have a value of zero if the file is available.

Simple Example of the FIXFORM Subcommand to Update a File

I will now introduce a new Focus file. This file is called the MOVIES file. You could use this file to catalog movies, TV programs, and shows on cassette tapes. The Master File Description for this file is as follows:

```
FILENAME=MOVIES   ,SUFFIX=FOC
SEGNAME= MOVIES   ,SEGTYPE=S1
FIELDNAME=TITLE, ,USAGE = A43,$
FIELDNAME=TAPE_NO, ,USAGE = D03,$
FIELDNAME=LENGTH, ,USAGE = D04,$
FIELDNAME=COMMENTS, ,USAGE = A20,$
FIELDNAME=RATING, ,USAGE = A04,$
```

This file has four fields. The first field, which is also the main sort key is the TITLE field. The title is 43 characters long and is, of course, unique. We are assuming that no two shows could have the same title. The next field is TAPE_NO. This is the number that has been assigned to each tape in our collection. A video cassette tape could contain one or more movies. The next field is the length. This is the length of the program on videotape cassette as measured by the counter on the videocassette recorder. Since a tape could contain more than one show, this would be helpful in trying to locate a given program. The last field is the rating field. This is denoted by a series of stars. One star means below average, two stars mean average, three stars mean good, and four stars mean excellent. No star means that the program was not rated.

Let us assume that we want to update the MOVIES file with additional records and change the value of some records as follows:

1. Add four new records to the file.
2. Change two records.

The following is the contents of the MOVIES data file before the update.

PAGE   1

TITLE	TAPE_NO	LENGTH	COMMENTS	RATING
48 HOURS	18	1,170	ACTION	**
CASABLANCA	6	4,817	DRAMA	****
CLASSICAL MUSIC	28	0		
COLUMBO A DEADLY STATE OF MIND	18	1,100	DRAMA	***
COLUMBO A FRIEND INDEED	15	853	DRAMA	***
COLUMBO AN EXERCISE IN FATALITY	15	0	DRAMA	***
COLUMBO BLUEPRINT FOR MURDER	35	1,535	MYSTERY	***
COLUMBO BY DAWN'S EARLY LIGHT	34	1,880	DRAMA	***
COLUMBO DEAD WEIGHT	24	1,254	DRAMA	***
COLUMBO DEATH LENDS A HAND	15	1,765	ACTION	***
COLUMBO DOUBLE EXPOSURE	18	1,870	DRAMA	***
COLUMBO ETUDE IN BLACK	21	1,506	DRAMA	***
COLUMBO IN SCOTLAND	34	0	DRAMA	***
COLUMBO LADY IN WAITING	24	880	DRAMA	***
COLUMBO LOVELY BUT LETHAL	18	1,349	MYSTERY	***
COLUMBO NEGATIVE REACTION	15	1,110	DRAMA	***
COLUMBO PUBLISH OR PERISH	24	1,885	DRAMA	***
COLUMBO SHORT FUSE	24	1,050	DRAMA	***
COLUMBO THE GREEN HOUSE JUNGLE	34	1,028	DRAMA	***
FOUR HORSEMEN OF APPOCALYPSE	31	0	DRAMA	***
GONE WITH THE WIND	14	4,120	DRAMA	****
HOGANS HEROES	29	0	COMEDY	**
JAMES BOND DIAMONDS ARE FOREVER	19	2,529	ACTION	***
JAMES BOND DOCTOR NO	22	2,949	ACTION	****
JAMES BOND GOLDFINGER	26	1,346	ADVENTURE	***
JAMES BOND THE SPY WHO LOVED ME	11	1,576	ACTION	***
JAMES BOND THUNDERBALL	33	2,750	ACTION	***
MALTESE FALCON	30	0	CLASSIC	****

```
SHERLOCK HOLMES DRESSED TO KILL        27     850    MYSTERY      ***
SHERLOCK HOLMES FACES DEATH            11   1,640    ACTION       ***
SHERLOCK HOLMES SECRET WEAPON          22      0    ACTION       ***
THE BIG SLEEP                          26   1,382    MYSTERY      ***
WAR WAGON THE                           8   2,232    WESTERN      ***
WIZARD OF OZ                           13   3,062    FANTASY     ****
```

I will use the following input transaction file to update this file.

```
COLUMBO GOODBYE MRS COLUMBO   (NEW)        331028DRAMA              ***
COLUMBO A FRIEND INDEED       (CHANGE)     281028DRAMA              ***
HOGANS HEROES                 (CHANGE)     291200COMEDY             ***
FATHER GOOSE                  (NEW)        271296COMEDY             ***
JAMES BOND LIVE AND LET DIE   (NEW)        121576ACTION             ***
SECRET OF NIMH                (NEW)        31   0CARTOON MOVIE      ***
```

The file above contains six records. Two of these records are new and need to be inserted in the file. The other four contain changes to the existing records. The program to update this file and add the new records follows.

```
-*CHAPTER 12
-*CHA12-4
-*
FILEDEF MOVIES DISK E:\MOVIES.DAT  ← This statement will identify the
MODIFY FILE MOVIES                    input file to focus.
FIXFORM TITLE/43 TAPE_NO/3
FIXFORM LENGTH/4 COMMENTS/20 RATING/4
MATCH TITLE           ← This statement compares the key input field
ON NOMATCH INCLUDE      against the key field in the Focus file.
ON MATCH UPDATE TAPE_NO LENGTH COMMENTS RATING
DATA ON MOVIES
END
```

The following message is displayed after the execution of the MODIFY request above.

```
E:MOVIES.FOC ON 06/12/91 AT 14.52.21

TRANSACTIONS:  TOTAL=   6  ACCEPTED=   6  REJECTED=   0
SEGMENTS:      INPUT=   4  UPDATED=    2  DELETED =   0
```

The messages above indicate that Focus received six records (transactions) from us. It accepted all of them. There were no errors and nothing was rejected. The segment line informs us that four new segments were added (i.e., input) and two segments were updated. There were no deleted segments in this MODIFY request.

TABLE 12.1 FIXFORM FORMATS

Format	Meaning
An	Alphanumeric. For example, A5 means that the field is five characters long. The letter "A" is optional.
In	Integer type. For example, I4 means an integer field that is four bytes long.
Dn	Double-precision floating point. For example, D6.
Pn	Packed decimal. For example, P10.
Zn	Zoned decimal. For example, Z6.

Elements of the FIXFORM Subcommand

FIXFORM. This subcommand informs Focus that there will be a string of fixed-format data (i.e., field names) following the statement. Each field name will be followed by a length format. For example, TITLE/43 means that the first field encountered will be the TITLE field and it will be 43 characters long. There are some optional format statements that could be used when we describe each field to Focus. We would describe the format by adding the format type as shown in Table 12.1.

MATCH and NOMATCH. The MATCH and NOMATCH verbs compare the key field(s) in the input file (the input file is also known as the *transaction file*) against the key field(s) in the Focus data file. Nonkey fields in a segment may also be included in a MATCH statement. Depending on the outcome of the comparison, the programmer could take several actions. In our example, if the TITLE field on the input file does not match the TITLE field on the Focus data file, a new segment with the input data information is created and inserted in the Focus data file. The INCLUDE verb is used to insert new segments. To delete a segment, the key fields are matched in the same way and the DELETE verb is used to erase the unwanted segment. If the TITLES match each other, the information from the input file is used to update the Focus data file. Remember that you cannot update a key field; only the nonkey fields could be updated. To update a key field, you should either use the SCAN or FSCAN facilities or delete the segment and then create a new segment with the new key. Some valid MATCH and NOMATCH actions are displayed in Table 12.2. As you will notice, statements such as "ON MATCH INCLUDE" are not acceptable since this would cause the entry of a duplicate key. However, many other statements are perfectly legal. For example, you could even have a FIXFORM within another FIXFORM.

DATA. This statement tells Focus where to find the input file that it will need to use in this program. In this case it was called the MOVIES. We must use the FILEDEF (CMS or PC) or ALLOCATE (TSO) statements to identify the files to Focus before start of the MODIFY command. As you will notice, I did that in my first line of code.

The MOVIES file has been updated as follows.

TABLE 12.2   MATCH AND NOMATCH ACTIONS

ON MATCH actions	ON NOMATCH actions
REJECT	REJECT
UPDATE	INCLUDE
DELETE	PROMPT
CRTFORM	CRTFORM
TYPE	TYPE
COMPUTE	COMPUTE
VALIDATE	VALIDATE
GOTO	GOTO
PERFORM	PERFORM
FIXFORM	FIXFORM
FREEFORM	FREEFORM
CONTINUE	
CONTINUE TO	
PROMPT	

```
TABLE FILE MOVIES
PRINT TAPE_NO AND LENGTH AND RATING
BY TITLE
END


    PAGE     1
                        UPDATED MOVIES FILE


    TITLE                                     TAPE_NO  LENGTH  RATING
    -----                                     -------  ------  ------
48 HOURS                                          18   1,170    **
CASABLANCA                                         6   4,817   ****
CLASSICAL MUSIC                                   28       0
COLUMBO A DEADLY STATE OF MIND                    18   1,100   ***
COLUMBO A FRIEND INDEED      Updated fields →     28   1,028   ***
COLUMBO AN EXERCISE IN FATALITY                   15       0   ***
COLUMBO BLUEPRINT FOR MURDER                      35   1,535   ***
COLUMBO BY DAWN'S EARLY LIGHT                     34   1,880   ***
COLUMBO DEAD WEIGHT                               24   1,254   ***
COLUMBO DEATH LENDS A HAND                        15   1,765   ***
COLUMBO DOUBLE EXPOSURE                           18   1,870   ***
COLUMBO ETUDE IN BLACK                            21   1,506   ***
COLUMBO GOODBYE MRS COLUMBO (New segment added)   33   1,028   ***
COLUMBO IN SCOTLAND                               34       0   ***
COLUMBO LADY IN WAITING                           24     880   ***
COLUMBO LOVELY BUT LETHAL                         18   1,349   ***
COLUMBO NEGATIVE REACTION                         15   1,110   ***
COLUMBO PUBLISH OR PERISH                         24   1,885   ***
COLUMBO SHORT FUSE                                24   1,050   ***
COLUMBO THE GREEN HOUSE JUNGLE                    34   1,028   ***
```

FATHER GOOSE	(New segment added)	27	1,296	***
FOUR HORSEMEN OF APPOCALYPSE		31	0	***
GONE WITH THE WIND		14	4,120	****
HOGANS HEROES	Updated field →	29	1,200	***
JAMES BOND DIAMONDS ARE FOREVER		19	2,529	***
JAMES BOND DOCTOR NO		22	2,949	****
JAMES BOND GOLDFINGER		26	1,346	***
JAMES BOND LIVE AND LET DIE	(New segment added)	12	1,576	***
JAMES BOND THE SPY WHO LOVED ME		11	1,576	***
JAMES BOND THUNDERBALL		33	2,750	***
MALTESE FALCON		30	0	****
SECRET OF NIMH	(New segment added)	31	0	***
SHERLOCK HOLMES DRESSED TO KILL		27	850	***
SHERLOCK HOLMES FACES DEATH		11	1,640	***
SHERLOCK HOLMES SECRET WEAPON		22	0	***
THE BIG SLEEP		26	1,382	***
WAR WAGON THE		8	2,232	***
WIZARD OF OZ		13	3,062	****

You will notice that we have updated two records and added four new records to our Focus file. In real-life applications, the add, delete, and change functions are not performed in the same MODIFY request. Usually, the delete and add are part of a separate program. Another method of updating Focus files is by using the CASE logic. In that case the same program would handle all the actions on the file (add, delete, change), but different parts of the program will be devoted to handling these functions.

Other Features of FIXFORM

There are several other features in FIXFORM. I discuss these below.

Skipping characters in a record. The letter "X" followed by a number in a FIXFORM statement instructs Focus to skip over as many characters as indicated by that number while reading the input record. Therefore, X4 would tell Focus to skip over the next four characters of input data. For example, if we wanted to skip the second field in our input file, which was the TAPE_NO field, we would have coded our FIXFORM subcommand as follows:

```
FILEDEF MOVIES DISK E:\MOVIES.DAT
MODIFY FILE MOVIES
FIXFORM TITLE/43 X3   ← Note: Focus will skip the next three characters.
FIXFORM LENGTH/4 COMMENTS/20 RATING/4
MATCH TITLE
ON NOMATCH INCLUDE
ON MATCH UPDATE LENGTH COMMENTS RATING
DATA ON MOVIES
END
```

This would have caused Focus to ignore that input field and update other fields in the segment.

You can also skip backward over transaction data with FIXFORM. To do that you place a minus sign next to the letter "X" and follow it by the number of characters that you want skipped. For example, X-3 means go back three characters in the input file. You could combine the skip forward and backward features of FIXFORM to read data from complex files. For example, our input file could have been prepared by another organization and they could have placed the TAPE_NO as the first field.

```
033COLUMBO GOODBYE MRS COLUMBO            1028DRAMA             ***
028COLUMBO A FRIEND INDEED                1028DRAMA             ***
029HOGANS HEROES                          1200COMEDY            ***
027FATHER GOOSE                           1296COMEDY            ***
012JAMES BOND LIVE AND LET DIE            1576ACTION            ***
031SECRET OF NIMH                            0CARTOON MOVIE      ***
```

This would have made our job much more difficult. One solution would be to write a program to flip the two fields into the order required. However, Focus provides a better solution. It allows you to process the second field first. If you were receiving tapes with tens of thousands of records, you would appreciate this facility.

```
FILEDEF MOVIES DISK E:\MOVIES.DAT
MODIFY FILE MOVIES
FIXFORM X3 TITLE/43 X-46 TAPE_NO/3 X43
FIXFORM LENGTH/4 COMMENTS/20 RATING/4
MATCH TITLE
ON NOMATCH INCLUDE
ON MATCH UPDATE TAPE_NO LENGTH COMMENTS RATING
DATA ON MOVIES
END
```

In the MODIFY request above, we performed the following tasks:

1. We skipped over the first three characters of every input record. This was the TAPE_NO. Since it is not the first field in our Focus data file, we will have to skip over it.

2. Next, we read the TITLE field for the length of 43 characters. This is the Focus data file key field for the MOVIES file. Because we skipped over the first three characters, this has effectively become the first logical field to be read from the input file.

3. The next part of the statement is X-46. This will direct Focus to go backward 46 characters. This will bring it to the beginning of the record.

4. Next, we will read the TAPE_NO field for three characters and place it as the second field in this file.

5. We will now have to skip over the TITLE field, which we have already read in step 2. Therefore, we coded X43 at the end of the first line.

6. The other lines of the FIXFORM statement are similar to the previous example.

Conditional fields. In many cases, in the input file, some field values may be available in one record but absent in another. For example, in updating the MOVIES file we used the following two input records to update the file:

```
COLUMBO A FRIEND INDEED              281028DRAMA          ***
HOGANS HEROES                        291200COMEDY         ***
```

You may remember that we updated the TAPE_NO and LENGTH fields with the first transaction record. The second transaction record only updated the LENGTH field. However, in both cases input records contained all the field values for each record that was already on the Focus MOVIES file.

However, most of the time, each input record will contain only the key field and the fields that are going to be changed. Other fields are left blank. The following displays the same two records as above, except that this time only the fields that are going to be changed are entered on the record.

```
COLUMBO A FRIEND INDEED              281028
HOGANS HEROES                        1200
```

This seems perfectly logical. If you are doing manual data entry, why enter data that are redundant? However, the problem in this case is that this time the first input record will update the TAPE_NO and LENGTH fields, but the comments and the rating fields will be changed to spaces. The second input record will update the Length field, but the other fields in this record in the Focus data file will be changed to spaces also. As a result, the original field values of those fields are permanently lost because no corresponding fields in the input file existed for these fields. Also, if any fields in the file originally contained numeric values, those values would be changed to zeros. To prevent unwanted space-filled and zero-filled fields, you must use the letter "C" after each FIXFORM field name.

```
MODIFY FILE MOVIES
FIXFORM TITLE/43 TAPE_NO/I3
FIXFORM LENGTH/C4 COMMENTS/C20 RATING/C4
MATCH TITLE
ON NOMATCH INCLUDE
ON MATCH UPDATE TAPE_NO LENGTH COMMENTS RATING
DATA ON MOVIES
END
```

The letter "C" tells Focus that it is handling a conditional field and should only update the field value of the corresponding Focus file fields if there is a value other than spaces or zeros in the input field which relates to that field. Otherwise, the value of the field in the Focus data file is left unchanged. Usually, if the value of a field has not changed, the data entry people do not key in the old values again.

For example, in the STAFF file, an employee's telephone number may have changed but his street address and city and zip code may not have changed. Since there is no point in reentering those fields into the file one more time, those fields are left blank. It is therefore a good practice to use the letter "C" to declare an input field conditional whenever you are in doubt about your input file.

Multiple segments. The MOVIES file was a single-segment file. It is almost just as easy to update multiple-segment files as single-segment files. The following MODIFY request adds new segments to the STAFF file, which, as you know, is a three-segment file.

```
-*CHAPTER 12
-*CHA12-6
-*
FILEDEF MODSTAFF DISK E:\MODSTAFF.DAT
MODIFY FILE STAFF
FIXFORM DEPRTMNT/C6 DEPT_NAME/C20 SECTION_ID/C6 SECTION_NAME/C20
FIXFORM EMPLOYEE_ID/C9 LAST_NAME/C20 FIRST_NAME/C10 JOB_TITLE/C20
FIXFORM STREET/C30 CITY/C16 STATE/C2 ZIP_CODE/C5
FIXFORM TELEPHONE/C10 DATE_BIRTH/C6 DATE_HIRE/C6 SALARY/C9
FIXFORM PCT_INC/C5 VACATION/C4
MATCH DEPRTMNT_ID
ON NOMATCH INCLUDE
ON MATCH CONTINUE
MATCH SECTION_ID
ON NOMATCH INCLUDE
ON MATCH CONTINUE
MATCH EMPLOYEE_ID
ON NOMATCH INCLUDE
ON MATCH REJECT
DATA ON MODSTAFF
END
```

As you will notice, the first MATCH statement compares the value in the DEPRTMNT_ID field in the transaction file against the value of DEPRTMNT _ID field, which is a key field, in the STAFF Focus file. If the values do not match, a department segment is created and the process will continue to the next MATCH statement. However, if the two fields match, this will mean that that segment is in existence, so the program will continue to the next segment. The action word CONTINUE is generally used to clarify the code. Next, the value of the SECTION_ID field is compared against the corresponding value in the input file. If the two values are not equal, a new section segment is created with the information from the input file and the process will continue to the next segment (employee segment). If the two values are equal, the process continues to the next segment.

In the employee segment, we cannot have duplicate EMPLOYEE_IDs. So if the value of EMPLOYEE_ID in the STAFF file is equal to the value of the EMPLOYEE_ID field on the input file record, the rest of the input record is rejected. If that happens, the employee segment will not get created, but if the previous segments (i.e., department and section segments) have been created, they will not be deleted. By the way, that will create a short path segment, which is not very desirable in Focus. However, if there is no match (i.e., the value of the EMPLOYEE_ID field on input file does not match the value of the EMPLOYEE_ID field on the STAFF file), a new employee segment is created. The entire procedure will then start from the first MATCH statement with the next record that will be read from the input file. This process will continue until all the input records have been read.

If you are initially loading a Focus file from a sorted external input file, it is not necessary to use the MATCH and NOMATCH statements. In the following example, an input (transaction) file called INMOVIES is used initially to load the MOVIES Focus file. Since this is an initial load and the transactions are in sequence, we do not need to use the MATCH and NOMATCH statements. This will make the processing much faster.

```
-*CHAPTER 12
-*CHA12-18
CMS FILEDEF INMOVIES DISK INMOVIES DATA A
MODIFY FILE MOVIES
FIXFORM TITLE/43 TAPE_NO/3
FIXFORM LENGTH/4 COMMENTS/20 RATING/4
DATA ON INMOVIES
END
```

COMPUTE Statement

The COMPUTE statement in the MODIFY environment is somewhat like the DEFINE command in the TABLE environment. It allows you to perform calculations on incoming input record fields, Focus data file fields, and temporary fields. The syntax of the COMPUTE statement is as follows:

$$
\texttt{COMPUTE FIELDNAME/FORMAT} = \left\{
\begin{array}{l}
\texttt{;} \\
\texttt{LITERAL ;} \\
\texttt{ARITHMETIC EXPRESSION ;} \\
\texttt{CONDITIONAL EXPRESSION ;} \\
\texttt{D.field name (data file field);}
\end{array}
\right\}
$$

There are a number of reasons for using the COMPUTE statement. Some of the more common reasons are listed below.

1. The input data need to be recomputed. For example, the salary field values on the input file may need to be adjusted before updating the Focus data file.

2. The input file may contain codes. In the Focus data file, these codes need to be translated to their full meaning. For example, we may decide that instead of typing the department name, which is 20 characters long, we will ask our data entry people to input department codes such as "1" for Accounting, "2" for Finance, and so on. We will need to translate these codes to their full value at update time, prior to entry into the Focus data file.

3. Some values may vary in predictable fashion. For example, employees in the accounting department may get an overtime pay rate of 1.5 times their hourly rates.

The following MODIFY request shows the application of the COMPUTE statement to convert codes to actual department names. The input file is coded with numbers 1 through 4 instead of actual department names. The COMPUTE statement following the FIXFORM statement converts the codes to actual department names. Note that this is not the only COMPUTE statement in this request. The first COMPUTE statement immediately follows the MODIFY FILE statement. The first COMPUTE statement is necessary to initialize (allocate) the size and identify the field (in this case INDEPT) to the second COMPUTE statement. A good rule to remember is that if a COMPUTE field is not a Focus data file field, it must be identified to Focus before it is referenced by the transaction description. That is why we declared the INDEPT field immediately after the MODIFY FILE statement.

```
-*CHAPTER 12
-*CHA12-7
-*
FILEDEF MODSTAFF DISK E:\MODSTAFF.DAT
MODIFY FILE STAFF

COMPUTE INDEPT/A20= ;              ← The first COMPUTE statement

FIXFORM DEPRTMNT/C6 INDEPT/C20 SECTION_ID/C6 SECTION_NAME/C20
FIXFORM EMPLOYEE_ID/C9 LAST_NAME/C20 FIRST_NAME/C10 JOB_TITLE/C20
FIXFORM STREET/C30 CITY/C16 STATE/C2 ZIP_CODE/C5
FIXFORM TELEPHONE/C10 DATE_BIRTH/C6 DATE_HIRE/C6 SALARY/C9
FIXFORM PCT_INC/C5 VACATION/C4

                    ─────────── The second COMPUTE statement

COMPUTE DEPT_NAME= IF INDEPT  EQ  '1'   THEN 'FINANCE'
ELSE IF INDEPT EQ '2'  THEN 'MIS'
ELSE IF INDEPT EQ '3' THEN 'OPERATIONS'
ELSE IF INDEPT EQ '4' THEN 'ADMINISTRATION'
ELSE 'NEW DEPT' ;
MATCH DEPRTMNT_ID
ON NOMATCH INCLUDE
ON MATCH CONTINUE
MATCH SECTION_ID
ON NOMATCH INCLUDE
ON MATCH CONTINUE
MATCH EMPLOYEE_ID
ON NOMATCH INCLUDE
ON MATCH REJECT
DATA ON MODSTAFF
END
```

In the case above, the format of the transaction file (MODSTAFF) has not changed. The INDEPT is 20 characters long, but the operator has only entered a number from 1 to 4 in that field. There are other uses for the COMPUTE statement. We will use this statement again when we discuss the CRTFORM subcommand.

FIXFORM and Repeating Groups

You can use FIXFORM to modify (change, add, and/or delete) multiple segment instances. You could use a repeating group transaction set within FIXFORM to perform these updates without having to explicitly enter each set of fields repeatedly. For example, if you look at the EMPLOYEE file, you will notice that there is a PAYINFO segment. Each time an employee receives a pay increase, these fields are updated. Let us assume that we want to update the PAYINFO segment with the history of the last four changes of the employees' salaries and job codes. The input file that we use would have four sets of PAYINFO segment data for each set of EMPINFO data (the root segment).

First, let us look at the EMPLOYEE file before we attempt to update that file. The following TABLE request will print the information about the two employees that we have selected to update.

```
TABLE FILE EMPLOYEE
PRINT EMP_ID AND LAST_NAME
AND DAT_INC AND PCT_INC AND SALARY AND JOBCODE
IF EMP_ID EQ '071382660' OR '117593129'

    PAGE    1


EMP_ID      LAST_NAME       DAT_INC  PCT_INC    SALARY   JOBCODE
------      ---------       -------  -------    ------   -------
071382660   STEVENS         82/01/01     .10  $11,000.00   A07
071382660   STEVENS         81/01/01     .12  $10,000.00   A07
117593129   JONES           82/06/01     .04  $18,480.00   B03
117593129   JONES           82/05/01     .00  $17,750.00   B02
```

As you will notice, the two employees in question have had two salary adjustments each.

Next, I created an input transaction file to update the record of these employees. Because the width of each page in this book is limited, I created only two new PAYINFO segment records per employee. Obviously you could create as many segments as you want with repeating groups. The following listing displays the two employee records that I used to update the EMPLOYEE file. Note that on each line I updated the same employee ID twice. The first employee number to be updated was 071382660. Here I added two subrecords with a new date of increase (DAT_INC) values. One date is 88/01/01 and the other is 90/01/01. For employee number 117593129, I added two sets of repeating records also. One recorded date of increase (DAT_INC) is 88/01/01, while the second one is 90/06/06. The data below provide a listing of the input records that will be used to update the PAYINFO segments.

```
071382660880101000.10000012000.00A0790010100.10000013200.00Z07
117593129880101000.12000012000.00A0790060600.11000013500.00X09
```

The program to update this file is listed below.

```
-*CHAPTER 12
-*CHA12-11
-* EXAMPLE OF HOW TO USE REPEATING GROUPS
-* WITH FIXFORM TO UPDATE A FILE
FILEDEF PAYINF DISK E:\PAYINF.DAT
MODIFY FILE EMPLOYEE
FIXFORM EMP_ID/A9
FIXFORM 4(DAT_INC/C6 PCT_INC/C6 SALARY/C12 JOBCODE/C3)
MATCH EMP_ID
ON MATCH CONTINUE
ON NOMATCH REJECT
MATCH DAT_INC
ON MATCH REJECT
ON NOMATCH INCLUDE
DATA ON PAYINF
END
```

Note the presence of the number 4 and the parentheses in the second FIXFORM
subcommand. The number 4 acts as a factor. It tells Focus that up to four sets of
DAT_INC segment data will be expected from the input file.

Notice that the format value for each FIXFORM subcommand in the
PAYINFO field is preceded with the letter "C." This will allow us to have
anywhere from one to four sets of DAT_INC segment information for each field.
If there are only one or two sets of PAYINFO data in the input file, only those
segments will be added to the EMPLOYEE file.

After the MODIFY request above was completed, I submitted the same
TABLE request as before. This time, the report created by this request shows
four additional segments that have been added to the EMPLOYEE file. These are
the new PAYINFO segments.

```
TABLE FILE EMPLOYEE
PRINT EMP_ID AND LAST_NAME
AND DAT_INC AND PCT_INC AND SALARY AND JOBCODE
IF EMP_ID EQ '071382660' OR '117593129'
```

```
PAGE      1


EMP_ID      LAST_NAME      DAT_INC    PCT_INC      SALARY    JOBCODE
------      ---------      -------    -------      ------    -------
071382660   STEVENS        90/01/01       .10   $13,200.00   Z07 (NEW)
071382660   STEVENS        88/01/01       .10   $12,000.00   A07 (NEW)
071382660   STEVENS        82/01/01       .10   $11,000.00   A07
```

```
071382660    STEVENS        81/01/01        .12     $10,000.00    A07
117593129    JONES          90/06/06        .11     $13,500.00    X09   (NEW)
117593129    JONES          88/01/01        .12     $12,000.00    A07   (NEW)
117593129    JONES          82/06/01        .04     $18,480.00    B03
117593129    JONES          82/05/01        .00     $17,750.00    B02
```

NEXT Statement

The NEXT statement allows us to step through a Focus data file sequentially. We can use the NEXT statement to modify or display an entire root segment or the first instances of descendent segments in a Focus data file. For example, if I wanted to increase the salary of every employee in the EMPLOYEE file, I could use the NEXT statement to step through the file logically and increase every employee salary by a certain percentage point.

The original value of the salary fields in the EMPLOYEE file is as follows:

```
     PAGE      1


     LAST_NAME                 CURR_SAL
     ---------                 --------
     STEVENS                 $11,000.00
     SMITH                   $13,200.00
     JONES                   $18,480.00
     SMITH                    $9,500.00
     BANNING                 $29,700.00
     IRVING                  $26,862.00
     ROMANS                  $21,120.00
     MCCOY                   $18,480.00
     BLACKWOOD               $21,780.00
     MCKNIGHT                $16,100.00
     GREENSPAN                $9,000.00
     CROSS                   $27,062.00
```

I will execute the following MODIFY request to increase every employee's salary by 12 percent. The value of the salary fields after the execution of this request is shown immediately following the MODIFY request.

```
-*CHAPTER 12
-*CHA12-13
-* EXAMPLE SHOWING HOW THE NEXT SUB COMMAND
-* CAN UPDATE ALL THE LOGICAL SEGMENTS IN A FOCUS
-* FILE.
MODIFY FILE EMPLOYEE
NEXT EMP_ID
ON NEXT
COMPUTE CURR_SAL = (D.CURR_SAL * 1.12) ;
ON NEXT UPDATE CURR_SAL
ON NONEXT GOTO EXIT
DATA
END
```

The EMPLOYEE file will be updated as shown below:

```
PAGE       1


LAST_NAME                   CURR_SAL
---------                   --------
STEVENS                  $12,320.00
SMITH                    $14,784.00
JONES                    $20,697.60
SMITH                    $10,640.00
BANNING                  $33,264.00
IRVING                   $30,085.44
ROMANS                   $23,654.40
MCCOY                    $20,697.60
BLACKWOOD                $24,393.60
MCKNIGHT                 $18,032.00
GREENSPAN                $10,080.00
CROSS                    $30,309.44
```

I wish to make a few points about the MODIFY request above. The phrase GOTO EXIT appearing near the end of this MODIFY request instructs Focus to stop processing. In a MODIFY request, EXIT is an implied statement. Basically, it means "go to the end." You do not have to code a paragraph in the MODIFY request to handle the EXIT. We could have created an exit paragraph as follows:

```
ON NEXT
COMPUTE CURR_SAL = (D.CURR_SAL * 1.12) ;
ON NEXT UPDATE CURR_SAL
ON NONEXT GOTO EXIT
DATA
-EXIT
END
```

The effects would have been the same. Focus would have stopped processing as soon as it reached the EXIT paragraph.

Also, the NEXT statement can only modify or display data in the first instance of each of the descendent segments. The MODIFY request above worked fine because the CURR_SAL field is in the root segment. If I had used the same logic to modify the SALARY field and/or the GROSS field which are in descendant segments of the EMPLOYEE file, only the first instance of each of those descendant segments would have been modified. If you want to display or modify the entire chain of descendent segments, you must use the CASE logic.

FREEFORM FACILITY

The logic of the FREEFORM subcommand is similar to the FIXFORM subcommand. However, FREEFORM is used for completely different reasons. There are really two primary uses for the FREEFORM subcommand.

1. To read comma-delimited external files. These files are usually created by dBase, Lotus, or other programming languages. Comma-delimited files can be used as input files to update a Focus file. These files usually contain variable-length fields. The fields are separated by commas from each other.

2. To enter a low volume of data from the MODIFY request into the Focus data file directly. Since this method does not leave a clear audit trail, it is not a very good practice for updating production files. It is perhaps acceptable for updating small personal files, but even there you may want to create a small file and use the FIXFORM subcommand.

The following file is a comma-delimited file created by another program. This file is used in the MODIFY request that follows to update the MOVIES file.

```
CASABLANCA,034,1200,DRAMA,****,$
COLUMBO MAKE ME A PERFECT MURDER,054,0700,DRAMA/THRILLER,****,$
STAR WARS,077,1250,ADVENTURE,****,$
LETHAL WEAPON,078,1500,ACTION,***,$
```

As you have noted, each field in this small file has a different length. Also, note that the fields are separated from adjacent fields by commas. The dollar sign ($) signifies the end of each record.

```
-*CHAPTER 12
-*CHA12-10
-* EXAMPLE OF FREEFORM UPDATE FROM AN EXTERNAL FILE
FILEDEF MOVIES2 DISK E:\FREEFORM.DAT
MODIFY FILE MOVIES
FREEFORM TITLE TAPE
FREEFORM LENGTH COMMENTS RATING
MATCH TITLE
ON NOMATCH INCLUDE
ON MATCH UPDATE TAPE LENGTH COMMENTS RATING
DATA ON MOVIES2
END
```

In the following MODIFY request, a similar update task is undertaken, but this time the data are coded directly into the MODIFY request.

```
-*CHAPTER 12
-*CHA12-9
-* EXAMPLE OF FREEFORM UPDATE
MODIFY FILE MOVIES
FREEFORM TITLE TAPE
FREEFORM LENGTH COMMENTS RATING
MATCH TITLE
ON NOMATCH INCLUDE
ON MATCH UPDATE TAPE LENGTH COMMENTS RATING
DATA
TITLE=CASABLANCA, TAPE_NO=026,RATING=****,$
```

```
TITLE=COLUMBO MAKE ME A PERFECT MURDER, TAPE_NO=054,
LENGTH=0700,COMMENTS=DRAMA/THRILLER,RATING=***,$
TITLE=STAR WARS, TAPE_NO=077, LENGTH=1250, COMMENTS=ADVENTURE,
RATING=****,$
END
```

Note the following:

1. The field values are identified by the field name, which appears to the left of each equal sign.

2. Alphanumeric fields do not have to be space-filled to the right as is the case with FIXFORM files.

3. Numeric fields do not have to be right-justified with leading zeros.

4. Each comma denotes the end of a field. As you will notice, the input data fields are all of different lengths. However, when these fields update a Focus data file, they are automatically converted to the correct format length as specified in the Master File Description.

START AND STOP

The START statement is used to start processing from a specific record in an input (transaction) file. The STOP statement will stop applying the input records to the Focus file that it is updating after a specified number of input records have been processed. The following MODIFY request will read the first five records from the input file and will update the first five Focus data file records. Processing will stop after input record number 5 has been completely processed.

```
-*CHAPTER 12
-*CHA12-17
-* EXAMPLE SHOWING THE START AND STOP COMMANDS
-* IN FOCUS
FILEDEF UPDSAL DISK E:\UPDSAL.DAT
MODIFY FILE STAFF
START   1
STOP    5
FIXFORM DID/6 SECID/6
FIXFORM EMPLOYEE_ID/9  SALARY/9
MATCH DID
ON MATCH CONTINUE
ON NOMATCH REJECT
MATCH SECID
ON MATCH CONTINUE
ON NOMATCH REJECT
MATCH EMPLOYEE_ID
ON MATCH UPDATE SALARY
ON NOMATCH REJECT
DATA ON UPDSAL    ← This is the name of the input file.
END
```

There are two major areas in which START and STOP should be used. The first one is in updating large files. It is always possible that halfway through an update program, the computer system may go down due to power failure or other hardware problems. You will then probably lose all your updated data and will have to start over. With the combination of these two statements, you can establish checkpoints in your program to stop the processing, say, every 5000 records or so and start it again from the next record. By using these techniques, if the computer system does go down, you will only have to go back to the point where the processing was stopped by the last STOP command and restart from that point. The following example will clarify the concept.

Let us assume that we have a large STAFF file with 10,000 records and are going to update all salary fields in this file. The input file is called UPDSAL and has 10,000 records. The first MODIFY request will read the first 5000 records from the transaction file and will update the STAFF file. The processing will then stop as soon as the 5000th input record has been processed.

```
CMS FILEDEF UPDSAL DISK UPDSAL DATA A
MODIFY FILE STAFF
START  1
STOP   5000
FIXFORM DID/6 SECID/6
FIXFORM EMPLOYEE_ID/9  SALARY/9
MATCH DID
ON MATCH CONTINUE
ON NOMATCH REJECT
MATCH SECID
ON MATCH CONTINUE
ON NOMATCH REJECT
MATCH EMPLOYEE_ID
ON MATCH UPDATE SALARY
ON NOMATCH REJECT
DATA ON UPDSAL
END
```

At this point, you should make a backup copy of the STAFF file. You could do that by using any utility that your operating environment provides. For example, in CMS, the following command would copy the STAFF file to a temporary file, which you could delete at the end of processing.

```
COPY STAFF FOCUS A BAKSTAFF FOCUS A (REP
```

Your next step would be to run the next program, which is almost identical to the first program except that it starts from input record number 5001 and will go to the end of the input file. If you are not sure how many records remain, you could always code the maximum number possible (i.e., STOP 99999 or higher) next to the STOP statement.

```
FILEDEF UPDSAL DISK UPDSAL DATA A
MODIFY FILE STAFF
```

```
START    5001
STOP     10000
FIXFORM DID/6 SECID/6
FIXFORM EMPLOYEE_ID/9  SALARY/9
MATCH DID
ON MATCH CONTINUE
ON NOMATCH REJECT
MATCH SECID
ON MATCH CONTINUE
ON NOMATCH REJECT
MATCH EMPLOYEE_ID
ON MATCH UPDATE SALARY
ON NOMATCH REJECT
DATA ON UPDSAL
END
```

If processing should fail in the second step, you could then restore the STAFF file by restoring it from the backup copy (BAKSTAFF).

```
COPY BAKSTAFF FOCUS A STAFF FOCUS A (REP
```

You could then restart your process at step 2 and the input record number at 5001. You could completely automate the process above by using the Focus Dialogue Manager, which we discuss in a future chapter.

The other use of START and STOP statements is to limit the number of transactions during the testing phase of program developments. In other words, you could test your MODIFY request against a large input file but read only the first 30 or 40 records. In that respect it is like the RECORDLIMIT phrase in the TABLE request, where only a few records from a large file are selected for processing.

The numbers appearing next to the START and STOP statements refer to physical records, not logical records. There could be two or more physical records for each logical record in an input file. As you know, most CRT terminals have a width of 80 characters across and it is therefore more convenient to limit the length of each record to 80 characters or less. This will make data entry and verification much faster. Now, your actual record in the Focus file may be 400 or 500 characters or more. Therefore, it may require several lines of 80 character full of physical data to complete one actual (logical) record. However, for smaller applications, each input record in an input file would represent one physical record as well as one logical record. Make sure that you are aware of the format and the record layout of the input file.

SUMMARY

In this chapter we discussed some advanced features of the Master File Description. We learned how to create permanent column titles in the Master File Description. We also discussed uses of the DEFINE statement in the Master File Description.

Another useful feature is the TITLE attribute. You can use it to override the field name and create more meaningful column titles.

DESC is an attribute that is used for documenting the purpose of each field. Since it is 44 characters long, you could almost create a minisentence with it. You should use this feature whenever possible in your Master File Description.

Context-sensitive help is available with the HELPMESSAGE attribute and should be used whenever possible. Finally, the ACCEPT attribute allows you to prescreen unwanted data. This feature does not take the place of validating each critical field of data in your MODIFY request since user requirements vary from program to program. However, ACCEPT can help you to perform your basic validation of input data.

There are a number of ways to update Focus files. In this chapter we concentrated on FIXFORM and FREEFORM. FIXFORM is the main method of updating Focus files with bulk batch data. The batch files are usually the by-products of various applications in a business. These applications could be the billing system, payroll system, savings accounts system, accounts receivable system, general ledger system, and so on. FIXFORM is very efficient for this type of update. The real application of the FREEFORM subcommand is in reading Comma-delimited files created by external files. In the PC world, Comma-delimited files are used extensively as a medium of transfer between various types of application software. For example, you could use these kinds of files to transfer data between Lotus and dBase. Focus also helps you to access these kinds of files. The added advantage is that you could then transmit these files to a mainframe computer and update a mainframe Focus file.

The START and STOP statements have two very useful purposes. One is to help you avoid costly reruns when you are updating large Focus files. The other is to allow you to test new programs with a subset of real production files.

INTERACTIVE FILE MAINTENANCE WITH THE PROMPT COMMAND

MAIN TOPICS:

- UPDATING FOCUS FILES INTERACTIVELY (PROMPT)
- DEFINING FIELD TYPES IN FOCUS MODIFY REQUESTS
- CASE LOGIC

In this chapter we discuss another method for updating Focus files. This method is the PROMPT subcommand. PROMPT is a fast, yet versatile method for maintaining a Focus file. With PROMPT you can update a Focus data file, usually one field at a time. Updating, adding, or deleting of data is done interactively via the terminal. All the other Focus MODIFY command features that we have reviewed in Chapter 12 also apply to PROMPT.

PROMPT

The PROMPT subcommand allows you to view and/or update Focus data files one field at a time. In fact, you can update more than one field at any given time, but once you update a field you cannot go back to that field without starting over from the beginning. The MODIFY prompt syntax is as follows:

```
MODIFY FILE file name
PROMPT field name
MATCH  key field(s)
  ON MATCH action
  ON NOMATCH action
DATA
```

The following MODIFY request will allow you to change the value of the department name field in the staff file.

```
-*CHAPTER 13
-*CHA13-1
-*
-* EXAMPLE OF PROMPT SUB COMMAND FOR UPDATING A FILE.
MODIFY FILE STAFF   ← This instruction will invoke the MODIFY
                       environment.

PROMPT DID          ← This command will ask the user to enter the
                       department ID.

PROMPT DEPT_NAME    ← This command will ask the user to enter the
                       department name.

MATCH DID           ← This instruction will try to find a record
                       in the file that matches the department ID
                       entered by you.

ON MATCH UPDATE DEPT_NAME   ← If a match is made, the department
                               name is updated.

ON NOMATCH REJECT           ← If Focus cannot find a match, it
                               will add a new record to the file.

DATA      ← This instruction means that data will follow the
             request. Data entry will be online. Notice that
             no END statement follows the DATA statement.
             The END is entered, by the user, on any prompted
             line, after the user has completed data entry.
```

If you execute the request above, Focus will prompt you to enter the department ID field and the department name. The department ID is a unique key field and cannot be changed. However, the department name can be changed. The following text displays the prompts issued by the program and the user's interaction or conversation with the system. Please remember that you must press the Enter key after each response to a prompt.

   Important note: Focus prompts the user slightly differently on its various versions. For example, in PC/Focus and MVS Focus, the cursor will stay next to the prompted message and will await data entry. This is shown below. However, under the VM/CMS operating system, the cursor will go to the bottom of the screen and await data entry. The results are the same. The slight difference in appearance is due to the characteristics of the various operating systems under which Focus is working. Throughout the rest of this chapter, I use the PC/Focus and MVS/Focus presentation of the PROMPT subcommand since it is easier to demonstrate and understand.

```
EX CHA13-1   ← This command will execute the MODIFY
                request above.
```

Focus will respond with the following series of prompts. The underlined text represent data entered by the operator.

TABLE 13.1   CHARACTERS USED WITH PROMPT

Character	Meaning
$	Cancels the current transaction. The "$" will not affect the previous transactions that may have been entered. Also, new transactions could be entered and the processing can continue.
``	This special character will repeat the value that was entered for the field on the previous transaction. For example, you may have several segments in a file, but some segments such as the department name may be common to all records. In this case you will enter the department name in response to the first prompt. In subsequent prompts, for the records that follow, you could just enter the `` in response to the prompt for the department field. Focus will pick the value of the department field from your first entry.
.	The period has several effects. If it is entered in response to a PROMPT instead of a field value, the old field value does not change. So if you are updating a series of fields in a Focus file and do not want to change the value of some of them, just enter the period in response to the prompt and press the Enter key. However, if you just enter space in response to a prompt, the current value of that field will be changed to either zeros or spaces, depending on the format of that field.
	If you enter the period in response to all the fields in a segment, none of the fields will be updated. If you are creating a new segment, then depending on the format of the fields, all fields will be either spaces-filled or zero-filled.
	If you enter a period in response to a key field but enter data for other fields, you could get either a space-filled or a zero-filled key field. This will be dependent on whether your key field was declared as numeric or alphanumeric in the Master File Description and is very undesirable, since it will introduce invalid key fields into your file. This problem could be avoided if you build good validation routines into the MODIFY request.
	In a good validation routine, you should basically reject a key field if its value is not greater than spaces or zeros.
END	Ends all processing. This will not affect previous updates to the segments.

```
-* CHAPTER 13
-* CHA13-16
-* EXAMPLE OF USING THE DDNAME WITH TYPE TO STORE
-* FOCUS MESSAGES TO A FILE.
FILEDEF ADDFILE DISK ADDFILE MOV A
FILEDEF REJFILE DISK REJFILE MOV A
MODIFY FILE MOVIES
PROMPT TITLE TAPE_NO
MATCH TITLE
     ON MATCH TYPE ON ADDFILE
     "<TITLE <TAPE_NO "
     ON MATCH UPDATE TAPE_NO
     ON NOMATCH TYPE ON REJFILE
     "<TITLE <TAPE_NO "
     ON NOMATCH REJECT
DATA
```

Each time you execute the request above, Focus will place the accepted titles and tape numbers on a file called ADDFILE. If the transaction is rejected, it is placed on a file called REJFILE. If you are writing the messages to a file as in this case, the message will begin in position 3 of the file. Positions 1 and 2 will be left blank. Each line of text in the TYPE statement can contain up to 256 characters. This includes the values of the embedded data fields as defined in their format entry in the Master File Description.

Following is another example of the PROMPT subcommand. In this example we step through two segment levels to reach the employee segment. Once there, we can update the salary of any employee within a section. To ensure against mistakes, we must enter both the employee identification number and the last name of an employee.

```
-*CHAPTER 13
-*CHA13-5
-* EXAMPLE OF USING THE PROMPT SUB COMMAND TO
-* UPDATE THE SALARY FIELD IN THE EMPLOYEE SEGMENT.
MODIFY FILE STAFF
PROMPT DID.PLEASE ENTER THE DEPARTMENT ID===.
MATCH DID      ← (1) The first match takes place at this level.
ON MATCH CONTINUE
ON NOMATCH REJECT
PROMPT SECID.PLEASE ENTER SECTION ID===.
MATCH SECID   ← (2) The second match takes place here.
ON MATCH CONTINUE
ON NOMATCH REJECT
PROMPT EID.PLEASE ENTER EMPLOYEE ID===.
PROMPT LN.PLEASE ENTER EMPLOYEE LAST NAME===.
PROMPT SALARY.PLEASE ENTER NEW EMPLOYEE SALARY===.
MATCH EID LAST_NAME   ← (3) This is the final match.
ON MATCH TYPE
"NEW SALARY IS  :<SALARY"  ← This statement reconfirms the new
                                 salary entered by you.
"OLD SALARY WAS :<D.SALARY  ← This statement will display the
                                 value of the salary field before
                                 the update takes place.

ON MATCH UPDATE SALARY
ON NOMATCH REJECT
DATA
```

The same logic, with minor modifications, could be used to add or delete records from this file. The following MODIFY request will delete an employee segment from the STAFF file.

```
-*CHAPTER 13
-*CHA13-6
-* EXAMPLE OF USING THE PROMPT SUB COMMAND TO
-* DELETE AN ENTIRE EMPLOYEE SEGMENT FROM THE STAFF FILE.
MODIFY FILE STAFF
```

```
PROMPT DID.PLEASE ENTER THE DEPARTMENT ID===.
MATCH DID
ON MATCH CONTINUE
ON NOMATCH REJECT
PROMPT SECID.PLEASE ENTER THE SECTION ID===.
MATCH SECID
ON MATCH CONTINUE
ON NOMATCH REJECT
PROMPT EID.PLEASE ENTER THE EMPLOYEE ID===.
PROMPT LN.PLEASE ENTER THE EMPLOYEE LAST NAME===.
MATCH EID LAST_NAME
ON MATCH TYPE

"EMPLOYEE SEGMENT FOR <25 <D.FN  <36 <D.LN"    ← These two lines
"        HAS BEEN DELETED "                     confirm that a segment
                                                has been deleted.

ON MATCH DELETE
ON NOMATCH REJECT
DATA
```

If you execute the request above, Focus will display the following messages on the terminal. After each message is displayed, the user should either enter the requested data or "END" to terminate the session. User responses have been printed in lowercase letters.

```
DATA FOR TRANSACTION    1

PLEASE ENTER THE DEPARTMENT ID===>12
PLEASE ENTER THE SECTION ID===>122
PLEASE ENTER THE EMPLOYEE ID===>504234521
PLEASE ENTER THE EMPLOYEE'S LAST NAME===>freeman
EMPLOYEE SEGMENT FOR  DIANE      FREEMAN
        HAS BEEN DELETED

DATA FOR TRANSACTION    2

PLEASE ENTER THE DEPARTMENT ID===>14
PLEASE ENTER THE SECTION ID===>141
PLEASE ENTER THE EMPLOYEE ID===>392345782
PLEASE ENTER THE EMPLOYEE'S LAST NAME===>greenstreet
EMPLOYEE SEGMENT FOR  JAMES      GREENSTREET
        HAS BEEN DELETED

DATA FOR TRANSACTION   3

PLEASE ENTER THE DEPARTMENT ID===>end
```

At the end of the update process Focus will display the following statistics about the file being accessed.

```
TRANSACTIONS: TOTAL=      2  ACCEPTED=      2  REJECTED=      0
SEGMENTS:      INPUT=      0  UPDATED =      0  DELETED =      2
```

In the following request, we are adding a complete new employee segment to the STAFF file.

```
-*CHAPTER 13
-*CHA13-8
-* EXAMPLE OF USING THE PROMPT SUB COMMAND TO
-* ADD ENTIRE NEW EMPLOYEE SEGMENT TO THE STAFF FILE.
MODIFY FILE STAFF
PROMPT DID.PLEASE ENTER THE DEPARTMENT ID===.
MATCH DID
ON MATCH CONTINUE
ON NOMATCH REJECT
PROMPT SECID.PLEASE ENTER SECTION ID===.
MATCH SECID
ON MATCH CONTINUE
ON NOMATCH REJECT
PROMPT EID.PLEASE ENTER EMPLOYEE ID===.
MATCH EID
ON MATCH TYPE
"EMPLOYEE SEGMENT FOR <25 <D.FN  <36 <D.LN"
"          ALREADY EXISTS   "
ON MATCH REJECT
PROMPT LN.PLEASE ENTER EMPLOYEE LAST NAME===.
PROMPT FN.PLEASE ENTER THE FIRST NAME===.
PROMPT TITLE.PLEASE ENTER THE JOB TITLE===.
PROMPT STREET.PLEASE ENTER THE STREET ADDRESS===.
PROMPT CITY.PLEASE ENTER THE CITY===.
PROMPT STATE.PLEASE ENTER THE STATE===.
PROMPT ZIP_CODE.PLEASE ENTER THE ZIP CODE===.
PROMPT PHONE.PLEASE ENTER THE TELEPHONE NO ===.
PROMPT DATE_BIRTH.PLEASE ENTER THE DATE OF BIRTH===.
PROMPT DATE_HIRE.PLEASE ENTER THE DATE OF HIRE===.
PROMPT SALARY.PLEASE ENTER ANNUAL SALARY===.
PROMPT PCT_INC.PLEASE ENTER PERCENT INCREASE OR ZERO===.
PROMPT VACATION.PLEASE ENTER ACCRUED VACATION HOURS===.
ON NOMATCH INCLUDE
DATA
```

If you execute the request above, the following messages will be displayed on the terminal. All user responses are entered in lowercase letters. Each message is followed by a user response.

```
DATA FOR TRANSACTION           1

PLEASE ENTER THE DEPARTMENT ID===>12
PLEASE ENTER SECTION ID===>121
```

```
PLEASE ENTER EMPLOYEE ID===>234532145
PLEASE ENTER EMPLOYEE LAST NAME===>thompson
PLEASE ENTER THE FIRST NAME===>carlos
PLEASE ENTER THE JOB TITLE===>staff analyst
PLEASE ENTER THE STREET ADDRESS===>345 JACKSON
PLEASE ENTER THE CITY===>beverly hills
PLEASE ENTER THE STATE===>ca
PLEASE ENTER THE ZIP CODE===>93214
PLEASE ENTER THE TELEPHONE NO ===>2135553421
PLEASE ENTER THE DATE OF BIRTH===>481212
PLEASE ENTER THE DATE OF HIRE===>910812
PLEASE ENTER ANNUAL SALARY===>45000
PLEASE ENTER PERCENT INCREASE OR ZERO===>0
PLEASE ENTER ACCRUED VACATION HOURS===>0

DATA FOR TRANSACTION      2


PLEASE ENTER THE DEPARTMENT ID===>20
PLEASE ENTER SECTION ID===>201
PLEASE ENTER EMPLOYEE ID===>514342896
PLEASE ENTER EMPLOYEE LAST NAME===>guttman
PLEASE ENTER THE FIRST NAME===>kaspar
PLEASE ENTER THE JOB TITLE===>manager
PLEASE ENTER THE STREET ADDRESS===>301 PAMLICO
PLEASE ENTER THE CITY===>irvine
PLEASE ENTER THE STATE===>ca
PLEASE ENTER THE ZIP CODE===>93422
PLEASE ENTER THE TELEPHONE NO===>7145553012
PLEASE ENTER THE DATE OF BIRTH===>551210
PLEASE ENTER THE DATE OF HIRE===>900105
PLEASE ENTER ANNUAL SALARY===>89000
PLEASE ENTER PERCENT INCREASE OR ZERO===>0
PLEASE ENTER ACCRUED VACATION HOURS===>0

DATA FOR TRANSACTION           3

PLEASE ENTER THE DEPARTMENT ID===>end


TRANSCATION: TOTAL=     2  ACCEPTED=     2  REJECTED=        0
SEGMENTS:    INPUT=     2  UPDATED=      0  DELETED  =       0
```

You may remember from a previous chapter that we used repeating groups with the FIXFORM subcommand to add and/or update multiple descendent segments in a file. You can accomplish the same outcome by using the PROMPT subcommand. The following MODIFY request will perform exactly the same function as the FIXFORM request that we performed in Chapter 12. This request will add up to four new PAYINFO segments, with associated fields, to the EMPLOYEE file.

Notice the number 4 following the PROMPT statement in the request. This is called a factor and it informs Focus that there will be up to four new PAYINFO segments for each EMPLOYEE ID segment. The fields in parentheses are the fields that will be added, as part of the update process, to each new PAYINFO segment. To break out of the repeating group during data entry, you should respond with the exclamation mark (!) to the Focus prompt. The exclamation mark will not terminate the request but will get you out of the particular repeating group that you are currently accessing. For example, if the factor is set at 4 and you have data for only two new segments, you need to enter the exclamation mark in response to the Focus prompt after the first two segments have been entered.

```
-*CHAPTER 13
-*CHA13-9
-* EXAMPLE OF USING THE PROMPT SUBCOMMAND WITH
-* REPEATNG GROUPS.
MODIFY FILE EMPLOYEE
PROMPT EMP_ID 4 (DAT_IN PCT_INC SALARY JOBCODE)
MATCH EID
    ON   NOMATCH REJECT
    ON   MATCH CONTINUE
MATCH DAT_INC
    ON MATCH REJECT
    ON NOMATCH INCLUDE
DATA

DATA FOR TRANSACTION            1

EMP_ID         =>117593129
DAT_INC        =>881215
PCT_INC        =>20
SALARY         =>22080
JOBCODE        =>B04

DATA FOR TRANSACTION            2

DAT_INC        =>891201      ← Note: You do not have to keep retyping
PCT_INC        =>10              the employee number with repeating groups.
SALARY         =>24288
JOBCODE        =>B04

DATA FOR TRANSACTION            3

DAT_INC        =>!           ← The "!" completes one repeating group.
EMP_ID         =>219984371   ← Start of another set of transactions
DAT_INC        =>881012         for another employee.
PCT_INC        =>18
SALARY         =>21806
JOBCODE        =>A08

DATA FOR TRANSACTION            4
```

```
DAT_INC        =>900601
PCT_INC        =>11
SALARY         =>24205
JOBCODE        =>A08


DATA FOR  TRANSACTION            5

DAT_INC        =>!
EMP_ID         =>end    ← The "END" statement signifies the
                           termination of the update session.


TRANSACTIONS: TOTAL     4  ACCEPTED=     4  REJECTED=       0
SEGMENTS:     INPUT     4  UPDATED  =     0  DELETED  =      0
```

The following TABLE request will print the contents of the EMPLOYEE file after the addition of the new segments.

```
-*CHAPTER 13
-*CHA13-10
TABLE FILE EMPLOYEE
PRINT EMP_ID   AS 'EMPLOYEE,ID'
AND LAST_NAME/A9 AS 'LAST NAME'
AND DAT_INC AS 'DATE,OF INCREASE'
AND PCT_INC AS 'PERCENT,INCREASE'
AND SALARY
AND JOBCODE
IF EMP_ID EQ '117593129' OR '219984371'
END
```

```
    PAGE     1


EMPLOYEE               DATE        PERCENT
ID          LAST NAME  OF INCREASE INCREASE     SALARY    JOBCODE
--------    ---------  ----------- --------     ------    -------
117593129   JONES       89/12/01    10.00    $24,288.00    B04
117593129   JONES       88/12/15    20.00    $22,080.00    B04
117593129   JONES       82/06/01     .04     $18,480.00    B03
117593129   JONES       82/05/01     .00     $17,750.00    B02
219984371   MCCOY       90/06/01    11.00    $24,205.00    A08
219984371   MCCOY       88/10/12    18.00    $21,806.00    A08
219984371   MCCOY       82/01/01     .15     $18,480.00    B02
```

FIELD TYPES IN FOCUS

Before we proceed with the next topic, we should discuss the three types of data or variable fields that could be specified in a MODIFY request. When we use the

...FY subcommand, we could specify a field in three different ways. These ...a entry fields, display fields, and turnaround fields. These field types have ...to do with the actual format of Focus data fields, such as alphanumeric, ...packed, and so on. The field types in MODIFY requests let Focus know ...t of actions that could be performed on data fields.

...try Fields

You use these fields to enter data for one of two purposes. One is to search a key field and display the rest of information for that record. The other is to enter data into a Focus file. We have so far been using these names in all our programs. Following are examples of display fields.

```
<LAST_NAME
<EMPLOYEE_ID
<DEPT_ID
```

Display Fields

When you specify a field as a display field, data are viewed only by the user. The field cannot be overwritten or changed in any way. Any field name prefixed with the letter "D" in a MODIFY request is considered a display field. These fields are used to display information about parts of a record, such as keys, that cannot or should not be changed, yet are important for accessing other fields in the record. Following are examples of Focus display fields.

```
<D.LAST_NAME
<D.DEPT_NAME
<D.FIRST_NAME
```

Turnaround Fields

Turnaround fields are used with the CRTFORM subcommand only. Any field name prefixed with the letter "T" in a MODIFY request is called a turnaround field. Turnaround fields can be displayed on the terminal and modified by the user. Turnaround fields are used extensively for making changes to records. Examples of turnaround fields follow.

```
<T.LAST_NAME.
<T.SALARY
<T.STREET
```

The left caret (<) in a turnaround field means that the field can be updated but will not change its original value if the user does not enter any values in response to the prompted field. This is known as a conditional field. However, if you end the field name with the right caret (>), then if the user does not enter a value for that field, the current value of the field will be changed to either zeros or spaces, depending on the original format of the field as defined in the Focus Master File

Description. These types of fields are known as *unconditional fields*. Following are examples of such fields.

```
<T.LAST_NAME>
<T.SALARY>
```

The turnaround fields are used only with the CRTFORM subcommand. You cannot use them with the PROMPT because PROMPT does not have full screen capabilities and you cannot go up and down on a screen. Once a field is displayed with the PROMPT statement and you enter data for that field, the cursor moves down one line and you cannot go back up to that field to change it.

Finally, you could also use fields created by the COMPUTE statement. These fields are defined by you and do not exist in the Focus Master File Description. These fields could also be defined as data entry, display or turnaround fields.

CASE LOGIC

So far, we have been dealing with Focus requests where only one action at a time takes place. There are occasions, in fact many, where the user needs to be more interactive with the program. Also, in many instances there is a need for the program to make a decision. These decisions are usually made as a result of one of the following:

1. A letter or word entered by the user in response to a program prompt
2. The value of the outcome of a computation
3. The current value of a certain field

Any one of the possibilities above could transfer control of the process to another part of the request. The transfer of control is also known as *branching*. For example, if the salary of a new employee is entered as greater than $200,000, you may want to highlight that field and execute a different part of the MODIFY request to make sure that the salary entered is not above the maximum range for that category of employee.

CASE logic is like having several MODIFY requests within the main MODIFY request. It can be said that with CASE logic users can create their own procedures in a nonprocedural environment such as Focus. With CASE logic, the programmer can break the request into simple logical sections or modules. Each module is performed independently. Any module can be executed by another module. The process is usually driven by the first module, also called the *main module*. This type of programming structure is known as *top-down structured programming* and is very popular in the third-generation language world. One of the main advantages of structured programming is that each module remains independent and can be changed without adversely affecting the entire program.

GOTO and IF Statements

The GOTO statement is really an integral part of CASE logic. This statement is used to transfer control from the current CASE module to another CASE module unconditionally. Control is transferred to the CASE module that follows the GOTO statement. For example, GOTO ADDNEW will branch to a CASE module named CASE ADDNEW.

If you are updating a file, depending on the code entered by the user, you may have to decide to transfer control of the program to either the module that adds records or the module that modifies them. The IF and ELSE IF statements are used in conjunction with the GOTO statement for conditional transfer of control to a module, depending on user input.

```
IF RECTYPE IS 'A' THEN GOTO ADD_REC
ELSE IF RECTYPE IS 'C' THEN GOTO CHNG_REC ;
```

In Focus, different modules for adding a record, deleting a record, or changing the value of fields within a record could be coded as CASEs. Each CASE is really an independent module and is generally performed by the main module. Each CASE module could also be called by other CASE modules to perform its predetermined function.

In brief, CASE logic allows you to perform the following:

1. Combine several MODIFY requests into one MODIFY request. In other words, instead of writing several independent MODIFY requests and branching from one to the other, you could write one bigger MODIFY request with many CASE modules or CASE routines within that request. Each of these CASE routines is like an independent MODIFY request.
2. Divide one MODIFY request into CASEs. You could then branch to each CASE independently.
3. Provide procedural control in a nonprocedural language.

The format of the CASE statement follows:

```
MODIFY FILE filename

CASE case name

ENDCASE

CASE case name

ENDCASE
```

For example:

```
MODIFY FILE STAFF
```

← The CASE TOP is implied in the beginning. You should not specify it.
← ENDCASE for TOP is also implied and should not be coded.

```
TYPE "PLEASE ENTER YOUR SELECTION BELOW"

COMPUTE SELECTION/A1= ;   ← The COMPUTE statement is needed to
                              to define "SELECTION" because it is
                              not a real field in this file.

PROMPT SELECTION

   IF SELECTION EQ 'A' GOTO ADDNEW ;     ← The IF statements will
   IF SELECTION EQ 'C' GOTO CHANGEREC ;  make a conditional
   IF SELECTION EQ 'D' GOTO DELETE ;        transfer of control
   ELSE GOTO TOP ;

CASE ADDNEW

               ← Code the module for adding new records here.

ENDCASE


CASE CHANGEREC

               ← Code the module for changing records here.
ENDCASE

CASE DELETE

               ← Code the module for deleting records from
                 the Focus data file here.

ENDCASE

DATA           ← Do not code END here.  END is a reserved
                 case name and will automatically end processing
                 as soon as it is entered, by the operator, in
                 response to a Focus prompt.
```

Each CASE routine starts with a CASE statement and ends with an ENDCASE statement. A CASE name could be up to 12 characters long. It should not contain special characters such as *, $, or @.

CASE TOP and CASE EXIT

These two CASEs are Focus reserved words. You should not use TOP and EXIT to name a CASE in a MODIFY request. Both these statements are implied. Therefore, if you code the statement GOTO TOP anywhere in your request, Focus will transfer control to the first statement following the MODIFY FILE statement. Similarly, GOTO EXIT will terminate the request.

CASE AT START

The CASE AT START is another Focus reserved phrase. It has a specific meaning in Focus, and unlike the CASE TOP, it must be coded in the request, if needed. The CASE AT START has the following attributes:

1. It can be coded anywhere in the request.
2. If coded in the request, it will automatically be the first CASE that is executed by Focus.
3. It is executed only once, at the beginning of the request. It cannot be executed again.
4. You cannot branch to it from another CASE statement.
5. You can branch from the CASE AT START to other CASEs. If you do not branch to another CASE, the control will be transferred to the CASE TOP as soon as the ENDCASE statement is encountered by the MODIFY request.

Other rules of CASE logic are as follows:

1. You cannot nest CASEs within one another. In other words, a CASE module cannot contain another CASE module. It can, however, pass control to another CASE module.

2. Other statements cannot be placed between two CASE modules. When one CASE module ends, another CASE module must start.

3. You can have as many CASE modules as you need in a MODIFY request.

4. You cannot transfer control (i.e., branch) to the middle of a CASE module. You can only branch to the beginning of a CASE module.

5. There are five MODIFY statements that refer to the entire MODIFY request. These are known as global statements and should be physically coded at the end of the request following the last CASE module. These statements are:

a. START (not to be confused with CASE AT START). This statement will inform Focus of the starting record number for this request.
b. STOP. This statement will tell Focus when to stop processing.
c. LOG. This statement is usually followed by other instructions which will tell Focus whether to perform or ignore certain logging activities. For example, you can use the LOG statement to record all your input transactions in a sequential file for review at a later date. You can even record your transactions on different files. One file could record all rejected transactions, while the other file could record deleted transactions, and so on. You can also control the display of rejected messages at the terminal and replace them with your own messages. For example, the following statement will prevent display of the automatic Focus message whenever you get a no-match condition.

```
LOG NOMATCH MSG OFF
```

d. CHECK. The Focus Check Point facility allows the programmer to ens
that the updated records are written to the Focus file more frequently. Inpu
transactions are usually written to a buffer in the main storage area of the
CPU before being written to the Focus data file or files on disk drives. The
programmer can establish check points to ensure that data are written at
more frequent intervals to the file. If the system crashes for any reason
during the update process, the user can restart the process at the point where
the last update had taken place by using the START command. The Check
Point facility attributes are:

$$
\text{CHECK} \left\{ \begin{array}{l} \text{ON} \\[1em] \text{OFF (the default)} \\[1em] \text{n (i.e., 10 which means write records to} \\ \quad \text{the file after every 10 transactions.)} \end{array} \right\}
$$

To find out how many transactions have been applied to the file after a crash
has been corrected, use the ? FILE filename query. For example ? FILE
STAFF will produce the statistic for the Staff file.

```
STATUS OF FOCUS FILE: C:\FOCUS\STAFF.FOC  ON 08/10/91 AT  18.52.48


                ACTIVE   DELETED   DATE OF     TIME OF    LAST TRANS
SEGNAME         COUNT    COUNT     LAST CHG    LAST CHG   NUMBER

DEPRTMNT           7               06/24/91    21.49.02       1
SECTION           12               04/24/91    00.26.06       6
EMPLOYEE          16               08/10/91    18.52.48       4


TOTAL SEGS        35
TOTAL CHARS     2964
TOTAL PAGES        3
LAST CHANGE                        08/10/91    18.52.48       4
```

The last line of the statistic will show the last transaction that was applied to
Focus.

e. DATA. This is always the last statement in a MODIFY request with the
PROMPT subcommand. This will tell Focus that the data will be following
the execution of the request. The data, of course, are entered interactively
by the user.

The following example illustrates the use of CASE logic with the PROMPT
subcommand. In this example we use the PROMPT subcommand, in conjunction
with CASE logic, to allow the user to perform any of the following activities on
the MOVIES file.

1. Add new records to the MOVIES file.

Make changes to the records in the MOVIES file.
Delete existing records from the MOVIES file.

```
 APTER 13
 IA13-13
 THE FOLLOWING ILLUSTRATES THE USE OF CASE LOGIC
 SUB COMMAND IN A SIMPLE REQUEST.
MODIFY FILE MOVIES
TYPE "PLEASE ENTER YOUR CHOICE BELOW"
TYPE "IF YOU WANT TO ADD A COMPLETE NEW RECORD, ENTER 'A'"
TYPE "IF YOU WANT TO CHANGE A RECORD, ENTER 'C'"
TYPE "IF YOU WANT TO DELETE AN ENTIRE RECORD, ENTER 'D'"
TYPE "IF YOU WANT TO END THE SESSION TYPE 'END'"
TYPE "THE PROGRAM WILL GUIDE YOU THROUGH YOUR SELECTION"

COMPUTE CHOICE/A1= ;
PROMPT CASE1.PLEASE ENTER YOUR CHOICE.
       IF CHOICE EQ 'A' THEN GOTO ADDNEW ;
       IF CHOICE EQ 'C' THEN GOTO CHANGEREC ;
       IF CHOICE EQ 'D' THEN GOTO DELETE ;
       ELSE GOTO  TOP ;

CASE ADDNEW
PROMPT TITLE.PLEASE ENTER THE TITLE===.
PROMPT TAPE_NO.PLEASE ENTER THE TAPE NUMBER===.
PROMPT LENGTH.PLEASE ENTER THE LENGTH OF THE SHOW OR 0===.
PROMPT COMMENTS.PLEASE ENTER YOUR COMMENTS===.
PROMPT RATING.PLEASE ENTER THE RATING OF THE SHOW ===.
MATCH TITLE
ON NOMATCH INCLUDE
ON NOMATCH GOTO ADDNEW
ON MATCH REJECT
ON MATCH GOTO TOP
ENDCASE

CASE CHANGEREC
PROMPT TITLE.PLEASE ENTER THE TITLE===.
PROMPT TAPE_NO.PLEASE ENTER THE TAPE NUMBER===.
PROMPT LENGTH.PLEASE ENTER THE LENGTH OF THE SHOW OR 0===.
PROMPT COMMENTS.PLEASE ENTER YOUR COMMENTS===.
PROMPT RATING.PLEASE ENTER THE RATING OF THE SHOW===.
MATCH TITLE
ON MATCH UPDATE TAPE_NO LENGTH COMMENTS RATING
ON MATCH GOTO TOP
ON NOMATCH REJECT
ON NOMATCH GOTO TOP
ENDCASE

CASE DELETE
PROMPT TITLE.PLEASE ENTER THE TITLE===.
```

```
MATCH TITLE
ON NOMATCH REJECT
ON NOMATCH GOTO TOP
ON MATCH DELETE TITLE
ON MATCH GOTO TOP
ENDCASE

DATA
```

If you execute this request, Focus will display the following information at the terminal. User responses have been entered in lowercase.

```
PLEASE ENTER YOUR CHOICE BELOW
IF YOU WANT TO ADD A COMPLETE NEW RECORD, ENTER 'A'
IF YOU WANT TO CHANGE A RECORD, ENTER 'C'
IF YOU WANT TO DELETE AN ENTIRE RECORD, ENTER 'D'
IF YOU WANT TO END THE SESSION TYPE 'END'
THE PROGRAM WILL GUIDE YOU THROUGH YOUR SELECTION

DATA FOR TRANSACTION    1

PLEASE ENTER YOUR CHOICE > a

PLEASE ENTER THE TITLE===>dick tracy
PLEASE ENTER THE TAPE NUMBER===>87
PLEASE ENTER THE LENGTH OF THE SHOW OR 0===>2300
PLEASE ENTER YOUR COMMENTS===>action
PLEASE ENTER THE RATING OF THE SHOW ===>***

PLEASE ENTER THE TITLE===>total recall
PLEASE ENTER THE TAPE NUMBER===>89
PLEASE ENTER THE LENGTH OF THE SHOW OR 0===>1890
PLEASE ENTER YOUR COMMENTS===>action
PLEASE ENTER THE RATING OF THE SHOW ===>***

PLEASE ENTER THE TITLE===>end

TRANSACTIONS: TOTAL=      1    ACCEPTED=    1    REJECTED=     0
SEGMENTS:     INPUT=      2    UPDATED =    0    DELETED  =    0
```

Please note that CASE logic for adding new records to the file (CASE ADDNEW) is somewhat different from CASE logic for changing existing records (CASE CHANGEREC). My assumption was that when you are adding new records, you have a bunch of them and are entering them one after another. Therefore, the logic in the CASE ADDNEW module allows you to keep adding new records until you enter the word "END" in response to the Focus prompt. On the other hand, the logic in the CASE CHANGEREC module will transfer control back to the beginning of the request (i.e., CASE TOP) after each record has been modified. Obviously, depending on your requirements, you could modify the logic of either of these modules.

The following is a longer and more complex MODIFY request. This request will perform the following tasks.

1. The request will first ask the user to make a selection.

a. The user can add a complete new record to the STAFF file. This will include all three segments. In this case the user must enter the letter "A" in response to the Focus prompt.

b. The user can change the information within the employee segment only. In this case the user must enter the letter "C" in response to the Focus prompt.

c. The user can delete an entire record from the STAFF file. In this case the user must enter the letter "D" in response to the Focus prompt.

d. If, at any time, the user enters the word "END" in response to the Focus prompt, the program will be terminated.

If the user makes any other entry, the request will loop back to the beginning and the user will again be asked to make a selection.

2. If the user enters the letter "A," control is transferred to the CASE called ADDNEW. This CASE statement will either pass control to the TOP CASE or the ADDSEC CASE. The TOP CASE is implied which means that the control will pass to the statement following the MODIFY FILE statement. In other words, processing will start from the beginning of the MODIFY request. The ADDSEC CASE module will pass control to the ADDEMP CASE, which is the next CASE statement. In this instance a new employee is added to the file. Since there could be many employees in each section, the ADDEMP CASE will transfer control back to the beginning of itself. In other words, you could keep on adding new employee segments for the same section segment as long as you want. If at any time you want to break out of this CASE module, you will need to enter "END" in response to the Focus prompt.

3. If the user enters the letter "C" in response to the prompt, control is transferred to the CHANGEREC CASE. This will allow the user to make changes by first stepping through the department and section segments for an employee. Once the existence of the employee ID has been verified, the user can change any field within the employee segment. Remember that you cannot change a key field (e.g., the EMPLOYEE_ID field). Another important point here is that there are no GOTO statements at the end of the CHANGEREC CASE. In this case, and any time that there are no GOTOs coded within a CASE, the CASE statement defaults to the TOP CASE. In other words, as soon as you finish updating the employee segment for one employee, control of the program is passed to the statement following the MODIFY FILE statement. Therefore, you will start from the beginning of the program. As I mentioned in the previous example, you can modify this code and make it loop within itself by adding a simple GOTO statement. For example, you could add ON MATCH GOTO CHANGEMP right before the ENDCASE statement in that CASE statement. This will ensure that control remains within the CHANGEMP CASE module until you enter the "END" statement in response to the Focus prompt.

4. If the user enters the letter "D" in response to the Focus prompt, control is passed to the DELETE CASE. Deleting entire records is much simpler and easier than any other update function. If you just delete the first key field in a Focus record, you will delete the entire record. In our example we have added another line of code that will force the user to enter the department name. This will guard against erroneous deletions.

```
-*CHAPTER 13
-*CHA13-12
-* PROGRAM ILLUSTRATING THE USE OF CASE WITH THE PROMPT
-* SUB COMMAND.
MODIFY FILE STAFF
TYPE "PLEASE ENTER YOUR SELECTION BELOW"
TYPE "IF YOU WANT TO ADD A COMPLETE NEW RECORD, ENTER 'A'"
TYPE "IF YOU WANT TO CHANGE THE EMPLOYEE SEGMENT, ENTER 'C'"
TYPE "IF YOU WANT TO DELETE AN ENTIRE RECORD, ENTER 'D'"
TYPE "IF YOU WANT TO END THE SESSION TYPE 'END'"
TYPE "THE PROGRAM WILL GUIDE YOU THROUGH YOUR SELECTION"

COMPUTE CHOICE/A1= ;
PROMPT CHOICE.PLEASE ENTER YOUR CHOICE.
      IF CHOICE EQ 'A' THEN GOTO ADDNEW ;
      IF CHOICE EQ 'C' THEN GOTO CHANGEREC ;
      IF CHOICE EQ 'D' THEN GOTO DELETE
      ELSE GOTO  TOP ;

CASE ADDNEW
PROMPT DID.PLEASE ENTER THE DEPARTMENT ID===.
PROMPT DEPT_NAME.PLEASE ENTER DEPARTMENT NAME===.
MATCH DID
ON MATCH REJECT
ON MATCH GOTO TOP
ON NOMATCH INCLUDE
ON NOMATCH GOTO ADDSEC
ENDCASE
CASE ADDSEC
PROMPT SECID.PLEASE ENTER SECTION ID===.
PROMPT SECTION_NAME.PLEASE ENTER SECTION NAME===.
MATCH SECID
ON MATCH GOTO ADDEMP
ON NOMATCH INCLUDE
ON NOMATCH GOTO ADDEMP
ENDCASE

CASE ADDEMP
PROMPT EID.PLEASE ENTER EMPLOYEE ID===.
MATCH EID
ON MATCH TYPE
"    "
"EMPLOYEE SEGMENT FOR <25 <D.FN   <36 <D.LN"
"        ALREADY EXISTS     "
ON MATCH REJECT
```

```
PROMPT LN.PLEASE ENTER EMPLOYEE LAST NAME===.
PROMPT FN.PLEASE ENTER THE FIRST NAME===.
PROMPT TITLE.PLEASE ENTER THE JOB TITLE===.
PROMPT STREET.PLEASE ENTER THE STREET ADDRESS===.
PROMPT CITY.PLEASE ENTER THE CITY===.
PROMPT STATE.PLEASE ENTER THE STATE===.
PROMPT ZIP_CODE.PLEASE ENTER THE ZIP CODE===.
PROMPT PHONE.PLEASE ENTER THE TELEPHONE NO ===.
PROMPT DATE_BIRTH.PLEASE ENTER THE DATE OF BIRTH===.
PROMPT DATE_HIRE.PLEASE ENTER THE DATE OF HIRE===.
PROMPT SALARY.PLEASE ENTER ANNUAL SALARY===.
PROMPT PCT_INC.PLEASE ENTER PERCENT INCREASE OR ZERO===.
PROMPT VACATION.PLEASE ENTER ACCRUED VACATION HOURS===.
ON NOMATCH COMPUTE PIN=PIN/100 ;
ON NOMATCH INCLUDE
ON NOMATCH GOTO ADDEMP
ENDCASE

CASE CHANGEREC
PROMPT DID.PLEASE ENTER THE DEPARTMENT ID===.
PROMPT DEPT_NAME.PLEASE ENTER DEPARTMENT NAME===.
MATCH DID
ON NOMATCH REJECT
ON NOMATCH GOTO TOP
ON MATCH GOTO CHANGSEC
ENDCASE
CASE CHANGSEC
PROMPT SECID.PLEASE ENTER SECTION ID===.
PROMPT SECTION_NAME.PLEASE ENTER SECTION NAME===.
MATCH SECID SECTION_NAME
ON MATCH GOTO CHANGEMP
ON NOMATCH GOTO CHANGEREC
ENDCASE

CASE CHANGEMP
PROMPT EID.PLEASE ENTER EMPLOYEE ID===.
MATCH EID
ON NOMATCH TYPE
"   "
"AN EMPLOYEE SEGMENT FOR THIS EMPLOYEE"
"         DOES NOT EXIST      "
"         PLEASE TRY AGAIN                "
ON NOMATCH REJECT
ON NOMATCH GOTO CHANGEMP
PROMPT LN.PLEASE ENTER EMPLOYEE LAST NAME===.
PROMPT FN.PLEASE ENTER THE FIRST NAME===.
PROMPT TITLE.PLEASE ENTER THE JOB TITLE===.
PROMPT STREET.PLEASE ENTER THE STREET ADDRESS===.
PROMPT CITY.PLEASE ENTER THE CITY===.
PROMPT STATE.PLEASE ENTER THE STATE===.
```

```
PROMPT ZIP_CODE.PLEASE ENTER THE ZIP CODE===.
PROMPT PHONE.PLEASE ENTER THE TELEPHONE NO ===.
PROMPT DATE_BIRTH.PLEASE ENTER THE DATE OF BIRTH===.
PROMPT DATE_HIRE.PLEASE ENTER THE DATE OF HIRE===.
PROMPT SALARY.PLEASE ENTER ANNUAL SALARY===.
PROMPT PCT_INC.PLEASE ENTER PERCENT INCREASE OR ZERO===.
PROMPT VACATION.PLEASE ENTER ACCRUED VACATION HOURS===.
ON MATCH UPDATE LAST_NAME FIRST_NAME TITLE STREET CITY
ON MATCH UPDATE STATE ZIP PHONE DOB DOH SALARY VACATION
ON MATCH COMPUTE PIN=PIN/100 ;

ON MATCH UPDATE PIN      ← Note that this is also an implied
ENDCASE                     GOTO TOP since there is no GOTO
                            statement in this CASE module.

CASE DELETE
PROMPT DID.PLEASE ENTER THE DEPARTMENT ID===.
PROMPT DEPT_NAME.PLEASE ENTER DEPARTMENT NAME===.
MATCH DID DEPT_NAME
ON NOMATCH REJECT
ON NOMATCH GOTO TOP
ON MATCH DELETE DID
ON MATCH GOTO TOP
ENDCASE
DATA
```

CASE Logic and the NEXT Statement

Previously we have demonstrated how to use the NEXT statement to update succeeding segments of the same segment type. We also stated that in a multisegment file, it was not possible to update beyond the first segment of any child segments with the NEXT statement. Each succeeding child segment within a chain can be updated only by using the CASE logic. Using the NEXT and CASE together is like having a MODIFY request just for one segment. The following example will illustrate how to update multiple child segments with the help of combination of the NEXT and CASE statements. The following MODIFY request is a program to increase the salaries of employees in various sections. Employees in different section may be eligible for different raises. The request, as written, performs the following tasks:

1. Prompts the user to enter the department number.
2. Prompts the user to enter the section number.
3. Prompts the user for the percentage increase in salary for employees in that section.
4. Uses the NEXT statement to step through the entire chain of employees for that section. In each instance it computes the new salary for an employee by applying the increase.
5. After all the employee records in one section have been processed, it will

return to the beginning of the program and will prompt the user for another department number. At any time during the entire process the user can stop the request by typing the END statement in response to a prompt.

```
-*CHAPTER 13
-*CHA13-15
-* EXAMPLE SHOWING HOW THE NEXT SUBCOMMAND
-* CAN UPDATE ALL THE LOGICAL SEGMENTS IN FOCUS
-* FILE.
MODIFY FILE STAFF

   COMPUTE INC/D4.3= ;

PROMPT DID.PLEASE ENTER THE DEPARTMENT NUMBER.
MATCH DID
ON MATCH GOTO NEXT_SEC
ON NOMATCH REJECT
ON NOMATCH GOTO TOP

CASE NEXT_SEC
PROMPT SECID.PLEASE ENTER THE SECTION NUMBER.
PROMPT INC.PLEASE ENTER INCREASE PERCENTAGE.

   COMPUTE INC=INC/100 ;

MATCH SECID
ON MATCH GOTO NEXT_EMP
ON NOMATCH GOTO TOP
ENDCASE

CASE NEXT_EMP
NEXT EMPLOYEE_ID SALARY
ON NONEXT GOTO TOP
ON NEXT
   COMPUTE SALARY = D.SALARY * INC + D.SALARY ;
ON NEXT UPDATE SALARY
ON NEXT
TYPE "<EMPLOYEE_ID CURRENT SALARY:<D.SALARY NEW SALARY:<SALARY"
ON NEXT GOTO NEXT_EMP
ENDCASE
DATA
```

PERFORM Statement

This statement forces the request to transfer control to another CASE. After that CASE is executed, control is returned back to the statement following the PERFORM statement that caused the branch. There are a few exceptions to this rule, as we shall see shortly. The PERFORM statement is similar to the GOTO statement in the sense that it transfers control to another part of the request. However, it has several advantages over the GOTO statement. The main advantage is that the control always returns to the statement following the PERFORM statement. PERFORM achieves this by building an internal table of return points to allow itself to find its way back up the chain. The other advantage is that nesting is allowed with PERFORM. Therefore, you can take full advantage of structured programming techniques and build programs that could be maintained easily. The syntax of the PERFORM statement is as follows:

```
              ⎧TOP
              ⎪ENDCASE
PERFORM       ⎨case name
              ⎪variable
              ⎩EXIT
```

PERFORM TOP.   In this case control is passed to the TOP CASE. With this option, control does not return back to the statement following the PERFORM statement. In other words, all PERFORM return points are cleared.

PERFORM ENDCASE.   This statement will branch to the end of the current CASE module. If the current CASE module was itself PERFORMed by another CASE module, control will return to the statement following that PERFORM. If the current CASE module was not called by another CASE module, the control will branch back to the TOP CASE.

PERFORM case name.   This statement will transfer control to the CASE module that was coded. For example, PERFORM SALCHEK will transfer control of the program to the CASE called SALCHEK.

PERFORM variable.   This statement will branch to the beginning of a CASE module with the name of a temporary field. The temporary variable field must have a format of A12.

EXIT.   This statement will immediately terminate the request.

A PERFORM statement can transfer control to a CASE module containing another PERFORM statement. That module can branch to other modules until eventually an ENDCASE is encountered. In that case, PERFORM will start transferring control back through the chain of PERFORMed cases until it finally transfers control to the statement following the original PERFORM statement.

A PERFORM statement can branch to a CASE module that contains a GOTO or an IF statement. Those CASE modules could branch to other CASEs, and so on. When the last module is executed and the request encounters an ENDCASE statement, the request will immediately transfer control to the statement following the original PERFORM statement.

Whenever possible, it is preferable to use the PERFORM statement instead of the GOTO statement. However, it may not be available on older versions of Focus. So, before attempting to use it, make sure that you have this statement available.

Example of PERFORM statement. The following request will selectively update the value of the salary fields of the STAFF file. The user is first asked for the department ID and the section ID numbers. The next step is identifying the employee by his employee ID number. The user is next prompted to enter the new salary. Focus will then perform two tasks. The first one is to perform the SALCHEK CASE module. This CASE module will check the employee's new salary. If the new salary is less than or equal to $60,000, the CASE module will increase it by 10 percentage points. If the new salary is more than $60,000, it is not adjusted further. In any case, control is returned to the statement following the first perform statement (SALCHEK). The next perform statement is UPDATESAL. This module will check the employee ID against the value in the Focus file, and if correct, will update the employee's salary field with the new value. If the employee ID is not entered correctly, this module will branch back to the CHANGEMP module and will prompt the user for the employee ID. If the match is successful, control is transferred to the TOP CASE since no other branch instructions are given.

```
-*CHAPTER 13
-*CHA13-14
-* PROGRAM ILLUSTRATING THE USE OF CASE WITH PROMPT
-* SUB COMMAND USING THE PERFORM STATEMENT.
MODIFY FILE STAFF
TYPE "PLEASE ENTER YOUR SELECTION BELOW"
PROMPT DID.PLEASE ENTER THE DEPARTMENT ID===.
PROMPT DEPT_NAME.PLEASE ENTER DEPARTMENT NAME===.
MATCH DID
ON NOMATCH TYPE "INCORRECT DEPARTMENT INFORMATION, "
ON NOMATCH TYPE "        PLEASE TRY AGAIN            "
ON NOMATCH REJECT
ON NOMATCH GOTO TOP
ON MATCH GOTO CHANGSEC
CASE CHANGSEC
PROMPT SECID.PLEASE ENTER SECTION ID===.
PROMPT SECTION_NAME.PLEASE ENTER SECTION NAME===.
MATCH SECID SECTION_NAME
ON MATCH GOTO CHANGEMP
ON NOMATCH TYPE "INCORRECT SECTION INFORMATION, "
ON NOOMATCH TYPE "        PLEASE TRY AGAIN           "
ON NOMATCH GOTO TOP
ENDCASE

CASE CHANGEMP
PROMPT EID.PLEASE ENTER EMPLOYEE ID===.
PROMPT SALARY.PLEASE ENTER NEW SALARY===.
PERFORM SALCHECK
PERFORM UPDATESAL
ENDCASE
```

`CASE UPDATESAL` ← The second PERFORMed CASE.

```
MATCH EID
ON MATCH UPDATE SALARY
ON NOMATCH TYPE
"    "
"AN EMPLOYEE SEGMENT FOR THIS EMPLOYEE"
"         DOES NOT EXIST      "
"         PLEASE TRY AGAIN                "

ON NOMATCH REJECT
ON NOMATCH GOTO CHANGEMP

ENDCASE
```

    ┌─────────────────┐
    │ CASE SALCHECK   │ ← The first PERFORMed CASE.
    └─────────────────┘

```
IF SALARY GT 60000 GOTO ENDCASE ;
COMPUTE
SALARY=(SALARY*PIN+SALARY) ;
ENDCASE

CASE AT START
COMPUTE PIN=(.10) ;
ENDCASE

DATA
```

Note: PERFORM CASEs do not have to be in any particular physical sequence. In the example above, the second PERFORMed CASE (UPDATESAL) is physically coded before the SALECHECK CASE but is performed first.

CASE Logic and Batch Transaction File Processing

You can use the CASE logic to update a Focus file with batch transactions with different record codes. In the following example, the transaction file contains two types of records. The first field of each record is the record type. Record type "A" denotes that the incoming record should be used to add a new record to the MOVIES Focus file. Record type "C" denotes a change record. These incoming transaction records will be used to change the Comments field in the MOVIES file. If the incoming record is coded with any other record type, it will be rejected. Rejected record types and records are displayed on the terminal. Remember that the record size for this file is 75 characters long.

```
-* CHAPTER 13
-* CHA13-17
-* PROGRAM DEMONSTRATING THE USE OF THE CASE
-* LOGIC TO UPDATE TRANSACTION FILES WITH DIFFERENT
-* RECORD TYPES.
FILEDEF INFILE DISK C:\FOCUS\TRANS.MOV
```

```
MODIFY FILE MOVIES

COMPUTE RECTYPE/A1= ;
COMPUTE DUMMY/A74= ;

FIXFORM RECTYPE/1 DUMMY/74      ← This is the original definition
                                  of the incoming records.


     IF RECTYPE IS 'A' THEN GOTO ADD_REC
ELSE IF RECTYPE IS 'C' THEN GOTO CHNG_REC ;
```

┌─────────────── If neither "A" nor "C" are present in the RETYPE
│   field, the following five statements are executed.
│
↓

```
TYPE "  "
TYPE "BAD RECORD TYPE VALUE "
TYPE "RECORD TYPE: <RECTYPE "
TYPE "<DUMMY"
GOTO TOP

CASE ADD_REC
   FIXFORM X-75 X1 TITLE/43      ← This entry redefines the original
                                   entry, skipping back 75 positions
                                   and starting the field
                                   definitions from position 1.

   FIXFORM TAPE_NO/3 LENGTH/4
   FIXFORM COMMENTS/20 RATING/4
   MATCH TITLE
   ON NOMATCH INCLUDE
   ON MATCH REJECT
ENDCASE

CASE CHNG_REC
FIXFORM X-75 X1 TITLE/43         ← This is similar to the
                                   entry above.
   FIXFORM TAPE_NO/3 LENGTH/4
   FIXFORM COMMENTS/20 RATING/4
   MATCH TITLE
   ON MATCH UPDATE COMMENTS
   ON NOMATCH REJECT
ENDCASE

DATA ON INFILE
END
```

Note: I have used two COMPUTE fields in this request. This was necessary because RECTYPE was not a defined name for this file. I also defined another field called DUMMY. This was necessary because I needed to label the rest of the incoming record for display, in case of error.

The TRACE Facility

The TRACE facility is a very useful debugging tool that is available with the MODIFY request. Trace works with CASE logic and when invoked will display the name of each CASE module that is being executed. To use the TRACE facility, all you will have to do is to add the word "TRACE" at the end of your MODIFY statement.

```
MODIFY FILE MOVIES TRACE
```

The following is the same example that I used a few pages back to demonstrate the NEXT statement. This time I have added the word "TRACE" to the end of the MODIFY statement. The resulting display, on the terminal, is shown directly following the request.

```
-*CHAPTER 13
-*CHA13-15
-* EXAMPLE SHOWING HOW THE NEXT SUBCOMMAND
-* CAN UPDATE ALL THE LOGICAL SEGMENTS IN FOCUS
-* FILE.
MODIFY FILE STAFF TRACE   ← Note: The TRACE facility is invoked
                                     here.
COMPUTE INC/D3.2= ;
PROMPT DID.PLEASE ENTER THE DEPARTMENT NUMBER.
MATCH DID
ON MATCH GOTO NEXT_SEC
ON NOMATCH REJECT
ON NOMATCH GOTO TOP
CASE NEXT_SEC
PROMPT SECID.PLEASE ENTER THE SECTION NUMBER.
PROMPT INC.PLEASE ENTER INCREASE PERCENTAGE.
MATCH SECID
ON MATCH GOTO NEXT_EMP
ON NOMATCH GOTO TOP
ENDCASE

CASE NEXT_EMP
NEXT EMPLOYEE_ID SALARY
ON NONEXT GOTO TOP
ON NEXT
COMPUTE SALARY = D.SALARY * INC + D.SALARY ;
ON NEXT UPDATE SALARY
ON NEXT
TYPE "<EMPLOYEE_ID CURRENT SALARY:<D.SALARY NEW SALARY:<SALARY"
ON NEXT GOTO NEXT_EMP
ENDCASE
DATA
```

The result of execution of this request follows.

```
**** START OF TRACE ****
TRACE ===> AT CASE TOP

DATA FOR TRANSACTION      1


 PLEASE ENTER THE DEPARTMENT NUMBER>12
TRACE ===> AT CASE NEXT_SEC
 PLEASE ENTER THE SECTION NUMBER>121
 PLEASE ENTER THE INCREASE PERCENTAGE>.10
TRACE ===> AT CASE NEXT_EMP
 294728305 CURRENT SALARY: 65,400.00 NEW SALARY: 71,940.00
TRACE ===> AT CASE NEXT_EMP
 513724567 CURRENT SALARY: 102,000,00 NEW SALARY: 112,200.00
TRACE ===> AT CASE NEXT_EMP
TRACE ===> AT CASE TOP

DATA FOR TRANSACTION      2

 PLEASE ENTER THE DEPARTMENT NUMBER>end
```

Trace is a very useful tool for debugging MODIFY requests with CASE logic.

SUMMARY

In this chapter we discussed a number of very important items. PROMPT is a very useful facility for producing quick MODIFY requests for updating or viewing Focus files. Unlike the FIXFORM and the FREEFORM sub commands, PROMPT is an interactive facility. It allows the user to enter data in response to preprogrammed prompts on the terminal. PROMPT has all the capabilities of FIXFORM and FREEFORM. PROMPT is versatile and powerful; however, it does not have full screen capabilities. It prompts the user one line at a time. The user cannot see all the fields that are being updated or added before making his or her decision to enter the data and transmit them. Because of these shortcomings, it is used for low-volume updating. Sometimes you may need to fix one or two fields that are entered incorrectly or add a few records to a small file that you are very familiar with. In those cases you can very easily create a MODIFY request with PROMPT and complete your work within an hour or so. For bulk data and also when input data are from external files, you should use the FIXFORM subcommand. For truly interactive user-friendly data entry, you should develop CRTFORM requests.

I introduced several new statements in this chapter. These were the TYPE, LOG, and CHECK statements. I also used the COMPUTE statement to create new fields. The computed fields were not part of the Focus data file but were created to make possible updating of the file. One good example was the use of the INC field to calculate the percentage salary increase for each employee.

I discussed Focus field types in this chapter. You should not confuse the field types as used in a MODIFY request with field formats as used in the Master File Description. Field types are basically a safeguard to ensure that fields that need to be viewed only are not accidentally corrupted and stop the user from attempting to update key fields and other fields that should not or could not be updated.

Finally, I discussed the CASE logic. The CASE logic concept is not merely a Focus feature. Other languages also use this concept. In essence, you can use CASE logic to divide your program into smaller, more manageable portions or subprograms and still retain them in one program. Each case is an independent module and could be called by other cases to perform its predefined function. CASE logic provides the GOTO and the IF, THEN, ELSE statements to facilitate navigation through the program. With the PERFORM statement Focus has given users more power to control the flow of the program. However, you should be careful when using the PERFORM statement. It is not always a one-for-one replacement for the GOTO statement. PERFORMed CASEs usually come back to the statement following the PERFORM statement. This may not be desirable in certain circumstances when you are trying to loop through a particular CASE until a certain condition is met or the user has entered the "END" statement.

CRTFORM: CREATING CUSTOMIZED DATA ENTRY AND DATA DISPLAY SCREENS

MAIN TOPICS:

- DEVELOPING ONLINE APPLICATIONS
- CRTFORM
- VALIDATE STATEMENT
- DATA VALIDATION
- DATA INQUIRY SCREENS
- FIND FUNCTION
- LOOKUP FUNCTION
- REPEATING GROUPS
- TEXT FEATURE

In this chapter we discuss the main method for updating Focus files online and interactively. While PROMPT is a versatile subcommand, its use is limited to low-volume input. Also, since you cannot back up to a previous field, it is not very easy to correct a data entry error on the fly. On the other hand, CRTFORM is fully interactive and allows the programmer to develop flexible data entry and inquiry screens.

CRTFORM FACILITY

The CRTFORM facility allows you to develop full-screen user-friendly online data entry and data inquiry applications. The user could then navigate through one or more screens of data and perform any of the following tasks:

1. *Data inquiry*. This involves just looking at the data in the file.
2. *Data entry*. This could be any one of three activities: (a) you could add new segments and/or records; (b) you could modify fields in existing records; and

(c) you could delete segments and records completely by deleting their key fields.

You could use the CRTFORM facility to display an entire Focus data file one record at a time. This may occupy anywhere from a few lines on the terminal to several screens of data for each record. You could use CRTFORM for adding new records, changing data already in the file, and deleting whole segments or records.

We have so far reviewed three methods—FIXFORM, FREEFORM, and PROMPT—for updating a Focus file. CRTFORM is the full-screen online method for updating files. CRTFORM, which runs under the Focus FIDEL (Focus Interactive Data Entry Language) facility, is fully interactive. With CRTFORM the users can move around one or more screens of data and make changes to various fields. CRTFORM also gives the programmer the ability to display the current value of a data field and allows the user to change that value by writing over it.

All Focus facilities that are available under the PROMPT, FIXFORM, and FREEFORM subcommands are also available under the CRTFORM facility. Additionally, we discuss additional features such as the VALIDATE statement, and the LOOKUP and FIND functions that are available under all MODIFY subcommands but are used primarily with CRTFORM.

CRTFORM INVOCATION WITH MODIFY

Full-screen data entry in Focus is invoked by using the CRTFORM statement following the MODIFY FILE statement. The syntax of this subcommand is as follows:

```
MODIFY FILE filename

CRTFORM [LINE #] [CLEAR   ] LOWER TYPE n
                 [NO CLEAR]
"                                               "
"                                               "
"   SCREEN FORMAT                               "
"                                               "
"                                               "
"                                               "
"                                               "
"                                               "
DATA VIA FIDEL
END
```

The CRTFORM works with FIDEL (Focus Interactive Data Entry Language). It generates the visual form (i.e., a full data entry or data inquiry screen) and it invokes FIDEL. CRTFORM starts the form. The form begins on the line specified in the line option part of the subcommand. If the line option is not coded, the form will begin on line 1 of the terminal.

It is important to note the similarities between the CRTFORM syntax and the heading option syntax in the TABLE request. Once you understand the similarities, you will find CRTFORM very easy to work with. Both the CRTFORM subcommand and the heading option in the TABLE request are enclosed in double quotation marks. Like the heading option, CRTFORM also uses spot markers to position the columns on the terminal. You use the caret sign (<) in both CRTFORM and heading to retrieve field values from the file and embed them in the heading or the screen, the difference being that with heading, the data are either printed on the printer or displayed on the terminal. With CRTFORM, the data are displayed on the terminal only. Also, with the CRTFORM you will have the option of modifying some of the fields. With the heading option, you can only look at the data. In fact, a MODIFY request with CRTFORM and with five lines of displayed data looks very much like a TABLE request with five lines of heading.

The following example is a simple MODIFY request with the CRTFORM subcommand. This request will add new records to the MOVIES data file. This request consists of one screen. The subcommand CRTFORM LINE 3 will create a screen for entering the data. The number 3 following the LINE statement means that the first two lines of the CRT screen will be left blank and the display of the form will start on line 3 of the screen. All the lines following this subcommand that are enclosed in double quotation marks will be displayed on the screen. Each line usually consists of a short text field and a data-entry field. The data-entry fields are identified by a left-hand caret (<). In the example that follows, the actual Focus codes follow the screen description. We have reviewed the MATCH and NOMATCH commands in previous chapters. Observe the statement: DATA VIA FIDEL. This statement is required on all MODIFY requests that utilize the CRTFORM facility. It simply invokes the full-screen online facilities of Focus.

```
-* CHAPTER 14
-* CHA14-1
-* SIMPLE EXAMPLE SHOWING HOW TO USE THE CRTFORM
-* IN FOCUS
-*
MODIFY FILE MOVIES
CRTFORM LINE 3        ← This command starts the form on line 3
                         of the screen.

"</1 "                ← This spot marker will skip one blank line
                         from the top of the screen before printing
                         the screen title shown below.

"                        SCREEN FOR ADDING NEW
                               TITLES TO THE MOVIES FILE"

"    "                ← This will display a blank line.
"    "
"    "                                    Text field.
                                              Data-entry field.

"Please Enter The Title: <TITLE"    ← The first displayed line
                                       of data on the screen.

  "Tape Number: <TAPE_NO "
  "Length:      <LENGTH"
  "Comments:    <COMMENTS"
  "Rating:      <RATING"            ← Last displayed line on
                                      the screen.
```

The instructions for displaying the form.

```
MATCH TITLE
    ON MATCH TYPE
                                    In case of error, this message will
                                    be displayed at the bottom of the
                                    screen.

    "Title is already on file: Please try again"
    ON MATCH REJECT
    ON NOMATCH INCLUDE
DATA VIA FIDEL

LOG DUPL MSG OFF  ← This command will turn regular Focus
                     duplicate messages off and replace them
                     with the messages encoded in the request.

END
```

The Focus code
to manipulate
the data on
the form.

If you execute the program above, Focus will first clear the screen and will then display the following screen:

```
        SCREEN FOR ADDING NEW TITLES TO THE MOVIES FILE


    Please Enter The Title:_  ← The cursor is positioned here.


    Tape Number:
    Length:
    Comments:
    Rating:
```

The cursor will be positioned at the first character position of the first field, in this case the TITLE field, ready for data entry. You can then enter the movie or show's title, followed by the tape number, the length of the movie, your comments, and your personal rating of the movie.

Data should be entered one field at a time. After you finish with one field, you should use the Tab key or one of the cursor keys to move the cursor to the next field and enter data for that field. If you do not have a value for a field, you can bypass it by tabbing over it to the next field. For example, you may not know the length of a particular movie. In that case, when you get to that field, you should press the Tab key once. This will take you to the next field. If you tab over a field, that field will be stored as either spaces or zeros in the file. That will depend on the format of the field as defined in the Master File Description. If the field was defined as an alphanumeric field (A type), it will be stored as spaces. If the field was defined as a numeric field, (i.e., I type, P type, D type, or F type), the field will be stored with a value of zeros. If you press the Enter key (the Return key on PCs) any time during data entry, data will be transmitted from the screen to the Focus data file. If you press the Enter key before completing all the entries, the remaining entries will be stored as either spaces or zeros.

Now let us use the screen above and enter some data. The following shows the screen after completion of data entry.

```
   SCREEN FOR ADDING NEW TITLES TO THE MOVIES FILE


Please Enter The Title:FLASH GORDON CONQUERS THE UNIVERSE


Tape Number:   97
Length:        1456
Comments:      SERIAL/ACTION
Rating:        ***
```

In the example above, I added a movie title called "Flash Gordon Conquers the Universe" to my movies collections library. Note that all entries on the screen are completed. After completing the rating entry, I can press the Enter key, and the data, if they pass the match test, will be transmitted to the disk drive to update the MOVIES data file. Note that only the data entered by the user, in this case me, is transmitted back to the file. These fields are also referred to as the unprotected fields or unprotected areas because information can be entered in these areas. By contrast, the text fields are not transmitted back. Those are the protected areas of the screen, because there is no way that a user can enter data in those areas. If you try to do that, the screen will probably freeze up and you will have to press the Reset key, Clear key, or PF2 key to unfreeze the screen and continue with data entry.

You can always clear the screen and restart data entry from the first field by pressing the PF2 key (F2 key on PCs). PF2 will simply cancel the transaction that is already on the screen. To terminate a request, you can enter the PF3 key (F3 on PCs). PF3 will also clear the current screen before terminating the MODIFY process. It has no effect on data that have already been accepted by Focus and have updated the data file. Alternatively, you could type the "END" statement in the title field and press the Enter key. This will also terminate the program.

If there is already another movie by the same title in the data file, Focus will display the error message defined in the MODIFY request. The data are rejected and Focus will clear the screen and display another fresh screen ready for data entry.

```
        SCREEN FOR ADDING NEW TITLES TO THE MOVIES FILE


   Please Enter The Title:CASABLANCA


   Tape Number:   54
   Length:        1206
   Comments:      DRAMA
   Rating:        ****




            Title is already on file: Please try again
```

As a matter of interest, I have coded a TABLE request with the Heading option, which basically mimics the MODIFY request above. It does not, of course, allow you to add data, but it displays the information from the data file one record at a time. Notice the similarities between the two programs.

```
-* CHAPTER 14
-* CHA14-2
-* SIMPLE EXAMPLE SHOWING THE SIMILARITIES BETWEEN
-* THE HEADING OPTION IN THE TABLE REQUEST
-* AND THE CRTFORM SUBCOMMAND.
-*
TABLE FILE  MOVIES
HEADING
"</1 "
```

```
"           SCREEN FOR DISPLAYING RECORDS IN THE MOVIES FILE"
"   "
"   "
"Please Enter The Title: <TITLE"
  "Tape Number: <TAPE_NO "
  "Length:      <LENGTH"
  "Comments:    <COMMENTS"
  "Rating:      <RATING"
BY TITLE NOPRINT PAGE-BREAK
END
```

If you execute this program, you will get a screen of data as shown below. Each time that you press the Enter key, the next record will be displayed on the screen.

```
PAGE:   1


      SCREEN FOR DISPLAYING RECORDS IN THE MOVIES FILE


Please Enter The Title: 48 HOURS
Tape Number:    18
Length:         1,178
Comments:       COMEDY
Rating:         **
```

Improving Our First MODIFY Request

The first MODIFY request that we created was an acceptable working program. It performed as planned. However, the problem with that program was that the operator had to enter all the data required for each record before Focus had an opportunity to find out if the title was already on file. In that program there was not much data since the user was only keying in five fields. Imagine having to enter 15 or 16 fields and then finding out that the key field is duplicated!

Focus provides a solution to this problem. You are allowed to have multiple CRTFORMs within one MODIFY request. Each CRTFORM is treated individually; therefore, you can end up with several forms on one screen, with each form following the previous one. You can even have forms overlaying part or all of a previous CRTFORM. I can now change my request slightly to take advantage of this feature. First, I will use one CRTFORM to prompt for entry of the title field. I will then need to add a MATCH statement to check any entry against the file immediately. If the title is a duplicate, Focus will immediately reject my entry and print the error message at the bottom of the screen. On the other hand, if the title does not already exist, Focus will display the second CRTFORM starting on line 9 of the terminal. I can then complete data entry and press the Enter key when I am done, confident that my efforts will not have been wasted.

```
-* CHAPTER 14
-* CHA14-3
-* A MORE SOPHISTICATED EXAMPLE SHOWING HOW TO USE
-* THE CRTFORM IN FOCUS
-*
MODIFY FILE MOVIES
CRTFORM LINE 3
"</1 "
"                    SCREEN FOR ADDING NEW TITLES TO THE MOVIES FILE"
"    "
"    "
"Please Enter The Title: <TITLE"
MATCH TITLE
    ON MATCH TYPE
          "Title is already on file: Please try again"
    ON MATCH REJECT
    ON NOMATCH CRTFORM LINE 9
  "Tape Number: <TAPE_NO "
  "Length:      <LENGTH"
  "Comments:    <COMMENTS"
  "Rating:      <RATING"
    ON NOMATCH INCLUDE
DATA VIA FIDEL
LOG DUPL MSG OFF
END
```

The following screens show the result of executing the foregoing request.

```
        SCREEN FOR ADDING NEW TITLES TO THE MOVIES FILE


Please Enter The Title:_
```

If you enter a title that is already on file, Focus will reject that title and will display the error message at the bottom of the screen. For my first title, I selected a new title, "GASLIGHT."

```
        SCREEN FOR ADDING NEW TITLES TO THE MOVIES FILE


Please Enter The Title:GASLIGHT
```

I entered the title of the movie and pressed the Enter key. Since I did not have this movie in my collection, there was no match and it was not rejected. Focus then displayed the second CRTFORM starting on line 9 of the screen. Note that with each succeeding CRTFORM the cursor moves to the first data entry field of that screen.

```
        SCREEN FOR ADDING NEW TITLES TO THE MOVIES FILE


Please Enter The Title:GASLIGHT


Tape Number:_← Note: the cursor is positioned here now.
Length:
Comments:
Rating:
```

Next, I entered the rest of the information about this movie on the screen using the Tab key to move from one field to the next.

```
        SCREEN FOR ADDING NEW TITLES TO THE MOVIES FILE


Please Enter The Title:GASLIGHT


Tape Number:185
Length:979
Comments:DRAMA
Rating:****
```

Once I was satisfied with my entries, I pressed the Enter key. This transmitted the data and updated the data file. To change any field, before pressing the Enter key, I could have used the cursor keys or the back Tab key to move backward through the fields on the screen. So you have a number of ways for modifying the data before pressing the Enter key. The operator can also completely clear all the data that have been entered by pressing the PF2 key.

Once data from one screen are transmitted, Focus will refresh the screen. In other words, it will display another data entry screen. You can continue entering data and pressing the Enter key until all the input data have been added to the Focus data file. Once there are no more data to be entered, you can enter "END" in response to the prompt.

```
         SCREEN FOR ADDING NEW TITLES TO THE MOVIES FILE


Please Enter The Title:END
```

Alternatively, you could press the PF3 or the F3 keys instead. Any one of those commands would cause Focus to complete the task and terminate the request.

Remember that the MOVIES file is a single-segment file. If I had to modify a multiple-segment file such as the STAFF file, I may have had to step through several segments and key fields to get to the segment that needed updating. As we go along in this chapter, we will try more difficult MODIFY requests.

Importance of the COMPUTE Statement

COMPUTE is very important in a MODIFY request. Basically, it performs the same functions as the DEFINE statement in a TABLE request. The DEFINE statement does not exist under the MODIFY request. You could use the COMPUTE statement to (1) create new fields, (2) decode data entered by the user, (3) perform arithmetic calculations, (4) perform logical IF, THEN, ELSE operations, and more. One of the main functions of the COMPUTE statement is to create new temporary fields for entering data or redefining the name of a group of fields that need to be accessed by a different name.

Review of CRTFORM Fundamentals

1. The Tab key or the cursor keys should be used for moving around the screen.

2. The Enter key (Return key on PCs) should be used to transmit data from the screen to the data file.

3. The PF8 and PF7 keys (F8 and F7 keys on PCs) should be used to scroll forward or backward on CRTFORMs that are longer than one screen (i.e., 24 lines).

4. The PF2 key (F2 key on PCs) should be used to clear the screen to reenter the data.

5. The PF3 (F3 key on PCs) should be used to terminate the request. Typing end on a key field will also terminate the request.

CRTFORM OPTIONS

You may remember the basic CRTFORM syntax from the beginning of this chapter. The syntax is repeated below.

```
MODIFY FILE file name

CRTFORM [LINE #] ⎡CLEAR   ⎤   LOWER TYPE n
                 ⎣NO CLEAR⎦
"                                              "
"                                              "
"   SCREEN FORMAT                              "
"                                              "
"                                              "
"                                              "
"                                              "
"                                              "

DATA VIA FIDEL
END
```

The CRTFORM has several facilities that we should review here. As we have already discussed, the LINE number option determines the beginning position of each form. We said before that you could have several CRTFORMs within one request, each occupying different parts of the screen.

   The CLEAR option, which is the default, will clear the screen after completion of each data entry operation. In all our examples so far, we defaulted to the CLEAR option. The NOCLEAR option will transmit the data, just like the CLEAR option, but will leave the data on the screen as initially entered by the user. This has its uses. For example, you may want to add to or change only one field and the other fields that you are adding are the same for all records. In this case, why bother to enter the same data over and over again. You can use the NOCLEAR option and since the data are left on the screen after transmission, only the fields that need changing are modified. However, when you press the Enter key, all the other fields are transmitted with the new record as part of it.

The TYPE option allows the programmer to control the number of lines that are available for use on the screen. As you know, most CRT screens can display up to 24 lines of information. Each line is 80 characters wide. Focus allows you to use 20 lines on each screen and 78 characters on each line. The remaining four lines are reserved for error messages. If the programmer determines that he or she needs more than 20 lines of display per screen, the height of the screen could be adjusted by using the TYPE statement. For example, TYPE 2 means that only two lines are reserved for Focus error messages and the programmer now has 22 lines for the program. The maximum number of lines for messages is 4; the minimum is 1.

I will now show you how to create a more complex MODIFY request with CRTFORM. I will use CASE logic to perform a complete data maintenance task. With the following request, I can add, change, or delete records from the MOVIES file. I have also added a few enhancements along the way that I will discuss later. But first, let's look at the following MODIFY request.

```
-* CHAPTER 14
-* CHA14-4
-* EXAMPLE SHOWING HOW TO USE CRTFORM TO
-* ADD, CHANGE AND DELETE RECORDS
-*
MODIFY FILE MOVIES
COMPUTE SELECTION/A1= ;
```

CRTFORM LINE 3   ← The first CRTFORM
```
"</1 "
"                              MOVIES FILE"
"                         FILE MAINTENANCE MENU"
"                         --------------------"
"</2  "
"                    1. Add new Records to the file"
"                    2. Change Existing Records "
"                    3. Delete Existing Records "
"                    X. Exit This Program   "
"    "
"    "
"  Please Enter Your Selection:<SELECTION"
" "

" "
IF SELECTION EQ '1' PERFORM ADD_NEW
ELSE IF SELECTION EQ '2' PERFORM CHNG_REC
ELSE IF SELECTION EQ '3' PERFORM DEL_REC
ELSE IF SELECTION EQ 'X' GOTO EXIT          ;
TYPE
"Wrong selection, please enter the correct selection or press PF3"
GOTO TOP
```

```
CASE ADD_NEW
CRTFORM LINE 3 NOCLEAR   ← The second CRTFORM
"                SCREEN FOR ADDING NEW TITLES TO THE MOVIES FILE"
"    "
"    "
"Please Enter The Title: <TITLE"
MATCH TITLE
    ON MATCH TYPE
"             Title is already on file: Please try again"
    ON MATCH REJECT
    ON MATCH GOTO ADD_NEW
    ON NOMATCH CRTFORM LINE 9
  "Tape Number: <TAPE_NO "
  "Length:      <LENGTH"
  "Comments:    <COMMENTS"
  "Rating:      <RATING"
    ON NOMATCH INCLUDE
    ON NOMATCH GOTO ADD_NEW
ENDCASE


CASE CHNG_REC
CRTFORM LINE 3  NOCLEAR   ← The third CRTFORM
"               SCREEN FOR CHANGING THE CONTENTS OF THE MOVIES FILE"
"    "
"    "
"Please Enter The Title: <TITLE"
MATCH TITLE
    ON MATCH CRTFORM LINE 9
  "Tape Number: <D.TAPE_NO "
  "Length:      <T.LENGTH"
  "Comments:    <T.COMMENTS"
  "Rating:      <T.RATING"
    ON MATCH UPDATE TAPE_NO LENGTH COMMENTS RATING
    ON MATCH GOTO CHNG_REC
    ON NOMATCH TYPE
"             This Title does not exist in the file"
    ON NOMATCH REJECT
    ON NOMATCH GOTO CHNG_REC
ENDCASE


CASE DEL_REC
CRTFORM LINE 3  NOCLEAR   ← The fourth CRTFORM
"               SCREEN FOR DELETING RECORDS FROM THE MOVIES FILE"
"    "
"    "
"Please Enter The Title: <TITLE"
MATCH TITLE
    ON MATCH TYPE
```

```
       " <TITLE  has been permanently deleted"
       ON MATCH DELETE
       ON MATCH GOTO DEL_REC
       ON NOMATCH TYPE
"                  This Title does not exist in the file"
       ON NOMATCH REJECT
       ON NOMATCH GOTO DEL_REC
ENDCASE
DATA VIA FIDEL
LOG DUPL MSG OFF
LOG NOMATCH MSG OFF
END
```

The first item to look at is the COMPUTE SELECTION entry. This field defines a temporary field named SELECTION with the format "A1." This field is needed to allow the user to make a selection. Remember that COMPUTE fields that refer to fields that are not part of the Focus file must be defined immediately after the MODIFY request. You will notice that there are four CRTFORM statements in this request.

1. The first CRTFORM displays a nice menu starting on line 3 of the terminal. This menu will allow the operator to make a selection. The operator can enter a number from 1 to 3 to perform file maintenance on this file. He or she can also enter the letter "X" to terminate the program. As always, pressing the PF3 key will also terminate the program. Also notice the use of the IF, ELSE statements in this part of the request.

2. The second CRTFORM displays the screen for adding new records to the MOVIES file. This is a CASE logic module. We have already seen how this is done in an earlier request. The only difference here is the use of the NOCLEAR with CRTFORM. This will ensure that the information keyed in will stay on screen even after transmission has taken place. The choice between CLEAR and NOCLEAR options is really application dependent. Sometimes, you may want to see what you have just added to the file. At other times, you want the screen cleared before the next data entry operation.

3. The third CRTFORM displays the screen for changing the current records in the MOVIES file. This is another CASE logic module. Note that in this module I have coded the NOCLEAR option with the CRTFORM subcommand. This will ensure that as records are changed the information will stay on the screen. This will help the data entry person to remember the fields that he or she has just changed. This time around, I defined the TAPE_NO field as a display (D-type) field. The other three fields, LENGTH, COMMENTS, and RATING, are defined as turnaround fields. The TAPE_NO is not a key field, but it is hardly likely to change. However, the other fields can change. By defining the TAPE_NO as display type, the operator will be able to view it (but not change it) while changing the other three fields. By defining the other three fields as turnaround fields, I have enabled the operator to view the value in each field and change them at the same time, online.

4. The fourth CRTFORM displays the screen for deleting a complete record. To delete a segment or a record, you need to delete that segment's key field. In this case there is really no need to display the other fields. However, in many cases you can construct your program in such a way as to force the operator to enter another field also. This will guard against erroneous deletions.

If we execute this request, we will first get the menu, which will prompt for additional entries.

```
                          MOVIES FILE
                   FILE MAINTENANCE MENU
                   --------------------

             1. Add new Records to the file
             2. Change Existing Records
             3. Delete Existing Records
             X. Exit This Program


   Please Enter Your Selection:_
```

The operator can then make any selection, as long as it is one of the four options on the menu. Any other letter or number will display the following message at the bottom of the screen:

```
Wrong selection, please enter the correct selection or press PF3
```

The operator then has the option of entering the correct entry or aborting the process by pressing the PF3 key. The other screens are similar to what we have seen earlier in the chapter.

VALIDATE STATEMENT

The VALIDATE statement is used to ensure that the data entered by the operator are not corrupted. The syntax of the statement is as follows:

```
VALIDATE
EXPRESSION =                    ;
```

Depending on the application, many types of validations could take place. For example, if the application is concerned with adding new records to the file, the programmer must ensure that the key field is greater than zeros or spaces. There may be other instances when salaries, dates of birth, or employee job titles need to be validated for accuracy. Another validation rule is to check for the correct range of employee numbers or the accuracy of department names. It is important to be able to verify and validate the data as they are being entered into the file. No user wants inaccurate records in an application. In certain circumstances such as payroll, it may even expose the organization to undue risks to have data that are not accurate.

The following example displays the use of the VALIDATE statement to prevent the operator from creating a record with blank (i.e., space-filled) title names. Also, note the similarities between the VALIDATE and the COMPUTE statements.

```
VALIDATE      ← Activates the validation logic in Focus
OKAY = IF TITLE GT ' ' THEN 1 ELSE 0 ;
ON INVALID TYPE
"              Blanks are not valid. Please enter the Title"
```

Without this statement during the data entry phase, if the operator presses the Enter key before entering any data for the title field, Focus will store a record with a blank key field. This is obviously bad and should be avoided.

The VALIDATE statement above will check the TITLE field. If the value of the TITLE field is greater than spaces (i.e., some real data have been entered), it will return a code of 1; otherwise, a code of 0 is returned. Focus will only accept a field with a return code of 1. Therefore, if the TITLE field has been left blank, it will be rejected and the following generic message will be displayed by Focus at the bottom of the screen:

```
(FOC421)  TRANS 2 REJECTED INVALID OKAY
```

In the example that follows, I managed to turn off the generic Focus invalid transaction message and substituted a more meaningful message.

```
-* CHAPTER 14
-* CHA14-5
-* EXAMPLE SHOWING THE VALIDATE STATEMENT
-* IN FOCUS
-*
MODIFY FILE MOVIES


CRTFORM LINE 3
"</1 "
"              SCREEN FOR ADDING NEW TITLES TO THE MOVIES FILE"
"    "
"    "
"Please Enter The Title: <TITLE"
```

```
VALIDATE
OKAY = IF TITLE GT ' ' THEN 1 ELSE 0 ;
                                    ┌───────────── My own Invalid message.
ON INVALID TYPE                     ↓
   "              Blanks are not valid. Please enter the Title"
MATCH TITLE
    ON MATCH TYPE
    "            Title is already on file: Please try again"
    ON MATCH REJECT
    ON NOMATCH CRTFORM LINE 9

  "Tape Number: <TAPE_NO "
  "Length:      <LENGTH"
  "Comments:    <COMMENTS"
  "Rating:      <RATING"
    ON NOMATCH VALIDATE
    OKAY = TAPE_NO GT 0  ;
ON INVALID TYPE
   "              Tape number must be greater than zero          "
    ON NOMATCH INCLUDE
DATA VIA FIDEL
LOG DUPL MSG OFF
LOG INVALID MSG OFF    ← Turns the Focus Invalid message off.
END
```

Note: You can also use the shorthand version of VALIDATE, which basically truncates the THEN and the ELSE statements:

```
OKAY = TITLE GT ' '
```

is the same as

```
OKAY = IF TITLE GT ' ' THEN 1 ELSE 0 ;
```

As you have noticed, the ON INVALID phrase follows the VALIDATE statement. You are allowed to perform other tasks if the data are invalid. Other ON INVALID options are shown below.

$$ \text{ON INVALID} \begin{cases} \texttt{GOTO Case name} \\ \texttt{IF expression GOTO Case name} \\ \texttt{TYPE} \\ \texttt{PERFORM Case name} \end{cases} $$

A brief explanation of each option follows.

GOTO CASE name. This statement will make an unconditional branch to a CASE statement.

```
ON INVALID GOTO ADD_CASE
```

The CASE does not have to be a different CASE. Control could be transferred to the beginning of the CASE that contains the VALIDATE statement, thereby creating a loop. For example:

```
CASE ADD_DEPT
Other Focus code ....
MATCH DID
GOOD = IF DID GT ' ' THEN 1 ELSE 0
ON INVALID GOTO ADD_DEP   ← Branches back to the beginning of the
                            same case, so the user could enter
                            the correct data.
```

IF expression GOTO CASE name. This statement branches to another CASE or the same CASE, depending on the result of the expression.

```
CASE ADD_EMP
Other Focus code.
VALIDATE
S_RANGE = IF SALARY GT 200000 THEN 0 ELSE 1 ;

ON INVALID IF TITLE NE 'MANAGER' GOTO EXIT
```

TYPE. This option will display a message at the bottom of the screen. The message could be up to four lines long.

```
VALIDATE
GOOD = IF LAST_NAME  GT ' ' THEN 1 ELSE 0 ;
ON INVALID TYPE
"  Last Name must be greater than spaces.  "
```

PERFORM CASE name. This option is similar to the GOTO option. The only difference is that control will return to the statement following the INVALID phrase after execution of the CASE name to which control was transferred.

There are many validation rules that you could build with the VALIDATE statement. One of the most common problems in any programming language is checking the validity of dates. Since a date field is basically a numeric field, any combination of numbers could be entered as values for date fields. However, obviously 905432 is not a valid date, though it is technically an acceptable numeric field. The following VALIDATE statement will ensure that any date entered by the user is at least in the correct format. It will not allow obvious mistakes. For example, 91/06/31 will be acceptable but 91/02/30 or 91/13/12 will be rejected. However, the operator could still enter an incorrect date in the correct format. In other words, the operator can enter 91/09/15 instead of 91/06/15, and since both dates are valid dates, they will be accepted.

```
VALIDATE
OKAY = IF YMD (010101,DOB) THEN 1 ELSE 0 ;
or:
OKAY = YMD (010101,DOB) ;     ← This is a Focus function that
                                checks any date against 01/0101
                                to validate its accuracy.
```

The VALIDATE statement could also be used to ensure that numeric fields such as salary fields have a value greater than zero. Also, it could be used to perform range checking as part of data entry validation. Some other examples of validating data follow.

```
VALIDATE
GOOD = IF SALARY GT 0 THEN 1 ELSE 0 ;
ON INVALID GOTO NEW_EMP

VALIDATE
T_DEPT = IF DEPT_NAME EQ 'MARKETING' THEN 1 ELSE 0 ;

VALIDATE
OKAY = IF SALARY GT D.SALARY THEN 1 ELSE 0 ;

VALIDATE with DECODE function:

VALIDATE
TEST_SEC = DECODE SECNAME  (PAYABLES 1 COLLECTIONS 1 ELSE 0 ) ;
```

DATA INQUIRY SCREENS

In the next example, I will use the CRTFORM to display a multiple-segment record. The user will be prompted to enter the department ID and the section ID. If the data entered are valid (i.e., the segments exist), the program will display all the employee segments within each section segment. Each time the Enter key is pressed, a new employee record will be displayed, until there are no more employee segments within that section.

```
-*   CHAPTER 14
-*   CHA14-7
-*   THIS PROGRAM DISPLAYS THE EMPLOYEE RECORDS.
-*   THERE ARE THREE SEGMENTS IN THE STAFF FILE.
-*   FIRST, THE DEPARTMENT ID IS ENTERED. THIS IS FOLLOWED
-*   BY SECTION ID.  THE PROGRAM DISPLAYS THE EMPLOYEE SEGMENT
-*   WITHIN EACH SEGMENT ONE SEGMENT AT A TIME.
MODIFY FILE STAFF
COMPUTE
CRTFORM LINE 1 TYPE 2
"<66 Date:&DATE"     ← Positions the current date on screen;
                       starting on column 66.
```

```
"                            Staff File          "
"                    File Inquiry By Department "
"                    ---------------------------"
"  "
"Please Enter Department ID:<DID "
MATCH DID
ON NOMATCH TYPE
"               Wrong Department ID, Please try again "
ON NOMATCH REJECT
ON MATCH GOTO SEC_SEG


CASE SEC_SEG
CRTFORM LINE 7 CLEAR TYPE 2
"Enter Section ID: <SECID "
MATCH SECID
ON NOMATCH TYPE
"               Wrong Section ID, Please try again "
  ON NOMATCH REJECT
  ON MATCH GOTO EMP_SEC
ENDCASE

CASE EMP_SEC
NEXT EID
ON NONEXT TYPE
"         No more employee segments in this Section     "
ON NONEXT GOTO TOP
ON NEXT CRTFORM LINE 9 CLEAR TYPE 2


  "Employee ID    : <D.EID"          ← Note: All these following
  "Last Name      : <D.LAST_NAME"    fields are defined as
  "First Name     : <D.FIRST_NAME"   display (D) type.
  "Job Title      : <D.JOB "
  "Street Address : <D.STREET"
  "City           : <D.CITY"
  "State          : <D.STATE"
  "Zip Code       : <D.ZIP_CODE"
  "Phone No.      : <D.TELEPHONE"
  "Date of Birth  : <D.DOB"
  "Date of Hire   : <D.DOH"
  "Salary         : <D.SALARY"
  "Pct_Inc        : <D.PIN"
  "Vacation       : <D.VACATION"
ON NEXT GOTO EMP_SEC
ENDCASE
LOG NOMATCH MSG OFF
DATA VIA FIDEL
END
```

The program that follows next ties everything together. This program is a file maintenance program to add new segments to the STAFF file. As you will remember, the STAFF file is a hierarchical file with three segment levels. The segments are the department, section, and employee. This program allows the user to add new segments to each of those levels. In other words, the user could create a new department, add one or many section segments to any department, and add one or many employees to any section in the file. The program consists of four main parts.

1. *Menu.* This is the main driver and is displayed as soon as the program is executed. It allows the operator to make a selection. The IF, ELSE statements, in conjunction with the GOTO statements, allow the operator to perform one of the CASE modules. The message at the bottom of the screen tells the operator that the PF2 key will return him or her to the menu screen and the PF3 key will terminate the session.

2. *New Department Module.* This CASE module—ADD_DEP—will allow entry of new department ID and new department names only. Here I used the VALIDATE statements to ensure that the operator does not enter blanks or duplicate department IDs. The user can enter as many departments as desired. To clear a screen and return to the main menu, the PF2 function key should be pressed. As always, to terminate the process, the PF3 function key should be pressed.

3. *New Section Module.* This part of the program consists of two CASE modules. The first module—ADD_SEC—checks for the presence of a valid department ID. Obviously, you cannot add a section to the file without a parent department. The second module—SECID1—adds a new segment. The second module also prevents the user from entering blanks or duplicate section IDs. As you will remember, CASE modules cannot be nested. However, you can transfer control from one CASE module to another CASE module.

4. *New Employees Module.* This part of the program consists of three CASE modules. The first module—ADD_EMP—will ensure that the department IDs and the section IDs are correctly entered. The second CASE module—ADD_EMP1—generates a new CRTFORM and prompts the user for the new employee number. This is important, because we do not want the operator to enter all the other information about a new employee before discovering that the employee ID number is a duplicate. Finally, the third module—ADD_EMP2—allows the operator to enter the rest of information about the new employee. I built some additional validation checks into this module. For example, the employee's name cannot be all blanks. The date of birth and date of hire must be valid dates. This is done by comparing the dates to 01/01/01 (January 1, 1901). Any invalid date format will be rejected. I could have performed other validation tasks, such as checking the salary range or the job title or ensuring that the vacation allowance of a new employee is always entered as zeros. Also notice that in ADD_EMP2 module, I used the CRTFORM statement with the NO-CLEAR option. In this case the NOCLEAR option will ensure that in case of errors, the entire screen is not cleared, so that the operator will only need to reenter the incorrect fields.

```
-* CHAPTER 14
-* CHA14-6
-* UPDATING MULTIPLE SEGMENT FILES WITH CRTFORM
-*
-*
MODIFY FILE STAFF
COMPUTE SELECTION/A1= ;
CRTFORM LINE 2 TYPE 2
"</1 "
"                          STAFF  FILE"
"                     FILE MAINTENANCE MENU"
"                     ---------------------"
"</2   "
"                    1. Add new Departments to the file"
"                    2. Add new Sections to the file "
"                    3. Add new Employees to the file "
"                    X. Exit This Program  "
"     "
"     "
"   Please Enter Your Selection:<SELECTION"
" "
" "
" "
"              To return to this menu press the PF2 key."
" "
"    To terminate the session, press the PF3 key from any screen"
IF SELECTION EQ '1' GOTO    ADD_DEP
ELSE IF SELECTION EQ '2' GOTO    ADD_SEC
ELSE IF SELECTION EQ '3' GOTO    ADD_EMP
ELSE IF SELECTION EQ 'X' GOTO EXIT          ;
TYPE
 "Wrong selection, please enter the correct selection or press PF3"
GOTO TOP

CASE ADD_DEP
CRTFORM LINE 3 TYPE 2
"         SCREEN FOR ADDING NEW DEPARTMENTS TO THE STAFF FILE"
"    "
"    "
"Please enter new Department ID:<DID> New Dept_Name:<DEPT_NAME>"
MATCH DID
VALIDATE
GOOD=IF DID GT ' ' THEN 1 ELSE 0 ;
ON INVALID TYPE
"              Department ID cannot be all blanks  "
ON INVALID GOTO ADD_DEP
VALIDATE
```

```
DEP_GOOD=IF DEPT_NAME GT ' ' THEN 1 ELSE 0 ;
ON INVALID TYPE
"              Department Name cannot be all blanks    "
ON INVALID GOTO ADD_DEP
    ON NOMATCH INCLUDE
    ON NOMATCH GOTO ADD_DEP
    ON MATCH TYPE
    "                        Department Already Exists"
    ON MATCH GOTO ADD_DEP
ENDCASE

CASE ADD_SEC
CRTFORM LINE 2  NOCLEAR
"       SCREEN FOR ADDING NEW SECTIONS TO THE STAFF FILE"
"   "
"   "
"Please Enter the Department Id:<DID Department Name:<DEPT_NAME"
MATCH DID
VALIDATE
GOOD=IF DID GT ' ' THEN 1 ELSE 0 ;
ON INVALID TYPE
"              Department ID cannot be all blanks"
ON INVALID GOTO ADD_SEC
ON NOMATCH TYPE
"          Department ID does not exist, try again"
ON NOMATCH REJECT
ON NOMATCH GOTO ADD_SEC
ON MATCH GOTO SECID1
ENDCASE

CASE SECID1
CRTFORM LINE 6 NOCLEAR
"Please enter new Section ID:<SECID> New Section Name:<SECN>"
MATCH SECID
VALIDATE
S_GOOD=IF SECN GT ' ' THEN 1 ELSE 0 ;
ON INVALID TYPE
"              Section Name cannot be all blanks "
ON INVALID GOTO SECID1
   ON NOMATCH INCLUDE
   ON NOMATCH GOTO SECID1
   ON MATCH TYPE
   "                        Section Already Exists"
   ON MATCH REJECT
   ON MATCH GOTO SECID1
ENDCASE

CASE ADD_EMP
CRTFORM LINE 2  NOCLEAR
"       SCREEN FOR ADDING NEW EMPLOYEES TO THE STAFF FILE"
```

Multiple-Segment File Maintenance Program   377

```
"    "
"    "
"Please Enter the Department Id:<DID Department Name:<DEPT_NAME"
MATCH DID
VALIDATE
GOOD=IF DID GT ' ' THEN 1 ELSE 0 ;
ON INVALID TYPE
"                 Department ID cannot be all blanks"
ON NOMATCH TYPE
"      Department ID incorrect, please enter the correct ID"
ON INVALID GOTO ADD_EMP
ON NOMATCH REJECT
ON NOMATCH GOTO ADD_EMP
ON MATCH CONTINUE
ON MATCH CRTFORM LINE 6 NOCLEAR
"Please Enter The Section ID:<SECID> Section Name:<SECN>"
MATCH SECID
ON NOMATCH TYPE
"      Section ID incorrect, please enter the correct ID"
ON NOMATCH REJECT
ON NOMATCH GOTO ADD_EMP
ON MATCH GOTO ADD_EMP1
ENDCASE

CASE ADD_EMP1
CRTFORM LINE 7 NOCLEAR
"Please Enter The New Employee ID: <EID"
MATCH EID
  VALIDATE
  E_GOOD=IF EID  GT ' ' THEN 1 ELSE 0 ;
  ON INVALID TYPE
  "                Employee ID cannot be all blanks    "
  ON INVALID GOTO ADD_EMP1
    ON MATCH TYPE
  "     Duplicate Employee ID. Please enter the correct number"

    ON MATCH REJECT
    ON MATCH GOTO ADD_EMP1
    ON NOMATCH GOTO ADD_EMP2
ENDCASE

CASE ADD_EMP2
  CRTFORM LINE 8  NOCLEAR
   "Last Name  : <LAST_NAME"
   "First Name : <FIRST_NAME "
   "Job Title  : <JOB "
   "Street Address : <STREET"
   "City       : <CITY"
   "State      : <STATE"
   "Zip Code   : <ZIP_CODE"
```

```
    "Phone No.  : <TELEPHONE"
    "Date of Birth : <DOB"
    "Date of Hire  : <DOH"
    "Salary      : <SALARY"
    "Pct_Inc     : <PIN"
    "Vacation    : <VACATION"
VALIDATE
N_GOOD=IF LAST_NAME GT ' ' THEN 1 ELSE 0 ;
ON INVALID TYPE
"          Last Name must contain at least one letter    "
ON INVALID GOTO  ADD_EMP2
VALIDATE
DOB_GOOD= YMD (010101,DOB) ;
ON INVALID TYPE
"           Error in Date of Birth, please correct        "
ON INVALID GOTO  ADD_EMP2

VALIDATE
DOH_GOOD= IF YMD (010101,DOH) THEN 1 ELSE 0 ;
ON INVALID TYPE
"           Error in Date of Hire, please correct        "
ON INVALID GOTO  ADD_EMP2
    MATCH EID
    ON NOMATCH INCLUDE
    ON NOMATCH GOTO ADD_EMP1
ENDCASE

DATA VIA FIDEL
LOG DUPL MSG OFF
LOG INVALID MSG OFF
LOG NOMATCH MSG OFF
END
```

The program above may seem like a lengthy MODIFY request, but it handles only the addition of new segments to the STAFF file. I have not coded the logic for changing the data and deleting segments and/or records, as we have already covered much of that logic in previous examples. It should be easy for you to make the necessary modifications to this program or to create two new programs for making changes and deletions.

ADDITIONAL FEATURES OF MODIFY REQUEST WITH CRTFORM

There are several other features that I cover in the remainder of the chapter. Some of them are used exclusively with CRTFORM. Others are used with other MODIFY subcommands as well, but you will find them most useful with the CRTFORM subcommand.

Use of the PFKEYs or Function Keys

You can use the PFKEYs (or the function keys on a PC) to transfer control of your program to various CASE modules. The coding for using the function keys is similar to the coding that we have done previously. However, this time, instead of selecting either a letter or a number and pressing the Enter key, the operator presses an appropriate PFKEY. You must also use the COMPUTE statement to define a four-character temporary field. This field must be called ''PFKEY'' with a format of A4. Then in the menu screen the operator should be instructed to press a specific PFKEY or FKEY to make a selection. A PFKEY can be tested for specific value. Based on the PFKEY pressed, control will pass to a particular CASE module. Following is an example of using the PFKEYs instead of entering numbers to make a selection. You may remember this example from a few pages back. Note that very few changes have been made in this program.

```
-*   CHAPTER 14
-*   CHA14-8
-*   Using the PFKEYs to control the execution of a program
MODIFY FILE MOVIES
COMPUTE PFKEY/A4= ;
CRTFORM LINE 3
"<1 "
"                            MOVIES FILE"
"                        FILE MAINTENANCE MENU"
"                        ----------------------"
"<2   "
"                    PF4. Add new Records to the file"
"                    PF5. Change Existing Records "
"                    PF6. Delete Existing Records "
"                    PF3. Exit This Program   "
"    "
"    "
"    "
"    "
"        Please Enter Your Selection by pressing a PFKEY "
"PF4 = Add a new movie, PF5 = Change record, PF6 = Delete a record"

"  "
IF PFKEY     EQ 'PF04' PERFORM ADD_NEW
ELSE IF PFKEY     EQ 'PF05' PERFORM CHNG_REC
ELSE IF PFKEY     EQ 'PF06' PERFORM DEL_REC
ELSE IF PFKEY     EQ 'PF03' GOTO EXIT          ;
TYPE
 "Wrong selection, please enter the correct selection or press PF3"
GOTO TOP
CASE ADD_NEW
.

.

The rest of the code.
```

Note: Do not redefine the PF2, PF3, PF7, and PF8 keys. These are generally reserved for use by Focus.

Screen Attributes

Screen attributes are characters that are encoded before a particular field on the CRTFORM. These characters could change the display characteristics of a field. They can cause a field to be highlighted, to blink, to be displayed in reverse video or be displayed in different colors on color monitors. The background of the fields could also be modified by using attributes. Attributes should be chosen carefully and only when appropriate. Screen design in data processing should not be treated the same way as the design of an arcade game. Multicolored flashing screens may look fancy on a demo, but there is nothing more annoying and frustrating to the operator who has to live with flashing data fields day after day. Also, blinking fields or use of inappropriate colors could make the data unintelligible. So when in doubt, do not use the attributes. Some of the most common attributes are as follows:

BLINK OR FLASH	F
REVERSE VIDEO	I
UNDERLINE	U (not available on color monitors)
NON DISPLAY	N (use them for password entry fields)
HIGHLIGHT OR INTENSIFY	H

Each attribute is preceded by a dot (or period) before and after the attribute letter.

```
"          SCREEN FOR CHANGING THE CONTENTS OF THE MOVIES FILE"
"    "
"    "
"Please Enter The Title: <TITLE"
 MATCH TITLE
     ON MATCH CRTFORM LINE 9
  "Tape Number: <.HD.TAPE_NO "     ← Highlighted display type field
  "Length:      <.FT.LENGTH "      ← Flashing turnaround field
  "Comments:    <.IT.COMMENTS "    ← Reverse video turnaround field
  "Rating:      <.FT.RATING"       ← Flashing turnaround field
     ON MATCH UPDATE TAPE_NO LENGTH COMMENTS RATING
```

CRTFORM LOWER Option

Usually, data entry is performed using the uppercase letters of the alphabet. In fact, the default in Focus is the uppercase. All lowercase data are automatically converted to uppercase prior to storage. However, Focus allows the programmer to specify the lowercase option with the CRTFORM subcommand. With this option, data will be stored as they are entered by the operator. Conversion will not take place. This may be a good option for many applications. However, please remember that it may not be worth the trouble, especially on the mainframes. If there is likely to be a need to transfer data between Focus and another application on a mainframe, it is best to stay with the default. Most mainframe languages do not handle lowercase data very elegantly. In fact, many mainframe printers will only print in uppercase or work at their rated speed only with uppercase characters. This, by the way, is a function of line or bar printers. The uppercase letters are repeated more often on the chain or bar, so there is a higher likelihood of character selection and printing. Example; of CRTFORM with LOWER option;

```
CRTFORM LINE 2 NOCLEAR LOWER
```

FIND Function

The FIND function allows you to check for the presence of data in another file to control execution of a program. FIND can only be used with the COMPUTE and VALIDATE statements. For example, in the STAFF file, you may want to update an employee's salary field. But first you may want to make sure that a record for that employee exists in the employee history (EMPHIST) file. By using the FIND function, you could check for the presence of the employee ID in the EMPHIST file. If the same employee ID also exists in the EMPHIST file, the transaction could proceed; otherwise, it will be rejected.

The syntax of the FIND function is as follows:

```
Field =  FIND(Field name [As dbfield] IN File) ;
```

Field is the name of the temporary field. It can really be any name that you chose, as long as it is not a Focus reserved word or a valid field name in your Focus file.

Field name is the full name of the incoming field that is being tested. This must be the full field name. Aliases or truncations are not allowed.

dbfield is the full name of database or file field containing values that will need to be compared to the incoming data field. You must select the full name. Aliases or truncations are not allowed.

No spaces are allowed between the keyword FIND and the left parenthesis. Also note that the file that is being interrogated or cross-referenced must be indexed on the field that is being tested for presence of values.

```
         Field name in file                        dbfield = fieldname in the file
         being updated. ⌐                        ⌐ being interrogated.
                        ↓                        ↓
SAL_GOOD= FIND(EMPLOYEE_ID AS SSN IN EMPHIST)     ;
                                                  └ Name of file being interrogated.
```

In the example above, the SSN field in the EMPHIST file is being tested for the presence of the same value as the value of data of the EMPLOYEE_ID field that the operator has entered.

To refresh your memory, the following is the listing of the EMPHIST Master File Description.

```
FILENAME=EMPHIST,SUFFIX=FOC
SEGNAME=ONE,SEGTYPE=S1
FIELDNAME=SSN,ALIAS=EID,FORMAT=A9,FIELDTYPE=I,$    ← Note: This
                                                    field is indexed.
FIELDNAME=MARITAL_STAT,ALIAS=MS,FORMAT=A1,$
FIELDNAME=SEX,ALIAS=SEX,FORMAT=A1,$
FIELDNAME=DEGREE,ALIAS=EDUCATION,FORMAT=A4,$
FIELDNAME=PREVIOUS_SAL,ALIAS=OLDSAL,FORMAT=D9.2C,$
```

The following program will update the salary field of the STAFF file and will calculate the percentage salary increase only if the employee has a record on the EMPHIST master file. Otherwise, the operator entry will be rejected.

```
-* CHAPTER 14
-* CHA14-9
-* UPDATING MULTIPLE SEGMENT FILES WITH CRTFORM
-* USING THE FIND FUNCTION
-*
MODIFY FILE STAFF
COMPUTE SELECTION/A1= ;
CRTFORM LINE 2 TYPE 2
"</1 "
"                          STAFF  FILE"
"                       Salary Update Menu"
"                       -------------------"
"</2  "
"                     1. Update Employee Salaries"
"                     X. Exit This Program  "
"     "
"     "
" Please Enter Your Selection:<SELECTION"
" "
" "
" "
" "
" "
"               To return to this menu press the PF2 key."
" "
"    To terminate the session, press the PF3 key from any screen"
IF SELECTION EQ '1' GOTO    UP_SAL
ELSE IF SELECTION EQ 'X' GOTO EXIT        ;
TYPE
 "Wrong selection, please enter the correct selection or press PF3"
```

```
GOTO TOP
CASE UP_SAL
CRTFORM LINE 2  NOCLEAR
"              SCREEN FOR UPDATING EMPLOYEE SALARIES     "
"   "
"   "
"Please Enter the Department Id:<DID Department Name:<DEPT_NAME"
MATCH DID
VALIDATE
GOOD=IF DID GT ' ' THEN 1 ELSE 0 ;
ON INVALID TYPE
"                  Department ID cannot be all blanks"
ON NOMATCH TYPE
"      Department ID incorrect, please enter the correct ID"
ON INVALID GOTO UP_SAL
ON NOMATCH REJECT
ON NOMATCH GOTO UP_SAL
ON MATCH CONTINUE
ON MATCH CRTFORM LINE 6 NOCLEAR
"Please Enter The Section ID:<SECID> Section Name:<SECN>"
MATCH SECID
ON NOMATCH TYPE
"      Section ID incorrect, please enter the correct ID"
ON NOMATCH REJECT
ON NOMATCH GOTO UP_SAL
ON MATCH GOTO UP_SAL1
ENDCASE

CASE UP_SAL1
CRTFORM LINE 7 NOCLEAR
"Please Enter The Employee ID: <EID"
MATCH EID
  VALIDATE
  E_GOOD=IF EID  GT ' ' THEN 1 ELSE 0 ;
  ON INVALID TYPE
  "               Employee ID cannot be all blanks    "
  ON INVALID GOTO  UP_SAL1
    ON NOMATCH TYPE
  "     Employee ID incorrect. Please enter the correct number"
    ON NOMATCH REJECT
    ON NOMATCH GOTO UP_SAL1
    ON MATCH GOTO UP_SAL2
ENDCASE

CASE UP_SAL2
 CRTFORM LINE 8  NOCLEAR
  "Last Name  : <D.LAST_NAME"
  "First Name : <D.FN       "
  "Job Title  : <D.JOB "
  "Street Address : <D.STREET"
```

```
"City        :  <D.CITY"
"State       :  <D.STATE"
"Zip Code    :  <D.ZIP_CODE"
"Phone No.   :  <D.TELEPHONE"
"Date of Birth :  <D.DOB"
"Date of Hire  :  <D.DOH"
"Salary      :  <T.SALARY"
"Pct_Inc     :  <T.PIN"
"Vacation    :  <D.VACATION"
```

VALIDATE ← Notice the VALIDATE statement before the FIND
                 function.

```
SAL_GOOD= FIND(EMPLOYEE_ID AS SSN IN EMPHIST)    ;
ON INVALID TYPE
 "            Error, No such employee in history file       "
ON INVALID GOTO   UP_SAL1
```
```
    MATCH EID
    ON MATCH COMPUTE
    PIN=  ( (SALARY / D.SALARY) -1 ) ;
    ON MATCH UPDATE SALARY
    ON MATCH UPDATE PIN
    ON MATCH GOTO UP_SAL1
    ON NOMATCH REJECT
    ON NOMATCH GOTO UP_SAL1
ENDCASE

DATA VIA FIDEL
LOG DUPL MSG OFF
LOG INVALID MSG OFF
LOG NOMATCH MSG OFF
END
```

There is also a NOT FIND function with the following syntax:

```
Field = NOT FIND(In field  [As dbfield] IN File)  ;
```

LOOKUP Function

The LOOKUP function is similar to the FIND function. It works with both
VALIDATE and COMPUTE statements. LOOKUP allows the program to look
for a field value in another file or database, and depending on the value of that
field, perform certain tasks. It can also use the value of that field in calculations.
The syntax of the LOOKUP command is as follows:

```
RCODE = LOOKUP(Field) ;
```

RCODE is a variable name assigned by you. Focus will place either a ''1'' for a successful lookup or a ''0'' for an unsuc-
cessful one in that field.

LOOKUP is the keyword that invokes the function.

Field is the name of the field in the cross-referenced file.

An example is

```
S_test = LOOKUP(DEGREE) ;
```

There are a few restrictions associated with using this function. First, no spaces are allowed between the word LOOKUP and the left parenthesis. Second, the cross-referenced file must be indexed. However, the indexed field cannot be used as a LOOKUP field. Third, both files must be cross-referenced to each other either dynamically (i.e., by using the JOIN command) or by static cross-referencing (through Master File Description); see Chapter 10. Fourth, the LOOKUP function can only specify one field at a time. You will need a separate LOOKUP function for each field that you want to retrieve.

In the program that follows some employees with special degrees are slated to receive a one-time increase of 5 percent of their current salaries. This is a selective process. In other words, employees without those degrees do not get the increase. Also, only some of the employees with those degrees will receive the increase; therefore, we cannot write a universal update program. Each employee who is on the list must be selected individually and his or her salary will then be automatically adjusted up by 5 percent.

The following program is similar to the previous program using the FIND function. There are, however, several differences between the two programs, as noted below.

1. The host file (STAFF) is dynamically joined to the cross-referenced file (EMPHIST).

2. The menu is driven by the PF key selections.

3. The LOOKUP function is used as part of a COMPUTE statement to access the DEGREE field in the EMPHIST database.

4. If the value of the DEGREE field in the EMPHIST database is equal to "MBA" or "MA" or "PHD," the salary field is increased by 5 percentage points. If the employee does not have one of these degrees, his or her salary is not adjusted.

5. The SALARY field is next updated. The PERCENTAGE INCREASE field is also recalculated and updated.

6. The program will also display the new salary amount, the percentage increase, and the employee's degree (from the cross-referenced database), immediately below the current salary field. I used reverse video for these fields. It makes them more conspicuous.

The operator must press the PF1 key to get to the main update screen. Once a section has been selected, one or all of the employees could be selected for automatic review. This is done one at a time, employee by employee. At any time, the process could be terminated by pressing the PF3 key. To move to a new

department and/or section, the PF2 key must be pressed. This will cancel the
current transaction and will return control to the main menu.

```
-* CHAPTER 14
-* CHA14-10
-* PROGRAM SHOWING THE USE OF THE LOOKUP FUNCTION
-* WITH THE COMPUTE STATEMENT
JOIN EMPLOYEE_ID IN STAFF TO SSN IN EMPHIST AS JJ      ← Notice the JOIN
MODIFY FILE STAFF                                        command
COMPUTE PFKEY/A4= ;
COMPUTE SAL1/D9.2= ;
CRTFORM LINE 2 TYPE 2
"</1 "
"                              STAFF  FILE"
"                      Special Salary Adjustment Menu"
"                      ---------------------------"
"</3   "
"                         PF1. Update Employee Salaries"
"                         PF3. Exit This Program   "
"    "
"    "
"    "
"    "
" "
" Please Enter Your Selection by pressing a PFKEY   "
" "
" "
" "
"                     To return to this menu press the PF2 key "
" "
IF PFKEY EQ 'PF01' GOTO    UP_SAL
ELSE IF PFKEY EQ 'PF03' GOTO EXIT           ;
TYPE
"Wrong selection, please enter the correct selection or press PF3"
GOTO TOP
CASE UP_SAL
CRTFORM LINE 3  NOCLEAR
"<6 SCREEN FOR UPDATING SALARIES OF EMPLOYEES WITH SPECIAL DEGREES"
"    "
"Please Enter the Department Id:<DID Department Name:<DEPT_NAME"
MATCH DID
VALIDATE
GOOD=IF DID GT ' ' THEN 1 ELSE 0 ;
ON INVALID TYPE
"                  Department ID cannot be all blanks"
ON NOMATCH TYPE
"      Department ID incorrect, please enter the correct ID"
ON INVALID GOTO UP_SAL
ON NOMATCH REJECT
ON NOMATCH GOTO UP_SAL
```

```
ON MATCH CONTINUE
ON MATCH CRTFORM LINE 6 NOCLEAR
"Please Enter The Section ID:<SECID> Section Name:<SECN>"
MATCH SECID
ON NOMATCH TYPE
"       Section ID incorrect, please enter the correct ID"
ON NOMATCH REJECT
ON NOMATCH GOTO UP_SAL
ON MATCH GOTO UP_SAL1
ENDCASE


CASE UP_SAL1
CRTFORM LINE 7 NOCLEAR
"Please Enter The Employee ID: <EID"
MATCH EID
  VALIDATE
  E_GOOD=IF EID  GT ' ' THEN 1 ELSE 0 ;
  ON INVALID TYPE
  "                Employee ID cannot be all blanks    "
  ON INVALID GOTO  UP_SAL1
    ON NOMATCH TYPE
  "      Employee ID incorrect. Please enter the correct number"
    ON NOMATCH REJECT
    ON NOMATCH GOTO UP_SAL1
    ON MATCH GOTO UP_SAL2
ENDCASE


CASE UP_SAL2
 CRTFORM LINE 8  NOCLEAR
  "Last Name      : <D.LAST_NAME"
  "First Name     : <D.FN      "
  "Job Title      : <D.JOB "
  "Street Address : <D.STREET"
  "City           : <D.CITY"
  "State          : <D.STATE"
  "Zip Code       : <D.ZIP_CODE"
  "Phone No.      : <D.TELEPHONE"
  "Date of Birth  : <D.DOB"
  "Date of Hire   : <D.DOH"
  "Current Salary : <D.SALARY"
  "Pct_Inc        : <D.PIN"
  "Vacation       : <D.VACATION"

  MATCH EID
```

```
  ON MATCH COMPUTE
S_TEST = LOOKUP(DEGREE) ;
ON MATCH COMPUTE                              ← Note the LOOKUP
SALARY= IF DEGREE CONTAINS 'MBA' OR 'PHD' OR 'MA'    command
        THEN D.SALARY * 1.05
        ELSE  D.SALARY ;
```

```
      ON MATCH COMPUTE
      PIN=  ( (SALARY / D.SALARY) -1 ) ;
      ON MATCH UPDATE SALARY
      ON MATCH UPDATE PIN
ON MATCH PERFORM SHOWCASE
      ON MATCH GOTO UP_SAL1
      ON NOMATCH REJECT
      ON NOMATCH GOTO UP_SAL1

ENDCASE

CASE SHOWCASE
      MATCH EID
      ON MATCH
      CRTFORM LINE 19  NOCLEAR TYPE 2
   "New Salary      : <.ID.SALARY"  ← Note the screen attribute.
   "Pct_Inc         : <.ID.PIN"
   "Degree          : <.ID.DEGREE"
      ON NOMATCH REJECT
ENDCASE

DATA VIA FIDEL
LOG DUPL MSG OFF
LOG INVALID MSG OFF
LOG NOMATCH MSG OFF
END
```

Repeating Groups with CRTFORM

We have already seen how you can update groups of fields with multiple occurrences using the FIXFORM and the PROMPT subcommands. Similar facilities are available with the CRTFORM subcommand. The following example accomplishes exactly the same results as our FIXFORM and PROMPT examples in previous chapters. This time we use the CRTFORM subcommand to display all those fields on the screen at once. The operator can then enter the data for one or all of these fields. All the data will be transmitted at once, as soon as the Enter key is pressed.

```
-*   CHAPTER 14
-*   CHA14-11
-*   REPEATING GROUPS WITH THE CRTFORM SUB COMMAND
MODIFY FILE EMPLOYEE
CRTFORM LINE 3 NOCLEAR
"<+6 SCREEN FOR UPDATING THE EMPLOYEE FILE WITH REPEATING GROUPS"
" "
" "
"Please Enter the Employee ID: <EID"
" "
" "
```

```
"Please Enter the following for the selected employee: "
" "
" "
"Date_Inc: <DI Pcnt_inc: <PI Salary: <SAL Job_Code: <JBC"
"Date_Inc: <DI Pcnt_inc: <PI Salary: <SAL Job_Code: <JBC"
"Date_Inc: <DI Pcnt_inc: <PI Salary: <SAL Job_Code: <JBC"
"Date_Inc: <DI Pcnt_inc: <PI Salary: <SAL Job_Code: <JBC"
MATCH EID
   ON NOMATCH REJECT
   ON MATCH CONTINUE
MATCH DAT_INC
   ON MATCH REJECT
   ON NOMATCH INCLUDE
DATA VIA FIDEL
END
```

USING THE TEXT FEATURE WITH CRTFORM

One of the newer features available in most versions of Focus is the TEXT feature. This feature allows you to create variable length text fields for descriptive information. For example, in the MOVIES file we could add another field called the abstract field. In this field we could enter information about the stars and the plot line of each show. TEXT fields are variable length and you can enter whatever you want in them. Basically, the TEXT field invokes the TED editor and gives the operator all the facilities of TED for entering and/or modifying the data. The following is a modified version of the MOVIES file. I have called it MOVIES2 to separate it from the other MOVIES file.

```
FILENAME=MOVIES2 ,SUFFIX=FOC
SEGNAME= MOVIES    ,SEGTYPE=S1
  FIELDNAME=TITLE, ,USAGE = A43,$
  FIELDNAME=TAPE_NO, ,USAGE = D03,$
  FIELDNAME=LENGTH, ,USAGE = D04,$
  FIELDNAME=COMMENTS, ,USAGE = A20,$
  FIELDNAME=RATING, ,USAGE = A04,$
  FIELDNAME=ABSTRACT, , USAGE = TXT40,$   ← New field added here.
```

Notice the new format of TXT. The size of this field has been declared as forty characters long. However, this is only to determine the number of columns that this field will occupy during a TABLE Request. It has nothing to do with the actual size of the field. As stated earlier, you basically have all the free format capabilities of TED during data entry.

The following program will add new records to the MOVIES2 file

```
-* CHAPTER 14
-* CHA14-20
-* EXAMPLE USING THE TEXT FIELD IN A FOCUS FILE TO
-* ADD LONG DESCRIPTIVE FIELDS TO THE FILE
```

```
MODIFY FILE MOVIES2
CASE ADD_NEW
CRTFORM LINE 3 NOCLEAR
"                    SCREEN FOR ADDING NEW TITLES TO THE MOVIES FILE
"   "
"   "
"Please Enter the Title: <TITLE"
MATCH TITLE
    ON MATCH TYPE
"             Title is already on file: Please try again"
    ON MATCH REJECT
    ON MATCH GOTO ADD_NEW
    ON NOMATCH CRTFORM LINE 9
  "Tape Number: <TAPE_NO "
  "Length:       <LENGTH"
  "Comments:     <COMMENTS"
  "Rating:       <RATING"
   ON NOMATCH TED ABSTRACT      ← This will invoke the TED text
                                  editor which will allow free
                                  format data entry by the operator.
    ON NOMATCH INCLUDE
    ON NOMATCH GOTO ADD_NEW
ENDCASE
DATA VIA FIDEL
LOG DUPL MSG OFF
LOG NOMATCH MSG OFF
END
```

If you execute the program above, the following six screens will be displayed consecutively.

```
     SCREEN FOR ADDING NEW TITLES TO THE MOVIES2 FILE


 Please Enter The Title: To have and have not
```

This is the first screen for data entry. The operator will enter the title of the movie and will press Enter key.

```
    SCREEN FOR ADDING NEW TITLES TO THE MOVIES2 FILE


Please Enter The Title: To have and have not


Tape Number:   387
Length:        1345
Comments:      Drama
Rating:        ***
```

The second screen displayed above will request additional information about the movie. As soon as the operator presses the Enter key the next screen is displayed.

```
 ABSTRACT TXTFLD   A1              SIZE=0    LINE=0
00000 * * * TOP OF FILE * * *
00001 * * * END OF FILE * * *













====> case m
                                       EDITING MODE
```

This, as you will remember, is the standard TED data entry screen. The operator can enter "case m" in the command line to allow mixed case (uppercase and lowercase) data entry.

```
/  ABSTRACT TXTFLD    A1                     SIZE=0     LINE=0

   00000 * * * TOP OF FILE * * *
   00001 * * * END OF FILE * * *








   ====> input
                                                   EDITING MODE
```

To get to the input mode, the operator should enter the word "INPUT" on the TED command line.

```
/  ABSTRACT TXTFLD    A1                     SIZE=1     LINE=1

   Humphrey Bogart gives a wonderful performance as a fishing boat
   owner in this tale of espionage, romance and intrigue set on the
   island of Martinique during World War II.  Howard Hawks directed.








   ====> * * * INPUT ZONE * * *
                                                   INPUT-MODE
```

TED provides the free format data entry screen. The operator can enter the information that he or she will need to enter.

```
ABSTRACT TXTFLD   A1                    SIZE=3     LINE=0

00000 * * * TOP OF FILE * * *
00001 Humphrey Bogart gives a wonderful performance as a fishing boat
00002 owner in this tale of espionage, romance and intrigue set on the
00003 island of Martinique during World War II.  Howard Hawks directed.
00004 * * * END OF FILE * * *







====> file
                                                        EDITING MODE
```

As soon as data entry is completed, the operator should press the Enter key *twice*. This will move the cursor to the TED command line. Next the operator should enter "file" and press the Enter key. This will store the movie record including the abstract field.

The following program will update the MOVIES2 file. Notice how TED has been invoked to make changes to the TEXT field.

```
-* CHAPTER 14
-* CHA14-21
-* EXAMPLE SHOWING THE USE OF TEXT FIELDS IN FOCUS
-* THIS PROGRAM WILL UPDATE ALL THE FIELDS INCLUDING THE TEXT FIELD
MODIFY FILE MOVIES2
CASE CHNG_REC
CRTFORM LINE 3  NOCLEAR
"          SCREEN FOR CHANGING THE CONTENTS OF THE MOVIES FILE"
"   "
"   "
"Please Enter the Title: <TITLE"
MATCH TITLE
    ON MATCH CRTFORM LINE 9
  "Tape Number: <D.TAPE_NO "
  "Length:       <T.LENGTH "
  "Comments:     <T.COMMENTS "
  "Rating:       <T.RATING"
```

```
ON MATCH TED ABSTRACT
ON MATCH UPDATE TAPE_NO LENGTH COMMENTS RATING ABSTRACT
ON MATCH GOTO CHNG_REC
ON NOMATCH TYPE
                This Title does not exist in the file"
ON NOMATCH REJECT
ON NOMATCH GOTO CHNG_REC
ENDCASE
DATA VIA FIDEL
LOG DUPL MSG OFF
LOG NOMATCH MSG OFF
END
```

SUMMARY

Creating full-screen data entry and retrieval programs is not a very easy task. In many other environments, it would take many months for an experienced batch programmer to learn the techniques for developing online programs. Additionally, writing online programs in, say, IBMs CICS (Customer Information Control Language) is usually time consuming. In Focus, on the other hand, with the CRTFORM subcommand, you can achieve the same results in a fraction of the time.

In this chapter we reviewed the following:

1. Coding the CRTFORM subcommand with its options
2. Developing screens and programs for adding, changing, and deleting fields, segments, and records
3. Developing data inquiry programs for displaying data online
4. Techniques for using the program function keys (PFKEYs) to cancel transactions or terminate the session
5. Techniques for updating multiple-segment records
6. Techniques for creating multiple CRTFORMs on one screen
7. Using CASE logic to improve program flow and provide added versatility
8. The COMPUTE statement and its importance in CRTFORM subcommand
9. Using the TYPE statement to convey meaningful messages to the operator
10. Using the PFKEYs to allow the operator to make processing decisions
11. Using the the VALIDATE statement to check input data
12. Using screen attributes
13. Using the FIND function for locating values in other files
14. Using the LOOKUP function to extract values from fields in other files and use them in processing
15. Repeating groups processing
16. Textfields with CRTFORM

This has been a long chapter. But it is important to learn all the major techniques that can be used to develop online programs in Focus. Focus also provides the ModifyTalk facility to assist you in developing screens and online programs. That facility is currently available on most Focus platforms. The code generated by ModifyTalk is not very compact and user friendly. In any case, once you have mastered what I have covered in this chapter, you will become more competent at handling bigger and more complex assignments by yourself without needing the ModifyTalk facility. Read this chapter twice and you may even become an expert!

COMPLETE APPLICATION DEVELOPMENT WITH THE DIALOGUE MANAGER

MAIN TOPICS:

- STORED PROCEDURES
- DIALOGUE MANAGER VARIABLES
- FULL SCREEN DATA ENTRY WITH –CRTFORM
- TESTING PROGRAMS WITH THE DIALOGUE MANAGER
- CURSOR POSITIONING

THE COMPLETE APPLICATION DEVELOPMENT TOOL

In this chapter we study the Focus Dialogue Manager. It has also been called the executive language of Focus. You can, in fact, look upon it as a procedural command language that will assist users in the execution of stored programs. The Dialogue Manager has all the facilities needed for developing complete applications. It has the capability to link several programs together and allow them to be run in any sequence. The Dialogue Manager is usually the vehicle for inputting systems and other variables into programs. It is the preferred method for creating default values and modifying them. The Dialogue Manager has the instruction set and the power to create full-screen data entry and data inquiry screens. In this respect it is like the CRTFORM subcommand.

INTRODUCTION AND CONVENTIONS

Every Dialogue Manager keyword starts with the dash (-) immediately to the left of the keyword. No spaces are allowed between the dash and the keyword.
    Examples:

–CRTFORM ← Very similar to the CRTFORM subcommand in MODIFY.

```
-RUN

-DEFAULT
```

The dash will invoke the Dialogue Manager environment. The Dialogue Manager commands and keywords could be intermixed with other Focus commands and codes. The Dialogue Manager statements are executed as soon as they are read from the disk. Regular Focus commands (i.e., TABLE and MODIFY) are stored or stacked temporarily in an area called FOCSTACK before execution.

Some of the functions of the Dialogue Manager facility are as follows:

1. Storing and executing frequently used Focus programs
2. Substituting variables and controlling the manner in which they are supplied
3. Validation of information supplied
4. Controlling the sequence of execution of commands
5. Executing system commands (i.e., passing TSO, CMS, or PC/DOS commands such as COPY, DELETE, RENAME, or other commands, for immediate execution, to the operating system from within the Focus environment)
6. Maintaining a dialogue between Focus and the operator

STORED PROCEDURES

A stored procedure is a Dialogue Manager program that is stored on magnetic media, usually disk unit. It contains a series of commands. Most of the programs that we have written in this book were stored programs. The Dialogue Manager programs are also called *procedures*. The Dialogue Manager commands may be one of three types.

1. Commands that are passed to one of the Focus environments, such as TABLE or MODIFY
2. Commands that are directly passed to the operating system, such as CMS COPY, TSO ALLOCATE, or DOS STATE
3. Commands used by the Dialogue Manager, such as –PROMPT or –DEFAULT

Following is an example of a simple Dialogue Manager procedure.

```
-* CHAPTER 15
-* CHA15-1
-* PROGRAM SHOWING THE USE OF THE DIALOGUE MANAGER
-*
-PROMPT  &STATE
-PROMPT &DEPT_NAME
TABLE FILE STAFF
HEADING CENTER
"REPORT OF SALARIES BY STATE OF RESIDENCE: <STATE"
"AND BY DEPARTMENT AS OF: &DATE"
```

```
"    "
PRINT LAST_NAME AND SALARY BY DEPT_NAME
IF STATE EQ  &STATE IF DEPT_NAME EQ &DEPT_NAME
END
```

When this program is executed, Focus will prompt the operator with the following messages. Operator responses are in lowercase.

```
PLEASE SUPPLY VALUES REQUESTED

STATE=>ca
DEPT_NAME=>finance
```

This is succeeded by the following report.

```
  PAGE      1

      REPORT OF SALARIES BY STATE OF RESIDENCE: CA
          AND BY DEPARTMENT AS OF: 09/01/91

                        EMPLOYEE
DEPT_NAME               LAST NAME                SALARY
---------               ---------                ------
FINANCE                 TURPIN                65,400.00
                        FREEMAN               34,500.00
```

Notice how the Dialogue Manager prompted the operator for the value of each of the fields requested. These fields then replaced the corresponding variables in the TABLE request.

DIALOGUE MANAGER VARIABLES

I briefly reviewed the different types of variables in a previous chapter when discussing the heading option and embedding data from a file in heading lines. I will review them here in more detail. Basically variables are temporary areas in the TABLE or MODIFY environment. Variables are always preceded by one or two ampersands (&). That is why they are also known as *amper variables*. Dialogue Manager variables, unlike fields, do not have data types, field lengths, or edit options. When a Focus program with Dialogue Manager variables is executed, the variables are substituted by their values. The variables can then be printed or be used in arithmetic or logical operations. We will shortly see how the values are supplied to the variables.

Syntax and Naming Conventions

1. All local variables must start with a single ampersand (&).
2. All global variables must start with double ampersands (&&).

3. The maximum number of characters in a variable name is 12. This does not include the && or &. Embedded blanks are not permitted.

4. The underscore (_) may be part of a variable name. Most special characters are not permitted in variable names.

5. If it is anticipated that the value of a variable may contain blanks, the entire variable must be enclosed in single quotation marks.

6. You can assign a number to a variable instead of a name. This will create a positional variable.

The syntax for a variable is as follows:

```
&variable [.format. [.text].]    ← Local variable

&&variable [.format. [.text].]   ← Global variable
```

or

```
&variable  [.(list) [.text].]

&&variable [.(list) [.text].]
```

&variable denotes the name of a local variable.

&&variable denotes the name of a global variable.

.format. denotes the type and maximum length of variable. Note that the format statement must be delimited by periods.

.text. specifies a programmer-defined prompt message that will be sent to the terminal at execution time. The text must also be delimited by periods.

.(list). refers to a list of allowable responses. The list must be enclosed in parentheses. Format and list are mutually exclusive.

Some examples of variables follow:

```
-PROMPT &STATE.A2.PLEASE ENTER STATE.
```

```
-PROMPT &CITY.(ANAHEIM,IRVINE,LAKEWOOD).
```

There are five types of variables:

1. *Local variables.* These variables are normally supplied by the user at program execution time. The values supplied remain in effect throughout a single FOCEXEC only. Local variables are identified by a single ampersand (&) preceding the variable. For example, &CITY and &DEPT_NAME are both local variables.

2. *Global variables.* These variables are also supplied at program execution time. The difference here is that once a value is entered it remains in effect throughout the entire Focus session. Therefore, other programs which later use one of these variables will access the same values. Global variables are identified by double ampersands (&&) preceding the variable name. For example, &&CITY and &&DEPT_NAME are both global variables. Once a value is placed in, say, the &&CITY variable, it will remain in the computer memory until the end of the Focus session.

3. *System variables.* These variables are reserved for the system. They are always available. If they are used in a program, the value will automatically be extracted from the system and will be made available to the Focus program for manipulation. For example, if you use the &DATE variable in a TABLE request, Focus will automatically place the current system date on your report. The main system variables and their meanings are listed in Table 15.1.

TABLE 15.1 SYSTEM VARIABLES

System variable	Meaning
&DATE	Displays the current date in MM/DD/YY format (e.g., 09/12/91). Note that the system automatically inserts the slashes in the variable.
&MDY	Displays the current date in MMDDYY format (e.g., 091291). *Note:* No slashes here.
&YMD	Displays the current date in YYMMDD format (e.g., 910912).
&DMY	Displays the current date in DDMMYY format (e.g., 120991).
&TOD	Displays the time of day. This is displayed in hours, minutes, and seconds (e.g., 10.14.12).
&RETCODE	Contains the value returned after an operating system command such as COPY, STATE, or RENAME is executed. Normally, a return code (&RETCODE) of 0 means a successful end. Anything higher than 0 is suspect.
&IORETRUN	Contains the value returned by the system after a -READ or a -WRITE operation. These are Dialogue Manager commands to read or write data from sequential files.
&ECHO	This is used in the test mode for debugging. This variable, if turned on, will display the Focus program lines that are expanded and stacked for Focus to execute.

4. *Statistical variables.* Like the System variables, these variables (see Table 15.2) are always available. They could be supplied whenever requested by the program. To see the value of current statistical variables, type ? STAT from the Focus > prompt.

TABLE 15.2 STATISTICAL VARIABLES

Statistical variable	Meaning
	Variables Available in the Table Environment
&RECORDS	Number of records retrieved in the last report
&LINES	Number of lines printed in the last report
	Variables Available in the Modify Environment
&TRANS	Number of transactions processed
&DUPLS	Number of transactions rejected as duplicates
&NOMATCH	Number of transactions rejected because they did not pass the MATCH test
&INVALID	Number of transactions rejected because of an invalid condition
&DELTD	Number of segments deleted
&READS	Number of reads from an external file
&ACCEPTS	Number of transactions accepted
&FORMAT	Number of transactions rejected because of format errors
&REJECTS	Number of other rejected transactions other than due to NOMATCH, DUPLICATE, INVALID, and format error
&CHNGD	Number of segments updated
&INPUT	Number of segments input
&BASEIO	Number of input/output operations

5. *Reserved variables.* The Dialogue Manager has access to the special variables listed in Table 15.3.

TABLE 15.3 SPECIAL (RESERVED) VARIABLES

Special variable	Meaning
&PFKEY	Returns the value of the PFKEY function.
&CURSOR	Identifies the cursor position
&CURSORAT	Reads the current cursor position
&QUIT	Can be manipulated to turn the QUIT function (or PF1 in -CRTFORM) off

You can always check for the current value of a variable from the Focus > prompt. To display the current value of global variables, issue the following query command.

```
> ? &&
```

To display statistical variables, issue the following query command:

```
> ? STAT
```

A typical display resulting from a ? STAT query command is shown below.

```
STATISTICS OF LAST COMMAND

RECORDS         =        0
LINES           =        0
BASEIO          =        5
READS           =        8
TRANSACTIONS    =        7
ACCEPTED        =        3
SEGS INPUT      =        1
SEGS CHNGD      =        0
SEGS DELTD      =        0
NOMATCH         =        1
DUPLICATES      =        1
FORMAT ERRORS   =        0
INVALID CONDTS  =        0
OTHER REJECTS   =        0
```

Supplying Values to Variables in Focus Programs

There are several ways to supply values to variables in a program. The use
depends on the user's requirements. The various methods are detailed below.

Supplying values to named variables at the Focus prompt > line. There
are three variables in the following example. If the operator types the values on
the Focus prompt line following the name of the program or the procedure, the
values supplied will be passed on to each variable.

```
-* CHAPTER 15
-* CHA15-2
-* PROGRAM SHOWING THE USE OF THE DIALOGUE MANAGER
-* USING THE FOCUS PROMPT LINE TO ENTER VARIABLES.
-*
DEFINE FILE STAFF
SSTAX/D9.2=IF SALARY GT 52000 THEN 52000 * .075
          ELSE IF SALARY LT 52000 THEN SALARY * .075 ;
END
TABLE FILE STAFF
HEADING CENTER
"SALARIES AND ANNUAL SOCIAL SECURITY SALARY TAXES "
" "
PRINT LAST_NAME AND SALARY AND SSTAX BY DEPT_NAME
IF STATE EQ &STATE IF DEPT_NAME EQ &DEPT_NAME
IF SALARY GT &SALARY
END
```

This is how the program is executed from the Focus prompt:

```
EX CHA15-2 STATE=CA, DEPT_NAME=MIS, SALARY=36000
```

The commas to delimit each entry are required. Always use the full field names. If the value contains embedded commas or the equal sign (=), enclose the values between single quotation marks.

```
PAGE     1

         SALARIES AND ANNUAL SOCIAL SECURITY SALARY TAXES

                       EMPLOYEE
DEPT_NAME              LAST NAME                SALARY       SSTAX
---------             ---------               ------       -----
MIS                    GREENSTREET           45,600.00    3,420.00
                       TAHANIEV              55,400.00    3,900.00
```

If the operator omits the name of any variable, Focus will prompt him or her for that name. Observe the following entry:

```
EX CHA15-2 STATE=CA, SALARY=36000
```

Focus will respond with the following prompt:

```
PLEASE SUPPLY VALUES REQUESTED

DEPT_NAME=>mis   ← The operator must enter a value here.
```

Supplying values to positional variables. In this case the name of each variable is a number indicating its position in the program. The following program is almost identical to the program above, the only difference being that I have used positional variables to indicate the position of each variable.

```
-* CHAPTER 15
-* CHA15-3
-* PROGRAM SHOWING THE USE OF THE DIALOGUE MANAGER
-* USING POSITIONAL VARIABLES.
-*
DEFINE FILE STAFF
SSTAX/D9.2=IF SALARY GT 52000 THEN 52000 * .075
ELSE IF SALARY LT 52000 THEN SALARY * .075 ;
END
TABLE FILE STAFF
HEADING CENTER
"SALARIES AND ANNUAL SOCIAL SALARY TAXES "
"   "
PRINT LAST_NAME AND SALARY AND SSTAX BY DEPT_NAME
```

```
IF STATE EQ &1 IF DEPT_NAME EQ &2    ← Note the difference between the
IF SALARY GT &3                      ← two lines and the previous
                                       program.
END
```

To execute this program, the operator will need to enter the following:

```
EX CHA15-3 CA, MIS, 36000
```

If the operator does not enter the positional variables as indicated, he or she will get prompted by Focus as follows:

```
EX CHA15-3

PLEASE SUPPLY VALUES REQUESTED

1=>ca
2=>mis
3=>36000
```

Implied prompting. In any of the foregoing methods, if the operator does not supply the needed values on the command line, he or she will be prompted by Focus to enter the values requested.

Supplying values with the -DEFAULTS control statement. The -DEFAULTS statement will provide the initial or default values for variable substitution. The values are hard coded in the Focus program. The purpose of using the -DEFAULTS statement is to ensure that the program will at least always execute with some predefined values. The operator will have the opportunity, but will not be required, to set new values for the program variables. The syntax of this statement is as follows:

```
-DEFAULTS &variable=value, &variable=value, &variable=value
```

&variable denotes the name of the variable.
Value denotes the initial or default value being assigned to the the variable.

The following program illustrates the use of -DEFAULTS to assign an initial value for a salary range.

```
-* CHAPTER 15
-* CHA15-4
-* USING THE -DEFAULT CONTROL STATEMENT
-*
-DEFAULTS &SALARY1=34000, &SALARY2=56000
-TYPE Default Range Values are 34000 and 56000
TABLE FILE STAFF
HEADING CENTER
"SALARY RANGES BY DEPARTMENT NAME"
"SALARY RANGE IS FROM: &SALARY1 TO: &SALARY2"
" "
PRINT LN AND SALARY BY DEPT_NAME
IF SALARY FROM &SALARY1 TO &SALARY2
END
```

The operator has two choices. He or she can execute this program from the command line by typing EX CHA15-4. In that case, the values supplied by the -DEFAULTS statement will replace the variables &SALARY1 AND &SALARY2, as shown below.

```
PAGE     1

             SALARY RANGES BY DEPARTMENT NAME
          SALARY RANGE IS FROM: 34000 TO: 56000

                         EMPLOYEE
        DEPT_NAME        LAST NAME              SALARY
        ---------        ---------              ------
        FINANCE          FREEMAN             34,500.00
        MARKETING        COLE                39,000.00
                         MORALES             39,400.00
                         ZARKOV              47,000.00
                         JAMESON             36,700.00
        MIS              GREENSTREET         45,600.00
                         BOCHARD             35,000.00
                         TAHANIEV            55,400.00
```

I included a -TYPE statement in this program. This will cause the following message to be printed prior to program execution.

```
Default Range Values are 34000 and 56000
```

The other option is to override the default values by entering new values on the command line, as shown below.

```
EX CHA15-4 SALARY1=24000, SALARY2=68000
```

In this case the program will execute with the new values.

The -DEFAULTS option can be combined with masking. This will allow all possible values to pass through. The dollar sign is used to indicate a mask. Masked defaults can also be overridden by the operator at execution time.

```
-*CHAPTER 15
-* CHA15-5
-* USING THE -DEFAULT CONTROL STATEMENT
-* WITH MASKED VALUES.
-DEFAULTS &STATE=$$, &DEPT_NAME=$$$$$$$$$$$$$$$$$$$$$
-TYPE This Procedure will print information about employees
-TYPE in all Departments in all states.
TABLE FILE STAFF
HEADING CENTER
"LIST OF EMPLOYEES, SALARIES AND LAST PERCENTAGE SALARY INCREASE"
"FOR DEPARTMENT: &DEPT_NAME STATE: &STATE"
"  "
```

```
PRINT LAST_NAME AND SALARY AND PIN
AND DEPT_NAME
IF STATE EQ &STATE
IF DEPT_NAME EQ &DEPT_NAME
BY STATE
END
```

This statement will override the
department name default.

```
EX CHA15-5 DEPT_NAME=FINANCE
```

```
PAGE    1

    LIST OF EMPLOYEES, SALARIES AND LAST PERCENTAGE SALARY INCREASE
                 FOR DEPARTMENT: FINANCE STATE: $$

           EMPLOYEE
    STATE  LAST NAME                   SALARY  PCT_INC  DEPT_NAME
    -----  ---------                   ------  -------  ---------
    CA     TURPIN                   65,400.00     .05   FINANCE
           FREEMAN                  34,500.00     .00   FINANCE
    NY     BORGIA                  102,000.00     .06   FINANCE
```

Note: Executing the foregoing program without overriding the defaulted values will cause printing of the entire file.

Supplying values with the -SET statement.   Values can be assigned to variables with the -SET statement. The -SET statement is similar to the COMPUTE statement in the MODIFY environment. You can use -SET to EDIT, DECODE, control loops, concatenate fields, and perform logical and arithmetic operations. The syntax of the -SET statement is as follows:

```
-SET &variable=expression ;
```

&variable denotes the name of the variable.

expression; may be any literal arithmetic or logical expression. Expressions may occupy more than one line. Always end the'expression with a semicolon. (*Note:* If the expression exceeds one line, you must start all subsequent lines with a dash.)

In the following program, the -SET statement is used to change the logic of the program, depending on the value of the department field, as input by the user. If the operator enters MIS or MARKETING in response to the prompt, the program will LIST the salaries by department. If the operator enters any other department name, the program will COUNT the employees and their salaries.

```
-* CHAPTER 15
-* CHA15-6
-* USING THE -SET STATEMENT TO ASSIGN VALUES.
-*
-SET &DEPT_CODE = IF &DEPT_NAME EQ 'MIS' OR 'MARKETING' THEN
-                 LIST ELSE COUNT  ;
TABLE FILE STAFF
HEADING CENTER
"&DEPT_CODE OF SALARIES FOR &DEPT_NAME DEPARTMENT"
" "
&DEPT_CODE LAST_NAME AND SALARY BY DEPT_NAME
IF DEPT_NAME EQ &DEPT_NAME
AND DEPT_NAME
END
```

The following command will produce the report that will follow.

```
EX CHA15-6 DEPT_NAME=MIS
```

```
          LIST OF SALARIES FOR MIS DEPARTMENT

                            EMPLOYEE
DEPT_NAME             LIST  LAST NAME            SALARY
---------            ----  ---------            ------
MIS                    1   GREENSTREET       45,600.00
                       2   BOCHARD           35,000.00
                       3   TAHANIEV          55,400.00
                       4   CAMPOS            32,000.00
```

Supplying values with the -READ statement. You can also read values from sequential files. The syntax for -READ is as follows:

```
-READ ddname[,] &variable[.format.][,]...
```

ddname[,] denotes the name of the sequential file. A space after the file name identifies it as a fixed-format file. A comma identifies it as a free-format file.

&variable refers to a list of variables.

.format. denotes the format of the variable. The format specifies the length of the variable.

If the list of variables is longer than one line, terminate the first line with a comma and start the next line with a dash followed by a comma (-,).

An example of a -READ statement follows:

```
-READ SEQFILE &DEPT_NAME.A20. &STATE.A2
```

This statement will read an external file called SEQFILE. There are two fields in that file. The DEPT_NAME field has a length of 20 characters. This is followed by the STATE field with a length of two characters. The external file must be identified to Focus with a FILEDEF or ALLOCATE command.

```
-* CHAPTER 15
-* CHA15-7
-* USING THE -READ STATEMENT TO ASSIGN VALUES.
-*
-READ SEQFILE &DEPT_NAME.A20. &STATE.A2.
TABLE FILE STAFF
HEADING CENTER
"LIST OF EMPLOYEES, THEIR SALARIES AND ACCRUED VACATIONS"
" "
PRINT LAST_NAME AND SALARY AND VACATION BY DEPT_NAME
IF DEPT_NAME EQ &DEPT_NAME
IF STATE EQ &STATE
END
```

The SEQFILE contains only one record and has the following layout:

```
FINANCE             CA
```

The following report is produced after the execution of the program above.

```
PAGE     1

       LIST OF EMPLOYEES, THEIR SALARIES AND ACCRUED VACATIONS

                         EMPLOYEE
DEPT_NAME                LAST NAME                SALARY   VACATION
---------                ---------                ------   --------
FINANCE                  TURPIN                65,400.00        120
                         FREEMAN               34,500.00         99
```

To detect the end of file, you can test &IORETURN. If its value equals 0, no more records remain to be read.

Supplying values directly with the -PROMPT statement. The -PROMPT statement prompts the user for values as soon as the -PROMPT statement is encountered. In the following example the -PROMPT is used to select a list of employees within a section of a department. The operator is prompted for the department ID and section ID of his or her choice. Once a selection is made, the variables are replaced by entered values and the program is executed. Notice the use of -SET to format the &YMD system variable. The &YMD system variable is always in the 999999 format. Therefore, January 14, 1991 will be displayed as 910114. I used the -SET statement to edit the value of this system variable and inserted slashes to make it more readable.

```
-* CHAPTER 15
-* CHA15-8
-* PROGRAM SHOWING THE USE OF DIRECT PROMPTING WITH -PROMPT
-*
-PROMPT &DID.A6.Please Enter the Department ID.
-PROMPT &SECID.A6.Please Enter the Section ID.      ← Also note use of –SET.
-SET &DATE1 = EDIT(&YMD,'99/99/99') ;
TABLE FILE STAFF
HEADING CENTER
"REPORT OF SALARIES BY DEPARTMENT : <DEPT_NAME <+3 DATE: &DATE1"
"BY SECTION: <SECTION_NAME"
"    "
PRINT LAST_NAME AND SALARY
IF DID EQ &DID IF SECID EQ &SECID
ON TABLE COLUMN-TOTAL
END
```

The result of execution of the program above is printed below.

```
EX CHA15-8

Please Enter the Department ID>15
Please Enter the Section ID>152



    PAGE     1

    REPORT OF SALARIES BY DEPARTMENT : OPERATIONS   DATE: 91/09/03
                    BY SECTION: CUSTOMER SERVICES


    EMPLOYEE
    LAST NAME                    SALARY
    ---------                    ------
    TRENT                     22,500.00
    TAYLOR                    26,550.00
    TOTAL                     49,050.00
```

FULL-SCREEN DATA ENTRY WITH -CRTFORM

As we discussed in Chapter 14, the full-screen data inquiry and entry form (CRT-FORM) is the most effective method for communicating with the operator. The Dialogue Manager also provides a similar environment. It is called -CRTFORM and it also operates under FIDEL. The Dialogue Manager's full-screen form is invoked by the keyword -CRTFORM. Each line of the form must begin with -" and must end with ". The first line without a -" terminates the -CRTFORM environment. The format of the -CRTFORM is as follows:

```
-CRTFORM, [LOWER]
```

-CRTFORM initiates the start of the screen form and invokes FIDEL.

LOWER will accept lowercase characters from the terminal. Without this option, all lowercase characters are converted to uppercase characters.

Note that in -CRTFORM, the WIDTH, LINE, and HEIGHT options are not available.

Variables in -CRTFORM are predeclared with the -SET statement. Remember that the Dialogue Manager variables do not have a predefined format. The size and the value of each &variable field must also be predeclared before usage, as shown below.

Note: there are eight spaces between the two single quotation marks.

```
-SET &ACCOUNT = '        ' ;
```

The entry above creates a variable called &ACCOUNT with a size of eight characters. Dialogue Manager variables do not have data types or length; therefore, the following is incorrect:

```
-SET &ACCOUNT/A8= ;
```

Variables within the -CRTFORM are identified by a left-hand caret ($<$). This is similar to the field definitions in CRTFORM. The following rules also apply.

$<$D.&VARIABLE displays the current value for a variable. The variable remains protected and cannot be changed.

$<$T.&VARIABLE displays the current value for a variable. The operator can change the value of the variable.

$<$&VARIABLE requests a value for a variable.

Frequently, a -CRTFORM procedure is used to create menus to control the flow of other programs. The following program is the main menu for the STAFF Focus database. The operator has many choices. Some choices lead to other menus, which allow more choices to be made.

```
-* CHAPTER 15
-* CHA15-9
-* PROGRAM SHOWING THE -CRTFORM. THIS PROCEDURE DISPLAYS
-* A MENU TO THE OPERATOR. EACH SELECTION COULD LEAD TO
-* OTHER MENUS AND PROGRAMS.
SET MSG=OFF      ← This command suppresses Focus messages.
SET PAUSE=OFF
-TOP1
-SET &SELECT = ' ' ;
-CRTFORM
-"                        The Staff File System    "
-"                             Main Menu              "
-" "
```

```
-"  "
-"   "
-"  "
-"   "
-"                          Q. Exit This Menu "
-"                          1. Inquire Into Staff File "
-"                          2. Update Staff File Salaries"
-"                          3. Add New Records to Staff File "
-"                          4. Delete Records from Staff File "
-"                          5. Print Reports  from Staff File"
-"                          6. Backup Your Data "
-"                          H. Help "
-"  "
-"Please make a selection===> <&SELECT> "
-"  "
-"  "
-"                          PRESS Q OR PF3 TO EXIT THE SYSTEM"
-IF &SELECT EQ   Q  GOTO KUIT ELSE IF &SELECT EQ 1 GOTO INQ
-ELSE IF &SELECT EQ 2 GOTO UP ELSE IF &SELECT EQ 3 GOTO ADDN
-ELSE IF &SELECT EQ 4 GOTO DEL ELSE IF &SELECT EQ 5 GOTO PRIN
-ELSE IF &SELECT EQ 6 GOTO UTIL ELSE IF &SELECT EQ H GOTO HELPM
-ELSE GOTO NONO ;
-KUIT
-EXIT
-TYPE   Thank You
-INQ
EXEC CHA14-7
-RUN
-GOTO TOP1
-UP
EXEC CHA14-9
-RUN
-GOTO TOP1
-ADDN
EXEC CHA14-6
-RUN
-GOTO TOP1
-DEL
EXEC CHA-DEL
-RUN
-GOTO TOP1
-PRIN
EXEC PRMENU1
-RUN
-GOTO TOP1
-UTIL
EXEC UTIL1
-RUN
-GOTO TOP1
-HELPM
```

```
-EXEC HELPM
-RUN
-GOTO TOP1
-NONO
-GOTO TOP1
```

As you have noticed, the Dialogue Manager's -CRTFORM is very much like the CRTFORM under the MODIFY environment. Note the importance of the -RUN control statement. The -RUN causes all the stacked Focus commands to be executed immediately. For example, look at the following code.

```
-UP
EXEC CHA14-9
-RUN
-GOTO TOP1
```

If the operator presses the number 2 key on the keyboard, the procedure will transfer control of the program to -UP paragraph. This paragraph executes a Focus program called CHA14-9. What really happens if CHA14-9 is invoked without the -RUN control statement is that it will sit there waiting to be executed. Dialogue Manager commands execute as the program is read from the storage (i.e., disk unit) area. Regular Focus program commands (i.e., MODIFY commands or TABLE request commands) are usually placed in a queue. These commands are executed at the end of the program. However, if as in the example above, there are a number of programs that need to be executed, Focus may not execute them in the correct order and you may get strange results. That is where the -RUN statement comes in. When you issue a -RUN statement, all the commands in the preceding program are immediately released and executed. Therefore, you can be sure that the program that was supposed to execute has really executed at this time. The other feature of the -RUN statement is that after the program has been executed, control will be transferred to the command following the -RUN statement. The -RUN statement is very important. It will ensure that programs that are part of a Dialogue Manager procedure are executed as they are invoked.

The following example should clarify the importance of the -RUN statement. The program below is a very simple Focus TABLE request. It will print the name of employees and their job titles by department. Notice the two -TYPE statements. There is one at the beginning of the program and one at the end. Normally, you would expect the program to display the first message, then print the report, and finally, display the second message. In reality, the first -TYPE statement is immediately executed because it is a Dialogue Manager statement. However, since the following lines are not Dialogue Manager statements (i.e., they do not begin with a dash), they are placed in a queue (FOCSTACK) to be executed later by Focus. The last program line starts with a dash, so the Dialogue Manager will execute it immediately, which will result in the display of the second message. The result is that the two Dialogue Manager -TYPE statements will be displayed one after the other before the TABLE request begins to process.

```
-* CHAPTER 15
-* CHA15-14
```

```
-* THE EFFECT OF -RUN CONTROL STATEMENT ON EXECUTION
-* OF PROGRAMS.
-TYPE THIS IS THE BEGINNING OF THE PROGRAM.
TABLE FILE STAFF
HEADING CENTER
"LIST OF EMPLOYEES BY DEPARTMENT "
" "
PRINT LAST_NAME AND TITLE
BY DEPT_NAME
IF RECORDLIMIT EQ 8
END
-TYPE THIS IS THE END OF THE PROGRAM.


EX CHA15-14


THIS IS THE BEGINNING OF THE PROGRAM.
THIS IS THE END OF THE PROGRAM.

  PAGE    1

              LIST OF EMPLOYEES BY DEPARTMENT

  EMPLOYEE
  DEPT_NAME              LAST NAME            JOB_TITLE
  ---------             ---------            ---------
  FINANCE               TURPIN               HEAD ACCOUNTANT
                        BORGIA               LIAISON MANAGER
                        FREEMAN              SUPERVISOR
  MARKETING             COLE                 SALES REPRESENTATIVE
                        MORALES              SALES REPRESENTATIVE
  OPERATIONS            HUNT                 MANAGER
                        TRENT                SERVICE REP.
                        TAYLOR               SERVICE REP.
```

To correct this problem and to ensure that the sequence of operations follows the logic of the program, as intended, we must add the -RUN statement immediately after the END command. This is shown below.

```
END

-RUN    ← This statement will release the Focus TABLE Request for
           immediate execution.

-TYPE THIS IS THE END OF THE PROGRAM.
```

The addition of this one statement will ensure that the first -TYPE message is followed by the printed report and then by the second -TYPE message, which announces the end of the program.

There are several other very important Dialogue Manager statements. I describe these commands below.

-GOTO. This statement will branch to the label (or paragraph) that was specified by the -GOTO statement. The syntax of the -GOTO is as follows:

```
-GOTO label
```

Label denotes the name of the paragraph to which control will be transferred. For example, -GOTO HELPM will transfer control to the paragraph labeled HELPM. Although similar to the GOTO command in the MODIFY environment, this command does not perform exactly the same function. The GOTO command in the MODIFY environment will perform a CASE module within a MODIFY request. The GOTO command will always default to the top of the program if there are no other instructions at the end of a CASE module. The -GOTO will not. It will just drop through to the next paragraph unless directed to go to the top of the program or to another paragraph.

-IF. This statement is a conditional GOTO. It transfers control to another paragraph based on evaluation of its attached expression. The syntax of the -IF statement is as follows:

```
-IF expression [THEN] GOTO label
[ELSE GOTO label] ;
```

Expression signifies a true or false test.

Then is optional and is used for clarity.

GOTO label specifies the paragraph that will be executed if the statement evaluates as being true.

ELSE GOTO label specifies the paragraph that will be executed if the statement evaluates as being false.

The following example illustrates the use of -IF.

```
-IF &SELECT EQ  Q  GOTO KUIT ELSE IF &SELECT EQ 1 GOTO INQ
-ELSE IF &SELECT EQ 2 GOTO UP ELSE IF &SELECT EQ 3 GOTO ADDN
-ELSE IF &SELECT EQ 4 GOTO DEL ELSE IF &SELECT EQ 5 GOTO PRIN
-ELSE IF &SELECT EQ 6 GOTO UTIL ELSE IF &SELECT EQ H GOTO HELPM
-ELSE GOTO NONO ;
```

Note that each new line in the statement above starts with a -. The -IF statement in the Dialogue Manager and the IF statement in Modify are quite similar in use and execution.

-INCLUDE. This statement allows the program or the procedure to invoke other Focus programs at execution time. This is a particularly good feature for writing one Focus program with a main heading option and including it in other programs. The syntax of this control statement follows.

```
-INCLUDE   filename
```

Filename denotes the Focus program (also known as the *called program*) that is included in the current Focus program (also known as the *calling program*).

You may want to incorporate a standard heading with your company and division name on every report. In this case, you can either code the report heading in each program separately or code it once and call it into other programs at execution time. You can also create common DEFINE statements and include them, as needed, in your requests. The following program is a partially coded program that prepares a standard heading that can be included in other programs.

```
-* CHAPTER 15
-* CHA15-10
-* USING THE -INCLUDE CONTROL STATEMENT.
-* THIS IS THE PROGRAM THAT CAN BE CALLED BY OTHER PROGRAMS.
TABLE FILE STAFF
HEADING CENTER
"FTA COMPUTER CONSULTANTS"
"    "
"MONTHLY SALARY REPORT BY DEPARTMENT"
"PREPARED BY THE FINANCE DEPARTMENT <55 &DATE"
"    "
```

The second program calls the first program at execution time and runs as if it were part of the second program. Note that the first program is run with the second program, but the original source code of each program is left intact.

```
-* CHAPTER 15
-* CHA15-11
-* USING THE -INCLUDE CONTROL STATEMENT.
-* THIS PROGRAM CALLS CHA15-10 AND INCORPORATES THE CODE FROM
-* THAT PROGRAM.
-INCLUDE CHA15-10
PRINT LAST_NAME AND FIRST_NAME AND CITY
BY DEPT_NAME
END
```

The following entry will execute the CHA15-11 program:

```
EX CHA15-11
```

```
                         FTA COMPUTER CONSULTANTS
               MONTHLY SALARY REPORT BY DEPARTMENT
      PREPARED BY THE FINANCE DEPARTMENT                 09/06/91
```

DEPT_NAME	EMPLOYEE LAST NAME	FIRST_NAME	CITY
ADMINISTRATION	DUXBURY	JILLIAN	IRVINE
	ANDERSEN	CHRISTINE	ANAHEIM
FINANCE	TURPIN	BENTON	LOS ANGELES
	BORGIA	CESARE	NEW YORK
	FREEMAN	DIANE	CANTON
MARKETING	COLE	ROBERT	GARDEN GROVE
	MORALES	CARLOS	LONG BEACH
	ZARKOV	WILLIAM	ANAHEIM
	JAMESON	CARLA	FOUNTAIN VALLEY
MIS	GREENSTREET	JAMES	LAKEWOOD
	BOCHARD	ROBERT	EL TORO
	TAHANIEV	RICHARD	SANTA ANA
	CAMPOS	CARLOS	LAGUNA NIGUEL
OPERATIONS	HUNT	CHARLES	ORANGE
	TRENT	RICHARD	LOS ANGELES
	TAYLOR	JUANITA	SANTA MONICA

Since -INCLUDE is a Dialogue Manager control statement, it is executed immediately. If the same program had been coded as part of the calling program, it would have been stacked for execution with the rest of the program.

You can have as many -INCLUDEs as you need. However, nested -INCLUDEs (-INCLUDEs containing -INCLUDEs within them) are limited to four levels deep in each program. An example of a nested -INCLUDE:

```
-INCLUDE PGM1
-RUN
-------------------------
PGM1
-INCLUDE PGM2
-RUN
-------------------------
PGM2
-INCLUDE PGM3
-RUN
-------------------------
```

```
PGM3
-INCLUDE PGM4
-RUN
---------------------------
PGM4
-RUN
```

As you will notice, each program in the procedure above calls and executes another program.

-EXIT. The -EXIT control statement forces the procedure to terminate. When this statement is encountered, all lines of code that may have been stacked for execution are executed immediately. The user is then returned to the Focus > prompt, or the calling program if the program was called from another program.

-QUIT. The -QUIT control statement forces an immediate termination of the procedure. Note that unlike -EXIT, the lines of code that may have been stacked are not executed. They are discarded. The -QUIT FOCUS statement will terminate the procedure and the Focus session. It will return the user to the operating system (i.e., CMS, TSO, or DOS).

Operating system commands. These commands allow you to issue operating system commands from within the Dialogue Manager procedure. The system commands are executed immediately by the operating system.

The syntax of these commands follows:

```
-CMS command
```

or

```
-TSO command
```

or

```
-DOS command
```

Examples:

```
-CMS COPY STAFF FOCUS A STAFF FOCUS B (REPL

-DOS STATE C:STAFF.FOC

-TSO ALLOC F(STAFF2) DA('STAFF2.DATA') SHR
```

While it is also possible to use TSO, DOS, or CMS commands from within Focus programs, it is more efficient to use the -TSO, -DOS, or -CMS commands. This is because the dash commands are passed directly to the operating system. The other commands are placed in the FOCSTACK for execution.

Both of the following statements are accurate and will allocate a CMS file as indicated. However, the Dialogue Manager statement starting with a dash is more efficient because it is passed on to CMS for immediate execution.

```
 CMS FILEDEF INFILE DISK INFILE DATA A

-CMS FILEDEF INFILE DISK INFILE DATA A
```

-WRITE. The write control statement allows you to write information to external sequential files. You may want to create a permanent record of operator identification or other pertinent data. The syntax of the -WRITE is as follows:

```
-WRITE filename text
```

Filename denotes the name of the file being written.

Text may be a combination of text and variables.

The -WRITE statement opens the file for writing and closes it when the procedure is terminated. If the same file is reopened during the next session, the previous information is overwritten with new information. To allow addition of new data to the file, you must define or allocate the file with a disposition of MOD (modifiable).

```
-* CHAPTER 15
-* CHA15-12
-* USING THE -WRITE CONTROL STATEMENT
-* TO WRITE INFORMATION TO EXTERNAL FILES.
-DOS FILEDEF INFO1 DISK C:\FOCUS\INFO1.DAT (DISP MOD
-PROMPT &DEPT_NAME.ENTER DEPARTMENT NAME.
-PROMPT &OPERATOR.ENTER OPERATOR LAST NAME.
-WRITE INFO1 &DEPT_NAME &OPERATOR &DATE &TOD
TABLE FILE STAFF
HEADING CENTER
"EMPLOYEE SALARIES BY DEPARTMENT: <&DEPT_NAME"
"  "
PRINT LAST_NAME AND SALARY
IF DEPT_NAME EQ &DEPT_NAME
END


PAGE     1

 EMPLOYEE SALARIES BY DEPARTMENT: OPERATIONS

 EMPLOYEE
 LAST NAME                SALARY
 ---------                ------
 HUNT                     57,000.00
 TRENT                    22,500.00
 TAYLOR                   26,550.00
```

Following is a list of the contents of the INFO1 file. It shows that the STAFF file was accessed three times by two different users or operators. The information is very useful because it shows the department they accessed, the date, and the time of day.

```
MIS DUXBURY 09/06/91 13.56.12
MIS DUXBURY 09/08/91 10.14.14
FINANCE HAMILTON 09/08/91 12.14.14
```

TESTING NEW PROGRAMS OR PROCEDURES IN FOCUS

The &ECHO facility within the Dialogue Manager will display the lines of code on the screen as they are being executed. The &ECHO can have one of the following variables.

$$\&ECHO = \left\{ \begin{array}{l} ON \\ ALL \\ OFF \end{array} \right\} \leftarrow \text{This is the default.}$$

ON will display the Focus lines that have been stacked and are ready for execution.

ALL will display the Dialogue Manager statement as well as stacked Focus lines that are ready for execution.

OFF suppresses display of both the Dialogue Manager and Focus stacked lines. This is the default.

There are three ways to invoke the debugging facility and assign values to the &ECHO variable.

1. From the Focus > prompt:

```
EX PROG1 ECHO=ON   or ECHO=ALL
```

2. Through the -DEFAULTS control statement:

```
-DEFAULTS &ECHO=ON
```

3. Through the -SET control statement:

```
-SET &ECHO=ALL ;
```

It is usually better to use the -SET control statement, especially in longer programs. Since you could use the -SET statement to turn the echo facility on and off, you could place a series of -SET statements throughout your program to debug your logic.

Use of the STACK Facility to Help with Debugging

The stacking or queuing of Focus program codes could be turned on and off. This is accomplished by one of the following methods.

1. Through the Focus > prompt:

```
EX PROG1 STACK=OFF
```

2. Through use of the -SET facility:

```
-SET STACK=ON ;
```

If the STACK is turned off, regular Focus codes do not get executed. Therefore, the STACK is usually turned off in conjunction with the ECHO=ALL parameter. In this way all the Dialogue Manager and Focus codes are displayed on the terminal but nothing is executed. This is an excellent method for reviewing the logic of the procedure or program.

Now let us take the last program that we used in this chapter (CHA15-12) and add debugging statements to it. First, we add the -SET &ECHO=ON; to it:

```
-* CHAPTER 15
-* CHA15-12
-* USING THE -WRITE CONTROL STATEMENT
-* TO WRITE INFORMATION TO EXTERNAL FILES.
-SET &ECHO=ON ;
-DOS FILEDEF INFO1 DISK C:\FOCUS\INFO1.DAT (DISP MOD
```

followed by the rest of the code.

If we execute this program, we will see the following display on the terminal (operator entries are shown in lowercase):

```
ENTER DEPARTMENT NAME>mis
ENTER OPERATOR LAST NAME>turpin
TABLE FILE STAFF
HEADING CENTER
"EMPLOYEE SALARIES BY DEPARTMENT"
" "
PRINT LAST_NAME AND SALARY
IF DEPT_NAME EQ MIS
END
```

This will be followed by the actual report.

If we execute this program with the -SET &ECHO=ALL statement, the Dialogue Manager commands will also be displayed on the terminal.

```
-DOS FILEDEF INFO1 DISK C:\FOCUS\INFO1.DAT (DISP MOD
ENTER DEPARTMENT NAME>mis
-PROMPT &DEPT_NAME.ENTER DEPARTMENT NAME.
```

Testing New Programs or Procedures in Focus

```
ENTER OPERATOR LAST NAME>turpin
-PROMPT &OPERATOR.ENTER OPERATOR LAST NAME.
-WRITE INFO1 MIS TURPIN 09/08/91 12.38.26
TABLE FILE STAFF
HEADING CENTER
"EMPLOYEE SALARIES BY DEPARTMENT"
"  "
PRINT LAST_NAME AND SALARY
IF DEPT_NAME EQ MIS
END
```

This will be followed by the actual report.

If we added the -SET &STACK=OFF statement to this program, Focus will display the same screen as above. However, because the STACK is set to the off position, nothing will get executed. This will reduce the computer resources needed to test and debug programs.

AUTOMATIC CURSOR POSITIONING

In Chapter 14, we learned two methods for selecting options from a menu for execution. One was using the PF keys to make a selection. The other method was entering the number that corresponded to the menu item on the screen and then pressing the Enter key.

Sometimes, the users may request that you design a screen where a selection could be made by moving the cursor to the required option and pressing the Enter key.

Focus allows you to satisfy this requirement. Focus provides a reserved field called CURSORAT which contains the address of the current cursor position. This field is 12 characters long and you can identify it to your program by attaching a label to each option line on the menu screen.

The syntax of the CURSORAT command in Dialogue Manager follows:

There must be exactly twelve spaces between the two single quotation marks.

```
-SET &CURSORAT= '            ' ;
```

&CURSORAT is a variable. This variable will contain the value of the field name or label on which the cursor is positioned.

The following is a menu program which uses the &CURSORAT facility to execute four options.

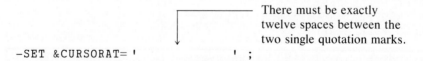

```
-*   CHAPTER 15
-*   CHA15-16
-*   THE DIALOGUE MANAGER VERSION OF CURSOR POSITIONING
-*   WITH CURSORAT.                  Must be exactly 12 spaces
-SET MSG=OFF ;                       wide
-SET &CURSORAT= '            ' ;
```

```
-SET &ADD= '-' ;
-SET &CHG = '-' ;
-SET &DEL = '-' ;
-SET &DON ='-'  ;
-GOTO MENU
-MENU
-CRTFORM LINE 1
-"</1 "
-"                          MOVIES FILE"
-"                      FILE MAINTENANCE MENU"
-"                      ----------------------
-"</2
-"                 <T.&ADD   Add New Records To The File"
-"                 <T.&CHG   Change Existing Records "
-"                 <T.&DEL   Delete Existing Records "
-"                 <T.&DON   Exit This Program   "
-"     "
-"     "
-"     "
-"     "
-"     "
-"     "
-"             Please select an option by moving the cursor     "
-"             to the desired line and pressing the Enter key    "

-"   "
-IF &CURSORAT EQ 'ADD' GOTO    ADD_NEW
-ELSE IF &CURSORAT EQ 'CHG' GOTO    CHNG_REC
-ELSE IF &CURSORAT  EQ 'DEL' GOTO    DEL_REC
-ELSE IF &CURSORAT  EQ 'DON' GOTO EXIT ;
-ADD_NEW
  EX ADDNEW
-RUN
-GOTO MENU

-CHNG_REC
  EX CHNGREC
-RUN
-GOTO MENU

-DEL_REC
  EX DELREC
-RUN
-GOTO MENU

-EXIT
EXIT
-DATA VIA FIDEL
-LOG DUPL MSG OFF
-LOG NOMATCH MSG OFF
END
```

When the above program is executed, the following screen will be displayed by the Dialogue Manager.

```
                        MOVIES FILE
                 FILE MAINTENANCE MENU
                 --------------------



        -     Add New Records To The File
        -     Change Existing Records
        -     Delete Existing Records
        -     Exit This Program




    Please select an option by moving the cursor
    to the desired line and pressing the Enter key
```

The cursor will automatically be positioned on the dash next to the first menu item (in this case the Add New Records To The File option). To select any of the four options, the operator must move the cursor to the desired line and simply press the Enter key. If the Exit option is selected, the program will terminate.

SUMMARY

The Dialogue Manager feature makes Focus a complete application development tool. It allows the programmer to develop complete procedures for executing a series of programs with minimal user intervention. As we have seen, it can even change the logic of the program based on user input parameters or system parameters such as date and time of day.

In this chapter we reviewed the following specific categories:

1. Naming conventions within the Dialogue Manager. Basically, the dash will invoke the Dialogue Manager. The & or && will identify variables.
2. The concept of stored procedures. We defined this concept initially several chapters ago. Once a program is stored or saved on magnetic media such as disk, it is possible to execute it over and over.
3. The Dialogue Manager variables. There are five types of variables. They all start with at least one ampersand (&). They are the local, global, system, statistical, and reserved variables.

4. The seven ways of supplying values to variables. Notice that -SET is a very important control statement. Basically, it performs the same functions as the COMPUTE statement.
5. -CRTFORM, the full-screen data entry and inquiry facility within the Dialogue Manager.
6. Other important Dialogue Manager control statements. These include the following:
   a. -GOTO
   b. -IF
   c. -INCLUDE
   d. -EXIT
   e. -QUIT
   f. The operating systems direct commands such as -TSO and -CMS.
7. Positioning the cursor with the &CURSORAT variable.

We also reviewed the ECHO facility for debugging the Dialogue Manager and Focus code.

ODDS AND ENDS

MAIN TOPICS:

- The LET Command
- The SET Command
- The Profile Focexec
- FSCAN and SCAN
- The REBUILD Utility
- Compile and Load
- The Focus Query Commands

In this chapter we wrap things up by presenting some other features of Focus. These are features that you could use to make your programming task easier and/ or improve the efficiency of your application.

LET FACILITY

Focus is a very easy, English-like language. However, the LET command allows you to simplify Focus further and make it even more user friendly. Additionally, the LET command is so powerful that it will allow the programmer to build a translation table of foreign words for non-English-speaking users. Finally, you could use the LET command to allow you to create a shorthand version of popular and commonly used commands and/or sentences. The syntax of the LET command follows:

```
LET word  =  Phrase
```

Using the LET Command to Create Shorthand Commands

If you use the STAFF and the EMPLOYEE files constantly during the day, you may want to create shorthand phrases for accessing and manipulating these Focus data files. The following LET commands will show you how.

```
LET
TFS=TABLE FILE STAFF
TFE=TABLE FILE EMPLOYEE
END
```

You can enter these commands directly from the Focus > prompt or store them as a procedure to be executed just like any other Focus program. Once the LET commands above are executed, you may refer to your files with the shorthand characters as follows:

```
TFS
PRINT LAST_NAME AND SALARY
END
```

As another example, under MVS/TSO, you usually have to type in the file type as well as the filename every time that you want to access FOCEXEC files and MASTER files. For example, if your Focus program is called PROG1, you must enter TED FOCEXEC(PROG1). Under CMS and DOS, all you have to enter is TED PROG1. To shorten the typing requirements under MVS/TSO, you could create a shorthand version for the TED access commands as follows:

```
LET
TF  =  TED FOCEXEC(<>)
TM  =  TED MASTER(<>)
END
```

The <> signs within parenthesis are placeholders. This means that there are or will be missing elements in the sentence or the phrase. You can then assign different values in their place in different Focus statements. In other words, they can be replaced by combination of letters.

After you define and ideally, store these commands in your profile, you can just use the abbreviated format of the commands as follows:

```
TF PROG1
TM STAFF
```

Translating Foreign Languages into Focus

You can build a rather extensive LET library of foreign words to allow users to enter Focus commands in their own languages. The following LET commands translate some of the basic Focus action words and commands into French.

```
-* CHAPTER 16
-* CHA16-2
-* PROGRAM SHOWING THE USE OF THE LET COMMAND
-* TO TRANSLATE FOREIGN LANGUAGES INTO FOCUS CODE
LET
CHARGER=TABLE
FICHIER=FILE
```

```
SOMMER=SUM
PAR=BY
AVEC=AND
DEPARTMENT=DEPT_NAME
TRAVERS=ACROSS
FIN=END
END
```

Once this table has been executed, the user can create a program in French, similar to the one shown below.

```
CHARGER FICHIER STAFF
SOMMER SALARY PAR CITY
TRAVERS DEPARTMENT
FIN
```

LET CLEAR FIN   ← This final command is necessary to reactivate the
                   original Focus FIN statement. Otherwise, you
                   will not be able to get out of Focus.

Creating More Flexible and User-Friendly Programs

The following Focus program will illustrate the use of LET to make Focus programs even more user friendly than they already are.

```
-* CHAPTER 16
-* CHA16-3
-* PROGRAM SHOWING THE USE OF THE LET COMMAND
-* TO SIMPLIFY USER PROGRAMMING EFFORTS.
LET
REPORT =TABLE FILE STAFF
TITLE="<22 SALARY RANGE REPORT BY DEPARTMENT"
BIGGEST=SUM MAX.< >
SMALLEST= MIN.< >
DEPARTMENT=DEPT_NAME
AVGSAL=SUM AVE.SAL
END
```

The user can then type the following program:

```
REPORT
TITLE
BIGGEST SALARY AND SMALLEST SALARY
BY DEPARTMENT
END
```

```
PAGE      1

                    SALARY RANGE REPORT BY DEPARTMENT
                         MAX           MIN
      DEPT_NAME         SALARY        SALARY
      ---------         ------        ------

      ADMINISTRATION   185,000.00    32,000.00
      FINANCE          102,000.00    34,500.00
      MARKETING         47,000.00    36,700.00
      MIS               55,400.00    32,000.00
      OPERATIONS        57,000.00    22,500.00
```

NULL Substitution

NULL words can also be defined by the LET command. NULL words are treated as comments by Focus and as such are ignored. The following shows how to define a NULL word:

```
LET  Word = ;
```

This arrangement allows you to make your reports more readable. The example below shows how we defined the word SHOW as a NULL word and used it to make our report more understandable.

```
-* CHAPTER 16
-* CHA16-4
-* PROGRAM SHOWING THE USE OF THE LET COMMAND
-* AND NULL WORDS SUBSTITUTION.
LET
SHOW= ;
AVGSAL= SUM AVE.SAL BY DEPT_NAME
REPORT=TABLE FILE STAFF
END
```

The user could then enter the following simple statements:

```
REPORT
SHOW AVGSAL
END


    PAGE    1


                              AVE
    DEPT_NAME                 SALARY
    ---------                 ------
    ADMINISTRATION        108,500.00
    FINANCE                67,300.00
    MARKETING              40,525.00
    MIS                    42,000.00
    OPERATIONS             35,350.00
```

LET Utilities

There are three useful LET utilities.

`? LET` ← This command will display all the current LET command
          substitutes that are in effect.

`LET CLEAR word` ← Will clear a specific LET statement.

`LET CLEAR *` ← Will clear all the LET statements in effect.

`LET ECHO` ← Will display the LET statements and
            substitutes.

SET COMMAND

SET is a powerful Focus command. It allows you to change standard Focus
parameters that control different environments of Focus. The syntax of the SET
command is as follows:

`SET Parameter=option, Parameter=option, ...`

Parameter represents Standard Focus parameter you wish to change.
Option represents one of the options available under Focus for that parameter.

If more than one line of SET commands is needed, you should repeat the SET
keyword on subsequent lines.
    Some of the more important SET commands are listed below. The default is
underlined.

1. SET ALL = $\begin{Bmatrix} \text{ON} \\ \underline{\text{OFF}} \\ \text{PASS} \end{Bmatrix}$

This parameter determines the handling of missing segments in Table requests. With the default (OFF), missing segments will not appear in reports. With the (ON) option, missing segments appear in reports if fields in segments are not screened by the IF or WHERE clauses. With the (PASS) option, missing segments will appear in the report. The IF or WHERE clauses will not screen the segments. (See Chapter 11 for a discussion about missing segments.)

2. SET CACHE = $\begin{Bmatrix} \underline{0} \\ n \end{Bmatrix}$

This parameter determines the amount of memory used to cache (store) Focus database pages. The default is 0. You can allocate cache memory in 4K (4000)-byte increments. Allocate CACHE memory whenever possible, since it will reduce the input and output access to disk by Focus.

3. SET CDN = $\begin{Bmatrix} \text{ON} \\ \underline{\text{OFF}} \end{Bmatrix}$

CDN stands for "continental decimal point." If CDN is turned on, the number 5,456,418.62 will be printed as 5.456.418,62.

4. SET filename = filename

This will allow you to declare a file as the main file that you will be using throughout the session. You do not then need to repeat the filename in TABLE requests. See the example below.

```
SET filename=STAFF
```

Then the subsequent TABLE requests could be coded as follows:

```
TABLE   ← The FILE STAFF phrase is not needed anymore.
PRINT LAST NAME etc.
END
```

5. SET FOCSTACK = $\begin{Bmatrix} \underline{8} \\ n \end{Bmatrix}$

This command can alter the size of FOCSTACK. FOCSTACK is the stack of Focus program lines and procedures queued and awaiting execution. The default size is 8000 characters or bytes. It can be changed to a higher or lower figure. For example, the following command will increase the FOCSTACK size to 12,000 characters.

```
SET FOCSTACK=12
```

6. SET LINES $= \left\{ \dfrac{57}{n} \right\}$

This command sets the number of printed lines per page on the printer. The default is 57 lines per page. The value should usually be less than the value set for the length of paper (see the SET PAPER command below). The value of this parameter could range from 1 to 999,999.

7. SET MESSAGE or MSG $= \left\{ \begin{array}{l} \text{ON} \\ \text{OFF} \end{array} \right\}$

This command displays or suppresses the Focus informational messages. Informational messages are messages that are usually displayed at the end of a TABLE or MODIFY request. These messages display useful information such as the number of records in the table or the number of segments updated. Following is a very common informational message that follows every TABLE request before display of data:

```
NUMBER OF RECORDS IN TABLE = 35   LINES = 35
```

Error messages such as duplicate or invalid conditions are not suppressed by this command. You will need to use the LOG DUPL MSG OFF and LOG INVALID MSG OFF to achieve that.

8. SET PAGE_NUM $= \left\{ \begin{array}{l} \text{ON} \\ \text{OFF} \\ \text{NOPAGE} \end{array} \right\}$

The default parameter assigns a number to each page and displays the page number on the upper left-hand corner of each page. The OFF parameter suppresses page numbers. The NOPAGE option will suppress page breaks. This will cause the report to be printed continuously without page breaks.

9. SET PAPER $= \left\{ \dfrac{66}{n} \right\}$

This command determines the physical length of the paper on the printer. The value of this parameter can range from 1 to 999,999. The value is determined by multiplying the number of lines per inch that your printer can print by the length of each sheet. If your printer paper is 11 inches long and the printer can print at six characters per inch, the value for this parameter will be 66. *Important:* If you are printing a footing on each page of your report, you should subtract 4 from the length of the paper (i.e., set the value at 62 instead of 66).

10. SET PAUSE $= \left\{ \begin{array}{l} \text{ON} \\ \text{OFF} \end{array} \right\}$

This command will make sure that Focus will pause before printing each report. The ON parameter was used initially for printing terminals. It is useless with CRT terminals and should always be set to OFF.

11. SET PRINT $= \begin{Bmatrix} \text{ONLINE} \\ \text{OFFLINE} \end{Bmatrix}$

This command directs the output of the TABLE request. The default displays the output on the terminal. The OFFLINE parameter will direct the output to the system printer.

12. SET SCREEN $= \begin{Bmatrix} \text{ON} \\ \text{OFF} \\ \text{PAPER} \end{Bmatrix}$

This command will affect the Hot Screen facility of Focus (see Chapter 4 for a detailed explanation of this facility). The default is ON and it activates the Hot Screen facility. The OFF parameter will turn the Hot Screen facility off. The PAPER parameter will activate the Hot Screen facility. With this parameter, Focus will use the LINES and PAPER parameter settings to format the screen display.

13. SET TEMP DISK $=$ disk

This parameter is only available in CMS and PC/Focus. It allows the user to assign a disk unit for temporary work area and to store extract files output by the HOLD and SAVE operations.

14. SET PANEL $= \begin{Bmatrix} 0 \\ n \end{Bmatrix}$

The maximum width in a report is determined by this parameter. If a report exceeds this limit, Focus will partition each page into sections called panels. These panels are printed as separate pages. If you are using an 80-column printer, you should set the panel width to 80. This will cause Focus to print the first 80 characters of a very wide report on the first panel, and the second 80 characters on the second panel, and so on. If you are working with 132 characters per line, the panel parameter should be set to 132. If you set the panel to 0, the report is not divided into panels.

PROFILE FOCEXEC

The PROFILE FOCEXEC is a special program that is executed automatically as soon as Focus is invoked. The PROFILE FOCEXEC could be an empty file without any code in it or it could have many lines of Focus coded within it. Because of this particular feature, it is possible to code within this program all the mundane and repetitive tasks that an operator needs to perform while using Focus to update or report from files. Through the PROFILE FOCEXEC program, you can direct Focus to access certain files or even execute certain Focus programs every time a Focus session is initiated. This feature is especially useful if you are creating a complete application, say, a payroll system for a user who does not need to be bothered with getting in and out of various files and/or programs. The following could be a typical PROFILE FOCEXEC:

```
-* PROFILE FOCEXEC
-* SHOWING THE USE OF PROFILE FOCEXEC TO
-* AUTOMATE FUNCTIONS.
USE
STAFF FOCUS A
END
FILEDEF INFO1 DISK C:\FOCUS\INFO1.DAT
EX CHA15-9
-RUN
FIN
```

As soon as Focus is invoked, the program above will access the STAFF file. It will also allocate the file called INFO1. Finally, it will find CHA15-9 and execute it. CHA15-9 is a Dialogue Manager procedure that calls several other programs. When the operator is finished with his or her activities, he or she will exit CHA15-9. The next step in the PROFILE FOCEXEC is the FIN statement, which will cause exit from Focus. So the operator has completed all his or her tasks within Focus without even being aware of the presence of Focus. He or she has no access to Focus and operates without having to remember any of the Focus or operating system commands.

The following is a typical PROFILE FOCEXEC under MVS/TSO.

```
TSO FREE F(HOLD)
TSO FREE F(HOLDMAST)
TSO FREE F(MASTER)
TSO FREE F(FOCEXEC)
TSO ALLOC F(HOLD) DA('TSRRT1.FOCUS.V60.MASTER.DATA') SHR REUSE
TSO ALLOC F(HOLDMAST) DA('TSRRT1.FOCUS.V60.MASTER.DATA') SHR REUSE
TSO ALLOC F(MASTER) DA('TSRRT1.MASTER.DATA' -
                       'TSRRT1.FOCUS.V60.MASTER.DATA') SHR REUSE
TSO ALLOC F(FOCEXEC) DA('TSRRT1.FOCEXEC.DATA' -
 'C3903RT.FOCEXEC.DATA2' 'TSRRT1.FOCUS.V60.FOCEXEC.DATA') SHR REUSE
TSO ALLOC F(ERRORS) DA('TSRRT1.FOCUS.V60.ERRORS.DATA') SHR REUSE
TSO ALLOC F(USERLIB) DA('TSRRT1.FOCUS.V60.FUSELIB.LOAD') SHR REUSE

LET TM= TED MASTER(<>)
LET TF= TED FOCEXEC(<>)
SET PAUSE=OFF
```

FSCAN AND SCAN

SCAN and FSCAN are facilities that allow you to make changes to fields in Focus files directly. These facilities have all the power of the MODIFY command;

however, you do not have to write a Modify request to make changes, add, or delete records. All you need to do is to invoke the SCAN or FSCAN facility with the name of the Focus database file and make the changes to the records directly on the terminal. SCAN and FSCAN have an added feature that MODIFY does not have. You can use these facilities to alter the keys of segments in a Focus database. With these commands, you can very easily delete an entire chain of records. Because of this power, and since very little audit trail is built into these commands, their use may be restricted in some sites. FSCAN is a full-screen database editor and is available on most versions of Focus. SCAN is a database line editor and is available on all versions of Focus.

The help screens that are part of FSCAN facility are quite adequate. However, I will review the FSCAN facility briefly here to familiarize you with the concept. To invoke the FSCAN facility, you must enter the following command from the Focus > prompt:

```
FSCAN file filename.
```

In the following example, I will use FSCAN to update the EMPHIST file, which is a single-segment file.

1. To invoke FSCAN, the following command is entered:

```
FSCAN file EMPHIST
```

Focus will display the following FSCAN screen:

```
FSCAN FILE EMPHIST FOCUS A                      CHANGES : 0


        SSN          MARITAL_STAT    SEX     DEGREE    PREVIOUS_SAL
        ---          ------------    ---     ------    ------------

==   213456682    M              M       MBA        50500.00
==   291345672    S              F       BS        142000.00
==   293245178    S              M       HS         36000.00
==   294728305    M              M       BA         49000.00
==   295738307    M              M       MBA        51300.00
==   297748301    S              M       HS         37600.00
==   312562345    S              M       HS         18000.00
==   312781122    W              M       PHD        42000.00
==   314562134    D              F       HS         24500.00
==   392345782    W              M       BA         41000.00
==   413267891    S              F       BA         34000.00

--------------------------------INPUT --------------------
==   ← The Input Line
==>  ← The Command Line
```

Prefix area →

Note the structure of this screen. On the upper left-hand side of the screen, the name of the file is displayed. On the upper right-hand side, the number of changes made to the file during the FSCAN session is displayed.

Eleven records are displayed in the middle part of the screen. Each field is individually identified by its field name. If there are more fields than could be displayed on the screen, the screen can be scrolled to the right to view and/or change the remaining fields. The prefix area is located on the left-hand side of the first field. It consists of two equal signs (==). This area is used for entering commands for deleting and changing key records. In multiple-segment files, this area is also used for entering a command to access the child segments.

Notice the INPUT line, the input area, and the command areas at the bottom of the screen. The INPUT line marks the lower one-third of the screen. The input area, which begins with two equal signs, is used primarily for entering new records. The command area is used to issue FSCAN commands, such as LOCATE, NEXT, and SINGLE. To exit FSCAN, you type one of these commands: END, FILE, QUIT, or QQUIT.

2. Entering new records is very easy. First, you move the cursor to the input area. Next, enter the letter ''I'' on the second equal sign, as shown below. The cursor will move to the first field location under the INPUT line, ready for data entry. As you complete entering data for a field, you press the Tab key to move to the next field, until all data have been entered. If the data being entered are as long as an entire field, the cursor will automatically move to the next field. Otherwise, you will have to press the Tab key to move to the next field. The following screen displays how a new record is added to the EMPHIST file.

```
FSCAN FILE EMPHIST FOCUS A                          CHANGES : 0


       SSN          MARITAL_STAT    SEX      DEGREE    PREVIOUS_SAL
       ---          ------------    ---      ------    ------------

  ==   213456682    M               M        MBA         50500.00
  ==   291345672    S               F        BS         142000.00
  ==   293245178    S               M        HS          36000.00
  ==   294728305    M               M        BA          49000.00
  ==   295738307    M               M        MBA         51300.00
  ==   297748301    S               M        HS          37600.00
  ==   312562345    S               M        HS          18000.00
  ==   312781122    W               M        PHD         42000.00
  ==   314562134    D               F        HS          24500.00
  ==   392345782    W               M        BA          41000.00
  ==   413267891    S               F        BA          34000.00

  ------------------------------------INPUT -------------------
 =I    333111222    S               F        BA          78000  ⇐
 ==>
```

You can continue to enter as many records as you want. Each time you complete one record, you press the Enter key. FSCAN will then refresh the screen and insert the record in its proper location, depending on its key value. FSCAN will also increment the CHANGES field display at the upper right-hand corner of the screen to denote the number of changes that have taken place so far.

```
 _____
/                                                                \
|  FSCAN FILE EMPHIST FOCUS A                    CHANGES : 1      |
|                                                                |
|       SSN          MARITAL_STAT    SEX     DEGREE    PREVIOUS_SAL|
|       ---          ------------    ---     ------    ------------|
|                                                                |
|  ==  213456682     M               M       MBA       50500.00   |
|  ==  291345672     S               F       BS       142000.00   |
|  ==  293245178     S               M       HS        36000.00   |
|  ==  294728305     M               M       BA        49000.00   |
|  ==  295738307     M               M       MBA       51300.00   |
|  ==  297748301     S               M       HS        37600.00   |
|  ==  312562345     S               M       HS        18000.00   |
|  ==  312781122     W               M       PHD       42000.00   |
|  ==  314562134     D               F       HS        24500.00   |
|  == [333111222     S  <-           F       BA        78000.00 ] |
|  ==  392345782     W               M       BA        41000.00   |
|                                                                |
|  ----------------------------------INPUT -------------------   |
|  ==                                                            |
|  ==>                                                           |
|   0 keys changed.      0 non-keys changed.                     |
|   0 records deleted.   1 records input.                        |
\                                                                /
 ----------------------------------------------------------------
```

Notice that at the bottom of the screen, FSCAN will display record maintenance statistics. In this case it shows that one record was added to the file.

3. In the following screen, I changed the value of the MARITAL_STAT field for SSN number 291345672 on the second line from S to M. I did that by typing over that field and then pressing the Enter key. Note that FSCAN altered the CHANGES field on the upper right-hand corner of the screen to the number 2.

```
┌─────────────────────────────────────────────────────────────────┐
│  FSCAN FILE EMPHIST FOCUS A                      CHANGES : 2      │
│                                                                   │
│                                                                   │
│        SSN          MARITAL_STAT   SEX    DEGREE    PREVIOUS_SAL  │
│        ---          ------------   ---    ------    ------------  │
│                                                                   │
│   ==   213456682    M              M      MBA        50500.00     │
│   ==  ┌291345672    M  ←           F      BS        142000.00┐    │
│   ==   293245178    S              M      HS         36000.00     │
│   ==   294728305    M              M      BA         49000.00     │
│   ==   295738307    M              M      MBA        51300.00     │
│   ==   297748301    S              M      HS         37600.00     │
│   ==   312562345    S              M      HS         18000.00     │
│   ==   312781122    W              M      PHD        42000.00     │
│   ==   314562134    D              F      HS         24500.00     │
│   ==   333111222    S              F      BA         78000.00     │
│   ==   392345782    W              M      BA         41000.00     │
│                                                                   │
│   --------------------------------INPUT --------------------      │
│   ==                                                              │
│   ==>                                                             │
│    0 keys changed.       1 non-keys changed.                      │
│    0 records deleted.    0 records input.                         │
└─────────────────────────────────────────────────────────────────┘
```

Note that at the bottom of the screen the statistics indicate that one nonkey field was changed.

4. To alter a key field, you must enter the letter "K" in the prefix area, as shown below. You can then change the key value of the key field and follow that by pressing the Enter key. FSCAN will accept the new key and will insert the record in its new position based on the new key value.

```
┌─────────────────────────────────────────────────────────────────┐
│  FSCAN FILE EMPHIST FOCUS A                      CHANGES : 2      │
│                                                                   │
│                                                                   │
│        SSN          MARITAL_STAT   SEX    DEGREE    PREVIOUS_SAL  │
│        ---          ------------   ---    ------    ------------  │
│                                                                   │
│   =K  ┌313456682    M  ←           M      MBA        50500.00┐    │
│   ==   291345672    M              F      BS        142000.00     │
│   ==   293245178    S              M      HS         36000.00     │
│   ==   294728305    M              M      BA         49000.00     │
│   ==   295738307    M              M      MBA        51300.00     │
│   ==   297748301    S              M      HS         37600.00     │
│   ==   312562345    S              M      HS         18000.00     │
│   ==   312781122    W              M      PHD        42000.00     │
│   ==   314562134    D              F      HS         24500.00     │
│   ==   333111222    S              F      BA         78000.00     │
│   ==   392345782    W              M      BA         41000.00     │
│                                                                   │
│   ------------------------------------INPUT ----------------      │
│   ==                                                              │
│   ==>                                                             │
└─────────────────────────────────────────────────────────────────┘
```

The following screen layout shows that the record was moved to its new position to keep the file in sequence. Also notice that the CHANGES field at the upper right-hand corner of the screen and the file statistics display at the bottom of the screen have been updated.

```
 FSCAN FILE EMPHIST FOCUS A                      CHANGES : 3


          SSN          MARITAL_STAT   SEX    DEGREE   PREVIOUS_SAL
          ---          ------------   ---    ------   ------------

    ==    291345672    M              F      BS       142000.00
    ==    293245178    S              M      HS        36000.00
    ==    294728305    M              M      BA        49000.00
    ==    295738307    M              M      MBA       51300.00
    ==    297748301    S              M      HS        37600.00
    ==    312562345    S              M      HS        18000.00
    ==    312781122    W              M      PHD       42000.00
    ==   | 313456682    M   ←          M      MBA       50500.00 |
    ==    314562134    D              F      HS        24500.00
    ==    333111222    S              F      BA        78000.00
    ==    392345782    W              M      BA        41000.00

 ----------------------------------------INPUT -----------------
    ==
    ==>
      1 keys changed.      0 non-keys changed.
      0 records deleted.   0 records input.
```

5. To delete a record or a segment, position the cursor on the prefix line next to the record or segment that must be deleted and press the Enter key.

```
FSCAN FILE EMPHIST FOCUS A                        CHANGES : 3


         SSN       MARITAL_STAT   SEX    DEGREE    PREVIOUS_SAL
         ---       ------------   ---    ------    ------------

=D     291345672   M              F      BS        142000.00
==     293245178   S              M      HS         36000.00
==     294728305   M              M      BA         49000.00
==     295738307   M              M      MBA        51300.00
==     297748301   S              M      HS         37600.00
==     312562345   S              M      HS         18000.00
==     312781122   W              M      PHD        42000.00
==     313456682   M              M      MBA        50500.00
==     314562134   D              F      HS         24500.00
==     333111222   S              F      BA         78000.00
==     392345782   W              M      BA         41000.00

-----------------------------------INPUT -----------------
==
==>
```

FSCAN will display the Delete Confirmation Screen, as shown below, to give you one more chance to reconsider your decision. If you confirm by pressing the Enter key, the record or the segment is deleted. Remember that if you delete a parent segment, you will automatically delete all the child segments associated with that parent segment.

```
FSCAN FILE EMPHIST FOCUS A                        CHANGES : 3

            Delete Confirmation Screen

       SSN  :  291345672 MARITAL_STAT : S
       SEX  :  F                DEGREE : BS
 PREVIOUS_SAL  : 142000.00




 ==>
  Enter To Delete
  Enter N(o) to abort
  Enter Q(uit) to quit session
```

6. To access multiple-segment records, you must make use of the prefix area. First, you must access the file in the normal way.

```
FSCAN file STAFF
```

```
  FSCAN FILE STAFF FOCUS A                    CHANGES : 0


        DEPRTMNT_ID  DEPT_NAME
        -----------  ---------

   ==   10           ADMINISTRATION
   =C   12           FINANCE
   ==   14           MIS
   ==   15           OPERATIONS
   ==   20           MARKETING




   --------------------------------INPUT -------------------
     ==
     ==>

```

Next, move the cursor to the prefix area next to the parent segment in which that you are interested. Enter the letter "C" and press the Enter key. FSCAN will display the child segments for that segment. In our example, since we were accessing the STAFF file, the first child segment would have been the section segments. Once again, enter the letter "C" on the prefix area next to the segment that you want and press the Enter key. This will display the next segment. You can then modify that segment as needed. To go back to the parent segment, move the cursor to the command area and type the word "PARENT" next to the ==> sign. This will take you back to the next parent level. By using the letter "C" on the prefix area and the PARENT command on the command line, you can look at an entire file and make any changes, deletions, and or additions that you may desire.

```
FSCAN FILE STAFF FOCUS A                    CHANGES : 0

  DEPRTMNT_ID  :   12

        SECTOPM_ID    SECTION_NAME
        ----------    ------------

=C    121          PAYABLES
==    122          COLLECTIONS




  -----------------------------------INPUT -------------------
  ==
  ==>
```

The following screen is a list of the employee segments of the PAYABLES section segment.

```
     FSCAN FILE STAFF FOCUS A                      CHANGES : 0

   DEPRTMNT_ID  :  12         SECTION_ID  :  121

        EMPLOYEE_ID  LAST_NAME     FIRST_NAME   JOB_TITLE
        -----------  ---------     ----------   ---------

   ==   294728305    TURPIN        BENTON       HEAD ACCOUNTANT
   ==   513724567    BORGIA        CESARE       LIAISON OFFICER




   --------------------------------INPUT ------------------
     ==
   ==>

                                           More ===>
```

To view a record or a segment individually, one record at a time, enter the command SINGLE at the command line. This will display one record on the screen. You can step through the rest of the segments via that screen by typing the NEXT command after the ==> sign. You can modify the fields in the segment by typing over them. To return to the multiple screen, type the command MULTIPLE at the command line.

```
     FSCAN FILE STAFF FOCUS A                      CHANGES : 0

   DEPRTMNT_ID  :  12         SECTION_ID  :  121

        EMPLOYEE_ID  LAST_NAME     FIRST_NAME   JOB_TITLE
        -----------  ---------     ----------   ---------

   ==   294728305    TURPIN        BENTON       HEAD ACCOUNTANT
   ==   513724567    BORGIA        CESARE       LIAISON OFFICER




   --------------------------------INPUT ------------------
     ==
   ==>SINGLE

                                           More ===>
```

The screen created by the SINGLE command is shown below.

```
   FSCAN FILE STAFF FOCUS A                      CHANGES : 0


   DEPRTMNT_ID : 12        SECTION_ID  :  121

    EMPLOYEE_ID : 294728305        LAST_NAME : TURPIN
    FIRST_NAME  : BENTON           JOB_TITLE : HEAD ACCOUNTANT
        STREET  : 121 LA CIENEGA BLVD.
          CITY  : LOS ANGELES          STATE : CA
      ZIP_CODE  : 91345         TELEPHONE_NO : 2135551232
    DATE_BIRTH  : 440315          DATE_HIRE : 781012
        SALARY  : 65400.00          PCT_INC :  .05
      VACATION  : 120



   ==>NEXT
```

REBUILD UTILITY

This utility has four associated subcommands, whose purpose it is to reorganize and/or enhance the efficiency of Focus databases. There are various reasons for reorganizing, and each subcommand will help you achieve a particular objective.
The syntax of the REBUILD command is as follows:

```
REBUILD
```

The Focus response is as follows:

```
Enter Option (REBUILD,REORG,INDEX,CHECK)=
```

REBUILD REBUILD Subcommand

The primary purpose of the REBUILD subcommand is to reorganize a Focus file. When a file is being used heavily, with many deletions and additions, the file becomes physically disorganized. The new segments may end up physically away from their logical parents. This is not disastrous, since Focus will keep track of all segments by internal pointers. It will, however, slow down file access and degrade system efficiency. The REBUILD subcommand allows the user or the programmer to restructure the file automatically and bring all related segments physically closer to each other. The following example shows how to REBUILD the STAFF file (the operator entries are in lower case).

```
>> rebuild

ENTER OPTION (REBUILD, REORG, INDEX OR CHECK) =>rebuild
ENTER NAME OF FOCUS FILE>staff
ANY RECORD SELECTION TESTS? (YES/NO) =>no
STARTING..
NUMBER OF SEGMENTS RETRIEVED=        35
NEW FILE STAFF FOCUS A  ON 06/16/91 AT 13.20.06
NUMBER OF SEGMENTS INPUT=        35
FILE HAS BEEN REBUILT
>>
```

You can use the record selection option of the REBUILD subcommand to filter out unwanted segments. For example, the following statement will ensure that only certain departments will be stored in the new file.

```
ANY RECORD SELECTION TESTS? (YES/NO) =>yes
dept_name eq 'mis' or 'finance' or 'administration' ,$
STARTING
NUMBER OF SEGMENTS RETRIEVED=        17
NEW FILE STAFF FOCUS A  ON  06/16/91 AT 13.38.34
FILE HAS BEEN REBUILT
```

Notice that the filtering statement must end with a comma and a dollar sign.

REBUILD REORG Subcommand

This subcommand is used to allow the programmer to perform one of the following activities:

1. Removing fields
2. Changing the order of fields within the Master File Description (i.e., changing the position of the vacation field and the salary field)
3. Adding new fields at the end of segments
4. Removing child segments
5. Adding new child segments
6. Changing the order of segments (i.e., making a child segment a parent segment, and vice versa)
7. Indexing fields
8. Increasing the size of alphanumeric fields

You cannot, however, change segment names or types or change an alphanumeric field to a numeric field, or vice versa.

The REORG subcommand has two phases, DUMP and LOAD. The DUMP phase lets Focus unload and store the data file records to an external file. The

LOAD phase will load the data back into a reorganized Focus data file. Following is an example of the REORG subcommand:

```
>>rebuild
ENTER OPTION (REBUILD, REORG, INDEX OR CHECK) =>reorg
ENTER THE REORG PHASE (DUMP OR LOAD) =>dump
ENTER THE NAME OF FOCUS FILE>staff
ANY RECORD SELECTION TESTS? (YES/NO)=>no
STARTING..
NUMBER OF SEGMENTS RETRIEVED=          35
```

The entry above is the DUMP phase of the REORG subcommand. Now you will have the opportunity to access the Master File Description for the STAFF file and make changes in the file, such as adding a new field or dropping a current field. The next step is to erase the current Focus data file. Otherwise, the LOAD phase of the REORG subcommand will add on top of current data the data that have been DUMPed. Therefore, you should issue an erase or delete command similar to the following VM/CMS command:

```
> CMS ERASE STAFF FOCUS A
```

The last step is to reload the dumped file back and create a new Focus STAFF file.

```
>>rebuild
ENTER OPTION (REBUILD, REORG, INDEX OR CHECK) =>reorg
ENTER THE REORG PHASE (DUMP OR LOAD) =>load
ENTER THE NAME OF FOCUS FILE>staff
STARTING..
NEW FILE  STAFF FOCUS A ON  06/16/91 AT 13.22.27
NUMBER OF SEGMENTS INPUT= 35
```

IMPORTANT NOTE: After reorganizing a file, you will notice that Focus is still using the original Master File Description. There are two ways of handling this situation:

1. Leave Focus by entering FIN and invoke Focus again.
2. A more elegant way is to issue the CHECK FILE command as shown below:

```
CHECK FILE STAFF
```

The above will serve two purposes: (1) it will check the validity of your changes and (2) will make the new Master File Description available to Focus.

REBUILD INDEX Subcommand

This command will allow the programmer to index up to seven additional fields in the file. The fields to be indexed must have the FIELDTYPE=I attribute in the

Master File Description. It is usually faster initially to load a file that will be indexed without the index option and later use the INDEX subcommand to index the required fields. The following example shows how the INDEX subcommand works.

```
>>rebuild
ENTER OPTION (REBUILD, REORG, INDEX, OR CHECK) =>index
ENTER NAME OF FOCUS FILE>emphist
ENTER NAME OF FIELD TO INDEX (OR * FOR ALL) =>ssn
STARTING..
INDEX INITIALIZED FOR: SSN
INDEX VALUES INCLUDED=          16
```

REBUILD CHECK Subcommand

This subcommand allows you to verify that the Focus file is not physically damaged. Following is an example of how this subcommand is used:

```
>>rebuild
ENTER OPTION (REBUILD, REORG, INDEX, OR CHECK) =>check
ENTER NAME OF FOCUS FILE>staff
STARTING..
NUMBER OF SEGMENTS RETRIEVED=      35
CHECK COMPLETED...
>
```

USE COMMAND

The USE command allows you to concatenate or attach several Focus files together for processing. Many times, data files used in one Focus program may reside in different disk directories. To ensure that Focus will find the right data file, you must use the USE command before executing the program. The USE command could be part of a TABLE or MODIFY request, or it could be issued from the Focus prompt >. The syntax of the USE command is as follows:

```
USE         ┌ ADD     ┐
            │ CLEAR   │
            └ REPLACE ┘

File ID     ┌ READ           ┐
            │ NEW            │
            │ AS master name │
            │ on user ID     │
            └ LOCAL          ┘

END
```

ADD adds one or more file IDs to the current directory being used.

CLEAR clears the current USE directories.

REPLACE replaces an existing file in the directory.

File ID, in CMS and PC/Focus, is the file ID of the Focus database. In MVS/TSO, this will be the ddname allocated to the Focus database.

READ allows only read access to a Focus database file.

NEW informs Focus that the Focus file is new and has not yet been created.

As Master Name identifies the Focus Master File Description that will be associated with this Focus data file.

On User ID specifies the user ID of the SINK machine. This has to do with concurrent access, which is outside the scope of this book. The MVS/TSO equivalent command is "On Communication."

LOCAL is an option used for accessing a sink database through the operating system.

An example of the USE command is

```
USE
STAFF FOCUS  A
EMPHIST FOCUS A
END

USE
EMPLOYEE FOCUS A AS EMP1
END

USE
STAFF FOCUS A READ
END

USE
NEWSTAFF FOCUS A NEW
END
CREATE FILE NEWSTAFF
```

COMPILE AND LOAD COMMANDS

Most versions of Focus allow you to compile your MODIFY requests. This means that the code will be translated into machine language, which will enable it to execute much faster. Remember that a noncompiled MODIFY request is basically translated into machine-language instructions and executed one statement at a time. To compile a MODIFY request, use the following syntax from the Focus > prompt:

```
COMPILE file
```

For example:

```
COMPILE CHA14-9
```

Focus will create a compiled program that can be loaded directly into the main storage of the computer and executed. The programs compiled by Focus have a file type of FOCCOMP. To execute a compiled program use the following syntax from the Focus > prompt.

```
RUN program name
```

For example:

```
RUN  cha14-9
```

It is much more efficient to compile and then execute a Focus program. It will take a little longer initially to load a compiled program, but once it is resident in the memory, execution will be much faster.

A LOAD feature is also available in certain versions of Focus. You can load a noncompiled program into the memory prior to running it. The results are similar to the COMPILE command. The loaded program will be compiled in memory and will be ready to run. However, with the LOAD option, the compiled program is not saved on disk. You can also load your Master File Description into main storage. The syntax for loading the Master File Description and the MODIFY requests is as follows:

```
LOAD file type filename1 ... (filename2 ...)
```

File type denotes the file type that needs to be loaded, such as MASTER, FOCEXEC or FOCCOMP.

Examples:

```
LOAD MASTER STAFF

LOAD FOCEXEC CHA14-9

LOAD FOCCOMP CHA14-6
```

You can load the MASTER file and the MODIFY request (FOCEXEC) one after the other. Focus will compile the MODIFY request and will bind it to the Master File Description to create an efficient memory resident program. The program will be slow to start, but once compilation and binding have taken place, execution will be very fast. Loaded programs can be unloaded by using the UNLOAD command. The LOAD option is not currently available on all versions of Focus, so check your system manual before attempting to use it.

TABLE 16.1 QUERY COMMANDS

Query	Meaning
? COMBINE	Shows the Focus files that have been combined for processing (COMBINE is similar to JOIN, but it is used only in the MODIFY request and can only attach Focus files together.)
? DEFINE	Shows the active DEFINE fields during the current session
?F	Displays the field names of the current Focus file that is being accessed
? FDT	Displays the File Directory Table for a Focus file
? FILE	Displays statistics about a Focus file: the number of segments and the date of last update
? HOLD	Displays the fields in the current HOLD file
? JOIN	Displays the join structure between files that are currently joined together
? LET	Displays active substitutions of the LET command
? LOAD	Displays statistics about all loaded files
? PFKEY	Displays a list of current PFKEYs and their values under the MODIFY environment
? SET	Displays all the active SET parameters in the Focus session
? SET GRAPH	Displays parameters controlling the graphs displayed by Focus
? STAT	Displays statistics about the activities on a file during the last Focus command
? USE	Displays the names of all files in use and their directories
? &&	Displays global variables that are in effect during the current Focus session

FOCUS QUERY COMMANDS

The Focus query commands provide information about the status of Focus parameters, variables, data files, DEFINE fields, and other attributes. The syntax of the query command is as follows:

```
? Query [filename]
```

The query commands and their meanings are shown in Table 16.1.

SUMMARY

In this, the final chapter of the book, we discussed various Focus utilities and commands that could help you design effective systems and programs in Focus. We discussed the following topics in this chapter.

1. *LET command.* This command is not used as often as it should be. Its main purpose is to make life easier for nonprogrammers.
2. *SET command.* There are many parameters under the SET command. SET controls practically all Focus environments.

3. *PROFILE FOCEXEC*. As soon as Focus is invoked, it looks for this program to execute. This gives you a golden opportunity to write commands that can control the environment that the operator is using.

4. *FSCAN facility*. FSCAN should be approached with caution. It is a powerful facility that allows the user to manipulate any Focus data file directly. It does not leave an audit trail and since it acts directly on the database, it can modify or delete segments that you do not even see. Nevertheless, it is extremely useful.

5. *REBUILD utility*. This utility and its four subcommands are at your disposal to reorganize or even reformat your Focus database. When you use the REORG subcommand, you must delete or rename the old Focus file before attempting to perform the load phase. Otherwise, you will have duplicate records all over the place.

6. *COMPILE and LOAD*. These two facilities speed up processing of Focus applications. COMPILE is universally available, but LOAD is not currently available on all Focus platforms. COMPILE and LOAD are available only for MODIFY requests. TABLE requests are always interpretive.

7. *Focus query commands*. These are useful commands that you will find handy, especially when you are programming interactively from the Focus > prompt.

Here the book ends. It has taken me a long time to complete this work and I do hope that the effort has been worth it. You, the reader, will determine that.

FILES, MASTER FILE DESCRIPTIONS, AND DATA USED IN THE BOOK

STAFF FILE

```
FILENAME=STAFF,SUFFIX=FOC
SEGNAME=DEPRTMNT,SEGTYPE=S1
FIELDNAME=DEPRTMNT_ID,ALIAS=DID,FORMAT=A6,$
FIELDNAME=DEPT_NAME,ALIAS=DEPT,FORMAT=A20,$
SEGNAME=SECTION,PARENT=DEPRTMNT,SEGTYPE=S1
FIELDNAME=SECTION_ID,ALIAS=SECID,FORMAT=A6,$
FIELDNAME=SECTION_NAME,ALIAS=SECN,FORMAT=A20,$
SEGNAME=EMPLOYEE,PARENT=SECTION,SEGTYPE=S1
FIELDNAME=EMPLOYEE_ID,ALIAS=EID,FORMAT=A9,$
FIELDNAME=LAST_NAME,ALIAS=LN,FORMAT=A20,$
FIELDNAME=FIRST_NAME,ALIAS=FN,FORMAT=A10,$
FIELDNAME=JOB_TITLE,ALIAS=TITLE,FORMAT=A20,$
FIELDNAME=STREET,ALIAS=STR,FORMAT=A30,$
FIELDNAME=CITY,ALIAS=TOWN,FORMAT=A16,$
FIELDNAME=STATE,ALIAS=ST,FORMAT=A2,$
FIELDNAME=ZIP_CODE,ALIAS=ZIP,FORMAT=A5,$
FIELDNAME=TELEPHONE_NO,ALIAS=PHONE,FORMAT=A10,$
FIELDNAME=DATE_BIRTH,ALIAS=DOB,FORMAT=I6YMD,$
FIELDNAME=DATE_HIRE,ALIAS=DOH,FORMAT=I6YMD,$
FIELDNAME=SALARY,ALIAS=INCOME,FORMAT=D9.2C,$
FIELDNAME=PCT_INC,ALIAS=PIN,FORMAT=D5.2C,$
FIELDNAME=VACATION,ALIAS=VAC,FORMAT=I4,$
```

MODIFIED STAFF FILE WITH ADVANCED FEATURES

```
FILENAME=STAFF,SUFFIX=FOC
SEGNAME=DEPRTMNT,SEGTYPE=S1
FIELDNAME=DEPRTMNT_ID,ALIAS=DID,FORMAT=A6,
DESC='DEPARTMENT IDENTIFICATION',$
FIELDNAME=DEPT_NAME,ALIAS=DEPT,FORMAT=A20,$
SEGNAME=SECTION,PARENT=DEPRTMNT,SEGTYPE=S1
FIELDNAME=SECTION_ID,ALIAS=SECID,FORMAT=A6,$
```

```
$ 'SECTION IDENTIFICATION',$
FIELDNAME=SECTION_NAME,ALIAS=SECN,FORMAT=A20,$
SEGNAME=EMPLOYEE,PARENT=SECTION,SEGTYPE=S1
FIELDNAME=EMPLOYEE_ID,ALIAS=EID,FORMAT=A9,$
FIELDNAME=LAST_NAME,ALIAS=LN,FORMAT=A20,
TITLE='EMPLOYEE,LAST NAME',$
FIELDNAME=FIRST_NAME,ALIAS=FN,FORMAT=A10,$
FIELDNAME=JOB_TITLE,ALIAS=TITLE,FORMAT=A20,$
FIELDNAME=STREET,ALIAS=STR,FORMAT=A30,$
FIELDNAME=CITY,ALIAS=TOWN,FORMAT=A16,$
FIELDNAME=STATE,ALIAS=ST,FORMAT=A2,$
FIELDNAME=ZIP_CODE,ALIAS=ZIP,FORMAT=A5,$
FIELDNAME=TELEPHONE_NO,ALIAS=PHONE,FORMAT=A10,$
FIELDNAME=DATE_BIRTH,ALIAS=DOB,FORMAT=I6YMD,$
FIELDNAME=DATE_HIRE,ALIAS=DOH,FORMAT=I6YMD,$
FIELDNAME=SALARY,ALIAS=INCOME,FORMAT=D9.2C,$
FIELDNAME=PCT_INC,ALIAS=PIN,FORMAT=D5.2C,$
FIELDNAME=VACATION,ALIAS=VAC,FORMAT=I4,$
DEFINE BIWEEKLY/D7.2=SALARY/26;$
DEFINE FULL_NAME/A31=FIRST_NAME ¦ LAST_NAME ;$
DEFINE ADDRESS/A26=CITY ¦  STATE ¦'  '¦ ZIP; $
```

EMPHIST (EMPLOYEE HISTORY) FILE

```
FILE=EMPHIST           ,SUFFIX=FIX
SEGNAME=EMPHIST
FIELDNAME   =EMPLOYEE_ID  ,E01        ,A9       ,A09      ,$
FIELDNAME   =LAST_NAME    ,E02        ,A20      ,A20      ,$
FIELDNAME   =MARITAL_STAT ,E03        ,A1       ,A01      ,$
FIELDNAME   =SEX          ,E04        ,A1       ,A01      ,$
FIELDNAME   =DEGREE       ,E05        ,A4       ,A04      ,$
FIELDNAME   =SALARY       ,E06        ,D9.2C    ,A09      ,$
FIELDNAME   =PREVIOUS_SAL ,E07        ,D9.2C    ,A09      ,$
```

MOVIES FILE

```
FILENAME=MOVIES  ,SUFFIX=FOC
SEGNAME= MOVIES  ,SEGTYPE=S1
FIELDNAME=TITLE, ,USAGE = A43,$
FIELDNAME=TAPE_NO, ,USAGE = D03,$
FIELDNAME=LENGTH, ,USAGE = D04,$
FIELDNAME=COMMENTS, ,USAGE = A20,$
FIELDNAME=RATING, ,USAGE = A04,$
```

MOVIES2 FILE WITH TEXT FIELD

```
FILENAME=MOVIES2 ,SUFFIX=FOC
SEGNAME= MOVIES  ,SEGTYPE=S1
FIELDNAME=TITLE, ,USAGE = A43,$
FIELDNAME=TAPE_NO, ,USAGE = D03,$
FIELDNAME=LENGTH, ,USAGE = D04,$
FIELDNAME=COMMENTS, ,USAGE = A20,$
FIELDNAME=RATING, ,USAGE = A04,$
FIELDNAME=ABSTRACT,ALIAS=ABS, USAGE = TX40,$
```


REGISTER FILE

```
FILENAME=REGISTER,SUFFIX=FOC
SEGNAME=MEMBER,SEGTYPE=S1
FIELDNAME=LAST_NAME,ALIAS=LN,FORMAT=A20,$
FIELDNAME=FIRST_NAMES,ALIAS=FN,FORMAT=A25,$
FIELDNAME=JOINT_NAME,ALIAS=JN,FORMAT=A1,$
FIELDNAME=DAY_PHONE,ALIAS=DPHONE,FORMAT=A10,$
FIELDNAME=ALT_PHONE,ALIAS=APHONE,FORMAT=A10,$
FIELDNAME=STREET,ALIAS=STR,FORMAT=A20,$
FIELDNAME=CITY,ALIAS=TOWN,FORMAT=A18,$
FIELDNAME=STATE,ALIAS=ST,FORMAT=A2,$
FIELDNAME=ZIP,ALIAS=ZIP,FORMAT=A5,$
SEGNAME=CARDS,PARENT=MEMBER,SEGTYPE=S2
FIELDNAME=CARD_TYPE,ALIAS=TYPE,FORMAT=A15,$
FIELDNAME=ACCOUNT_NO,ALIAS=ACNO,FORMAT=A20,$
FIELDNAME=NO_ISSUED,ALIAS=NO_ISS,FORMAT=I1,$
FIELDNAME=ISSUER,ALIAS=ISSUER,FORMAT=A30,$
FIELDNAME=EXPIRE_DATE,ALIAS=XPDATE,FORMAT=I6MDY,$
FIELDNAME=800_NUMBER,ALIAS=800,FORMAT=A10,$
FIELDNAME=PHONE_NO,ALIAS=PHONE,FORMAT=A10,$
FIELDNAME=CREDIT_LIMIT,ALIAS=CREDIT,FORMAT=D6,$
FIELDNAME=I_STREET,ALIAS=IST,FORMAT=A20,$
FIELDNAME=I_CITY,ALIAS=ICIT,FORMAT=A18,$
FIELDNAME=I_STATE,ALIAS=ISTATE,FORMAT=A2,$
FIELDNAME=IS_ZIP,ALIAS=IZIP,FORMAT=A5,$
```


CUSTOMER FILE

```
FILENAME=CUSTOMER,SUFFIX=FOC
SEGNAME=CUSTOM,SEGTYPE=S1
FIELDNAME=CUSTOMR_NAME,ALIAS=LN,FORMAT=A20,$
FIELDNAME=ACCOUNT_NO,ALIAS=ACNO,FORMAT=I9,$
FIELDNAME=PHONE_NO,ALIAS=FN,FORMAT=A10,$
FIELDNAME=STREET,ALIAS=STR,FORMAT=A20,$
FIELDNAME=CITY,ALIAS=TOWN,FORMAT=A18,$
```

```
FIELDNAME=STATE,ALIAS=ST,FORMAT=A2,$
FIELDNAME=ZIP,ALIAS=ZIP,FORMAT=A5,$
FIELDNAME=YTD_PURCHASE,ALIAS=YTD,FORMAT=D12,$
FIELDNAME=OUTSTANDING,ALIAS=BAL,FORMAT=D12,$
FIELDNAME=COMMENTS,ALIAS=COMM,FORMAT=A60,$
```

STUDENT FILE

```
FILENAME=STUDENT,SUFFIX=FOC
SEGNAME=STUDENT,SEGTYPE=S1
FIELDNAME=STUDENT_ID,ALIAS=ID,FORMAT=A9,$
FIELDNAME=LAST_NAME,ALIAS=LN,FORMAT=A20,$
FIELDNAME=FIRST_NAME,ALIAS=FN,FORMAT=A10,$
FIELDNAME=STREET,ALIAS=ST,FORMAT=A25,$
FIELDNAME=CITY,ALIAS=TOWN,FORMAT=A15,$
FIELDNAME=STATE,ALIAS=ST,FORMAT=A2,$
FIELDNAME=DATE_ENROLLD,ALIAS=ENR,FORMAT=I6MDY,$
FIELDNAME=MAJOR,ALIAS=MAJOR,FORMAT=A15,$
FIELDNAME=ACCUM_CREDIT,ALIAS=CRED,FORMAT=I4,$
SEGNAME=COURSES,PARENT=STUDENT,SEGTYPE=S1
FIELDNAME=COURSE_ID,ALIAS=CID,FORMAT=A8,FIELDTYPE=I,$
FIELDNAME=CREDITS,ALIAS=CR,FORMAT=D5.1,$
FIELDNAME=COMPL_CODE,ALIAS=COMP,FORMAT=A1,$
FIELDNAME=GRADE,ALIAS=GR,FORMAT=A5,$
```

COURSES FILE

```
FILENAME=COURSES,SUFFIX=FOC
SEGNAME=ONE,SEGTYPE=S1
FIELDNAME=COURSE_ID,ALIAS=CID,FORMAT=A8,FIELDTYPE=I,$
FIELDNAME=DESCRIPTION,ALIAS=DESC,FORMAT=A60,$
FIELDNAME=DEPARTMENT,ALIAS=DEP,FORMAT=A15,$
FIELDNAME=INSTRUCTR_ID,ALIAS=INSTR,FORMAT=A25,FIELDTYPE=I,$
FIELDNAME=START_DATE,ALIAS=SDATE,FORMAT=I6MDY,$
FIELDNAME=END_DATE,ALIAS=EDATE,FORMAT=I6MDY,$
FIELDNAME=SESSIONS,ALIAS=NO_SESSIONS,FORMAT=I2,$
FIELDNAME=CONTACT_HRS,ALIAS=NO_HOURS,FORMAT=I3,$
FIELDNAME=CREDIT,ALIAS=CR,FORMAT=D5.1,$
```

EMPLOYEE FILE

```
FILENAME=EMPLOYEE ,SUFFIX=FOC
SEGNAME=EMPINFO, SEGTYPE=S1
 FIELDNAME=EMP_ID      ,ALIAS=EID    ,FORMAT=A9     ,$
 FIELDNAME=LAST_NAME   ,ALIAS=LN     ,FORMAT=A15    ,$
 FIELDNAME=FIRST_NAME  ,ALIAS=FN     ,FORMAT=A10    ,$
```

EMPLOYEE File

```
 FIELDNAME=HIRE_DATE     ,ALIAS=HDT      ,FORMAT=I6YMD  ,$
 FIELDNAME=DEPARTMENT    ,ALIAS=DPT      ,FORMAT=A10     ,$
 FIELDNAME=CURR_SAL      ,ALIAS=CSAL     ,FORMAT=D12.2M ,$
 FIELDNAME=CURR_JOBCODE  ,ALIAS=CJC      ,FORMAT=A3      ,$
 FIELDNAME=ED_HRS        ,ALIAS=OJT      ,FORMAT=F6.2    ,$
SEGNAME=FUNDTRAN, SEGTYPE=U, PARENT=EMPINFO
 FIELDNAME=BANK_NAME     ,ALIAS=BN       ,FORMAT=A20     ,$
 FIELDNAME=BANK_CODE     ,ALIAS=BC       ,FORMAT=I6S     ,$
 FIELDNAME=BANK_ACCT     ,ALIAS=BA       ,FORMAT=I9S     ,$
 FIELDNAME=EFFECT_DATE   ,ALIAS=EDATE    ,FORMAT=I6YMD   ,$
SEGNAME=PAYINFO,SEGTYPE=SH1,PARENT=EMPINFO
 FIELDNAME=DAT_INC       ,ALIAS=DI       ,FORMAT=I6YMD   ,$
 FIELDNAME=PCT_INC       ,ALIAS=PI       ,FORMAT=F6.2    ,$
 FIELDNAME=SALARY        ,ALIAS=SAL      ,FORMAT=D12.2M ,$
 FIELDNAME=JOBCODE       ,ALIAS=JBC      ,FORMAT=A3      ,$
SEGNAME=ADDRESS,SEGTYPE=S1,PARENT=EMPINFO
 FIELDNAME=TYPE          ,ALIAS=AT       ,FORMAT=A4      ,$
 FIELDNAME=ADDRESS_LN1   ,ALIAS=LN1      ,FORMAT=A20     ,$
 FIELDNAME=ADDRESS_LN2   ,ALIAS=LN2      ,FORMAT=A20     ,$
 FIELDNAME=ADDRESS_LN3   ,ALIAS=LN3      ,FORMAT=A20     ,$
 FIELDNAME=ACCTNUMBER    ,ALIAS=ANO      ,FORMAT=I9L     ,$
SEGNAME=SALINFO,SEGTYPE=SH1,PARENT=EMPINFO
 FIELDNAME=PAY_DATE      ,ALIAS=PD       ,FORMAT=I6YMD   ,$
 FIELDNAME=GROSS         ,              ,FORMAT=D12.2M ,$
SEGNAME=DEDUCT,SEGTYPE=S1,PARENT=SALINFO
 FIELDNAME=DED_CODE      ,ALIAS=DC       ,FORMAT=A4      ,$
 FIELDNAME=DED_AMT       ,ALIAS=DA       ,FORMAT=D12.2M ,$
SEGNAME=JOBSEG,CRFILE=JOBFILE,CRKEY=JOBCODE,PARENT=PAYINFO,
SEGTYPE=KU,$
SEGNAME=SECSEG,CRFILE=JOBFILE,PARENT=JOBSEG,SEGTYPE=KLU,$
SEGNAME=SKILLSEG,CRFILE=JOBFILE,PARENT=JOBSEG,SEGTYPE=KL,$
SEGNAME=ATTNDSEG,CRFILE=EDUCFILE,CRKEY=EMP_ID,PARENT=EMPINFO,
SEGTYPE=KM,$
SEGNAME=COURSEG ,CRFILE=EDUCFILE,PARENT=ATTNDSEG,SEGTYPE=KLU,$
```

CAR FILE

```
FILENAME=CAR,SUFFIX=FOC
SEGNAME=ORIGIN,SEGTYPE=S1
 FIELDNAME=COUNTRY,COUNTRY,A10,$
SEGNAME=COMP,SEGTYPE=S1,PARENT=ORIGIN
 FIELDNAME=CAR,CARS,A16,$
SEGNAME=CARREC,SEGTYPE=S1,PARENT=COMP
 FIELDNAME=MODEL,MODEL,A24,$
SEGNAME=BODY,SEGTYPE=S1,PARENT=CARREC
 FIELDNAME=BODYTYPE,TYPE,A12,$
 FIELDNAME=SEATS,SEAT,I3,$
 FIELDNAME=DEALER_COST,DCOST,D7,$
```

```
FIELDNAME=RETAIL_COST,RCOST,D7,$
FIELDNAME=SALES,UNITS,I6,$
SEGNAME=SPECS,SEGTYPE=U,PARENT=BODY
FIELDNAME=LENGTH,LEN,D5,$
FIELDNAME=WIDTH,WIDTH,D5,$
FIELDNAME=HEIGHT,HEIGHT,D5,$
FIELDNAME=WEIGHT,WEIGHT,D6,$
FIELDNAME=WHEELBASE,BASE,D6.1,$
FIELDNAME=FUEL_CAP,FUEL,D6.1,$
FIELDNAME=BHP,POWER,D6,$
FIELDNAME=RPM,RPM,I5,$
FIELDNAME=MPG,MILES,D6,$
FIELDNAME=ACCEL,SECONDS,D6,$
SEGNAME=WARANT,SEGTYPE=S1,PARENT=COMP
FIELDNAME=WARRANTY,WARR,A40,$
SEGNAME=EQUIP,SEGTYPE=S1,PARENT=COMP
        FIELDNAME=STANDARD,EQUIP,A40,$
```

STAFF FILE DATA

Dept	Department	Div	Division	Title	First Name	ID / Last Name	Account	Salary	Rate	Qty	City	Address
12	FINANCE	121	PAYABLES	HEAD ACCOUNTANT	BENTON	294728305TURPIN	CA9134521355123440315781012	65400.00	.05	120	LOS ANGELES	121 LA CIENEGA BLVD.
12	FINANCE	121	PAYABLES	LIAISON OFFICER	CESARE	513724567BORGIA	NY100012125554665707088411110	102000.00	.06	15	NEW YORK	347 SOUTH ROMA AVENUE
12	FINANCE	122	COLLECTIONS	SUPERVISOR	DIANE	504234521FREEMAN	CA94107714555123452096791208	34500.00	.00	99	CANTON	22 SOUTH DEAN DRIVE
15	OPERATIONS	151	ENGINEERING	MANAGER	CHARLES	213456682HUNT	CA93199714559842843099870713	57000.00	.11	140	ORANGE	87A NEWTON
15	OPERATIONS	152	CUSTOMER SERVICES	SERVICE REP.	RICHARD	312562345TRENT	CA91287213555291164023821012	22500.00	.08	50	LOS ANGELES	93 LA CIENEGA BLVD
15	OPERATIONS	152	CUSTOMER SERVICES	SERVICE REP.	JUANITA	314562134TAYLOR	CA91278108555477168092284091 5	26550.00	.10	10	SANTA MONICA	1901 LAKE AVE. #132
20	MARKETING	201	SALES	SALES REPRESENTATIVE	ROBERT	293245178COLE	CA93110714555012360101787081 5	39000.00	.04	43	GARDEN GROVE	37 EXETER DRIVE
20	MARKETING	201	SALES	SALES REPRESENTATIVE	CARLOS	297748301MORALES	CA91230714555171395019881118	39400.00	.06	80	LONG BEACH	883 MANNER DRIVE
20	MARKETING	201	SALES	SALES REPRESENTATIVE	WILLIAM	312781122ZARKOV	CA91422714555421042120880502	47000.00	.11	63	ANAHEIM	544 E. KATELLA #4
20	MARKETING	201	SALES	SALES REPRESENTATIVE	CARLA	413267891JAMESON	CA91205714555987581012821215	36700.00	.10	22	FOUNTAIN VALLEY	727 STROMBRG ROAD
10	ADMINISTRATION	101	EXECUTIVE	PRESIDENT	JILLIAN	291345672DUXBURY	CA93217145551003911138121018	85000.00	.05	110	IRVINE	1020 JEFFRIES
10	ADMINISTRATION	101	EXECUTIVE	EXECUTIVE ASSISTANT	CHRISTINE	515478922ANDERSEN	CA94127145551234650915880107	32000.00	.07	35	ANAHEIM	640A KATELLA STREET
14	MIS	141	DEVELOPMENT	SENIOR PROGRAMMER	JAMES	392345782GREENSTREET	CA95124213555345139032182080 7	45600.00	.06	10	LAKEWOOD	1247 LAKEWOOD DRIVE
14	MIS	141	DEVELOPMENT	OPERATOR	ROBERT	621893221BOCHARD	CA93106714555021250908821215	35000.00	.09	40	EL TORO	561 SANTOS
14	MIS	142	OPERATIONS	MANAGER, DATA CENTER	RICHARD	295738307TAHANIEV	CA93002714555789310385080 9	55400.00	.09	85	SANTA ANA	100 BEVERLY DRIVE
14	MIS	142	OPERATIONS	OPERATOR	CARLOS	432568023CAMPOS	CA94087145558126210028702 3	32000.00	.08	60	LAGUNA NIGUEL	54 CLUB AVENUE

EMPHIST DATA

```
213456682MMMBA   50500.00
291345672SFBS   142000.00
293245178SMHS    36000.00
294728305MMBA    49000.00
295738307MMMBA   51300.00
297748301SMHS    37600.00
312562345SMHS    18000.00
312781122WMPHD   42000.00
314562134DFHS    24500.00
392345782WMBA    41000.00
413267891SFBA    34000.00
432568023MMAA    30000.00
504234521MFBS    28000.00
513724567WMMA    95000.00
515478922SFAA    28000.00
621893221MMHS    31200.00
```

FOCUS LOAD PROGRAM

This program will load the EMPHIST Focus file from the data in the EMPHIST data file above.

```
-*EMPHISUP
-*PROGRAM TO ADD RECORDS TO THE EMPHIST FILE
CMS FILEDEF EMPHIST DISK EMPHIST DATA A (PERM
MODIFY FILE EMPHIST
FIXFORM SSN/9 MS/1 SEX/1 DEGREE/4 OLDSAL/9
MATCH SSN
ON MATCH REJECT
ON NOMATCH INCLUDE
DATA ON EMPHIST
END
```

TABLETALK TUTORIAL

TableTalk is an automated facility that allows the Focus user to produce reports from Focus files. The user does not need to know Focus or understand much about computers, other than knowing how to type letters on a keyboard or use a mouse.

In this appendix I create a report from the STAFF file with TableTalk. Focus will automatically create a TABLE request based on my requirements which will include field selection, record filtering, and a meaningful heading for the report. Let's say that I want to look at the STAFF file and print a report identifying employees who are earning more than $40,000 a year. I want to find out who they are, their job titles, and for which department they work. Finally, I want to print my report in department ID sequence but I do not want to print the department ID numbers themselves. The final report will look as follows:

```
PAGE     1

      LIST OF EMPLOYEES MAKING MORE THAN $40,000 BY DEPARTMENT
EMPLOYEE
LAST NAME       DEPT_NAME        JOB_TITLE                  SALARY
---------       ---------        ---------                  -------
DUXBURY         ADMINISTRATION   PRESIDENT             185,000.00
TURPIN          FINANCE          HEAD ACCOUNTANT        65,400.00
BORGIA          FINANCE          LIAISON MANAGER       102,000.00
GREENSTREET     MIS              SENIOR PROGRAMMER      45,600.00
TAHANIEV        MIS              MANAGER, DATA CENTER   55,400.00
HUNT            OPERATIONS       MANAGER                57,000.00
ZARKOV          MARKETING        SALES REPRESENTATIVE   47,000.00
```

As you will notice in the following pages, there is no need to have Focus expertise to use TableTalk. In fact, it is not even necessary to know the structure of the STAFF file. Focus will display all the field names to the user. The user can pick and choose any combination of fields.

There are two ways to invoke the TableTalk facility. One way is to type the command TableTalk, by itself, at the Focus prompt (>). In that case Focus will display the initial TableTalk menu. This menu will also display the name of Focus files available to you and will allow you to select one of these files by moving the cursor to the file requested and pressing the Enter or Return key, as shown below.

```
+----------------------------------------------------------------------+
|                                                                      |
| : INSTRUCTIONS : 1-Move cursor to name of the field with tab keys :  |
| :                2-Depress ENTER to Select a file                 :  |
| :                3-Depress PF3 or PF12 to QUIT                     :  |
| :                4-Use PF8 to go down a page, PF7 to go back up    :  |
| +------------------------------------------------------------------+  |
| +------------------------------------------------------------------+  |
| :Select         :                                                 :   |
| :Filename       :                                                 :   |
| :---------------------------------------------------------------+     |
| :CALLDET        :                                                 :   |
| :CAR            :                                                 :   |
| :CUSTOMER       :                                                 :   |
| :CUST1          :                                                 :   |
| :DDA            :                                                 :   |
| :DIR_DEP        :                                                 :   |
| :EMPLOYEE       :                                                 :   |
| :FINAL          :                                                 :   |
| :GRADES         :                                                 :   |
| :STAFF       <-------                                             :   |
| :STUDENT        :                                                 :   |
| :SWITCH         :                                                 :   |
| +(MORE)------------------------------------------------------------+  |
|                                                                      |
+----------------------------------------------------------------------+
```

However, if you already know the name of the Focus file that you would like to report from, you can go the main TableTalk menu directly by typing the following command from the Focus prompt (>):

```
TABLETALK FILE filename
```

that is,

```
TABLETALK FILE STAFF.
```

The main TableTalk menu looks as follows:

```
+-------------------------------------------------------------------+
¦ Keys: ENTER      Select      PF1 Field Definitions   PF2 Revise mode  ¦
¦       PF3, PF12 Undo         PF4 Top                 PF5 Bottom       ¦
¦       PF7        Scroll Up PF8 Scroll Down           PF9 Multi-select ¦
+-------------------------------------------------------------------+

                                        +-----------------------+
                                        ¦ Select a data field   ¦
+-----------------------------------+   ¦                       ¦
¦ Do you want to:                   ¦   ¦ --------------------- ¦
¦                                   ¦   ¦DEPRTMNT_ID            ¦
¦ --------------------------------- ¦   ¦DEPT_NAME             ¦
¦PRINT the individual values of <------ ¦SECTION_ID            ¦
¦SUM the values of                  ¦   ¦SECTION_NAME          ¦
¦COUNT the instances of             ¦   ¦EMPLOYEE_ID           ¦
¦WRITE the PERCENT of               ¦   ¦LAST_NAME             ¦
¦WRITE the AVERAGE of               ¦   ¦FIRST_NAME            ¦
¦QUIT                               ¦   ¦JOB_TITLE             ¦
+(MORE) ----------------------------+   +-----------------------+

+-------------------------------------------------------------------+
¦TABLE FILE STAFF                                                   ¦
¦                                                                   ¦
¦                                                                   ¦
¦                                                                   ¦
+-------------------------------------------------------------------+
```

The PC/Focus TableTalk menu is functionally similar to the mainframe version; however, it is more user friendly and has better graphics, as shown below.

```
+-------------------------------------------------------------------+
¦ KEYS:     CURSOR UP        ⊔   SELECT    F1     DEFINITIONS        ¦
¦           CURSOR DOWN      ESC ERASE     F2     REVISE             ¦
+-------------------------------------------------------------------+

+-----------------------------------+   +-----------------------+
¦ IN THE FIRST REPORT COLUMN:       ¦   ¦ SELECT A DATA FIELD   ¦
¦                                   ¦   ¦                       ¦
¦ PRINT THE INDIVIDUAL VALUES OF    ¦   ¦ DEPRTMNT_ID           ¦
¦ PRINT ALL FIELDS                  ¦   ¦ DEPT_NAME             ¦
¦ SUM THE VALUES OF                 ¦   ¦ SECTION_ID            ¦
¦ COUNT THE INSTANCES OF            ¦   ¦ SECTION_NAME          ¦
¦ COUNT THE INSTANCES OF ALL FIELDS ¦   ¦ EMPLOYEE_ID           ¦
¦ WRITE THE PERCENT OF              ¦   ¦ LAST_NAME             ¦
¦ WRITE THE AVERAGE OF              ¦   ¦ FIRST_NAME            ¦
+-----------------------------------+   ¦ JOB_TITLE             ¦
                                        +-----------------------+
+-------------------------------------------------------------------+
¦ TABLE FILE STAFF                                                  ¦
¦                                                                  ¦
¦                                                                  ¦
¦                                                                  ¦
+-------------------------------------------------------------------+
```

TableTalk consists of a series of full-screen menus. Each screen is divided into several sections. The upper area of the screen is reserved for instructions for using the TableTalk control keys (these are the PF keys, the cursor keys, the Enter key, and the Escape key). These keys vary slightly from mainframe Focus to PC/Focus. On the whole, the PC/Focus layout is less complicated and the graphics are more pleasing to the eye. The middle part of the screen is reserved for pop-up menus or little windows. These windows appear from time to time to help you make a selection or guide you in your work. The bottom part of the screen is reserved for the Focus code, which is generated automatically based on your selections. This is one of the nice features of Focus, since it allows you to see the code and learn Focus at the same time.

CONTROL KEYS IN TABLETALK

Following are the important control keys in TableTalk.

1. The Enter or Return key will select the field or option currently being highlighted by the cursor.

2. The PF3 or PF12 keys (or the Escape key in PC) will undo your previous selections. You can keep pressing the Escape or PF3 key to back out of all your selections, all the way to the beginning of the TableTalk main menu.

3. The PF7 and PF8 keys are the scroll-up and scroll-down keys. These keys are generally used to scroll screens up and down in all Focus environments. In TableTalk you can use them to scroll up or down the windows that open up in the middle part of the screen.

4. The PF1 key is the field definition key. This function key is useful only if you have a field description, in addition to the field name, in the Master File Description. In that case, PF1 will display that field description.

5. By pressing the PF5 key, you can go to the bottom of any window to which the cursor is currently pointing. Wherever you see the word "More" at the bottom of a window, you can be certain that more fields or options are available for review and/or selection. PF4 and PF5 keys will take you to the top and bottom of the list of choices or fields, respectively.

6. The PF2 key allows the user to insert, change, and/or delete a selected field without backing out all the way to that field. By using the PF2 key, Focus will present a new menu that will allow you to change, insert, or delete fields. Frankly, I am not very keen on using the PF2 key. I find the Revision screen displayed by this key rather confusing. It is much easier either to back out of that particular instruction by using the PF3 key or wait to the end, save the TABLE request created by TableTalk, and then edit it with TED. The following shows an example of the Revision mode screen invoked by pressing the PF2 key.

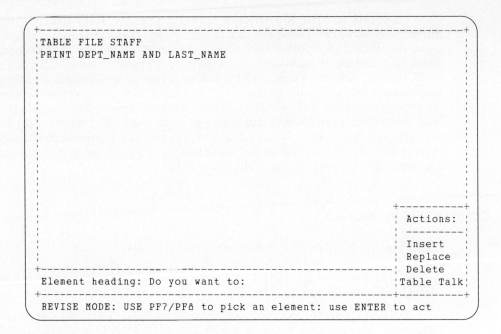

```
+-------------------------------------------------------------------+
|TABLE FILE STAFF                                                   :
|PRINT DEPT_NAME AND LAST_NAME                                      :
:                                                                   :
:                                                                   :
:                                                                   :
:                                                                   :
:                                                                   :
:                                                                   :
:                                                                   :
:                                                                   :
:                                                                   :
:                                                                   :
:                                                        +----------+
:                                                        : Actions: :
:                                                        : -------- :
:                                                        : Insert   :
:                                                        : Replace  :
+--------------------------- ---------------------------- : Delete  :
 Element heading: Do you want to:                         :Table Talk:
+------------------------------------------------------+--+----------+
 REVISE MODE: USE PF7/PF8 to pick an element: use ENTER to act
```

7. Finally, the PF9 key allows you to make multiple selections. If you are printing or summing a number of fields, once you get to the data selection window, you can select each field individually by pointing to it with your cursor and pressing the PF9 key. The alternative is to press the Enter key and select your fields one field at a time. This will swap you between the two main windows: the logic selection window on the left-hand side of the screen and the data field selection window on the right-hand side of the screen. The PF9 key is currently available on mainframe Focus only. You do not miss much in other versions of Focus by not having it available.

In the main TableTalk menu, the cursor always highlights the first selection line, which in this case states.

"And Print the individual values of" ←

During the rest of this tutorial, I will use an arrow (←) to indicate highlighted cursors. You can, of course, move the cursor down to make other selections within that window. Also, since the word "More" is at the bottom of this window, you can use the PF8 key to scroll down and see other options that are currently invisible to you.

On the right-hand side of the screen, the small pop-up menu or window will list the fields in the STAFF file. In this case there are many more fields that could be displayed on one screen, so you could always scroll down by using the PF8 key (or just the down cursor key in PC/Focus) to locate the other fields.

Focus will start the first line of code by putting the TABLE FILE STAFF statement in the program window at the bottom third of the screen. Since the first item that I want to print is the employee last name, I must select the first item on the list by pressing the Enter key:

```
And PRINT the individual values of  ←
```

This action will move the cursor to the right-hand side of the screen to the data field selection window. Since the employee last name is in the current window, I will need to use the cursor key to go down the list of fields until I reach the LAST_NAME field. Here, I must stop and press the Enter key. Having selected the field, Focus will automatically update the code at the bottom of the screen.

```
+-----------------------------------------------------------------+
¦ Keys: ENTER      Select      PF1 Field Definitions  PF2 Revise mode  ¦
¦       PF3, PF12 Undo        PF4 Top                 PF5 Bottom       ¦
¦       PF7        Scroll Up  PF8 Scroll Down         PF9 Multi-select ¦
+-----------------------------------------------------------------+

                                    +-----------------------+
+---------------------------------+ ¦ Select a data field   ¦
¦ Do you want to:                 ¦ ¦                       ¦
¦                                 ¦ ¦ ---------   --------- ¦
¦ ------------------------------- ¦ ¦DEPRTMNT_ID            ¦
¦No more                          ¦ ¦DEPT_NAME              ¦
¦And PRINT the individual values of¦ ¦SECTION_ID            ¦
¦And WRITE the PERCENT of         ¦ ¦SECTION_NAME           ¦
¦And COMPUTE the RATIO of         ¦ ¦EMPLOYEE_ID            ¦
¦And COMPUTE the PRODUCT of       ¦ ¦LAST_NAME ←———————     ¦
¦And COMPUTE the DIFFERENCE between¦ ¦FIRST_NAME             ¦
¦Underneath the last column       ¦ ¦JOB_TITLE              ¦
+(More --------------------------+ +-----------------------+
+-----------------------------------------------------------------+
¦TABLE FILE STAFF                                                 ¦
¦PRINT LAST_NAME                                                  ¦
¦                                                                 ¦
¦                                                                 ¦
¦                                                                 ¦
+-----------------------------------------------------------------+
```

Next, the cursor will move back to the left-hand side of the screen to the options window and will highlight the "No more" option.

```
+------------------------------------------------------------------+
¦ Keys: ENTER      Select     PF1 Field Definitions  PF2 Revise mode  ¦
¦       PF3, PF12 Undo        PF4 Top                PF5 Bottom       ¦
¦       PF7       Scroll Up PF8 Scroll Down          PF9 Multi-select ¦
+------------------------------------------------------------------+

                                        +----------------------+
+-----------------------------------+   ¦ Select a data field  ¦
¦ Do you want to:                   ¦   ¦                      ¦
¦                                   ¦   ¦  -------------------- ¦
¦  ------------------------------   ¦   ¦DEPRTMNT_ID            ¦
¦No more ←-------                   ¦   ¦DEPT_NAME             ¦
¦And PRINT the individual values of ¦   ¦SECTION_ID            ¦
¦And WRITE the PERCENT of           ¦   ¦SECTION_NAME          ¦
¦And COMPUTE the RATIO of           ¦   ¦EMPLOYEE_ID           ¦
¦And COMPUTE the PRODUCT of         ¦   ¦LAST_NAME             ¦
¦And COMPUTE the DIFFERENCE between ¦   ¦FIRST_NAME            ¦
¦Underneath the last column         ¦   ¦JOB_TITLE             ¦
+(More -------------------------+       +----------------------+
+------------------------------------------------------------------+
¦TABLE FILE STAFF                                                  ¦
¦PRINT LAST_NAME                                                   ¦
¦                                                                  ¦
¦                                                                  ¦
¦                                                                  ¦
+------------------------------------------------------------------+
```

As you will notice, the pop-up menu or window on the left-hand side of the screen has several new options. For now, however, we will ignore the other choices. We need to print the next field, which is the department name. I must therefore move the cursor down to the following field.

And PRINT the individual values of ←

I must next press the Enter key. The cursor will move to the right-hand side or data field window. This time I will select the DEPT_NAME and press the Enter key again. Focus will update the code and will display the following screen.

```
+-------------------------------------------------------------------+
| Keys: ENTER      Select     PF1 Field Definitions  PF2 Revise mode |
|       PF3, PF12 Undo        PF4 Top                 PF5 Bottom     |
|       PF7        Scroll Up PF8 Scroll Down          PF9 Multi-select |
+-------------------------------------------------------------------+
                                        +----------------------+
+-----------------------------------+   | Select a data field  |
| Do you want to:                   |   |                      |
|                                   |   | ---------------------|
| ----------------------------------|   |DEPRTMNT_ID           |
|No more                            |   |DEPT_NAME  <--------- |
|And PRINT the individual values of |   |SECTION_ID            |
|And WRITE the PERCENT of           |   |SECTION_NAME          |
|And COMPUTE the RATIO of           |   |EMPLOYEE_ID           |
|And COMPUTE the PRODUCT of         |   |LAST_NAME             |
|And COMPUTE the DIFFERENCE between |   |FIRST_NAME            |
|Underneath the last column         |   |JOB_TITLE             |
+(More ----------------------   -+      +----------------------+
+-------------------------------------------------------------------+
|TABLE FILE STAFF                                                   |
|PRINT LAST_NAME AND DEPT_NAME                                      |
|                                                                   |
|                                                                   |
|                                                                   |
+-------------------------------------------------------------------+
```

As you will notice, Focus is building the program at the bottom of the screen. I must now follow the same procedure as before and continue to select the other fields that I need to select for my report. These fields are the JOB_TITLE and SALARY fields. For every field that the user decides to print, he or she will first have to select the following option:

```
And PRINT the individual values of ←
```

and then select the field that is needed from the data field window. Note that the SALARY field is not in the initial data field window. To select this field, you must use the PF8 key (or the cursor key in PC/Focus) to scroll down that window to locate and select the SALARY field. At the end of this phase, my screen will look as follows:

```
+----------------------------------------------------------------+
¦ Keys: ENTER      Select     PF1 Field Definitions  PF2 Revise mode ¦
¦       PF3, PF12 Undo        PF4 Top                PF5 Bottom      ¦
¦       PF7       Scroll Up PF8 Scroll Down          PF9 Multi-select ¦
+----------------------------------------------------------------+

                                    +-----------------------+
                                    ¦ Select a data field    ¦
  +-----------------------------------+  ¦                       ¦
  ¦ Do you want to:                   ¦  ¦ --------------------- ¦
  ¦                                   ¦  ¦                       ¦
  ¦ --------------------------------- ¦  ¦CITY                   ¦
  ¦No more ←------                    ¦  ¦STATE                  ¦
  ¦And PRINT the individual values of ¦  ¦ZIP_CODE               ¦
  ¦And WRITE the PERCENT of           ¦  ¦TELEPHONE_NO           ¦
  ¦And COMPUTE the RATIO of           ¦  ¦DATE_BIRTH             ¦
  ¦And COMPUTE the PRODUCT of         ¦  ¦DATE_HIRE              ¦
  ¦And COMPUTE the DIFFERENCE between ¦  ¦SALARY                 ¦
  ¦Underneath the last column         ¦  ¦PCT_INC                ¦
  +(More ----------------------------+  +-----------------------+
  +----------------------------------------------------------------+
  ¦TABLE FILE STAFF                                                ¦
  ¦PRINT LAST_NAME AND DEPT_NAME AND JOB_TITLE AND SALARY          ¦
  ¦                                                                ¦
  ¦                                                                ¦
  ¦                                                                ¦
  +----------------------------------------------------------------+
```

Next, I will need to sequence my report by the department ID. So I must stop the field selection process by selecting the "No more" option from the window. This option will open up another window, called the "Select a sort order action" window, that will allow me to sequence or sort a report based on the values of fields in the Focus data file.

```
+---------------------------------------------------------------+
| Keys: ENTER      Select    PF1 Field Definitions  PF2 Revise mode |
|       PF3, PF12 Undo       PF4 Top                PF5 Bottom      |
|       PF7       Scroll Up PF8 Scroll Down         PF9 Multi-select |
+---------------------------------------------------------------+


+------------------------------------------+
|Select a sort order action                |
|                                          |
| ---------------------------              |
|None or no more                           |
|Sort the rows ALPHABETICALLY BY field...  <-------
|Sort the rows HIGH to LOW (Z-A 9-0)       |
|Sort the columns ACROSS the page          |
|Sort the columns across high to low       |
+(More)---   -----------------------------+


+-----------------------------------------------------------+
|TABLE FILE STAFF                                           |
|PRINT LAST_NAME AND DEPT_NAME AND JOB_TITLE AND SALARY      |
|                                                           |
|                                                           |
|                                                           |
+-----------------------------------------------------------+
```

In this case I will select the second option, which is titled

```
Sort the rows ALPHABETICALLY BY field  ←
```

This is because I am trying to sort my report by department ID. So the cursor must be moved to this field. The selection is made by pressing the Enter key.

```
+-------------------------------------------------------------------+
¦ Keys: ENTER      Select    PF1 Field Definitions  PF2 Revise mode ¦
¦       PF3, PF12 Undo       PF4 Top                PF5 Bottom      ¦
¦       PF7       Scroll Up PF8 Scroll Down         PF9 Multi-select¦
+-------------------------------------------------------------------+
                                      +-----------------------+
                                      ¦ Select a data field   ¦
                                      ¦                       ¦
    +------------------------------------+ ---------------------¦
    ¦Select a sort order action        ¦ ¦DEPRTMNT_ID ←———————  ¦
    ¦----------------------------------¦ ¦DEPT_NAME             ¦
    ¦None or no more                   ¦ ¦SECTION_ID            ¦
    ¦Sort the rows ALPHABETICALLY BY field...¦ ¦SECTION_NAME      ¦
    ¦Sort the rows HIGH to LOW (Z-A 9-0)¦ ¦EMPLOYEE_ID           ¦
    ¦Sort the columns ACROSS the page  ¦ ¦LAST_NAME             ¦
    ¦Sort the columns ACROSS high to low¦ ¦FIRST_NAME            ¦
    +(More -------------------------------+ ¦JOB_TITLE             ¦
                                         +-----------------------+
    +--------------------------------------------------------------+
    ¦TABLE FILE STAFF                                              ¦
    ¦PRINT LAST_NAME AND DEPT_NAME AND JOB_TITLE AND SALARY        ¦
    ¦BY DEPRTMNT_ID                                                ¦
    ¦                                                              ¦
    +--------------------------------------------------------------+
```

Focus will now know that I want to sequence my data by a field from high to low. The next screen displayed will present further options.

```
+-------------------------------------------------------------------+
| Keys: ENTER       Select      PF1 Field Definitions  PF2 Revise mode |
|       PF3, PF12 Undo        PF4 Top                PF5 Bottom       |
|       PF7         Scroll Up PF8 Scroll Down        PF9 Multi-select |
+-------------------------------------------------------------------+


               +------------------------------------------+-----------+
               |Select an option when sort order changes  | ta field  |
+----------+   |                                          |           |
|          |   | ---------------------------------------- |  -------- |
|Select a s|   |None or no more                           |           |
|----------|   |Do not print the sort field value (NOPRINT) <------    |
|None or no|   |SKIP one LINE                             |           |
|Sort the r|   |SKIP to a new PAGE                        |           |
|Sort the r|   |SUB TOTAL the numerical fields            |           |
|Sort the c|   |Draw an UNDER LINE across page            |           |
|Sort the c|   |FOLD the print LINE into two lines        |           |
+----------+   +(More)------------------------------------+           |
                                                  +-------------------+


+-------------------------------------------------------------------+
|TABLE FILE STAFF                                                    |
|PRINT LAST_NAME AND DEPT_NAME AND JOB_TITLE AND SALARY              |
|BY DEPRTMNT_ID NOPRINT                                             |
|                                                                   |
|                                                                   |
+-------------------------------------------------------------------+
```

Since I do not plan to print the value of this sort field (i.e., the department number), I must select the NOPRINT option, as shown in the preceding screen. Next, since I have completed sorting my report, I must select the "None or no more" option from this window.

```
+----------------------------------------------------------------+
¦ Keys: ENTER      Select      PF1 Field Definitions  PF2 Revise mode ¦
¦       PF3, PF12 Undo         PF4 Top                PF5 Bottom   ¦
¦       PF7        Scroll Up PF8 Scroll Down          PF9 Multi-select ¦
+----------------------------------------------------------------+


+-------------------------------------------+----------+
¦Select an option when sort order changes   ¦ ta field ¦
+----------¦                                          ¦          ¦
¦          ¦ --------------------------------------- ¦  -------- ¦
¦Select a s ¦None or no more  ←———                   ¦           ¦
¦----------¦Do not print the sort field value (NOPRINT)¦
¦None or no ¦SKIP one LINE                            ¦
¦Sort the r ¦SKIP to a new PAGE                       ¦
¦Sort the r ¦SUB TOTAL the numerical fields           ¦
¦Sort the c ¦Draw an UNDER LINE across page           ¦
¦Sort the c ¦FOLD the print LINE into two lines       ¦
+---------- +(More)-------------------------------------+
                                        +-----------------------+


+----------------------------------------------------------------+
¦TABLE FILE STAFF                                                ¦
¦PRINT LAST_NAME AND DEPT_NAME AND JOB_TITLE AND SALARY          ¦
¦BY DEPRTMNT_ID NOPRINT                                          ¦
¦                                                                ¦
¦                                                                ¦
+----------------------------------------------------------------+
```

The initial sort window is displayed one more time. I must choose the
"None or no more" option to terminate the sort operation.

```
+------------------------------------------------------------------+
| Keys: ENTER      Select     PF1 Field Definitions  PF2 Revise mode |
|       PF3, PF12 Undo        PF4 Top                PF5 Bottom      |
|       PF7        Scroll Up PF8 Scroll Down         PF9 Multi-select |
+------------------------------------------------------------------+


+-------------------------------------------------+
|Select a sort order action                       |
|                                                 |
|  -----------------------                        |
|None or no more          <--------               |
|Sort the rows ALPHABETICALLY BY field...         |
|Sort the rows HIGH to LOW (Z-A 9-0)              |
|Sort the columns ACROSS the page                 |
|Sort the columns across high to low              |
+(More)-------------------------------------------+


+------------------------------------------------------------------+
|TABLE FILE STAFF                                                  |
|PRINT LAST_NAME AND DEPT_NAME AND JOB_TITLE AND SALARY            |
|BY DEPRTMNT_ID NOPRINT                                            |
|                                                                  |
|                                                                  |
+------------------------------------------------------------------+
```

Next, the record selection window is displayed by TableTalk. In this window, the user is given the opportunity to filter records based on values in one or more data fields. As seen on the following screen, I requested filtering by selecting the "Yes—WHERE test" option. Note: On some version of Focus, this window will be called the "IF field value" option.

```
+------------------------------------------------------------------+
| Keys: ENTER      Select     PF1 Field Definitions  PF2 Revise mode |
|       PF3, PF12 Undo        PF4 Top                PF5 Bottom      |
|       PF7       Scroll Up PF8 Scroll Down          PF9 Multi-select|
+------------------------------------------------------------------+

                                          +--------------------+
                                          |Select a data field |
                                          |                    |
                                          |------------------- |
                                          |DEPRTMNT_ID         |
        +----------------------------------+ |DEPT_NAME           |
        |Do you want to select only certain records? | |SECTION_ID          |
        |----------------------------------- | |SECTION_NAME        |
        |No                                | |EMPLOYEE_ID         |
        |Yes - WHERE test  <-------        | |LAST_NAME           |
        +----------------------------------+ |FIRST_NAME          |
                                          |JOB_TITLE           |
                                          +--------------------+


  +------------------------------------------------------------------+
  |TABLE FILE STAFF                                                  |
  |PRINT LAST_NAME AND DEPT_NAME AND JOB_TITLE AND SALARY            |
  |BY DEPRTMNT_ID NOPRINT                                            |
  |                                                                  |
  |                                                                  |
  +------------------------------------------------------------------+
```

In the following screen, I selected the SALARY field from the data field window to use in my filtering test. Note that the SALARY field was not in the list of initial data fields that was displayed by TableTalk. To get there, the user will have to use the PF8 key to scroll down the list of data fields. In PC/Focus, you can use the cursor down key to scroll down the list of data fields.

```
+------------------------------------------------------------+
| Keys: ENTER      Select    PF1 Field Definitions  PF2 Revise mode  |
|       PF3, PF12 Undo       PF4 Top                PF5 Bottom       |
|       PF7       Scroll Up PF8 Scroll Down         PF9 Multi-select |
+------------------------------------------------------------+

                                        +--------------------+
                                        |Select a data field |
                                        |                    |
                                        |(More)----------    |
                                        |CITY                |
                                        |STATE               |
                                        |ZIP_CODE            |
                                        |TELEPHONE_NO        |
                                        |DATE_BIRTH          |
                                        |DATE_HIRE           |
                                        |SALARY   <--------  |
                                        |PCT_INC             |
                                        +--------------------+

+------------------------------------------------------------+
|TABLE FILE STAFF                                            |
|PRINT LAST_NAME AND DEPT_NAME AND JOB_TITLE AND SALARY      |
|BY DEPRTMNT_ID NOPRINT                                      |
|WHERE (                                                     |
|                                                            |
+------------------------------------------------------------+
```

The next screen allows the user to select a relation. I selected the "Is GREATER THAN" option since I was looking for salaries greater than $40,000.

```
+-----------------------------------------------------------------+
¦ Keys: ENTER       Select    PF1 Field Definitions  PF2 Revise mode ¦
¦       PF3, PF12 Undo        PF4 Top                PF5 Bottom    ¦
¦       PF7         Scroll Up PF8 Scroll Down        PF9 Multi-select ¦
+-----------------------------------------------------------------+

                    +--------------------------------+-----+
                    ¦ Select a relation:             ¦ield ¦
                    ¦--------------------            ¦     ¦
                    ¦Is EQUAL to                     ¦---  ¦
                    ¦Is NOT EQUAL to                 ¦     ¦
                    ¦Is GREATER THAN    <--------    ¦     ¦
                    ¦Is LESS THAN                    ¦     ¦
                    ¦Is GREATER THAN or EQUAL to     ¦     ¦
                    ¦Is LESS THAN or EQUAL to        ¦     ¦
                    +--------------------------------+     ¦
                                      ¦                    ¦
                                      ¦PCT_INC             ¦
                                      +--------------------+

+-----------------------------------------------------------------+
¦TABLE FILE STAFF                                                 ¦
¦PRINT LAST_NAME AND DEPT_NAME AND JOB_TITLE AND SALARY           ¦
¦BY DEPRTMNT_ID NOPRINT                                           ¦
¦WHERE (SALARY                                                    ¦
¦                                                                 ¦
+-----------------------------------------------------------------+
```

The next window will allow the user to choose either a specific value or the value of another field for comparing against the selected field. Remember that on all Focus versions below release 6.00 you cannot compare the values of two fields in the same file against each other. Only Focus release 6.00 and above allow you to use the WHERE clause to do so. In the earlier releases of Focus, you will have to use the DEFINE statement for comparing two field values in the same file. However, this should not present a problem since most of you will be working with release 6.00 or higher releases of Focus. In the following window, I chose the "A specific value" option.

```
+-----------------------------------------------------------------+
| Keys: ENTER      Select    PF1 Field Definitions  PF2 Revise mode |
|       PF3, PF12 Undo       PF4 Top                PF5 Bottom      |
|       PF7       Scroll Up PF8 Scroll Down         PF9 Multi-select|
+-----------------------------------------------------------------+

    +---------------------------------------------+------------+-----+
    |What do you want to compare the field with?  |            |ield |
    |---------------------------------------------|            |---- |
    |A specific value  <———                       |            |---  |
    |Another field                                |            |     |
    +---------------------------------------------+            |     |
                              |Is LESS THAN                    |     |
                              |Is GREATER THAN or EQUAL to     |     |
                              |Is LESS THAN or EQUAL to        |     |
                              +-------------------------------+     |
                                                             |     |
                                           |PCT_INC           |     |
                                           +--------------------+---+

+-----------------------------------------------------------------+
|TABLE FILE STAFF                                                  |
|PRINT LAST_NAME AND DEPT_NAME AND JOB_TITLE AND SALARY            |
|BY DEPRTMNT_ID NOPRINT                                            |
|WHERE (SALARY   GT                                               |
|                                                                 |
+-----------------------------------------------------------------+
```

The next screen simply prompted me to enter the desired value. I entered 40,000.

```
+----------------------------------------------------------------+
¦ Keys: ENTER      Select     PF1 Field Definitions  PF2 Revise mode ¦
¦       PF3, PF12 Undo       PF4 Top                 PF5 Bottom      ¦
¦       PF7       Scroll Up PF8 Scroll Down          PF9 Multi-select ¦
+----------------------------------------------------------------+

                    +-----------------------+------------+-----+
                    ¦Enter a value:         ¦            ¦ield ¦
                    ¦-----------------------¦            ¦     ¦
                    ¦40000      ←————————    ¦            ¦---  ¦
                    ¦-----------------------¦            ¦     ¦
                    +-----------------------+            ¦     ¦
                     ¦Is LESS THAN                       ¦     ¦
                     ¦Is GREATER THAN or EQUAL to        ¦     ¦
                     ¦Is LESS THAN or EQUAL to           ¦     ¦
                     +-----------------------------------+     ¦
                                                               ¦
                                               ¦PCT_INC        ¦
                                               +---------------+

+----------------------------------------------------------------+
¦TABLE FILE STAFF
¦PRINT LAST_NAME AND DEPT_NAME AND JOB_TITLE AND SALARY
¦BY DEPRTMNT_ID NOPRINT
¦WHERE (SALARY   GT
¦
+----------------------------------------------------------------+
```

TableTalk will allow the user, in the following screen, to make additional selections and continue the filtering process. Notice that the so-called compound conditions (i.e., OR and AND) are also allowed. This is also known as the *Boolean logic test*. I selected the "No" option and pressed the Enter key.

```
+--------------------------------------------------------------------+
¦ Keys: ENTER      Select      PF1 Field Definitions  PF2 Revise mode ¦
¦       PF3, PF12 Undo        PF4 Top                 PF5 Bottom      ¦
¦       PF7       Scroll Up PF8 Scroll Down           PF9 Multi-select ¦
+--------------------------------------------------------------------+


              +-----------------------------------------+-----+-----+
              ¦Any additional record selection tests?   ¦     ¦ield ¦
              ¦-----------------------------------------¦     ¦     ¦
              ¦No  ←_____                             ¦     ¦---  ¦
              ¦Yes - OR another condition               ¦     ¦     ¦
              ¦Yes - AND another condition              ¦     ¦     ¦
              +-----------------------------------------+     ¦     ¦
                        ¦Is GREATER THAN or EQUAL to           ¦     ¦
                        ¦Is LESS THAN or EQUAL to              ¦     ¦
                        +------------------------------+       ¦     ¦
                                                              ¦     ¦
                                              ¦PCT_INC         ¦     ¦
                                              +---------------- --+

+--------------------------------------------------------------------+
¦TABLE FILE STAFF                                                    ¦
¦PRINT LAST_NAME AND DEPT_NAME AND JOB_TITLE AND SALARY              ¦
¦BY DEPRTMNT_ID NOPRINT                                              ¦
¦WHERE (SALARY  GT 40000                                            ¦
¦                                                                    ¦
+--------------------------------------------------------------------+
```

The following screen displays the initial record selection window again. This allows you to continue the record filtering process. In this example, I had already made my selection in the previous window and did not need to make another selection. Therefore, I selected the "No" option.

```
+----------------------------------------------------------------------+
¦ Keys: ENTER       Select      PF1 Field Definitions  PF2 Revise mode ¦
¦       PF3, PF12 Undo          PF4 Top                PF5 Bottom       ¦
¦       PF7       Scroll Up PF8 Scroll Down            PF9 Multi-select ¦
+----------------------------------------------------------------------+


                              +--------------------------------+
                              ¦ Select a relation:             ¦
                              ¦--------------------            ¦
                              ¦Is EQUAL to                     ¦
+---------------------------------------------+                ¦
¦Do you want to select only certain records? ¦                ¦
¦-------------------------------------------- ¦                ¦
¦No  <----------                      ¦r EQUAL to             ¦
¦Yes - WHERE test                     ¦QUAL to                ¦
+---------------------------------------------+ ---------------+


+----------------------------------------------------------------------+
¦TABLE FILE STAFF                                                      ¦
¦PRINT LAST_NAME AND DEPT_NAME AND JOB_TITLE AND SALARY                ¦
¦BY DEPRTMNT_ID NOPRINT                                                ¦
¦WHERE (SALARY  GT 40000);                                            ¦
¦                                                                      ¦
+----------------------------------------------------------------------+
```

The main coding for this Focus TABLE request is now completed. The next few screens will give the user the opportunity to create a report heading or a report footing for this TABLE request. For my report, I selected the third option, which allowed me to center the heading that I had chosen on top of the report. This is a very useful option because it will save the user the arduous task of counting the columns on each side of the heading line.

```
+------------------------------------------------------------+
| Keys: ENTER      Select     PF1 Field Definitions  PF2 Revise mode |
|       PF3, PF12 Undo        PF4 Top                PF5 Bottom      |
|       PF7        Scroll Up  PF8 Scroll Down        PF9 Multi-select|
+------------------------------------------------------------+


                             +--------------------------------+
+----------------------------------------------------+        |
|Do you want a page HEADING or FOOTING ?             |        |
|----------------------------------------------------|        |
|None or no more                                     |        |
|Yes , HEADING                                       |        |
|Yes , and CENTER HEADING   <------                  |        |
|Yes , a FOOTING                                     | AL to  |
|Yes , a CENTERED FOOTING                            | to     |
|Yes , a FOOTING at the page BOTTOM                  | ------+
|Yes , a CENTERED FOOTING at page BOTTOM             |
+----------------------------------------------------+

+------------------------------------------------------------+
|TABLE FILE STAFF                                            |
|PRINT LAST_NAME AND DEPT_NAME AND JOB_TITLE AND SALARY      |
|BY DEPRTMNT_ID NOPRINT                                      |
|WHERE (SALARY  GT 40000);                                   |
|                                                            |
+------------------------------------------------------------+
```

The next window will prompt the user to enter the heading text on the screen.

```
+-------------------------------------------------------------------+
¦ Keys: ENTER      Select     PF1 Field Definitions  PF2 Revise mode ¦
¦       PF3, PF12 Undo        PF4 Top                PF5 Bottom      ¦
¦       PF7       Scroll Up PF8 Scroll Down          PF9 Multi-select¦
+-------------------------------------------------------------------+


                        +---------------------------------+
+-----------------------------------------------------------------+
¦Enter your text:                                                 ¦
¦-----------------                                                ¦
¦  <----- The user can start entering the heading text on this line.
¦---------------------------------------------------------------- ¦
+-----------------------------------------------------------------+
                        ¦                                 ¦
                        ¦Is GREATER THAN or EQUAL to      ¦
                        ¦Is LESS THAN or EQUAL to         ¦
                        +---------------------------------+


+-----------------------------------------------------------------+
¦PRINT LAST_NAME AND DEPT_NAME AND JOB_TITLE AND SALARY           ¦
¦BY DEPRTMNT_ID NOPRINT                                           ¦
¦WHERE (SALARY  GT 40000);                                        ¦
¦HEADING CENTER                                                   ¦
¦                                                                 ¦
+-----------------------------------------------------------------+
```

The following screen shows the heading text that I entered.

```
+--------------------------------------------------------------------+
| Keys: ENTER      Select    PF1 Field Definitions  PF2 Revise mode  |
|       PF3, PF12 Undo       PF4 Top                PF5 Bottom        |
|       PF7       Scroll Up PF8 Scroll Down         PF9 Multi-select  |
+--------------------------------------------------------------------+


                          +--------------------------------+
+--------------------------------------------------------------------+
|Enter your text:                                                    |
|----------------                                                    |
| list of employees making more than $40,000 a year by department    |
|------------------------------------------------------------------- |
+--------------------------------------------------------------------+
                          |Is GREATER THAN or EQUAL to    |
                          |Is LESS THAN or EQUAL to       |
                          +--------------------------------+


+--------------------------------------------------------------------+
|PRINT LAST_NAME AND DEPT_NAME AND JOB_TITLE AND SALARY              |
|DY DEPRTMNT_ID NOPRINT                                              |
|WHERE (SALARY  GT 40000);                                          |
|HEADING CENTER                                                     |
|                                                                    |
+--------------------------------------------------------------------+
```

The next window prompts the user for more heading lines to this request. I selected the "No" option.

```
+----------------------------------------------------------------------+
¦ Keys: ENTER      Select      PF1 Field Definitions   PF2 Revise mode ¦
¦       PF3, PF12 Undo         PF4 Top                 PF5 Bottom       ¦
¦       PF7       Scroll Up PF8 Scroll Down            PF9 Multi-select ¦
+----------------------------------------------------------------------+

                            +-----------------------------------+
+------------------------------------------------------------------+
¦Ente +-------------------------------+                            ¦
¦     ¦Any more text lines ?          ¦                            ¦
¦---- ¦                               ¦                            ¦
¦list ¦----------------------         ¦      0 a year by department ¦
¦-----¦No   ←————————                 ¦      --------------------- ¦
+-----¦Yes                            ¦      --------------------- +
      +-------------------------------+ THAN or EQUAL to          ¦
                            ¦Is LESS THAN or EQUAL to             ¦
                            +-----------------------------------+

+----------------------------------------------------------------------+
¦BY DEPRTMNT_ID NOPRINT                                                 ¦
¦WHERE (SALARY  GT 40000);                                              ¦
¦HEADING CENTER                                                         ¦
¦"LIST OF EMPLOYEES MAKING MORE THAN $40,000 A YEAR BY DEPARTMENT"      ¦
¦                                                                       ¦
+----------------------------------------------------------------------+
```

The following is the initial HEADING or FOOTING request window. TableTalk will display this window again to give the user the opportunity to add other headings and/or footings to the report. Since I had completed my heading, I selected the "None or no more" option.

```
+----------------------------------------------------------------+
| Keys: ENTER       Select    PF1 Field Definitions  PF2 Revise mode |
|       PF3, PF12 Undo         PF4 Top               PF5 Bottom   |
|       PF7        Scroll Up PF8 Scroll Down          PF9 Multi-select |
+----------------------------------------------------------------+


                          +--------------------------------+
+----------------------------------------------------+ +-----------+
|Do you want a page HEADING or FOOTING ?             | |           |
|--------------------------------------------        | |           |
|None or no more     <-------                        | | tment     |
|Yes , HEADING                                       | |-----------|
|Yes , and CENTER HEADING                            | |-----------+
|Yes , a FOOTING                                     | | AL to |
|Yes , a CENTERED FOOTING                            | | to    |
|Yes , a FOOTING at the page BOTTOM                  | | ------+
|Yes , a CENTERED FOOTING at page BOTTOM             | |
+----------------------------------------------------+


+----------------------------------------------------------------+
|BY DEPRTMNT_ID NOPRINT                                          |
|WHERE (SALARY  GT 40000);                                       |
|HEADING CENTER                                                  |
|"LIST OF EMPLOYEES MAKING MORE THAN $40,000 A YEAR BY DEPARTMENT" |
|                                                                |
+----------------------------------------------------------------+
```

Finally, as you will notice in the following screen, TableTalk provides the user with a host of options as what to do with the TABLE request that has just been created. Usually, the best choice for a first-time report is the second option. This is especially important if the user is accessing large files. This option will allow the user to select only a few records to run the report with. If you try to execute your TableTalk request with a large file of, say, 50,000 or more records, you may find that it may take awhile, and you will affect access by other users. So always select a limited number of records for your first try at any report. I chose the second option, which is

```
Execute, as a test with limited records?  ←
```

```
+----------------------------------------------------------------------+
¦ Keys: ENTER      Select      PF1 Field Definitions  PF2 Revise mode ¦
¦       PF3, PF12 Undo         PF4 Top                 PF5 Bottom      ¦
¦       PF7        Scroll Up PF8 Scroll Down          PF9 Multi-select ¦
+----------+------------------------------------------------∠-+-----+
           ¦Do you want to -                                    ¦
          ·¦                                                     ¦
           ¦-----------------------------                        ¦
           ¦Execute this request?                                ¦
           ¦Execute, as a test with limited records? ←───────   ¦
           ¦Send the report to the system printer?               ¦
           ¦Save this request?                                   ¦
           ¦Save this session for later revision?                ¦
           ¦Retrieve the data but HOLD it in a file?             ¦
           ¦Retrieve the data but SAVE it in a file?             ¦
           ¦Clear this request?                                  ¦
           ¦QUIT                                                 ¦
           +-------------------------------------------------+
+----------------------------------------------------------------------+
¦BY DEPRTMNT_ID NOPRINT                                               ¦
¦WHERE (SALARY  GT 40000);                                           ¦
¦HEADING CENTER                                                       ¦
¦"LIST OF EMPLOYEES MAKING MORE THAN $40,000 A YEAR BY DEPARTMENT"   ¦
¦                                                                    ¦
+----------------------------------------------------------------------+
```

The next window displayed by TableTalk will request that the user enter the number of records that need to be selected for this TABLE request. For a large file, you should select 50 to 100 records.

```
+----------------------------------------------------------------+
! Keys: ENTER      Select    PF1 Field Definitions  PF2 Revise mode !
!       PF3, PF12 Undo       PF4 Top                PF5 Bottom      !
!       PF7       Scroll Up PF8 Scroll Down         PF9 Multi-select !
+----------+-------------------------------------------+-----+
           !Do you want to  +------------------------------! !
           !                ! Enter RETRIEVED RECORD LIMIT! !
           !---------------!                              ! !
           !Execute this req!----------------------------  ! !
           !Execute, as a te                               ! !
           !Send the report !---------------------------  ! !
           !Save this reques+---------------------------+ !
           !Save this session for later revision?          !
           !Retrieve the data but HOLD it in a file?       !
           !Retrieve the data but SAVE it in a file?       !
           !Clear this request?                            !
           !QUIT                                           !
           +-----------------------------------------------+
+------------------------------------=-  ---------------------+
!BY DEPRTMNT_ID NOPRINT                                       !
!WHERE (SALARY   GT 40000);                                   !
!HEADING CENTER                                               !
!"LIST OF EMPLOYEES MAKING MORE THAN $40,000 A YEAR BY DEPARTMENT" !
!IF RECORDLIMIT EQ                                            !
+-------------------------------------------------------------+
```

The STAFF file is a very small file, so I selected six records for my test.

```
+-------------------------------------------------------------------+
¦ Keys: ENTER      Select     PF1 Field Definitions  PF2 Revise mode ¦
¦       PF3, PF12 Undo        PF4 Top                 PF5 Bottom      ¦
¦       PF7        Scroll Up PF8 Scroll Down          PF9 Multi-select¦
+---------+------------------------------------------------+-----+
          ¦Do you want to  +------------------------------¦ ¦
          ¦                ¦ Enter RETRIEVED RECORD LIMIT¦ ¦
          ¦---------------¦                                ¦ ¦
          ¦Execute this req¦----------------------------  ¦ ¦
          ¦Execute, as a te 6                              ¦
          ¦Send the report ¦----------------------------  ¦ ¦
          ¦Save this reques+----------------------------+ ¦
          ¦Save this session for later revision?          ¦
          ¦Retrieve the data but HOLD it in a file?       ¦
          ¦Retrieve the data but SAVE it in a file?       ¦
          ¦Clear this request?                            ¦
          ¦QUIT                                           ¦
          +----------------------------------------------+
+-------------------------------------------------------------------+
¦BY DEPRTMNT_ID NOPRINT                                             ¦
¦WHERE (SALARY  GT 40000);                                         ¦
¦HEADING CENTER                                                     ¦
¦"LIST OF EMPLOYEES MAKING MORE THAN $40,000 A YEAR BY DEPARTMENT"  ¦
¦IF RECORDLIMIT EQ                                                  ¦
+-------------------------------------------------------------------+
```

TableTalk will then display the following report:

```
PAGE     1
        LIST OF EMPLOYEES MAKING MORE THAN $40,000 BY DEPARTMENT
EMPLOYEE
LAST NAME        DEPT_NAME          JOB_TITLE               SALARY
---------        ---------          ---------              -------

DUXBURY          ADMINISTRATION     PRESIDENT              185,000.00
TURPIN           FINANCE            HEAD ACCOUNTANT         65,400.00
BORGIA           FINANCE            LIAISON MANAGER        102,000.00
GREENSTREET      MIS                SENIOR PROGRAMMER       45,600.00
TAHANIEV         MIS                MANAGER, DATA CENTER    55,400.00
HUNT             OPERATIONS         MANAGER                 57,000.00
```

Note that only six employees have been selected for this request. In fact, there are seven records in the STAFF file that would meet the selection criteria of this TABLE request. However, since I asked for a limit of six, only six records were processed by Focus.

After the report is displayed on your terminal, TableTalk will return to its final menu one more time. You can, once again, make a selection from the list of options.

```
+-----------------------------------------------------------------+
¦ Keys: ENTER      Select     PF1 Field Definitions  PF2 Revise mode ¦
¦       PF3, PF12 Undo        PF4 Top                PF5 Bottom      ¦
¦       PF7        Scroll Up PF8 Scroll Down          PF9 Multi-select ¦
+----------+--------------------------------------------------+-----+
           ¦Do you want to -                                  ¦
           ¦                                                  ¦
           ¦--------------------------                        ¦
           ¦Execute this request?                             ¦
           ¦Execute, as a test with limited records?          ¦
           ¦Send the report to the system printer?            ¦
           ¦Save this request?                                ¦
           ¦Save this session for later revision?             ¦
           ¦Retrieve the data but HOLD it in a file?          ¦
           ¦Retrieve the data but SAVE it in a file?          ¦
           ¦Clear this request?                               ¦
           ¦QUIT                                              ¦
           +--------------------------------------------------+
+-----------------------------------------------------------------+
¦BY DEPRTMNT_ID NOPRINT                                            ¦
¦WHERE (SALARY  GT 40000);                                         ¦
¦HEADING CENTER                                                    ¦
¦"LIST OF EMPLOYEES MAKING MORE THAN $40,000 A YEAR BY DEPARTMENT"  ¦
¦                                                                  ¦
+-----------------------------------------------------------------+
```

If the report displayed, with a small subset of records, has been successful, you may want to choose option number 1: "Execute this request?". This option will execute the TABLE request against the entire file. However, you have other options. One of the options is to save the file and use it over and over in the future. Among the other choices is the option of creating a HOLD file. Focus can create a temporary file called a HOLD file that can be used by other applications. For example, the output of this TABLE request can be saved automatically in LOTUS format or word-processing format. You could even create a Focus database file from the output of your report. These files could then be merged with other Lotus or word-processing files to create other business reports.

If you choose the HOLD option from the menu, TableTalk will display another window and will offer you a choice of formats that are currently available.

```
+-----------------------------------------------------------------+
¦ Keys: ENTER     Select    PF1 Field Definitions  PF2 Revise mode ¦
¦       PF3, PF12 Undo       PF4 Top               PF5 Bottom      ¦
¦       PF7       Scroll Up PF8 Scroll Down        PF9 Multi-select¦
+----------+--------------------------------------------+-----+----+
           ¦Do you want to  -                                ¦
           ¦         +-----------------------------+        ¦
           ¦-------- ¦Select the hold file format:  ¦        ¦
           ¦Execute  ¦-----------------------------  ¦        ¦
           ¦Execute, ¦None                          ¦        ¦
           ¦Send the ¦DIF format                    ¦        ¦
           ¦Save thi ¦LOTUS format                  ¦        ¦
           ¦Save thi ¦CALC format                   ¦        ¦
           ¦Retrieve ¦Word Processor format         ¦        ¦
           ¦Retrieve ¦As a FOCUS File               ¦        ¦
           ¦Clear th +------------------------------+        ¦
           ¦QUIT                                             ¦
           +-------------------------------------------------+
+-----------------------------------------------------------------+
¦BY DEPRTNT_ID NOPRINT                                            ¦
¦WHERE (SALARY  GT 40000);                                        ¦
¦HEADING CENTER                                                   ¦
¦"LIST OF EMPLOYEES MAKING MORE THAN $40,000 A YEAR BY DEPARTMENT" ¦
¦                                                                 ¦
+-----------------------------------------------------------------+
```

For example, if you select the Lotus option, TableTalk will produce a Lotus 1 2 3 format file on disk. You can then manipulate this file with your spreadsheet program just like any other Lotus spreadsheet file.

ORDERING
THE PROGRAM DISKETTE

There are several Focus files used in this book. The two main ones are the STAFF file and the MOVIES file. Most of the programs that work with the STAFF file will also work with the EMPLOYEE file which Information Builders Inc., provides as part of the product with every shipment of Focus. You could, therefore, execute most of these programs with the EMPLOYEE file. You could also make your own STAFF file by keying in the data that is provided in Appendix A. This data could be loaded into a Focus file by coding in any one of the following programs: CHA12-6 in Chapter 12, CHA13-12 in Chapter 13, or CHA14-6 in Chapter 14.

Alternatively, you could order the diskette which includes most of the Focus data files, Master File Descriptions, and over 180 programs. The diskette is available for IBM PC's or compatible computers. It can also be easily uploaded to the mainframe environment by using one of the many data communication packages such as MSKERMIT. All the programs on the diskette have been fully tested on both the PC and the mainframe environments and are ready to run under most conditions. Additionally, you can modify the programs for your own personal use.

The diskette is available for a nominal sum of $25 plus the appropriate state taxes. To receive your copy, send your check or money order to the following address:

FTA Computers
P. O. BOX 1463
San Carlos, Ca 94070

Please specify either the 5.25 or 3.5 inch diskette size when ordering.

INDEX

Index   495